THE LARDER

EST. 75 1938
YEARS
THE UNIVERSITY OF GEORGIA PRESS 2013

SOUTHERN FOODWAYS ALLIANCE
STUDIES IN CULTURE, PEOPLE, AND PLACE

The series explores key themes and tensions in food studies—
including race, class, gender, power, and the environment—
on a macroscale and also through the microstories of men
and women who grow, prepare, and serve food. It presents
a variety of voices, from scholars to journalists to writers of
creative nonfiction.

SERIES EDITOR

John T. Edge

SERIES ADVISORY BOARD

Brett Anderson | Nieman Fellow, Harvard University;
New Orleans *Times-Picayune*

Elizabeth Engelhardt | University of Texas at Austin

Psyche Williams-Forson | University of Maryland at College Park

THE LARDER

Food Studies Methods
from the American South

EDITED BY JOHN T. EDGE, ELIZABETH S. D. ENGELHARDT, AND TED OWNBY

The University of Georgia Press   Athens & London

Chapter 3 was first published in *Gastronomica* 10, no. 4 (2010). Chapter 7 was first published in *Southern Cultures* 14, no. 4 (2008). Chapter 5 includes a modified version of "Food for Thought: Race, Region, Identity, and Foodways in the American South," by Beth A. Latshaw, *Southern Cultures* 15, no. 4 (Winter 2009): 106–28. Chapter 9 was first published as "Mechanized Southern Comfort: Touring the Technological South at Krispy Kreme," in Anthony J. Stanonis, ed., *Dixie Emporium: Tourism, Foodways, and Consumer Culture in the American South* (Athens: University of Georgia Press, 2008). Parts of chapter 13 are adapted from chapter 2, "'Who Dat Say Chicken in Dis Crowd': Black Men, Visual Imagery, and the Ideology of Fear," in *Building Houses Out of Chicken Legs: Black Women, Food, and Power* by Psyche A. Williams-Forson (Chapel Hill: University of North Carolina Press, 2006).

Published by the University of Georgia Press
Athens, Georgia 30602
www.ugapress.org
Designed by Erin Kirk New
Set in Minion Pro by Graphic Composition, Inc., Bogart, Georgia
Manufactured by Sheridan Books
The paper in this book meets the guidelines for permanence
and durability of the Committee on Production Guidelines
for Book Longevity of the Council on Library Resources.

Most University of Georgia Press titles are
available from popular e-book vendors.

Printed in the United States of America
18 17 16 15 14 P 6 5 4 3 2

Library of Congress Cataloging-in-Publication Data
The larder : food studies methods from the American South / [edited by]
John T. Edge, Elizabeth S. D. Engelhardt, Ted Ownby. — First edition.
388 pages : illustrations ; 23 cm. — (Southern foodways alliance studies in culture, people, and place)
Includes bibliographical references and index.
ISBN-13: 978-0-8203-4554-3 (hardback)
ISBN-13: 978-0-8203-4555-0 (paperback)
1. Food habits—Southern States. 2. Food preferences—Southern States. 3. Food—Southern States—Psychological aspects. 4. Southern States—Social life and customs. I. Edge, John T. II. Engelhardt, Elizabeth Sanders Delwiche, 1969– III. Ownby, Ted.
GT2853.U5L37 2013
394.1'20975—dc23   2013015150

British Library Cataloging-in-Publication Data available

Contents

Acknowledgments

This collection emerged from the desire to bring together work in the emerging academic field of southern foodways. Our first thanks are thus to the numerous scholars, teachers, and students who have helped that field develop to a point that it can support and, we hope, benefit from its first collection of scholarly essays. For their interest, creativity, research, and patience, we thank the scholars whose essays are included here. We first imagined that this would be a collection of previously published essays, so we are grateful both to the authors of the four published essays (and the publications where they appeared) and to the authors of the essays first published here. We thank our friends at the University of Georgia Press, beginning with Erika Stevens, who was the first to show interest in the project, and also Laura Sutton, Regan Huff, Pat Allen, and John Joerschke. Thanks also to Lori Rider for her careful and thoughtful copyediting and Valerie Jones for her help with the index. We thank our colleagues in the Department of American Studies at the University of Texas at Austin and in the Center for the Study of Southern Culture at the University of Mississippi. Finally, we thank the people who helped produce the volume itself: Southern Studies graduate student Madelyn Duffey, Center for the Study of Southern Culture staffer LaTonya Pittman, Southern Foodways Alliance assistant director Melissa Hall, and Southern Foodways Alliance editor and project-finisher Sara Camp Arnold.

THE LARDER

Redrawing the Grocery

Practices and Methods for Studying Southern Food

ELIZABETH ENGELHARDT

As scholars of the U.S. South and southern food, my coeditors and I frequently engage popular and academic audiences. Recently I taught a class on southern food studies for adult learners in Austin, Texas. Attended by eight adults and one ten-year-old, the class was part of a program designed to encourage older and low-income men and women to apply for college admission.[1] The adults' ages ranged from the thirties to the seventies. They were single parents, retirees on fixed incomes, immigrants starting over at the bottom of their chosen fields, everyday men and women who recently pulled themselves out of health or life crises.

Natalia, the ten-year-old, came with her mother. Her body language and facial expressions telegraphed that she was not, at first, interested in participating. For the first fifteen minutes the adults brainstormed possible questions. I presented John Egerton's observation that "To learn what has gone on in the kitchen and the dining room—and what still goes on there—is to discover much about a society's physical health, its economic condition, its race relations, its class structure, and the status of its women."[2]

I also supplied a straightforward definition of foodways: the study of why we eat, what we eat, and what it means. The class added its own definitions: how we eat, how we prepare what we eat, who gathered the goods we cook, who cooks our food, what we do not eat, the rituals we create around food, who taught us to cook, what they were talking about when they taught us to cook, who is welcome at the table and who is not, where people sit when they eat, what people think and feel when they eat, what we remember about the dishes we eat, and, most importantly, why we care.

The class talked about who can afford food, where we get it, where we cannot, and how and why access can be conscribed. We added questions about what chemicals farmers spray on crops, who harvests crops, who profits from the harvest, how quickly and easily foods can be prepared, and whether a sustainable diet is a civil right. The class grasped quickly that the word "foodways" is useful because it is shorthand for *cultural processes*. They understood that the term "foodways" may be used to describe the social interactions and cultural exchanges that define food, drink, and nutrition.

Soon the seminar table was stacked with cookbooks, and the room was full of questions. Why does this book from North Carolina boast a Native American on the cover if there are no indigenous recipes in it? (And why is he wearing a headdress, associated with Western Plains tribes?) Why does the author of a Louisiana book from the 1930s wax poetic about white-gloved male servants? What is the story behind the Watergate salad in the South Carolina Junior League cookbook from the 1980s? And why does another recipe in that same book specify fat-free mayonnaise to go with the full-fat sour cream and cream cheese?

Later, to connect the community gardens of today with the curb markets, canning clubs, and household economies of one hundred years ago, we studied photographs and diary pages published in the 2009 food issue of the journal *Southern Cultures*.[3] We ended with mock oral history interviews. The class compared food traditions based in Ecuadorian, Pacific Northwest, Texan, Mexican, and southern homes.

Conversations swung wildly. We talked interview practices. (How do I record birthdates and family relations without stopping the flow of the conversation?) We compared bread practices and techniques. (Biscuits-versus-cornbread battles sound a lot like flour-versus-corn tortilla debates.) That night, everything was on the table and on topic.

As the class came to a close, I learned that Natalia had been paying attention after all. After carefully paging through the issue of *Southern Cultures*, Natalia had moved to a quiet corner and drawn a pen-and-ink version of the cover illustration, a 1936 Walker Evans photograph of a country grocery store.[4]

Attracted by photographs of girls who enrolled in early twentieth-century canning clubs, Natalia had been drawn into the journal and had, in turn, drawn her own rendition of the cover. Her artwork kept the basics of the original but revised and emphasized elements that must have seemed more important to a girl in 2011 Austin, Texas: she deleted the advertisements for roe and herring scrawled on the shop window. She moved the car, parked to the side of the store in the original, toward the center. More melons and vegetables were stacked outside the store, while fewer things were inside.

Growing up with limited means in landlocked Austin, Natalia probably does not regularly eat roe or herring. In her world, grocery stores are reached by car, not on foot. Recently chosen to join her school's gardening club, Natalia had spent this past growing season planting a vegetable patch and working a community garden with her mother.

Natalia's version of the cover offers truths about foodways, just as the conversation did 'that evening. What she did—what the whole class modeled at that seminar table—was choose, revise, combine, modify, practice, and embrace what has come before to make sense of where we are now. Literally: one group copied out an 1840s sweet potato dish to serve for a Thanksgiving potluck. And figuratively: we questioned how to study food today, how to use the processes of foodways to a researcher's advantage.

Herein, we propose that both strategies are worthy of your attention. Narratives and histories that complicate our understanding of southern food populate these pages. Rather than adhere to a strict chronological or geographical organization, we arranged the pieces to encourage conversation about methods and strategies. As we travel across the region, and across topics, we aim to rethink and reorder tools and practices that were previously stacked inside the silos of academic disciplines.

The State of Southern Food Studies

We, the editors of *The Larder*, assert that the food studies discipline has matured. Our colleagues in the South have been vigorously studying the region's foodways long enough to claim a national leadership role. Instead of fretting about the legitimacy of the field, we focus on how to grow and strengthen scholarship and methodologies. With that charge in mind, we stand ready to aid compatriots as they develop best practices.

This collection is organized by methodology. We have chosen articles that represent a range of disciplines, including history, geography, social sciences, American studies, gender studies, literary theory, visual and aural studies, cultural studies, and technology studies. Our aim was to place those essays in a context that catalyzes conversations about best methodological practices.

We cover a wide range of subjects. Krispy Kreme, the doughnut chain born of North Carolina mill-village culture, shares space with nineteenth-century Charleston markets, depicted in postcards and songs. A Waco, Texas, cookbook, published in multiple editions between 1888 and 1978, abuts a 2006 telephone survey.

We are neither chronologically nor geographically comprehensive. The Civil War gets little notice, although we believe that researchers focused on that sectional divide may gain insights from Psyche Williams-Forson's analysis of World War II–era Farm Security Administration photographers. Similarly, the state of Tennessee gets short shrift. Yet Justin Nystrom's careful oral history–driven study of immigrant entrepreneurs doing business along the Mississippi River in Louisiana might help with projects focused on other river cities such as Memphis or Chattanooga.

Southern identity is now being fractured and reconceived to reflect a twenty-first-century South informed by, but not wholly defined by, nineteenth- and twentieth-century racial politics. Even as we wonder whether the South coheres, southern food traditions do not appear to be imperiled. For popular audiences, southern foodways evoke positive associations and enjoy wide popularity. For academic audiences focused on examining and criticizing dietary habits and patterns of exclusion, southern food studies offer approaches to race, class, gender, and ethnicity.

Work in the popular and academic realms is gaining momentum. The Southern Foodways Alliance, a University of Mississippi institute, has, since its inception in 1999, collected more than seven hundred digitized oral histories and produced more than thirty documentary films. Foodways Texas, a member-supported, University of Texas–based organization, claims 250 members in its second year of operations. Sabores Sin Fronteras, based at the University of Arizona, now documents and studies the borderlands foodways of Mexico and the United States.

Many local communities are organizing food studies projects, including the Triangle University Food Studies group in North Carolina. Organizations such as the American Studies Association, the Modern Language Association, and the American Historical Association stage panels and caucuses dedicated to the study of food. The Association for the Study of Food and Society regularly hosts its annual conference in the South as recognition, in part, of the scholars working on southern foodways. Academic journals publish special food issues, which rank among their highest circulation numbers.[5]

The Larder argues that food studies does not simply help us understand more about the foods we eat and the foodways we embrace. Merit lies also in the methods and strategies developed that use food and foodways as lenses to examine culture. The resulting conversations provoke a deeper understanding of our overlapping, historically situated, and ever-evolving cultures and societies.

Organizing Principles

We organized this volume in five sections. Each of the first four approaches the study of food in the South from a different cluster of methods. We introduce each section with a discussion of how the methods developed and what they promise when deployed.

First, we examine *Cookbooks and Ingredients*. While scholars have turned to these sources repeatedly, we believe the essays collected here model new strategies and approaches to the materials. A section on *People and Communities* follows, with social science techniques, oral history practices, labor analysis, and demographic tools, all employed to bring individual and community voices into the discussion.

The third section focuses on *Spaces and Technologies*; the essays included analyze the rhetoric of science and technology and foreground geographical methods. The fourth section brings us to the *Material Cultures* of southern food, especially as that has changed over hundreds of years of growing, selling, cooking, and eating food in the South.

The final section, *On Authenticity*, containing one essay and our conclusion, steps back to perform more metatextual analysis on the field itself—asking pointed but promising questions based on the past, present, and future of the field. In so doing, it models the potential of southern food studies to generate theoretical methods and insights as well.

We can take several messages from that November class and our group conversation about processes in food studies. One is that food studies, especially southern food studies, has arrived on both the academic and the popular cultural scenes. Another is that we all can and should choose the methods most suited to any given food study. We mix and match, reading pieces against each other and in changing combinations.

Just as Natalia took a photograph of a grocery store in early twentieth-century Alabama and redrew it to reflect her experience of food in early twenty-first-century Texas, we encourage you to join us in redrawing the limits, emphases, and possibilities of food studies. Emergent methodologies, whether borrowed from the papers included here or fused from these models and others, will carry the field forward and foster a thoughtful future that is interdisciplinary, rigorous, and revealing.

NOTES

1. The class was part of the Free Minds Project of the University of Texas at Austin. For more information, see http://www.utexas.edu/cola/insts/humanitiesinstitute/programs/former -programs/free-minds-project.php.

2. John Egerton, *Southern Food: At Home, on the Road, in History* (1987; repr. Chapel Hill: University of North Carolina Press, 1993), 3.

3. A selection of the cookbooks we used includes Lydia Maria Child, *The American Frugal Housewife* (Boston: Carter, Hendee, 1833); Eastatoe Community Club, *Our Country Recipes* (Rosman, N.C., 1992); Eleanore Ott, *Plantation Cookery of Old Louisiana* (New Orleans: Harmanson, 1938); Louise Henderson, *Just Like Mother Made: Ozark Recipes* (Cassville, Mo.: Litho Printers, n.d.); The Ladies of the Palmetto State (South Carolina) Unit, Inc., of W.B.C.C.I., *Palmetto Cooking from the Mountains to the Sea* (Greer, S.C.: Ben Franklin Printers, 1975). The full name of W.B.C.C.I. is never spelled out, but it appears to be a group of Airstream Trailer enthusiasts.

4. See "The Edible South," ed. Marcie Cohen Ferris, special issue, *Southern Cultures* 15, no. 4 (Winter 2009); its cover photograph is "McCollum Grocery, Greensboro, Alabama" (1936) by Walker Evans.

5. See Southern Foodways Alliance (www.southernfoodways.org), Foodways Texas (www .foodwaystexas.com), Sabores Sin Fronteras (www.saboresfronteras.com).

PART 1

Cookbooks and Ingredients

JOHN EGERTON kicked off the modern era of southern food studies with an epic regional road trip. He catalogued the recipes, cookbooks, restaurants, and forgotten cooks of the region. In 1987's *Southern Food: At Home, on the Road, in History,* he foreshadowed the concentration on cookbooks and recipes that has since dominated food studies. In the popular vein, Scott Peacock, a white Alabamian, and Edna Lewis, a black Virginian, wrote a 2003 book, *The Gift of Southern Cooking,* that made connections across races, eras, and stereotypes. Cookbooks have been helpful in building theoretical frameworks for judging when and where national or regional cuisines emerge, as anthropologist Arjun Appadurai did in his 1988 study "How to Make a National Cuisine: Cookbooks in Contemporary India."

Cookbooks have been central to the feminist and gender studies of Sherrie Inness, Anne Bower, and contributors to the collection *From Betty Crocker to Feminist Food Studies.*[1] In recent years, studies of recipes have gotten stuck in the mire. Questions of intent and audience have been the focus. We believe there is more to explore in the recipes, ingredients, and cooking practices of the region. Rien Fertel, Rebecca Sharpless, David Shields, and Wiley Prewitt open these avenues of exploration.

Sometimes we should, in fact, judge a book by its cover, as Rien Fertel demonstrates in "'Everybody Seemed Willing to Help': *The Picayune Creole Cook Book* as Battleground, 1900–2008." Fertel highlights one edition of this New Orleans cookbook, featuring a smiling male chef on the dust jacket. (He was likely white.) Underneath the dust jacket, engraved on the boards of the book itself, remained an image of a black woman, inspired by an earlier edition of the book. As metaphor, the imbricated images allow Fertel to explore the changing definitions of race, ethnicity, Creolization, and community on New Orleans palates and in local social hierarchies. Fertel interrogates meanings beyond mere recipes when he sketches profiles of the various contributions from writers and readers of the *Times-Picayune* newspaper.

Thorny questions persist for readers interested in community cookbooks produced in the South: What do we make of the very brief attributions of individual recipes? What can we ask if all we have is a woman's name at the end of a recipe? Was she making a statement about race, class, gender, or ethnicity? Did she join with fellow contributors to police the boundaries of society or community through the cookbook? Or did she hope to open those boundaries?

Rebecca Sharpless applies the tools of social historians to provide one answer in "The Women of St. Paul's Episcopal Church Were Worried." She examines an 1888 cookbook from Waco, Texas, and its subsequent updated editions. Using church records, telephone directories, community interviews, letters, and diaries, she reconstructs the social history of the women who produced the cookbook. Sharpless uses stories of missionary trips to explain the inclusion of Asian recipes. She recovers networks of political appointments to clarify the role of celebrities in the cookbooks. She traces employment records and addresses of contributors to understand the racial hierarchies undergirding how women's names are listed under their recipes. That final detail, which becomes a map of the racial politics among domestic workers, established white families, and newly arrived residents, proves that the relatively terse narratives in community cookbooks can and should be the objects of scholarship.

Sometimes the most interesting questions come from stepping back and readjusting the frame of study. David Shields performs such a move in "Prospecting for Oil." Rather than focus on the cuisines that coalesced in the late eighteenth and early nineteenth centuries, Shields wonders what agricultural breakthroughs informed the dishes and recipes of that era. He finds some answers in coastal, agricultural communities of South Carolina as they worked to produce a sustainable source of cooking oil. Scanning early cookbooks, newspapers, general store records, and plantation accounts, Shields documents both the failures and successes that were later erased in blanket directions to "heat oil in large skillet" or "grease pan and preheat it."

Frequently politicized but rarely analyzed, hunting is the subject of "Bodies of the Dead: The Wild in Southern Foodways," by Wiley Prewitt. Examining what was hunted, how substantially, by whom, and to what ends, Prewitt asks questions about the changing relationship of humans and animals in the U.S. South. Such questions lead to shifting definitions of "wild" and "domesticated" food supply, as well as changes in our symbolic and metaphoric languages. Using game warden records, newspaper reports of noteworthy hunts, accounts of significant migrations, and scant traces of game in the region's cookbooks, Prewitt theorizes practices and values.

The source materials useful for southern food studies are myriad. We can begin by examining the food and its documents. We can return to classic sources such as cookbooks, or we can gather previously overlooked community memories. From oral histories to sociological surveys, histories, and texts, we have only begun to explore the sources available to us.

NOTES

1. John Egerton, *Southern Food: At Home, on the Road, in History* (Chapel Hill: University of North Carolina Press, 1987, 1993); Arjun Appadurai, "How to Make a National Cuisine: Cookbooks in Contemporary India," *Comparative Studies in Society and History* 30, no. 1 (January 1988): 3–24; Sherrie Inness, *Dinner Roles: American Women and Culinary Culture* (Iowa City: University of Iowa Press, 2001); Anne Bower, ed., *Recipes for Reading: Community Cookbooks, Stories, Histories* (Amherst: University of Massachusetts Press, 1997); Arlene Voski Avakian and Barbara Haber, eds., *From Betty Crocker to Feminist Food Studies: Critical Perspectives on Women and Food* (Amherst: University of Massachusetts Press, 2005).

CHAPTER 1

"Everybody Seemed Willing to Help"

The Picayune Creole Cook Book *as Battleground, 1900–2008*

RIEN T. FERTEL

In 1900, for just twenty-five cents, a freshly published copy of the "compendium of our local culinary science . . . an authentic and complete account of the Creole kitchen" could be obtained from any New Orleans newsstand. The *Picayune's Creole Cook Book*, boasted a promotional article in the *Daily Picayune*, would be "the first that has even been attempted, and probably the only one that can ever be made." The demographics of New Orleans were shifting rapidly. The formerly enslaved people who toiled in the kitchens of their masters, including the many who continued to do so as freedwomen and men throughout the city, were fading away, and just "a few years more will witness the disappearance of the last one." With the demise of this "race of Creole cooks," the paper warned, New Orleans would lose "the secrets of the Louisiana Kitchen." To combat this potential loss, an anonymous *Daily Picayune* staff member visited "the kitchen of more than one aristocratic Creole mansion in the district below Canal street." The interviewer consulted "the old Creole 'mammies'" and took down "from their lips the exact formulae by which the famous Creole dishes are prepared." The *Daily Picayune* then sent the recopies of these black domestic workers to a chef, "A man whose knowledge of cookery is encyclopaediac [*sic*]." Once this male, presumably white, chef "vouched for the authenticity, and guaranteed the practicability of a receipt [recipe]," the dish would be added to the cookbook's contents. Though the preparation of this recipe book hinged on methods and goals of power and knowledge, the *Daily Picayune* assured its readers that "everybody seemed willing to help."[1]

Republished in sixteen later editions through 1989, the *Picayune Cre-*

ole Cook Book's recipes have rarely changed. The introductory texts and illustrations, however, shifted over time to suit changing political, social, and cultural relationships in New Orleans, the South, and the nation. Editors of the cookbook repeatedly reordered the words and images within in order to assign and reassign authorship of these Creole recipes. Recipes were purportedly gathered community wide from those previously appearing in the paper, and from family cooks and leading restaurant chefs.[2] But the cookbook's recipes, as with its compilers and editors, always appeared anonymously. By ascribing authorship to a recipe collection without a true author and ownership to a Creolized culinary culture with historically ambiguous origins, this cookbook reinterpreted the history of New Orleans and accredited dominion over the city's Creole culture. The *Picayune Creole Cook Book* became a Crescent City urtext, "a compendium of food customs, race relations, religious observations, and festivals . . . to countless men and women."[3] This essay will examine the roles "everybody" (editors, cooks, and readers) played in constructing race, ethnicity, class, and gender relations within the *Picayune*.

The *Picayune Creole Cook Book*'s publication history proceeded in four distinct phases. The first four editions (1900, 1901, 1906, 1910), originally labeled *The Picayune's Creole Cook Book*, reinforced white southern racism by incorporating contemporary moonlight-and-magnolias imagery. Though this book was written with the white female consumer in mind, these earliest editions granted agency to a mammy character as chief cook, the creator of recipes within the kitchen and, thus, within the text. The second phase comprised a sole printing. The 1916 edition was characterized by a marked shift in the assigned authorship of recipes from the femininity of the household private sphere to the masculinity of the private restaurant kitchen. Here culinary proprietorship changed hands from African American female domestics to white (mostly) male professional chefs and businessmen. The sixth and seventh editions (1922 and 1928) encompassed the most progressive years in the cookbook's history. In the interwar period the book's text ascribed multiple peoples and cultures—as well as the reaffirmation of African American women—as architects of New Orleans's culinary heritage. From 1936 onward (1938, 1942, 1945, 1947, 1954, 1966, 1971) the *Creole Cook Book* reverted to a standardized white, male-centric historical narrative of

New Orleans cooking. It was not until the last two editions (1987 and 1989) that this racialized and gendered history disappeared.

Though the *Picayune Creole Cook Book* saw frequent representational changes throughout its nearly century-long publication history, every edition contained two interconnected ideas. The *Cook Book* promoted the exceptionality of New Orleans cuisine and culture. In June 1929 the *Times-Picayune* advertised the "famous recipes of the aristocratic" French and Spanish "emigres." The dishes of their "gastronomic culture," though now centuries old, had "retained their popularity because of their superior tastiness."[4] For another local commentator, it "is cooking, the art that sets us apart," and not Mardi Gras or jazz music, that marks "the joy of life in New Orleans."[5] Not only were New Orleans's Creole cooking and culture uniquely superior to other American forms, they were slowly slipping into dissolution. The city's cuisine and its practitioners were "now rapidly becoming extinct," according to the original advertisement that introduced the cookbook.[6] The cookbook blamed changing social conditions and gender norms, as well as the Americanization and modernization of the kitchen. These thematic threads of exceptionality and extinction are hardly unique to the *Picayune Creole Cook Book*. Since the publication of the first Creole cookbooks in 1885, nearly every interpreter—insiders and outsiders both—of the city's cooking style has boasted that "New Orleans cuisine is unique, without a doubt."[7] Lafcadio Hearn, compiler of one of the 1885 cookbooks, contrasted "the mysteries" of the Creole kitchen with those recipes found in "the average cook-book."[8] Concurrently, gourmands have invariably stressed that Creole cooking needs to be rescued from oblivion. The second 1885 cookbook, written by a religious women's organization, cautioned that New Orleans and the South were being overtaken by a proliferation of northern recipe collections.[9] Defenders of New Orleans's culinary culture have seen that culture as under threat and worth saving, a sentiment forcefully made in the *Times-Picayune*'s latest cookbook. In *Cooking Up a Storm: Recipes Lost and Found from the Times-Picayune of New Orleans* (2008), the city's culinary heritage is rescued once again from the flooding caused by the failure of the federal levee system following Hurricane Katrina.[10] This same duality of being exceptional and facing extinction is hardly unique to its cooking; New Orleans is, according to historian Lawrence Powell, "an American Pompeii," continually under threat from fire, floods, violence, and governmental corruption and undersight on all levels.[11]

The *Picayune Creole Cook Book*, though neither the first New Orleans cookbook nor the most widely circulated, has retained a long shelf life and is perhaps the most critically important to the history of cooking in Louisiana. It has been called not only "the ultimate cook book on Creole cuisine" but the "most notable among early-twentieth-century food writings."[12] Similar to authoritative, all-encompassing collections such as *The Joy of Cooking* (first published in 1931) and newspaper-derived tomes such as those by the *Los Angeles Times* (1902) and the *New York Times* (1961), the *Picayune* takes the home cook from drinks to dessert over the course of hundreds of recipes; recipes that will not only tell the reader how to cook a chicken but also how to buy, clean, and prepare the bird.

Anonymously compiled, the *Picayune's* authorship has remained, until now, unknown and the cause of considerable speculation. Credit should be given to Marie Louise Points, a wealthy white New Orleanian. A member of the white Creole aristocracy, Points's ancestors included elite Virginia and Gulf Coast landholders. A frequently published reporter for the *Daily Picayune* and several Catholic publications,[13] Marie Louise Points was undoubtedly aided by others, many of whom will forever remain unnamed.[14]

However, the future publication and success of the *Picayune Creole Cook Book* can furthermore be traced back to the business acumen of Eliza Jane Nicholson. In 1876 Nicholson became the first woman newspaper publisher in the South, inheriting the *New Orleans Daily Picayune* from her late husband. As editor and majority owner for twenty years, Nicholson, who sometimes wrote poetry under the pen name Pearl Rivers, modernized and feminized the city's premier journal. She hired woman writers, most famously the journalists Catherine Cole and Dorothy Dix; scandalously brought a society column (the Society Bee) to New Orleans; and added a weekly Household Hints feature. The first Household Hints editorial, appearing in late 1882, formulated the same housewife uplift gospel that the cookbook would repeat nearly two decades later: "Women do know how to combine for themselves in household service, where the incapable cook, chambermaid or waiter will demand and get as good pay as the capable girl. Here the scale tilts the wrong way."[15]

The tensions inherent in the household kitchen—and the cookbook's text and illustrations—paralleled that of fin-de-siècle New Orleans. In the Crescent City, as across the nation, former political enemies were forging bonds of white solidarity.[16] Lost Cause clubs and memorials sprang up across the city, with the resurgence of a white-supremacist Carnival tradition being one of the most openly visible practices.[17] Political and social gains made by African Americans during Reconstruction were widely overturned. Nearly two centuries of white Creole demographic dominance, and its accompanying political power, were erased by a burgeoning population of Americans who could not trace their roots back to the original settlers of Louisiana. Racial conflicts were numerous and especially ferocious in the last decade of the nineteenth century.[18]

Cookbooks can and do mirror history, as this essay on the *Picayune Creole Cook Book* will show. Simply put, cookbooks, like other forms of mass print culture, reflect social changes; historians should explore cookbooks as they do periodicals and novels. In a groundbreaking essay, Arjun Appadurai sees the formation of national cuisines—imagined communities of eaters— as "postindustrial, postcolonial" processes of modernization that emerge through the rise of a definite textual corpus and a consumption-driven middle class.[19] This intersection of race, class, and gender during the era when modernity, capitalism, and print culture arose guided several recent academic explorations in the field of food studies, including this essay.[20] As modern cookbooks came of age in the early twentieth century, this print medium often acted, according to Doris Witt, as "a battleground where the social barriers of class, race, and generation (as well as ethnicity, sexuality, religion, and nationality) were not eradicated but more nearly constructed, maintained, and fortified."[21] Today, too few scholars view cookbooks as fertile ground for analyzing these battles.

A Very Vexing Problem

The foreword to the 1900 edition of the *Picayune Creole Cook Book* reiterated the main themes explained in the beginning of this essay: the generational loss of black Creole cooks, the necessity of documenting Creole recipes lest they disappear, and the exceptionality of the New Orleans cooking style. In its entirety, the foreword reads:

> The question of "a good cook" is now becoming a very vexing problem, and the only remedy for this state of things is for the ladies of the present day to do as their grandmothers did, acquaint themselves thoroughly with the art of cooking in all its important and minutest details, and learn how to properly apply them. To assist them in this, to preserve to future generations the many excellent and matchless receipts of our New Orleans cuisine, to gather these up from the lips of the old Creole negro cooks and the grand old housekeepers who still survive, ere they, too, pass away, and Creole cookery, with all its delightful combinations and possibilities, will have become a lost art, is, in a measure, the object of this book.[22]

In 1,560 recipes spread over 352 pages, the cookbook's goal to "gather" and "preserve" local dishes benefited a new generation of middle-class home cooks.[23] Following the Reconstruction era, New Orleans and its residents endeavored to think of themselves as a city reborn. This rebirth began with the World's Industrial and Cotton Centennial Exposition of 1884–85, that year's World's Fair, which celebrated the hundredth anniversary of the first southern cotton shipment to Europe. Over the next several decades, promotions (re-)imagined New Orleans as the "Paris of America" and the "City of Progress, Beauty, Charm, and Romance."[24] The city enjoyed a burgeoning metro population and new economic possibilities in the nation's second busiest port. With this cosmopolitan reawakening came the rise of a new New Orleans middle class.

As a modern form of commercial print culture, the *Picayune Creole Cook Book* reflected and encouraged changes in the New South middle-class household. The most significant change was the move away from the employment of African American domestic cooks and servants. Modern middle-class housewives endeavored to do as their antebellum grandmothers did, to study and apply "the art of cooking." The modern cookbook industry increasingly "redefine[d] cooking as an important and pleasurable part of the modern woman's domestic duties—a signal feature of white middle-class womanhood."[25] As literary and cultural historian Nicola

Humble argues, the rise of a twentieth-century cookbook culture, in England just as in the United States, was tied to the shifting structures of middle-class life and identity.[26]

African Americans, too, were gradually becoming more socially and economically mobile. The Great Migration of six million African American southerners to other regions of the United States made black cooks less common in white households.[27] For those African American New Orleanians who could not escape the South, or those who actively decided to remain, it was women who could not enjoy the same occupational mobility as men. According to the cookbook's introduction, the Civil War and Reconstruction brought "vast upheavals of social conditions" that drastically altered the "household economy" of New Orleans. The South's white-owned domestic kitchens experienced two trends: the impoverished lean times that changed what and how much a family could eat, and the social mobility of the formerly enslaved. In the last decades of the nineteenth century, according to the cookbook's telling of history, the "younger darkies" fled their white owners, leaving their "mistresses behind" to fend for themselves in the kitchen. However, "older Creole négresse[s]" would not leave and pledged fidelity to both the "ancient families" and the "old cuisine." These "faithful old negro cooks" remained behind to keep their white masters fed and guard the legacy of Creole cooking from extinction. Those who would pass their days hovering over the stove with "pride and honor" were the mythical mammies.[28]

The cookbook's use of the word "Creole" deserves a mention. Since at least the mid-eighteenth century, with the cession of French Louisiana to Spain, "Creole" has been imbued with controversy. Used today, and historically, as both a noun and an adjective to signify racial, cultural, ethnic, and local identity, "Creole" can also be used to refer to social standing. During the colonial era, the term was applied as a signifier to denote both excellence, by New Worlders, and degeneracy, by colonial Europe. In French and Spanish colonial Louisiana, "Creole," in its simplest iteration, designated local birth—be it people, animals, or vegetables—from a fusion of American, African, or European parentage; "Creole" became a way to commodify local products. In 1900 New Orleans, two main groups used the word to identify themselves.[29] First were the Afro-Creoles, peoples with Afro-French

Caribbean and white ancestry who self-identified or were legally classified as mixed race and, before the Civil War, *gens de couleur libre* (free people of color). The white Creoles were a large group of New Orleanians who could purportedly trace their heritage to colonial French and Spanish settlers; beginning before the Civil War and culminating in the nineteenth century's last two decades, white Creoles and their circle of non-Creole followers mythologized, in a body of literature, their beginnings and insisted that "Creole" referred to pure-blooded whiteness.[30] Though reserving the noun "Creole" for themselves, the white Creole elite still frequently used the adjectival modifier "Creole" to refer to peoples of African heritage, a practice exemplified—besides in the *Picayune*'s cookbook—in Grace King's *New Orleans: The Place and the People* (1895), where the phrases "African Creole songs," a "Tignon Créole," "A Creole Darky," and "Creole mammies" appear.[31]

The *Picayune Creole Cook Book*, and similar southern cookery literature of the period, made the kitchen safe for a new generation of white bourgeois homemakers by reinforcing their presumed cultural and racial superiority over African American women, who had long presided over the stovetop. This symbolic whitening of the kitchen manifested itself in the mammy character. Between the 1820s and 1935, a century the American popular cultural scholar Kimberly Wallace-Sanders deems the "Mammification" era of the nation, the mammy figure was used to sell a multiplicity of southern food commodities.[32] In the *Picayune*, as elsewhere, mammy became "the grand old house-keeper," the devoted second mother to her white family. The first pictorial representation of mammy occurred in the cookbook's second edition (1901) and was a typical portrait: smiling in a clean white dress with a tignon gathering up her hair; she was here presented, as always, voluptuous but asexual. In this black-and-white portrayal, labeled "A Creole Negro Cook (Tante Zoe, with Tureen of Gumbo File)," she, of course, carried an enormous pot of that quintessential New Orleans dish.

Thus, before Creole cookery became a "lost art," it was up to white women to rescue the city's culinary heritage from demise. With the help of the Creole cookbook editors, middle-class whites could "acquaint themselves" with the recipes and thus "preserve [them] for future generations." Just as there was a "new colored woman" who refused to cook in white households, the cookbook promised a "new white" that needed "to do as their grandmothers did." The *Picayune* encouraged white housewives to rise up and take back their lost recipes. This coterie of middle-class white housewives, by using the cookbook, would immerse themselves in the "gastronomic lore" of the French and the "rich and stately dishes" of the Spanish. The high culture of these two European nations, or "races," in this narrative, once descended on colonial Louisiana and through their "amalgamation" transmitted to their "progeny," the Creoles, the glory of "a new school of cookery."[33]

Romance and a Golden Glamour

The first four editions of the cookbook were, if we take the biased opinions of the newspaper, an overwhelming success. In 1916 the fifth edition, now subtly retitled *The Picayune Creole Cook Book*, dramatically changed functions from a tutorial cookbook for modern housewives to a glamorized account of the professional restaurant kitchen and its impact on New Orleans cuisine. Mrs. Florence Russ gushed, "The best way to get a glimpse into [the city's] inner life and many of its social customs is to read the Picayune Cook Book [*sic*]." A local hotel proprietor exclaimed that it was "one of the best cook books I have ever seen," while another hotel owner added, "it will prove very valuable to the housekeeper." But the *Picayune Creole Cook Book* was not just for locals. The *United Service Magazine* labeled the cookbook "the most practical and useful to ordinary people of all the books of its class. . . . Every caterer of a wardroom mess in the Navy should send for this volume." Not just for the housewife, the *Picayune* also sold well to kitchen professions nationally: "It has found quite a large sale among . . . the hotel and restaurant chef."[34] In the fifth edition, the introduction and illustrations change but hardly the recipes. Though still addressed to the diligent homemaker ("Study, madame, and follow the path laid down"), the introduction transfers the cookbook from "that black-raftered kitchen of the long ago" to the New South charm of the modern urban environment. The kitchen of the 1910s is ultraluxe. Now the "rosy girls" and "stately ladies" of New Orleans cook within kitchens filled with "tiled walls and . . . rows of aluminum and graniteware." But from these shiny pots and pans still come the recipes of another time and place; the 1916 cookbook promises "romance and a golden glamour" by transporting the reader to a mystical "old New Orleans."

Expanding on the moonlight-and-magnolia literary device, the book's pre-
amble captures "glimpses of long-gone festivals, and of the graces and cour-
tesies that made them charming; of the wit and wisdom that flashed back
and forth across the mahogany; of the bright eyes, now asleep for this many
a year; of the gallant hearts that have long ceased to beat." The frontispiece,
titled "Old Creole Days in New Orleans," contains a drawing of a couple of
fashionable "beruffled gentlemen and crinolined ladies" occupying a table in
an elegant French Quarter courtyard; an African American waiter, with an
Uncle Tom smile, stands at attention waiting to present the gumbo tureen.
The portrait of the male servant merged the memory of prewar wealth and
entitlement with the ceremony of the fine-dining modern restaurant.[35] This
shift corresponded with the hardening of the color line in 1910s New Orleans. Whites continued to solidify their power in post-*Plessy* America. As
historian Adam Fairclough notes, the conservative political machine of the
pre–Huey Long era, the Regular Democratic Organization, that dominated
local politics watched as black disenfranchisement, lynchings, and white
supremacy organizations grew nearly unabated.[36]

Alterations in the cookbook reflected recent changes in the newspaper
ownership and the demographics of the city. In April 1914 the *Daily Picayune* newspaper merged with the *Times-Democrat* to become the *Times-
Picayune* that remains today. The *Picayune* had been New Orleans's cheap,
everyman's paper since its founding in 1837; named for the Spanish silver
coin, the daily paper originally cost just one picayune, or six and one-fourth
cents. The *Times-Democrat* owed its creation to an unlikely 1881 merger
of two city dailies: the *Times*, a pro-Union paper during the war, and the
Democrat, a Reconstruction-era, pro-Southern daily. The *Times-Democrat*
continued as a Republican paper in Gilded Age New Orleans. It was the
city's financial paper, dedicated to helping New Orleans regain its status
as America's per capita wealthiest city. The *Times-Democrat* carried more
advertisements than the *Picayune* and appealed to upper-class sensibilities
beyond the finance reports; a Shakespeare quote always appeared just above
the daily cotton prices.[37]

The unified *Times-Picayune* provided its cookbook readership with a
newly constructed Great Man theory of history. In the 1916 *Picayune Cook
Book*, the ingenious private restaurateur replaced the domesticated mammy

or housewife as the creator of the city's culinary capital. This new introduction focuses on "the names of the great chefs which became identified
with New Orleans in those long-gone years." These solely Latinate (French
and Spanish) chefs collaborated to form a Creole culinary culture, and the
result, according to the narrative, "was beyond speech." The introduction
proceeded to call the roll of these "great chefs" from Spain, "the best cooks
from that sunny clime," and the "artists" of France. Though the list of eleven
chefs and restaurant owners comprised mostly men, two women were given
the lengthiest biographies: Madame Eugene and Madame Begué. Still, this
short history credited the male chefs with creating New Orleans cuisine: "It
is the lore of such men as this which has made the Creole Cook Book possible. Men who have began [*sic*] to learn to cook at 10 or 12 years of age have
grown up, and have passed their knowledge to their sons." It was from these
male primogenitors that this Creole "art" spread into home kitchens.[38] In
the next edition of the *Picayune Creole Cook Book*, these romantic notions
of restaurants and professional service disappeared. Because of social and
economic pressures, the history of Creole cooking would be rewritten once
again.

An All-Inclusive School of Cookery

The completely redesigned sixth and seventh editions of the *Picayune Creole Cook Book* (1922 and 1928) presented a novel history of New Orleans:
the editors, because of Prohibition, excised all prior recipes that included
alcohol, reworked the introduction, and included two new images of the
mammy caricature. For the first time in the history of the cookbook, several
peoples and ethnicities were seen as contributing to the invention of a distinct culinary heritage. Along with the conventional praise of French and
Spanish cuisines, African Americans, Native Americans, and, oddly enough,
the Polish (for the baba cake) were included in the Creole mélange.[39] In the
1920s city boosters likewise seized on this cosmopolitan side of New Orleans; in 1922 the Convention and Tourist Bureau branded the city as "New
Orleans—America's Most Interesting City."[40] In addition, Creole cooking
was refeminized; "her magic" once again became the product of white and
African American women.[41] An article in the *Times-Picayune* stated that

"the old, tested formulae were handed along from mother to daughter in the Creole mansions of New Orleans and the stately plantation homes of Louisiana and Mississippi."[42] Alongside the cookbook's feminization, the mammy caricature returned as a more prominent character in the cookbook, a practice that would be repeated in all later editions.

The two 1920s cookbooks gave more agency to African Americans in the formation of a New Orleans "school of cookery." The cookbook now declared that Creole recipes were "a large part . . . the product of the cooks of the vast plantations" of the antebellum enslaved. This history even mentioned two long-past African American cooks by name. It described Aunt Chloe as the typical mammy whose greatest passions were cooking and caring for her master family's children. After Chloe retired, her "great copper preserving kettle" joined other historical "curiosities . . . of the plantation kitchen of Creole days" in the Louisiana State Museum; according to a risibly nostalgic story told in the *Picayune*, she would frequently return to the archives to keep her treasured kettle polished. Matilda, "the cook of cooks," likewise dutifully served her Creole family, who purchased her at the age of seventeen, and excelled at the making of French bread and flaky biscuits. A lengthy description of Matilda's baking techniques followed.[43] Despite the recognition given these unique women, their voices were suppressed by their mammification. Furthermore, two new examples of mammy iconography appear within the cookbook. A four-color mammy portrait illustrates the book's frontispiece (fig. 1); from 1922 to 1971 this sentimental study of mammy at a roaring hearth-fire, titled "A Creole Kitchen of Sixty Years Ago," would occupy the first printed page of the cookbook.

Surrounded by her cooking instruments, this unnamed domestic kitchen worker, head down, devotedly stirs her copper pot. Contrasted with this solemn portrayal is an image that would remain permanently stamped, front and center, on the cover of the cookbook until the fifteenth edition of 1971: another mammy stirring with a long wooden spoon. This time she looks directly at the reader, smiling with laughter.

The introduction to the sixth edition opened with a passage on perhaps the most lauded ingredient of New Orleans cooking, its abundant use of local seafood, the "fish, scale-fish, and shell fish, and many varieties of marine food." Each "finny tribe" was described as possessing a different attribute:

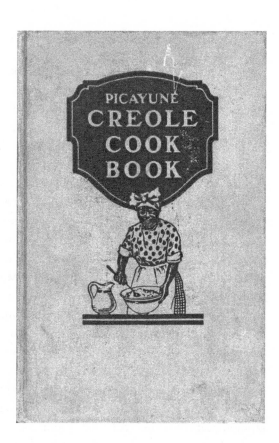

FIGURE 1. From 1922 to 1971 this image occupied the first printed page of the cookbook. From the author's personal collection.

croakers always issue "rebellious utterances"; the redfish was "handsome" and easily identifiable by "a single black dot"; Spanish mackerel were "aristocrats" and "[noblemen] indeed beside their plebeian relative[s]"; while the pompano is "supreme among fish."[44] The symbolism behind this passage cannot be ignored; New Orleans, like its surrounding waters, teemed with a limitless variety of inhabitants. The city and its seas resembled several contemporary sociopolitical and cultural ideas of the Progressive Era, especially those of Horace Kallen and Randolph Bourne. During a period when the government, corporations, and social organizations encouraged the second great wave of American immigrants to join the melting pot, philosopher Kallen contended that ethnic and cultural differences strengthened the nation.[45] Bourne similarly envisioned a "Trans-National America" where citizens would be united through their connections to their ethnic heritages.[46] Both Kallen and Bourne saw great potential in the cultural plurality of the United States. Likewise, the very Creoleness of New Orleans was the multiculturalism of the cosmopolitan city; like the mingling of fish in the sea, distinct people mixed to form an American Creole culture—or, as the cookbook designated, "a delicious combination."[47] The 1920s likewise saw another mingling of cultures in the city. In the summer of 1924, local business and civic leaders, with the blessing of President Calvin Coolidge, proclaimed that they would build "the only permanent and continuous trade fair in the Americas." The International Trade Exhibition, or Intrex, opened in early 1926, was organized to develop domestic and foreign trade relations. The International Trade Exhibition would open up American commerce globally but also, just as importantly, "sell New Orleans to the nation and to the world."[48]

Occurring at the same time as these culturally and commercially progressive sentiments were two reform movements: the backlash against the consumption of alcohol and a turn toward a domestic science revolution based on nutrition. The Eighteenth Amendment and the Volstead Act (both of 1919) prohibited the legal sale of intoxicating beverages and forced many famous New Orleans restaurants to shutter. A city used to the inebriated life was devastated. A New Orleans without Sazeracs and Ramos gin fizzes, to quote a headline from a 1925 *New York Times* article, "loses its convivial life."[49]

With the closing of many professional kitchens, the *Picayune*'s cookbook refocused its attention on the private arena of the household. Meanwhile, cookbooks and food experts were promoting a new style of cookery in American home kitchens, relying on nutritional content by counting calories, technological advancements such as cooking with gas and electricity rather than fire, and processed prepackaged foods such as canned and frozen items.[50] The *Picayune* shunned these advances: "Today cooking has taken its place as a science to be taught in dignified colleges with much talk of calories and proteids [*sic*: proteins] and other scientific jargon; but there is missed from the new cookery a something, a je ne sais quoi, that was brought together by the old Creole cooks."[51] The very symbol of culinary modernity, the cookbook, was being rewritten by physicians and a mass-market food scene. The city's newspaper of record continued its fight against the household as laboratory by opening the *Times-Picayune* Cooking School in 1932; the academy's goal was to teach housewives the "right way" to cook Creole.[52] The *Picayune's* cookbook maintained that New Orleans remained the "undisputed . . . culinary capital of America . . . for more than a century," and that little needed to be changed.[53]

More than a Memory

The two 1920s progressive editions can be considered failures, as the *Picayune Creole Cook Book's* editors quickly abandoned both the all-inclusive narrative and the attack on the scientific reform movement. The eighth edition (1936), renamed *The Original Picayune Creole Cook Book*, marked a turn back to earlier volumes that remained through the fifteenth edition of 1971. The recipes stayed basically the same, with the pre-Volstead alcoholic dishes brought back, thus enlarging the edition to more than two thousand entries.[54] The post-1930s editions kept the stamped front-cover mammy image and frontispiece illustration that first appeared in 1922. The cookbook's introduction reverted to the same praise of professional, mostly male, chefs and restaurateurs first found in the 1916 edition. One major change during this fourth phase in the evolution of the *Picayune* was the introduction of a dust jacket in 1947. The yellow-colored dust jacket (fig. 2) portrays a rosy-cheeked Caucasian man. He is surrounded by the foodstuffs of Louisiana cookery: shrimp, oysters, crawfish, crabs, turtles, sugarcane, strawberries, and a frog. With an upturned mustache and wearing a traditional toque hat, he looks unmistakably Francophone, the ideal Creole chef.

This dust jacket not only protects the book's hardcover but also physically conceals the cover's mammy image underneath. African American contributions to Creole cooking were ultimately and symbolically eclipsed beneath a masculine, white, Eurocentric-dominated narrative of New Orleans culture. Beginning in the early 1930s, the civic and business leadership of New Orleans embraced recreation as a way to entice visitors to the city; New Orleans would no longer be classified as a well-connected port city in which to do business. A new generation of middle- and upper-class American tourists would be encouraged to visit New Orleans to partake in a wide

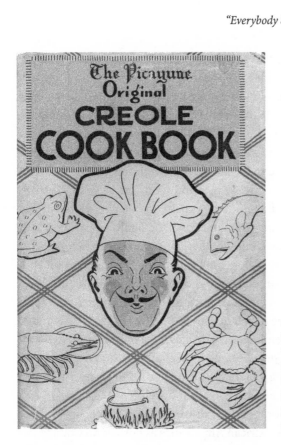

FIGURE 2. This dust jacket image was introduced in 1947. With an upturned mustache and wearing a traditional toque hat, the character looks unmistakably Francophone, the ideal Creole chef. From the author's personal collection.

range of leisure activities.[55] This new spirit was reflected in the post-1920s editions of the *Picayune*'s cookbook. With Prohibition repealed, New Orleans could once again be defined by the white, Latinate, professional male chef. Furthermore, the changing of the cookbook's title harked back to a distant era, an "original" time and place defined by its culinary and cultural connections to the Old World. The newspaper marketed the cookbook to visitors like never before. Advertisements in the *Times-Picayune* encouraged tourists to carry a piece of New Orleans "home with you. . . . Take away with you more than a memory. You needn't say 'Goodbye.'"[56]

By the next decade, civil rights and gender equality consciousness eased the tensions within the *Original Picayune Creole Cook Book*. The patriarchy and racism that defined the first fifteen editions were eliminated from the two final printings. The portraits of Mammy and the Latinate chef were replaced with romanticized archival photographs of turn-of-the-century New Orleans. To celebrate their newspaper's sesquicentennial anniversary, the *Times-Picayune* editors issued, in 1987, a sixteenth volume with a new title: *Picayune's Creole Cook Book*. For the first time, they contracted out the editorial duties to an outsider, local food journalist Marcelle Bienvenu. The cookbook now had a named author who reformatted the recipes for the contemporary kitchen. In her new introduction to the cookbook, Bienvenu is unable to escape the ties between race and food. She begins by relating a story from her childhood: the Sundays spent on her family's plantation near St. Martinville, Louisiana. Her aunt Cina, the family's matron de cuisine, would be joined in her duties by "her constant kitchen helpers" Yola and La Vielle (the Old One), who would supply the Bienvenu brood with their café au lait, freshly churned butter, and cornbread.[57] Bienvenu's *Creole Cook Book*, as a battleground for racial matters, thus hardly differs from previous editions. Although she names her family's African American domestic workers, by designating them merely as "helpers" Bienvenu fails to write an honest story about their contributions to her family's kitchen. Bienvenu, though she provides a loving memory, ultimately fails at offering a peek into Yola and La Vielle's lives as not just cooks but people.[58]

Another cookbook author used the *Picayune Creole Cook Book* for other means. Nathaniel Burton, an African American, was born in McComb, Mississippi, in 1914. He fled McComb, a racially volatile city that would later become the site of the first Student Nonviolent Coordinating Committee (SNCC) voter registration drive, for New Orleans in 1939. He took a busboy position at Canal Street's Hotel New Orleans. He moved to washing dishes, and in the kitchen he studied the expertise of Chef Dan Williams. With Williams's help and "the knowledge gained from reading every book he could find," especially the *Picayune's* cookbook, Burton eventually became a master chef. Burton oversaw kitchens in the Navy and throughout New Orleans, became an instructor at the prestigious Culinary Institute of America in Hyde Park, New York, and ended up as the chef de cuisine at New Orleans's famed Broussard's restaurant, overseeing the production of its fine French Creole fare.[59]

In 1978 Chef Nathaniel Burton coauthored, with leading New Orleans civil rights activist Rudy Lombard, *Creole Feast: Fifteen Master Chefs of*

New Orleans Reveal Their Secrets. Edited by Toni Morrison, *Creole Feast* was the first cookbook to significantly spotlight the contributions of African American cooks to New Orleans cuisine.[60] As Lombard tells it, he set out to document the unnamed: "My mother cooked for the president of the Cotton Exchange, so I knew black people were cooking in homes and restaurants like Broussard's and Galatoire's. I couldn't name names, so I set out to discover who they were." Lombard linked up with Chef Burton, and "the godfather of all the chefs in town" was placed on the cover of their cookbook.[61] Unsmiling and dressed in full chef's whites, the image of Burton both harked back to and contrasted with the mammy/Francophone chef dichotomy featured on the covers of the *Original Picayune Creole Cook Books.* In his introduction to *Creole Feast,* Lombard smashed one hundred years of racist exclusion by reclaiming Creole recipes:

> It is difficult to arrive at a universally satisfying definition of Creole cuisine. All such attempts in the past have failed to achieve a consensus, and have seldom been used twice; several key influences or individuals are always left out or changed. The one feature, however, that all previous definitions have in common is a curious effort to ascribe a secondary, lowly or nonexistent role to the Black hand in the pot, in spite of the fact that everything that is unique about New Orleans culture—its food, music, architecture, carnivals, voodoo and life style—can be traced to that city's Black presence. Quiet as it is kept, it is this fact that is at the center of the "Creole controversy."[62]

NOTES

1. "Creole Cookery. A Book Which Reveals the Secrets of the Louisiana Kitchen," *Daily Picayune,* April 15, 1900, 6.

2. Marie Louise Tobin, "Creole Cook Book Issued by *Times-Picayune* Passes on Delicious Cookery Art," *Times-Picayune,* January 25, 1937, F6.

3. Susan Tucker, with Cynthia LeJeune Nobles, Karen Trahan Leathem, and Sharon Stallworth Nossiter, "Setting the Table in New Orleans," in *New Orleans Cuisine: Fourteen Signature Dishes and Their Histories,* ed. Susan Tucker (Jackson: University of Mississippi Press, 2009), 19.

4. "Creole Cook Book, 5th Edition [*sic*]," *Times-Picayune,* June 16, 1929, *Creole Cook Book* section insert, 1.

5. Frank Schneider, "Picayune Cookbook Caters to Passion of Orleanians," *Times-Picayune,* February 24, 1988, E-4.

6. "Creole Cookery," *Daily Picayune,* April 15, 1900, 6.

7. Sue Baker, "Creole Cookery," *Dixie* magazine insert, *Times-Picayune*, February 8, 1970, 32.

8. Lafcadio Hearn, *La Cuisine Creole: A Collection of Culinary Recipes from Leading Chefs and Noted Creole Housewives, Who Have Made New Orleans Famous for Its Cuisine* (New York: W. H. Coleman, 1885), n.p.

9. The Christian Woman's Exchange of New Orleans, La., *The Creole Cookery Book* (New Orleans: T. H. Thomason, 1885), iii.

10. Marcelle Bienvenu and Judy Walker, eds., *Cooking Up a Storm: Recipes Lost and Found from the Times-Picayune of New Orleans* (San Francisco: Chronicle, 2008).

11. Lawrence N. Powell, "New Orleans: An American Pompeii?" in *Satchmo Meets Amadeus*, ed. Reinhold Wagnleitner (Innsbruck: StudienVerlag, 2006), 142–56; for recent discourse on the loss of Creole cuisine, see Ian McNulty, "Orleans Goes Nouvelle," *Gambit Weekly*, February 15, 2011, www.bestofneworleans.com/gambit/orleans-goes-nouvelle/Content?oid=1571467; Tom Fitzmorris, *Tom Fitzmorris's Hungry Town: A Culinary History of New Orleans, the City Where Food Is Almost Everything* (New York: Stewart, Tabori & Chang, 2010).

12. Marcelle Bienvenu, ed., *The Picayune's Creole Cook Book: Sesquicentennial Edition* (New Orleans: Times-Picayune, 1987), 4; Tucker et al., "Setting the Table," 19.

13. "Dr. J. F. Points Rites Arranged," *Times-Picayune*, April 9, 1946, 2; May W. Mount, *Some Notables of New Orleans: Biographical and Descriptive Sketches of the Artists of New Orleans, and Their Work* (New Orleans, 1896), 116–17; Glenn R. Conrad, *Cross, Crozier, and Crucible: A Volume Celebrating the Bicentennial of a Catholic Diocese in Louisiana* (New Orleans: Archdiocese of New Orleans, 1993), 196, 627.

14. "Ex-Professor, Newsman Dies," *Times-Picayune*, April 21, 1965. Kendall was also a distant cousin of George Wilkins Kendall, a cofounder of the *Daily Picayune*.

15. "Household Hints. Parlor and Kitchen Chow-Chow," *Daily Picayune*, October 1, 1882, 11. For Nicholson, see Patricia Brady, "Eliza Jane Nicholson (1843–1896): New Orleans Publisher," in *Louisiana Women: Their Lives and Times*, ed. Janet Allured and Judith F. Gentry (Athens: University of Georgia Press, 2009), 94–113.

16. W. Fitzhugh Brundage, *The Southern Past: A Clash of Race and Memory* (Cambridge, Mass.: Harvard University Press, 2005); David W. Blight, *Race and Reunion: The Civil War in American Memory* (Cambridge, Mass.: Harvard University Press, 2001).

17. In 1891 the city government erected the Battle of Liberty Place Monument to commemorate an 1874 insurrection by the Crescent City White League, a racist paramilitary group, which shared membership rolls with several nascent Mardi Gras Krewes. See James Gill, *Lords of Misrule: Mardi Gras and the Politics of Race in New Orleans* (Jackson: University Press of Mississippi, 1997), chapters 7 and 8; Joy J. Jackson, *New Orleans in the Gilded Age: Politics and Urban Progress, 1880–1896* (Lafayette: Louisiana Historical Association, 1969, 1997), chapter 12.

18. Dennis C. Rousey, *Policing the Southern City: New Orleans, 1805–1889* (Baton Rouge: Louisiana State University Press, 1996); Eric Arnesen, *Waterfront Workers of New Orleans: Race, Class, and Politics, 1863–1923* (New York: Oxford University Press, 1991); William Ivy

Hair, *Carnival of Fury: Robert Charles and the New Orleans Race Riot of 1900* (Baton Rouge: Louisiana State University Press, 1976).

19. Arjun Appadurai, "How to Make a National Cuisine: Cookbooks in Contemporary India," *Comparative Studies in Society and History* 30 (January 1988): 5.

20. Carol Gold, *Danish Cookbooks: Domesticity and National Identity, 1616–1901* (Seattle: University of Washington Press, 2007); Nicola Humble, *Culinary Pleasures: Cook Books and the Transformation of British Food* (London: Faber & Faber, 2005); Jessamyn Neuhaus, *Manly Meals and Mom's Home Cooking: Cookbooks and Gender in Modern America* (Baltimore: Johns Hopkins University Press, 2003); Janet Theophano, *Eat My Words: Reading Women's Lives through the Cookbooks They Wrote* (New York: Palgrave, 2002); Susan Williams, *Savory Suppers and Fashionable Feasts: Dining in Victorian America* (Knoxville: University of Tennessee Press, 1996).

21. Doris Witt, *Black Hunger: Soul Food and America* (Minneapolis: University of Minnesota Press, 1999, 2004), 11.

22. *The Picayune's Creole Cook Book* (New Orleans: The Picayune, 1900), 1.

23. "Advertisement," *Daily Picayune*, June 20, 1900, 12.

24. Kevin Fox Gotham, *Authentic New Orleans: Tourism, Culture, and Race in the Big Easy* (New York: New York University Press, 2007), 46–47.

25. Neuhaus, *Manly Meals*, 2.

26. Nicola Humble, "A Touch of Bohème: Cookery Books as Documents of Desires, Fears and Hopes," *Times Literary Supplement*, June 14, 1996, 15–16.

27. Isabel Wilkerson, *The Warmth of Other Suns: The Epic Story of America's Great Migration* (New York: Random House, 2010).

28. *The Picayune's Creole Cook Book* (1900), 2.

29. I use the words "main groups" because a wide range of persons in Louisiana identified as Creole; see the sources in the following note.

30. Joseph G. Tregle Jr., "Creoles and Americans," in *Creole New Orleans: Race and Americanization*, ed. Arnold R. Hirsch and Joseph Logsdon (Baton Rouge: Louisiana State University Press, 1992); Tregle, "Early New Orleans Society: A Reappraisal," *Journal of Southern History* 18 (February 1952): 20–36.

31. Though Grace King was not born a Creole, her lengthy writing career made her the most vocal and voracious white Creole myth proponent; Grace King, *New Orleans: The Place and the People* (New York: Macmillan, 1895), ix, 84, 117, 316.

32. Kimberly Wallace-Sanders, *Mammy: A Century of Race, Gender, and Southern Memory* (Ann Arbor: University of Michigan Press, 2008), 1. The recent historical literature on mammy is burgeoning; see Micki McElya, *Clinging to Mammy: The Faithful Slave in Twentieth-Century America* (Cambridge, Mass.: Harvard University Press, 2007); M. M. Manring, *Slave in a Box: The Strange Career of Aunt Jemima* (Charlottesville: University Press of Virginia, 1998); Deborah Gray White, *Ar'n't I a Woman? Female Slaves in the Plantation South* (New York: Norton, 1985, 1999).

33. *The Picayune's Creole Cook Book* (1900), 1–4.

34. "Compliments to the Picayune," *Daily Picayune*, April 16, 1900, 10; "Advertisement," *Daily Picayune*, February 4, 1902, 12; "The Creole Cookbook," *Daily Picayune*, August 12, 1905, 5; "Praises the Creole Cookbook," *Daily Picayune*, October 16, 1910, 16.

35. *The Picayune Creole Cook Book* (New Orleans: The Times-Picayune, 1916), i–iv.

36. Adam Fairclough, *Race and Democracy: The Civil Rights Struggle in Louisiana, 1915–1972* (1995; Athens: University of Georgia Press, 2008), 8–9.

37. Thomas Ewing Dabney, *One Hundred Great Years: The Story of the Times-Picayune from Its Founding to 1940* (New York: Greenwood, 1968), 1, 15, 119, 378–79.

38. *The Picayune Creole Cook Book* (1916), iii–v.

39. *The Picayune Creole Cook Book* (New Orleans: The Times-Picayune, 1922), vii.

40. Anthony J. Stanonis, *Creating the Big Easy: New Orleans and the Emergence of Modern Tourism, 1918–1945* (Athens: University of Georgia Press, 2006), 28.

41. *The Picayune Creole Cook Book* (1922), vii.

42. "Cooking Here Still a Fine Art," *Times-Picayune*, June 6, 1926, 2.

43. *The Picayune Creole Cook Book* (1922), v–vi.

44. Ibid., iii.

45. Horace M. Kallen, "Democracy Versus the Melting-Pot: A Study of American Nationality," *The Nation* (February 25, 1915).

46. Randolph Bourne, "Trans-National America," *Atlantic Monthly* 118 (July 1916): 86–97.

47. *The Picayune Creole Cook Book* (1922), iii.

48. Dabney, *One Hundred Great Years*, 423–26, quote on 423; Gary A. Bolding, "New Orleans Commerce: The Establishment of the Permanent World Trade Mart," *Louisiana History* 8, no. 4 (Autumn 1967): 354–56; Stanonis, *Creating the Big Easy*, 28–69.

49. Beatrice Cosgrove, "New Orleans Loses Its Convivial Life," *New York Times*, August 23, 1925, SM12; Joy Jackson, "Prohibition in New Orleans: The Unlikeliest Crusade," *Louisiana History* 19, no. 3 (Summer 1978): 261–84.

50. Laura Shapiro, *Perfection Salad: Women and Cooking at the Turn of the Century* (New York: Random House, 2001), 4–7.

51. *The Picayune Creole Cook Book* (1922), vi–vii.

52. Podine Schoenberger, "Times-Picayune Cooking School Now Institution," *Times-Picayune*, January 25, 1937, F1.

53. "Cooking Here Still a Fine Art."

54. "Advertisement," *Times-Picayune*, May 30, 1936, 17.

55. Stanonis, *Creating the Big Easy*, 70–103.

56. "Advertisement," *Times-Picayune*, February 14, 1931; also January 6, 1941, and February 26, 1941.

57. Bienvenu, *The Picayune's Creole Cook Book*, 1.

58. For a recent discussion on the inability of community cookbooks to talk about race, see John T. Edge, "Looking for Honest Stories: The Trouble with Community Cookbooks," *Oxford American* 69 (May 2010): 20–23.

59. Nathaniel Burton and Rudy Lombard, *Creole Feast: Fifteen Master Chefs of New Orleans Reveal Their Secrets* (New York: Random House, 1978), 3–4.

60. Lolis Eric Elie, "The Black Presence," *Oxford American* 49 (Spring 2005): 125–27.

61. Betsy Andrews, "Soul Food, Baby," On the Line in New Orleans: A Post-Katrina Restaurant Chronicle (December 20, 2005), http://foodandwine.blogs.com/neworleans/2005/12/soul_food_baby.html.

62. Burton and Lombard, *Creole Feast*, xv.

CHAPTER 2 ▶

The Women of St. Paul's Episcopal Church Were Worried

Transforming Domestic Skills into Saleable Commodities in Texas

REBECCA SHARPLESS

The women of St. Paul's Episcopal Church were worried. Their fine new building in downtown Waco, Texas, was nine years old, and the congregation remained in debt. They pledged as a group to raise the great sum of $800 to help reduce the church's financial embarrassment. But they had a problem. What could they, as upper-class white women, do to raise money? An unidentified person suggested publishing and selling a book of household hints and recipes, and in June 1888 the 328-page *Household Manual and Practical Cook Book* appeared. The women must have been pleased with their venture, for they brought out a second book, titled *The Guild Cook Book*, a mere thirteen years later, observing that "the kindly reception given the Guild Cook Book of fifteen years ago, encourages the hopes that a like fate may await the present volume." Almost half a century, including economic boom and bust and two huge wars, passed before the women of St. Paul's published their third cookery book, *Out of This World Recipes*, which came out in 1949. And in 1978 a fourth cookbook issued from the church, in honor of the congregation's centennial, simply titled *St. Paul's Episcopal Church Cookbook*. Individually, each of these cookbooks is an artifact of its time and place, with a unique raison d'être and content. Taken as a group, they provide a rich record of the lives of privileged white men and women in Central Texas, and to a limited extent the people who worked for them, over the ninety years between 1888 and 1978.[1] The St. Paul's cookbooks demonstrate the relationships of women to food, food preparation, and household management, and their connections with family, friends, employees, and employers. All are crucial elements in understanding the lives of southern women during a period of dramatic changes in American and southern society. Directly or indirectly, the women presented their values and their beliefs to the public that bought or read their books. Their voices were no longer reserved only for their private lives.[2]

When they decided to publish a cookbook, the women of St. Paul's entered into a genre of writing by women well established in English-speaking countries. Recipes were part of the transition from oral to written communication, and in 1672 Englishwoman Hannah Wolley was the first woman professional culinary writer to enter the realm of print publication.[3] Other English food professionals followed Wolley throughout the eighteenth century, including Eliza Smith, author of *The Compleat Housewife: Or Accomplished Gentlewomen's Companion*. In 1742 Williamsburg printer William Parks altered Smith's cookbook to suit colonial tables and made *The Compleat Housewife* the first cookbook printed, although not written, in America.[4] In 1796 New Englander Amelia Simmons published the first bona fide American cookbook in the United States, simply titled *The American Cookbook*.[5] And in 1824 Washington, D.C., boardinghouse keeper Mary Randolph gave her cookery book a southern twist by titling it *The Virginia House-Wife*.[6] An array of other regional cookbooks, such as *The Kentucky Housewife* and *The Carolina Housewife*, began popping up across the antebellum South.[7]

All of the earliest cookbooks in England and America were the work of one exemplary individual who spoke with authority and reassurance. During the American Civil War, however, a new genre arose in the form of the compiled or community cookbook. Enterprising northern women gathered their favorite recipes and sold the collections at their fund-raising bazaars to help the Union effort. After the war ended, other types of groups took notice of the collections' success and set out to create their own books.[8] By 1900 community groups across the United States had published more than two thousand titles. The number swelled to perhaps six thousand by World War I.[9] These community cookbooks function as "nonliterary print" texts that, much like quilts, can be read as documents of women and their milieu.[10] From the beginning, community cookbooks played dual roles: their overt purpose was to raise money for worthy causes, and their secondary importance was to present culinary content to appreciative audiences. Cookbooks have lasting value as the record of the foodways in particular places and times.

Southern women began publishing community cookbooks in the 1870s. The movement picked up steam rapidly.[11] Filtered through a variety of charity organizations and churches, the raising of money through cookbooks was clearly associated with the activism that propelled female reformers into both secular causes and religious missionary societies.[12] In print, however, Texas women downplayed the activist aspects of their work. The first community cookbook in the state came from the Ladies Association of the First Presbyterian Church of Houston in 1883.[13] Although the Houston editors probably intended to make money from their book, their stated concern was culinary. Articulating regional concerns, the editors observed in the preface that many cookbooks "contain receipts [recipes] not suited to the requirements of our climate" and that they aimed to "supply this deficiency" of instructions for the subtropical humidity of the Texas Gulf Coast. Their offerings included "yeast that will not sour" and tomato catsup that "does not mold."[14] Perhaps the guise of charity became a cover for women to demonstrate their cooking prowess. Or maybe the cloak of domesticity concealed an agenda of social justice or civic ambition. Irrespective of the purposes or the possible deception, the community cookbook took hold in Texas and thrived.

Five years later, the women of St. Paul's bravely followed their Presbyterian sisters into the world of publication, producing the state's second cookbook. Like the creators of many early community cookbooks, the first St. Paul's editors had two goals. First, they wanted to raise money, and writing about household topics was clearly one way of doing so. But second, they wished to showcase the culinary and housekeeping skills of the women whose recipes appeared therein. The women of St. Paul's carefully explained to their readers the need to raise eight hundred dollars. But they would raise the money through their domestic expertise: "The members and friends of the Guild were many experienced housekeepers, who could doubtless give much valuable information in the various departments of domestic economy, which information would bring a pecuniary collateral. . . . Do not forget that good cooking means good health and pleasant dispositions in the household."[15] By compiling a cookbook, the women transformed their domestic skills into saleable commodities.

In the succeeding St. Paul's volumes, mentions of money disappeared. In 1901 and 1949 the women did sell ads and did sell books. Some financial considerations existed, but they remained below the surface. In the 1901 volume the unnamed editors appeared to be concerned only about the food, writing that they were presenting "Tested Recipes ... the good and tried," culled from "all sources." They touted the "wisdom and experience of our skilled housewives." And they tantalized readers with the promise that a number of the recipes were "seen in print for the first time."[16] Premiering a recipe gave the book cachet, for it meant that a contributor had entrusted the editors with something precious that she had previously declined to share in print. In 1949 the volume was clearly about cooking and eating. The editors called their production an "epicurean delight" and assured purchasers that they would enjoy "many hours of cooking and eating the best."[17] Perhaps creators were celebrating the end of decades of economic uncertainty and war and the return of abundance and steady supplies of meat and milk. The editors spoke of the perceived increasing complexity of women's lives in the postwar world, writing that they were trying to make things easy for busy housewives: "We have endeavored to meet the needs of simple cookery, and to lift the everyday cookery out of the commonplace."[18] In 1978 the sole purpose of the volume was to celebrate the church's centennial by asking "for personal or family recipes of our members." The editors ornamented the sections with line drawings of the crosses found in various places in the church and observed, "As the crosses represent the faith we share, the recipes represent the food and fellowship we share as a church."[19] The cookbook honored the church as a community, an inward-looking entity contemplating itself.

Gathering evidence from a cookbook requires several steps. First I note the table of contents, if there is one, recording the major sections. Next I examine front matter—forewords, prefaces, et cetera—for any information about the project's creation or the attitudes of the editors. Then I proceed to recipes. Other researchers look for other topics in the recipes. For my project I concentrate on regionally identified dishes, those that merit special praise, and those attributed to someone other than the donor. Finally, I look at advertisements to see what they reveal, particularly about food in the local community.

Community cookbooks reflect their sources. They demonstrate how women's networks functioned. When a group of women decided to create a cookbook, they had to acquire recipes to publish. They culled their own personal archives, asked their friends and relatives, and sometimes wrote to well-known public figures, some of whom apparently kept files of recipes that could be sent out to answer requests. In 1888 the women of St. Paul's solicited and received recipes from across the United States—particularly but not exclusively from Texas and the rest of the South—and from Mexico. They published an alphabetical list of all contributors that ran to five pages. The women's network spanned far and wide, indicating perhaps a sort of nationwide unity with women with whom they shared similar values and resources.[20] In 1901 they received recipes from numerous Waco women and other points in the South. Mrs. Sam Sanger, who was a member of Waco's Reform Temple Rodef Sholom, contributed five recipes, and the unnamed "Baltimore" gave four, including the fanciful Bird-nest Salad, featuring eggs made of cream cheese, nests from "the heart of the lettuce," topped with French dressing.[21] Most notably, the editors lifted wholesale recipes from already published cookbooks: at least forty from the *Century Cook Book* by Mary Ronald, published in New York in 1895; at least twenty-five from the previous *St. Paul's Cookbook* (called the *Old Cook Book* and some-times shortened to "*O.C.B.*"); three from prolific novelist and cookbook writer Virginia Terhune, known as Marion Harland; and two taken from Sarah Tyson Rorer, author of seven cookbooks, as though she lived down the street.[22] Such widespread borrowing or even outright plagiarism, jar-ring to the twenty-first-century sensibility, was commonplace throughout the nineteenth century and into the twentieth.[23] A correction came with the 1978 cookbook, in which all contributors were members of St. Paul's. The recipe donors did, however, include recipes from two internationally known cooking authorities: Craig Claiborne and James Beard.[24] The women of St. Paul's linked themselves to other women across the United States as early as the 1880s, when letters were the only means of communication and sometimes took weeks to arrive. The women were also consumers of nationally distributed cookbooks, knowledgeable about the latest trends.

Like the volumes from First Presbyterian of Houston and St. Paul's of Waco, many of the early community cookbooks lacked the name of an editor or compiler, making the women appear modest and unassuming. Yet the nineteenth century was a time when literature written by women flourished, and the women who wrote cookbooks individually usually had no problem with publishing under their own names (although some wrote under pen names).[25] The women of St. Paul's knew about the grand success by Virginia Alexander Gurley, wife of prominent Waco citizen and former Confederate colonel Edward J. Gurley. Gurley won two hundred dollars when she published her six-part series on how to manage servants in *Good Housekeeping* magazine in 1886. Therein she challenged housewives to manage both household affairs and the servants in their employ.[26]

Recipes are often handed from friend to friend or from family member to family member. Women sometimes gave attribution for the recipes they collected.[27] Recipe writers rarely cite the originator's family name, which may indicate a familiarity on the part of the recipe donor. Occasionally they give a family relationship, connecting the originator and the donor by blood. While the women of St. Paul's practiced recipe attribution in the earlier cookbooks—Cousin Emily's Tea Cakes, Grandma's Pound Cake—they took particular care to do so in the 1978 cookbook.[28] At least twenty-three recipes have another woman's name attached. Elizabeth Webb contributed Audine's Sandwich Spread, consisting of cream cheese, nuts, green pepper, onion, pimento, catsup, grated hard-boiled eggs, and salt, while Mrs. William W. Taylor Jr. offered Larayne's Sour Cream Cake, a fairly straightforward concoction of sour cream, butter or oleo, sugar, egg yolks, flour, soda, almond extract, vanilla extract, and egg whites. Ruth Miller even noted somewhat ironically the renaming of her contribution as "Priscilla's Cake," writing, "This is really Italian Cream Cake."[29] Some contributors were either more zealous about gathering recipes from other women, more scrupulous about making sure to give credit where it was due, or more sentimental. Mary Ruth Duncan added attributions to five of her contributions, for yeast rolls, hush puppies, dumplings, green goddess salad dressing, and boiled custard.[30] Perhaps the women of the late twentieth century documented their recipes to preserve family recipes. Perhaps they were viewing cooking less as a daily imperative and more of a performance. The women of the late twentieth century proved much more sentimental than their predecessors.

Rather than a paean to their friends and neighbors, the women of St. Paul's likely had a different motivation in 1888 when they garnered a Boston brown bread recipe from the sitting first lady of the United States, Frances Folsom Cleveland.[31] Cleveland was not likely an acquaintance, nor was she a member of the St. Paul's immediate circle. By stretching the boundaries of their community to the White House, the women of St. Paul's may have had multiple motives. First, they enhanced their own social status. Second, by pointing out Cleveland's domesticity, they elevated esteem for cooking and creating good food. A similar dynamic may have been at work in 1978, when a recipe for a date cake frosted with brown sugar, butter, and cream, attributed to Queen Elizabeth II, found its way to Waco. The writer observed, "On occasion, Queen Elizabeth goes into the royal kitchens and bakes this cake. It is her request that the recipe not be given to others, but that it be sold for charitable purposes."[32] While the Waco women claimed no ties to royalty, they did have access to the inside of the kitchen at Buckingham Palace.[33]

Many community cookbooks, irrespective of their place of publication, show strong regional elements.[34] In the South these elements were particularly pronounced, because regional allegiance carried political as well as culinary overtones. Nostalgia for the Old South, which became increasingly strong through the late nineteenth and early twentieth centuries, diminished but did not disappear after the civil rights movement.

In the nineteenth century the women of St. Paul's reproduced recipes either named for or attributed to famous southerners. They copied from the *Creole Cookery Book* of the Women's Exchange in New Orleans. The recipe for Chickens Royal declared, "The following receipt was taken from a cooking book, 'The gift' of Mrs. Frances Dandridge to Anna Maria Dandridge, 15th December 1756, having belonged to Mrs. Martha Washington, and now in the library of Mount Vernon."[35] They included the Gen. Robert E. Lee Cake, a lemon-filled white cake which appeared in numerous southern cookbooks in the late nineteenth century, as well as a Stonewall Jackson Cake, made with an astonishing eighteen egg whites and flavored with lemon and brandy, contributed by Mrs. Dr. Early of Lynchburg, Virginia. They also included two recipes for wine from Mrs. Robert E. Lee herself, one for fox grape wine, "from an autograph recipe of Mrs. Lee, furnished by her daughter," and one for blackberry wine "from a recipe in her own hand."[36] Lest the love of the Lees be considered merely a nineteenth-century phenomenon, however, Mrs. J. L. Staton Jr. contributed a vegetable soup recipe in 1978 that she noted was "General Lee's favorite soup." Staton does not give any evidence for her assertion, and the recipe did not appear in a Lee family cookbook.[37]

Other recipes received the appellation of "South" or a place name as part of their titles. Early on, the women of St. Paul's got busy commemorating the old ways. The 1888 cookbook contains recipes for Dixie Bread, made with yeast, and several quick breads: Old Virginia Batter Bread, Southern Corn Bread, Dixie Hoe Cake, and Spoon Bread—Southern Style. The 1888 cookbook also had recipes for Stuffed Cabbage—Southern Style, which translated as a head of cabbage filled with cornbread and bacon, boiled, and served with drawn butter, as well as "Artichaux—A Southern Dish" of artichokes covered with chopped chicken, egg yolks, mushrooms, and cream.[38] The early appearance of "southern" dishes takes on added significance when one considers that Waco had the earliest Confederate monument in the state, erected in 1893. Furthermore, the donor of the spoon bread and cabbage recipes was Sarah Davis Robertson, whose husband, Felix Robertson, had been a Confederate general.[39] The hoecake and Robertson's spoon bread recipes were reprinted in the 1901 cookbook.[40] The fascination with spoon bread continued through the last two cookbooks. The 1949 cookbook had four recipes: one without a regional identifier, one called Virginia Spoon Bread, and two for Southern Spoon Bread, all some variations of milk, cornmeal, salt, and butter or shortening. One used egg whites for leavening, two used baking soda, and one used baking powder.[41] By 1978 the number of recipes was down to one, labeled Netsy's Virginia Spoonbread, sporting both a regional identifier as well as the name of the creator. The 1978 cookbook also had two recipes for hush puppies, both from the Lowcountry: St. Simon's Hush Puppies and one from a Junior League cookbook published in Charleston in 1950.[42]

In addition to quick breads, other recipes bore the southern label. The

1949 cookbook featured a recipe for Plantation Sweet Potatoes, flavored with butter and sherry, as well as beef à la mode, "one of the delicacies kept on hand during Christmas and Thanksgiving holidays in Tennessee 100 years ago."[43] Three other recipes touted their regional origins: Mississippi French Dressing, Mississippi Smothered Broiled Chicken—both the contribution of a woman whose family came from the Magnolia State—and Woodford County Kentucky Summerfried Cake, a confection of butter, flour, eggs, brown sugar, baking powder, salt, canned coconut, pecans, and vanilla extract, topped with sweetened, bourbon-laced whipped cream.[44]

Perhaps the strongest evocation of "Old South" sentiment was the line drawings that illustrated the 1949 cookbook. The cover featured an African American man, dressed in a white tuxedo jacket, balancing a tray of steaming food on his head. The chapter divider for soups and salads was illustrated with a portly African American woman, dressed in matching dress and head rag, bearing a tray loaded with a hot bowl of soup. The drawing of the male is more fully developed. He appears to be magically balancing the tray. The female is less skillfully rendered. She is wearing garb that African American women had eschewed half a century before. The editors of the St. Paul's cookbook tapped into the casual racism of a time when African Americans were the symbol of hospitality, commodified to further the financial aims of their white employers.[45]

The women of St. Paul's also used recipes to commemorate events and celebrate the church itself. Perhaps because of the church's centennial celebration, the 1978 cookbook reflected the recipes used over the decades for church events. The St. Paul's Wassail was served on Christmas Eve and a green goddess dressing recipe was "used as a fresh vegetable dip at Women of the Church picnic."[46] Large-quantity recipes fed crowds at the Lenten Luncheons: beef spaghetti, tossed salad, coleslaw, and two varieties of meat loaf. One of the latter came from Mrs. R. E. Lee Glasgow, who attributed it to "Mrs. Gregory," an English-born longtime member of St. Paul's. "She made this meat loaf for Lenten Luncheons and other functions as her contribution. When she could no longer do it herself, she gave us this recipe."[47] Also in 1978, Mrs. Robert Russell contributed a recipe for terrapin white stew originally printed in the 1888 cookbook. Turtle soup was merely a curiosity by the 1970s. The recipe's inclusion indicated a circularity, as one generation referenced another.[48] Despite the congregational focus of the 1978 book, the terrapin recipe is the only nod to the three prior cookbooks.

Even as the women of St. Paul's extolled the southernness and hominess of their recipes, they also extended their culinary range to include locales far from central Texas. Affluent, well educated, and well traveled, they demonstrated their cosmopolitan natures in their books. In addition to gathering recipes from relatives and friends from outside their homes, they brought together recipes from both the United States and beyond. The 1888 cookbook brought to central Texas dishes from Louisiana: spicy gumbo, stuffed baked fish, and "Jumballaya (A Spanish Creole Dish)" donated by "Mrs. M., New Orleans."[49] The 1888 cookbook also featured recipes from New York (roast veal, beef hash, and gingersnaps) and Boston (two recipes for brown bread and one for baked beans). The Louisiana connection is likely explained by proximity. The New York–Boston connections might be due to the strong impact of those two cities on American cooking in the late nineteenth century. The roast veal recipe from New York is attributed to the New York Cooking School, whose proprietor, Juliet Corson, published eight cookbooks in the last quarter of the nineteenth century; Boston also had an influential cooking school, which opened in 1879. The unnamed contributor of the baked bean recipe commented, "They will be done just right for Saturday night's supper, and of a rich brown color, fragrant and appetizing, as we have proved weekly, with exceptions in hot weather, for many years."[50] Deep in the heart of Texas, at least one Waco family regularly enjoyed undisputedly Yankee cuisine only thirty years after the Civil War.

Mexican cuisine was popular in Texas even in the 1880s. The 1888 St. Paul's cookbook featured a four-page chapter of "Mexican Recipes." The recipes came from domestic and international sources: eight from Mary Louise Ford Maddox of San Antonio, whose father, John Salmon "Rip" Ford, was a famous Texas Ranger; and six from "Mrs. Catalina de Leon, of Monterey, Mexico, who vouches for their superiority."[51] The fanciful spelling of the recipes—"trijoles" for *frijoles* (refried beans), "guajatale" for *guajolote* (turkey), "rollina" for *rellena* (stuffed or filled), and so on—may indicate an unfamiliarity with the recipes on the part of the editor, or a phonetic spelling or remarkable sloppiness by the contributors. The 1901 editors eschewed the Mexican dishes, but in 1949 the recipes stretched for seven pages, and most of the contributors apparently were from Waco. Directions for chili con carne and enchiladas came from a contributor in Harlingen, on the Texas-Mexico border. One of the odder contributions was French Dressing for Guacamole, a dish of mashed avocado and spices. The dressing included a base of chili sauce, hot sauce, or tomato sauce, and might include Roquefort or bleu cheese—a tasty but unorthodox take on Mexican cuisine.[52]

By 1978 the numerous "Mexican" dishes were tinged with chili flavoring but otherwise appear to be entirely American in derivation. The sheer volume of recipes makes clear that Mexican food was integral. Most recipes used traditional Mexican seasonings such as onion, garlic, chili powder, cumin, and oregano. They also made use of late twentieth-century commercial products, including corn chips made by companies such as Frito-Lay, canned enchilada sauce, and RO*TEL tomatoes. They also used cheddar and "Old English" cheese rather than Mexican cheeses.[53] To these home cooks, "Mexican" apparently meant anything with chili powder.

In the expansive years after World War II, the women of St. Paul's demonstrated their interests in exotic fare. The 1949 cookbook featured a twenty-page section of "foreign foods." Most of the collections of recipes were from individual women: nine English recipes from Jessie Green; two Syrian dishes, including "kipbe" (rather than kibbeh) from Lillian Andress, and Scandinavian dishes from Dorothea Borchers. A local grocer, Mariano Losavio, contributed the menu for a "Complete Italian Dinner."[54] While the ethnicities of the contributors remain unknown, at least two women had significant international experiences. Wartime adventure gave Margaret Barclay Megarity her international knowledge. The Chilean recipes she contributed to the cookbook came from her year and a half with the U.S. Foreign Service in Santiago during World War II.[55] Mary Tyng Higgins, who contributed four Chinese recipes, was the daughter of American Episcopalian missionaries to China. With her husband Charles Higgins she served as a missionary to China before World War II, and the two were interned as prisoners of war by the Japanese for ten months. In 1949 Charles Higgins was the pastor of St. Alban's, a newly founded Episcopal parish in Waco.[56]

In 1978 the St. Paul's cookbook reflected and acknowledged the ethnic roots of some members. Ann Thayer, the wife of associate rector Richard

Thayer, immigrated to the United States from England after her marriage. Not only did she contribute recipes for Welsh rarebit, hot cross buns, English Bath buns, Cornish pastries, and Yorkshire pudding, but she also included a substantial paragraph with each, discussing its origins and significance in English culinary history.[57] Four women who married into the Khoury family contributed recipes for Middle Eastern specialties. Although the Khoury family immigrated to the United States in 1901, not all of the daughters-in-law were Middle Eastern. They had nonetheless learned to make the dishes of their husbands' ancestral country. Clearly bicultural, some of the Khoury women emphasized the American iterations of their recipes. Others foregrounded the old names. Recipes for baba ghanoush and tabbouleh appeared with their Arabic names first and English explanations appended, but Lebanese Bread (Khubuz) and Stuffed Squash (Mih-Sheh Koosa) were given English titles first. Other St. Paul's members who were not of Middle Eastern ethnicity contributed recipes for Persian lamb stew and Greek moussaka, made with "Munster" (likely meaning Muenster) or Monterey Jack cheese.[58]

A third international cuisine with a prominent role in the 1978 cookbook was Spanish, albeit decidedly Americanized. Waco women contributed recipes for Spanish-sounding dishes with American ingredients such as gazpacho made with Clamato, a tomato juice–clam broth mixture invented in the late 1960s, and a paella recipe specifying Eckrich sausage, a product of Indiana. A recipe for spinach and pine nuts called for Serrano ham or prosciutto as a substitute. The dry-cured Spanish ham was likely unavailable in Waco on a regular basis, but the substitution seems to indicate that prosciutto, an Italian product, had wider availability in the late 1970s.[59]

A smattering of French recipes were not haute cuisine but rather a homelier type of provincial cooking. Broiled eggplant Provencale [*sic*] and aioli sauce spoke of southern France. "Walnut Bread from Southern Burgundy" featured a savory yeast dough from the wine region. Other European regions also appeared in the 1978 cookbook. "Swiss fondue" could be served in a chafing dish, and "Glühwein" brought the traditional German holiday drink into Waco homes. Cooking influences extended past Europe, too. Latin American tastes showed up in Cuban Black Beans and Apple Crisp, a "Pre-Lenten or Carnival Specialty" from Nancylu Bennett, who had traveled extensively in Mexico. And Chinese-inspired dishes included Chinese Chicken Salad, made with canned La Choy Fancy Chinese Vegetables and soy sauce, and zucchini pancakes, which the donor said had a "definite oriental taste."[60]

In addition to individual recipes, the four cookbooks reflect changes in American society. Only the 1888 cookbook contained a chapter, typical for the time, on "Cookery for the Sick," which included an "Excellent Substitute for Mother's Milk" composed of sweet milk, boiling water, and a little sugar.[61] Even the financially comfortable women of St. Paul's had to worry about a baby who could not receive nourishment from its mother. The editors of the 1901 cookbook chose to leave that chapter out, although it likely still had use, and by 1949 this type of material had largely dropped from general American culinary discussions.

The departure of basic cooking practices from the home factored into the number of recipes for breads, pickles, and jellies. Yeast breads have always presented difficulty for cooks, and the 1888 cookbook had sixteen pages of recipes for various types of breads; the 1901 cookbook increased its offerings to twenty pages. Despite the availability and popularity of bakery bread, the wealthy families of Waco expected home-baked bread, almost surely the painstaking labor of a domestic worker. In the post–World War II period, loaf bread made with yeast disappeared completely from the St. Paul's collection; four recipes for yeast rolls were the only offerings.[62] By 1978 bread baking reappeared as a leisure activity.[63] Those recipes included seven for yeast bread and eight for rolls. The decline in home preservation through making pickles, jellies, and other types of preserves is graphically illustrated by the numbers of pages devoted to them: twenty-three in 1888, ten in 1901, three in 1949, and only a smattering in 1978. Coming out of the lean years of World War II, prosperous central Texas women did make pickles. The 1949 cookbook includes recipes for the chopped cabbage preserve known as chowchow as well as other types of relishes and pickles made from beans, watermelons, peaches, and cucumbers.[64] By 1978 the number had dwindled to one recipe each for relish, cucumber pickles, and jelly, with an additional formula for "Idiot Pickles," a way of spicing up commercially prepared kosher dills.[65]

Foodways are subject to fads, and the recipes in St. Paul's cookbooks reflect trends. In 1888 the dish du jour was "Heavenly Hash (The Newest Fashionable Dish)," attributed to "New York": oranges, bananas, lemons, apples, raisins, and pineapples cut into tiny bits, seasoned with nutmeg, and served in a hollowed-out orange shell.[66] The 1901 book reflected the rage for chafing-dish cooking, in which dishes were prepared in the kitchen and finished at the table, presumably to the delight of the assembled guests. Thirteen pages of recipes, including numerous recipes for oysters and dishes à la Newburg (in a sherry-laced cream sauce), followed a discussion of the "well established reputation" of the chafing dish and a lecture on care in preparing dishes tableside.[67] The 1949 cookbook shows liberal use of prepared foods: Velveeta cheese, cream of mushroom soup in casseroles, and gelatin in congealed salads. Five variations of chicken spaghetti graced the pages. "Sailboat potatoes" inspired the mothers of the new baby boom to entice Junior with a clever entrée: make the potatoes look like boats, create a sail from a slice of cheese, and use a square hamburger for the dock, two pieces of bacon for the waves, and "carrot rings for rocks along the shore." Tellingly, amid the postwar prosperity, an eighteen-day reducing diet also appeared.[68] Reflecting an increased awareness of gender roles, the 1978 cookbook had a section on "Men's Specialties," ranging from barbecue sauce to blueberry muffins.[69]

While the recipes tell much about the foods that the people of Waco ate, the narrative elements also hold much detail about life in central Texas. Some of these elements are the work of the editor(s), while others come from the recipe contributors. The amount of narration varies widely from cookbook to cookbook, and the St. Paul's collection is no exception. The 1888 cookbook has by far the strongest editorial voice, but each volume has its own prejudices and revelations.

The science of nutrition made great gains in the last quarter of the nineteenth century. That development informed the growing home economics movement.[70] In the South authors such as Mary Stuart Harrison Smith, in her 1885 *Virginia Cookery-Book*, argued for regularity and order in the kitchen.[71] The women of St. Paul's titled their first publication *Household*

Manual and Practical Cook Book, for it was full of pages of advice in addition to recipes. An unnamed writer from St. Paul's proclaimed the virtues of this new scientific method of household management:

> Nature evidently endowed woman to be the presiding genius of the household, and she should regard housekeeping as a noble science, unsurpassed in its importance to comfort and health.... So it has become expedient that every girl should learn cooking as a science. Intelligence and resolution will unravel all its mysteries, and then her own works will praise her.... It means inventiveness, watchfulness and willingness—the economy of your grandmother and the science of modern chemists.[72]

Many of the tenets of the domestic science movement became commonplace, and subsequent publications had no such direct commentary. The 1901 authors editorialized little, weighing in only on the topic of pie preparation: "Pie is purely an American dish, and as intelligent, patriotic people, we should strive to make it a progression and not adhere too rigidly to old methods in its preparation."[73] The 1949 and 1978 volumes list only weights and measures, with no advice save for the Bible verses at the beginning of each section of the later book.

While cookbooks can be a valuable source in documenting the lives and work of domestic servants, only the 1888 St. Paul's volume alludes to the presence of paid staff in the kitchen. Household manuals of the late nineteenth century often assumed that a cook would do the preparation of food but that the housewife should know enough to train the domestic workers. The authors of the 1888 cookbook observed that "servants are few" and asserted that many housewives "must be their own housekeepers and often cooks." Servants needed to be well managed, and experience and "a good cook-book" could be the guide.[74]

The depiction of domestic workers in cookbooks by employers is often highly questionable. The creations of domestic workers often appeared in their employers' publications without proper attribution. Many times, employers simply lifted recipes without giving the cook any credit at all. When they did assign credit to the creator, they usually did it in the most cursory fashion possible.[75] Very few cookbooks that use African American recipes and voices identify the cooks by anything but first name, mirroring daily face-to-face practice in the Jim Crow South. White authors erased the women's identities and conflated their persons with their duties. In the 1888 cookbook, "Clara" and "Manerva" are in the list of contributors, but they appear in the list alphabetized under their first names and with "Cook" following their first names as though it were their family name. The latter appears in the body of the text as "'Manerva'" (in quotation marks), "Manerva Cook," and "Minerva Cook." The recipes reveal that Manerva/Minerva lived in Missouri and that she made potato stuffing, fried chicken, and smothered chicken of high quality. "Clara Cook," from St. Louis, prepared a custard cake with a sweet cream filling. The sender(s) of the recipes thought enough of the cooks to include their recipes and to attribute them to their creators (as opposed to taking credit for the recipes themselves). They could not bring themselves, however, to give these women family names, and someone grafted the women's occupation onto their names as if it adequately identified them.[76] Although Manerva and Clara lived in Missouri, not Waco, their employers were almost surely peers of the women in Texas, who likely had access to domestic help in their homes.

Much of the character of a community cookbook depends on the editor and how much license she allows recipe contributors with their prose. One of the ways a recipe contributor could express herself was by extolling the high merit of her offering. Many times from 1888 to 1978 the writers simply attached adjectives to their recipes: "very fine," "delicious," "excellent," or "exceedingly fine."[77] Others shared the number of times they had succeeded with a recipe: "Doughnuts (Well Tried)" and "Sponge Gingerbread—Tried and True."[78] At the other end of the spectrum, women touted their abilities as the creators of new formulas; in 1888, about her Chocolate Layer Cake, filled with Baker's chocolate, "sweet milk," sugar, and vanilla, Mrs. J. J. See wrote "(Original)." Lavonia Jenkins Barnes bragged on her sister's creation in a recipe for Raisin Sauce (onion, margarine or butter, vinegar, seeded raisins, chopped apple, salt, cinnamon, cloves, allspice, and Worcestershire sauce), served with "fresh or cured ham." Either Barnes or the editor wrote, "This recipe of Mrs. Barnes' sister won a $35.00 Good Housekeeping recipe prize."[79] Women were proud of their cooking and wanted others to know it.

By the late 1970s contributors felt the need to justify the time they spent cooking elaborate recipes from scratch. Ruth Warner wrote of her apricot bread, which required chopping dried apricots, "This takes time, but it is worth it." Sammie Pierce said the same of her Danish Twists, leavened with yeast and topped with margarine, powdered sugar, and chopped pecans. Pam and Cappy Crow, a married couple, assured readers that their jalapeño dill pickles were "crisp and worth the work," and they also felt the need to counsel their peers on the timing of pickling: "Make in May or early June. Latter part of June is too late for canning size cucumbers and fresh dill." Since pickling skills were largely artifacts of the past, the Crows wanted to make sure that housekeepers in the 1970s had the proper information needed to succeed.[80]

Still other annotations give glimpses into particular domestic situations. In 1888 a "young housekeeper" sent a recipe for scalloped oysters, observing: "They are not novel or extravagant, but through them I have been enabled, to some extent, to maintain the good humor of my very particular husband, and therefore have an abiding faith in their good results." The fact that oysters would seem commonplace in 1888 demonstrates the efficacy of rail transportation, bringing them from the seaside to everyday dinner tables. This young woman was placating a hard-to-please husband with food.[81] (The editor included this testimony in her commentary on the importance of domestic bliss but did not append it to the recipe.) In 1978 Margaret Boyce Brown published her recipe for "Mama B's Punch," made from frozen orange juice, frozen lemonade, canned pineapple juice, club soda, and ginger ale, to serve forty guests. The Boyce family was socially prominent in Amarillo and had a considerable number of entertaining obligations during Brown's girlhood in the late 1930s. Brown wrote: "My mother worked out this recipe when I was in high school to take care of numerous parties with 'sliding' guest lists. I brought it to Waco as a bride and we used it at a Garden Club tea. From then on it has been used at St. Paul's Church and School, PTAs, funerals, weddings, etc." She went on to note, "The beauty of this is that you can buy [for?] several recipes and make only one ahead. There is very little waste." Mrs. Boyce (and almost surely her cook) carefully developed a recipe that could be made from nonperishable items and serve a crowd at relatively little expense and difficulty. Brown's observations give a glimpse into the considerations that a socially prominent family gave to frequent entertaining and staying on budget.[82]

A final element in the content of many cookbooks was advertising, either clustered in one section of the book or scattered throughout. In 1888, 1901, and 1949 the women of St. Paul's sold advertising to local businesses, many of them food related, to fund their cookbooks. How ads were sold remains a matter of speculation. The women might have conducted their business by mail (for example, with Church and Dwight, the New York company that made Arm and Hammer baking soda) or through their husbands, but the image of a proper woman calling on a businessman in his office is compelling. Regardless of their method, the women engaged in commerce. Assuredly, it was for a good cause, but they were treading the boundaries of propriety.

The ads provide fascinating glimpses into the world of groceries. Twenty-two different entities appeared in the ads for the 1888 cookbook. Two were generic ads for local grocers, but the remainder defined a cornucopia of goods available to the housewife with a sufficient household budget. Some local grocers advertised fresh meats, from chicken to game, and fresh fish and oysters. Other advertisers touted staples such as flour, baking powder, and processed pork products, from lard to cured hams (all of which were highly competitive in the late nineteenth century).[83] Fancy groceries also abounded in Waco in 1888: various types of mustards, spices, "choicest catsup," teas, many kinds of coffee, "tropical fruits," canned fruits and vegetables, cocoa, and "Caracas" chocolate.[84] The solicitors for the 1901 cookbook were equally enterprising. At least two of the businesspeople who bought space in that edition—a local grocery wholesaler and the manager of the local ice plant—were husbands of recipe contributors. They created a transfer of wealth from the husband's business to the wife's charity, one that might not have occurred under different circumstances. The wife could offer the husband a tangible return—a print ad—for his investment.[85] While the types of ads generally remained the same as the previous edition, others indicated changes in cooking technology. The Waco Gas Company advised readers to "Do Away with the Danger of an Oil Stove; Gas Ranges Do Not Explode." And local hardware company Harrison and Winchell's advertised the availability of Mrs. Van Deusen Cake Molds. Widely touted Van Deusen Cake Molds appeared in *Table Talk* magazine, a periodical devoted largely to culinary matters, as early as 1891 and were espoused by the Boston Cooking School as late as 1915. Local merchants believed that national brands mattered to the women in Waco.

The 1949 cookbook featured ads from various retail establishments. Appliance advertising was brisk, letting customers know that new stoves and refrigerators were once again available in the postwar years. Several local food processors boasted of pasteurized milk, custom meat slaughtering, and chickens "dressed fresh daily." Local grocers also advertised, but they had reason to worry, for the most eye-catching notice was from the San Antonio–based HEB Grocery, calling attention to itself with a full-page ad as "Waco's Newest Super Market." Chain groceries were continuing to make inroads in central Texas. Also denoting postwar prosperity were ads for local restaurants. Youngblood's Chicken asked potential patrons to "Let us serve your next party or social. . . . We do a complete job . . . food, drink, serving" (ellipses in original). Servants no longer cooked or served, but Youngblood's would do so for a fee. And Moran's Coffee Shop appealed to young families: "Your entire family will enjoy eating out! Wholesome atmosphere and good food await you."[86] Since the 1978 cookbook concerned commemoration rather than fund-raising, it contained no ads. The women of St. Anne's Guild, a service group within the church who sponsored the cookbook, had access to enough financial resources within their own families and the church. They had no need to solicit external funding.

Across nine decades, the women of St. Paul's Episcopal Church shared food with their families, their friends, and the members of their congregations. Few of them left memoirs or paper collections for scholars. In addition to public records, the four cookbooks they published may be the only print sources that bear the names of most of them. By examining the cookbooks we can learn not only about the foods that they and their domestic workers prepared but also about their relationships to other people and to the marketplace. Taken as a group, the four cookbooks of St. Paul's create an invaluable record of change over time in one organization in one place.

A personal word: I grew up in St. Paul's, and I left the church when I was twenty to begin my religious search. As a child, I received my first communion in the building for which the women raised money in 1888. As I read the 1978 cookbook, I, like many readers of many community cookbooks, return to another place and time. The women whose names appear were my Sunday school teachers, youth leaders, and friends of my family. I remember my first taste of broccoli in Sandra Coleman's turkey divan when she hosted a college group in her home on one of Waco's finest streets; the recipe isn't in the book, but others by her are. Although my mother contributed no recipes to this or any other cookbook that I'm aware of, she gave numerous copies as gifts, including the one that sits on my desk now. Giving this cookbook to her college-age daughter was something she thought appropriate to do: a grown-up gift for a nearly grown-up girl. Mother and Sandra Coleman are both dead now, but the modest plastic-bound, loose-leaf cookbook is tangible evidence of their influence on me and surely others as well.

NOTES

1. St. Paul's Guild, Waco, Texas, *Household Manual and Practical Cook Book. Embracing many hundreds of valuable recipes, contributed and endorsed by the best housekeepers of Texas and other states* (Waco, Tex.: Brooks and Wallace Steam Print, 1888); St. Paul's Guild of St. Paul's Episcopal Church, Waco, Texas, *The Guild Cook Book of Tested Recipes* (Waco, Tex.: Knight Printing Co., 1901), quotation from unpaged preface; St. Anne's Guild, St. Paul's Episcopal Church, *Out of This World Recipes* (Waco, Tex.: Grove Printing Company, 1949); *St. Paul's Episcopal Church Cookbook* (Waco, Tex.: St. Paul's Episcopal Church, 1978). Like many—probably most—community cookbooks, these books are scarce, with only two or three copies found in libraries.

2. Anne L. Bower, "Bound Together: Recipes, Lives, Stories, and Readings," in *Recipes for Reading: Community Cookbooks, Stories, Histories*, ed. Anne L. Bower (Amherst: University of Massachusetts Press, 1997), 2.

3. Steven M. Tobias, "Early American Cookbooks as Cultural Artifacts," *Papers on Language and Literature* 34 (winter 1998): 7; Janet Theophano, *Eat My Words: Reading Women's Lives through the Cookbooks They Wrote* (New York: Palgrave, 2002), 197.

4. http://digital.lib.msu.edu/projects/cookbooks/html/intro_essay.html#1, accessed December 13, 2010; http://www.history.org/history/jdrlweb/exhibits/treasurecook.cfm, accessed December 13, 2010.

5. Theophano, *Eat My Words*, 202–3; Mary Tolford Wilson, "Amelia Simmons Fills a Need: *American Cookery*, 1796," *William and Mary Quarterly*, 3rd Series, 14, no. 1 (January 1957): 16–30.

6. Mary Randolph, *The Virginia House-Wife* (Washington, D.C.: Davis and Force, 1824).

7. Lettice Bryan, *The Kentucky Housewife* (Cincinnati: Shepard & Stearns, 1839); Sarah Rutledge, *The Carolina Housewife, or House and Home* (Charleston: W. R. Babcock and Co., 1847).

8. Margaret Cook, *America's Charitable Cooks: A Bibliography of Fund-raising Cook Books Published in the United States (1861–1915)* (Kent, Ohio, 1971), 7.

9. Lynne Ireland, "The Compiled Cookbook as Foodways Autobiography," *Western Folklore* 40 (1981), 107; Janice Bluestein Longone, "'Tried Receipts': An Overview of America's Charitable Cookbooks," in *Recipes for Reading: Community Cookbooks, Stories, Histories*, ed. Anne L. Bower (Amherst: University of Massachusetts Press, 1997), 18–20. The genre of course continues to flourish today.

10. Bower, "Bound Together," 4–5.

11. According to Margaret Cook, the oldest charitable cookbooks in each southern state are Jane Grant Gilmore Howard, *Fifty Years in a Maryland Kitchen* (Baltimore: Turnbull Brothers, 1873); *The Housekeeper's Manual: Collection of Valuable Receipts, Carefully Selected and Arranged* (Nashville: Pub. House of the Methodist Episcopal Church, South, 1875); Mrs. E. F. Richards, *My Mother's Cook Book: Compiled by Ladies of St. Louis and Sold for the Benefit of the Women's Christian Home* (St. Louis: Woodward, Tiernan & Hale, 1875); *Housekeeping in the Blue Grass* (Cincinnati: Geo. E. Stevens, 1875); *Housekeeping in Old Virginia: Containing Contributions from Two Hundred and Fifty Ladies in Virginia and Her Sister States*, ed. Marion Cabell Tyree (New York: G. W. Carleton & Co., 1877); *Gulf City Cook Book Compiled by the Ladies of the St. Francis Street Methodist Episcopal Church South, Mobile, Alabama* (Dayton, Ohio: United Brethren Publishing House, 1878); First Presbyterian Church (Raleigh, N.C.) Woman's Auxiliary, *Capital City Recipes* (Raleigh, 1880); Augusta, Ga., Second Presbyterian Church, *Choice Recipes of Georgia Housekeepers by the Ladies of the Second Presbyterian Church, Augusta, Ga.* (New York: Trow's Printing and Bookbinding Co., 1880); *265 Choice Recipes, Trinity Church (Washington, D.C.)* (Washington, D.C.: Wm. H. Morrison, Publisher & Bookseller, 1883); *The Creole Cookery Book, Christian Woman's Exchange* (New Orleans: T. H. Thomason, 1885); Louisa Cheves Smythe Stoney, *Carolina Rice Cook Book* (Charleston, S.C.: Carolina Rice Kitchen Association, 1901); *Souvenir Cook Book, Ladies' Aid Society, Presbyterian Church, Milton, Florida* (n.p., 1906); *Tried and True Cookbook, Ladies Aid Society, First Presbyterian Church, Gulfport, Miss.* (Galveston, Tex.: Clarke and Courts, 1906); *Border City Cook Book, Ladies of Central Methodist Church, Fort Smith*, (n.p., 1907) (Cook, *America's Charitable Cooks*, 19, 21, 49, 51, 52, 90, 94, 101, 144, 145, 196, 240, 243, 258).

12. The literature on women in church societies during the nineteenth century includes Carol Crawford Holcomb, "Mothering the South: The Influence of Gender and the Social Gospel on the Social Views of the Leadership of the Woman's Missionary Union, Auxiliary to Southern Baptist Convention, 1888–1930" (PhD diss., Baylor University, 1999); Elizabeth Hill Flowers, "Varieties of Evangelical Womanhood: Southern Baptists, Gender, and American Culture" (PhD diss., Duke University, 2007); Dana Robert, *American Women in Mission: A Social History of Their Thought and Practice* (Macon, Ga.: Mercer University Press, 1997);

Patricia Hill, *The World Their Household* (Ann Arbor: University of Michigan Press, 1995); Louis A. Boyd and R. Douglas Brackenridge, *Presbyterian Women in America: Two Centuries of a Quest for Status* (Westport, Conn: Greenwood, 1983); Mary Sudman Donovan, *A Different Call: A History of Women's Ministries in the Episcopal Church, 1850–1920* (Wilton, Conn.: Morehouse, 1986); Jean Miller Schmidt, *Grace Sufficient: A History of Women in American Methodism* (Nashville: Abingdon, 1999); and John Patrick Dowell, *Social Gospel in the South: The Women's Home Mission Movement in the Methodist Episcopal Church, South, 1866–1939* (Baton Rouge: Louisiana State University Press, 1982).

13. *The Texas Cook Book: A Thorough Treatise on the Art of Cookery* (Houston: First Presbyterian Church Ladies Association, 1883).

14. Ibid., unpaged preface, 47, 73.

15. *St. Paul's Waco*, unpaged preface.

16. *Guild Cook Book*, unpaged preface.

17. *Out of This World*, unpaged foreword.

18. Ibid.

19. *St. Paul's* 1978, unpaged foreword.

20. Bower, "Cooking Up Stories," 31.

21. *Guild Cook Book*, 129.

22. The *Century Cook Book* was published by the Century Company, producers of the popular *St. Nicholas* magazine, and little is known about Mary Ronald. The Harland/Terhune recipes are attributed to "Common Sense"—the popular *Common Sense in the Household: A Manual of Practical Housewifery*, published by Charles Scribner in New York in 1871. The cherry soufflé, however, appears to be from another Harland/Terhune cookbook, *The Dinner Year-Book*, published by Scribner's Sons in 1883.

23. Damon Lee Fowler, "Historical Commentary," introduction to *Mrs. Hill's Southern Practical Cookery and Receipt Book* by Annabella P. Hill (Columbia: University of South Carolina Press, 1995), xxvi.

24. *St. Paul's* 1978, 106, 178.

25. The literature on American women's writing in the nineteenth century is voluminous. For an overview of women's writing, see Elaine Showalter, *A Jury of Her Peers: Celebrating American Women Writers from Anne Bradstreet to Annie Proulx* (New York: Vintage Books, 2010).

26. Mrs. E. J. [Virginia Alexander] Gurley, "Mistress Work and Maid Work, Which Is Mistress and Which Is the Servant?" published serially in *Good Housekeeping*: vol. 2, no. 11 (April 3, 1886), 311–13; vol. 2, no. 12 (April 17, 1886), 339–40; vol. 2, no. 13 (May 1, 1886), 365–66; Vol. 3, no. 1 (May 15, 1886), 11–12; vol. 3, no. 2 (May 29, 1886), 39–40; and vol. 3, no. 3 (June 12, 1886), 66–67.

27. Ann Romines, "Growing Up with the Methodist Cookbooks," in *Recipes for Reading: Community Cookbooks, Stories, Histories*, ed. Anne L. Bower (Amherst: University of Massachusetts Press, 1997), 82.

28. *St. Paul's Waco*, 163; *Out of This World*, 122.

29. *St. Paul's* 1978, 1, 123–24. Italian cream cake, of unknown origin, consists of sugar, shortening, margarine, eggs, buttermilk, soda, flour, coconut, chopped nuts, and vanilla, frosted with cream cheese, powdered sugar, nuts, margarine, and vanilla.

30. Ibid., 44, 73, 78, 85, 142.

31. *St. Paul's Waco*, 86–87. It is difficult to imagine the newlywed Mrs. Cleveland, barely twenty-one years old, going into the White House kitchen and whipping up a batch of brown bread, but her staff in the White House likely kept a recipe on hand to dispatch to interested inquirers. A similar but slightly different version of Cleveland's recipe appeared in 1908 in Jacqueline Harrison Smith, *Famous Old Receipts Used a Hundred Years and More* (Philadelphia: John C. Winston, 1908), 46.

32. *St. Paul's* 1978, 128. Dozens of iterations of this recipe appear on the Internet in 2010, generally with some version of the same story.

33. Colleen Cotter, "Claiming a Piece of the Pie: How the Language of Recipes Defines Community," in *Recipes for Reading: Community Cookbooks, Stories, Histories*, ed. Anne L. Bower (Amherst: University of Massachusetts Press, 1997), 71.

34. Anne Bower, "Cooking Up Stories: Narrative Elements in Community Cookbooks," in *Recipes for Reading: Community Cookbooks, Stories, Histories*, ed. Anne L. Bower (Amherst: University of Massachusetts Press, 1997), 33.

35. *St. Paul's Waco*, 52; *Creole Cookery Book*, edited by the Christian Women's Exchange of New Orleans (1885), 204.

36. *St. Paul's Waco*, 154, 156, 250, 253. Dozens of recipes for the Robert E. Lee cake appear on the Internet in 2010. Not surprisingly, given the number of eggs required, the Stonewall Jackson has faded into culinary oblivion. The blackberry wine recipe is similar to that reproduced in Ann Carter Zimmer, *The Robert E. Lee Family Cooking and Housekeeping Book* (Chapel Hill: University of North Carolina Press, 1997), which reproduces recipes from the Lee family recipe notebook. Fox grapes, *Vitis labrusca*, are native to the eastern United States but not to Texas.

37. *St. Paul's* 1978, 29. The soup was fairly ordinary, consisting of tomatoes, celery, carrots, parsley, chopped pepper, onion juice, salt, pepper, "1 wineglass sherry wine," and water.

38. *St. Paul's Waco*, 92, 100, 101 119, 126.

39. Kelly McMichael, *Sacred Memories: The Civil War Monument Movement in Texas* (Denton: Texas State Historical Association, 2009), 206; Robert Maberry Jr., "Robertson, Felix Huston," *Handbook of Texas Online*, accessed November 25, 2010, http://www.tshaonline.org/handbook/online/articles/fro26.

40. *Guild Cook Book*, 227, 228.

41. *Out of This World*, 86–87.

42. *St. Paul's* 1978, 72–74, 181.

43. *Out of This World*, 79, 52.

44. Ibid., 30, 58, 122.

45. Among the literature on African American stereotyping, particularly concerning

Mammy, see Doris Witt, *Black Hunger: Food and the Politics of U.S. Identity* (New York: Oxford University Press, 1999); Psyche Williams-Forson, *Building Houses Out of Chicken Legs: Black Women, Food, and Power* (Chapel Hill: University of North Carolina Press, 2006); Patricia A. Turner, *Ceramic Uncles and Celluloid Mammies: Black Images and Their Influence on Culture* (Charlottesville: University of Virginia Press, 1994); Kenneth Goings, *Mammy and Uncle Mose: Black Collectibles and American Stereotyping* (Bloomington: Indiana University Press, 1994); Michael D. Harris, *Colored Pictures: Race and Visual Representation* (Chapel Hill: University of North Carolina Press, 2003); and Kate Haug, "Myth and Matriarchy: An Analysis of the Mammy Stereotype," in *Dirt and Domesticity: Constructions of the Feminine* (New York: Whitney Museum of American Art, 1992), 38–47. For a particularly perceptive discussion of southern nostalgia, see Stephanie Yuhl, *A Golden Haze of Memory: The Making of Historic Charleston* (Chapel Hill: University of North Carolina Press, 2005).

46. *St. Paul's* 1978, 16, 176.

47. Ibid., 173, 174, 175, 176.

48. Ibid., 29.

49. *St. Paul's Waco*, 22, 28, 51. The Louisiana dishes differ from other southern cuisine because of their distinctive derivation and spices. See Gene Bourg, "New Orleans Foodways," in *The Encyclopedia of Southern Culture*, vol. 7, *Foodways*, ed. John T. Edge (Chapel Hill: University of North Carolina Press, 2007), 83–86.

50. *St. Paul's Waco*, 45, 58, 86, 87, 126, 165; quotation on 127.

51. Ibid., 244–48.

52. *Out of This World*, 155.

53. http://www.texmex.net/Rotel/main.htm, accessed December 27, 2010. Old English cheese is a soft sharp cheddar product still manufactured by Kraft.

54. *Out of This World*, 149–68.

55. *Oral Memoirs of Margaret Barclay Megarity* (Waco, Tex.: Baylor University Institute for Oral History, 1977), 21–24.

56. http://www.nytimes.com/1985/08/11/us/charles-a-higgins.html, http://www.thecathedral school.com/who-we-are/history/index.aspx; http://www.chattanoogan.com/articles/article 52363.asp, accessed December 27, 2010.

57. *St. Paul's* 1978, 12, 80, 83, 87, 97; http://obit.porterloring.com/obitdisplay.html?id=510178, accessed December 28, 2010.

58. *St. Paul's* 1978, 6, 27, 37, 45, 56, 69, 105, 108.

59. Ibid., 26, 59, 180; http://www.clamato.com/en/about/historyofclamato.aspx, accessed December 5, 2010; http://www.eckrich.com/heritage, accessed December 5, 2010.

60. *St. Paul's* 1978, 11, 13, 19, 30, 48, 51, 64, 70, 137.

61. *St. Paul's Waco*, 273.

62. *Out of This World*, 90–91.

63. One example of the resurgence of bread baking in the 1970s is the popularity of *The Tassajara Bread Book* by Edward Espe Brown (Boston: Shambhala, 1974).

64. *Out of This World*, 72–76.

65. *St. Paul's* 1978, 17, 19, 20, 21.

66. *St. Paul's Waco*, 204–5.

67. *Guild Cook Book*, 261.

68. *Out of This World*, 78, 173–77.

69. *St. Paul's* 1978, 155–65.

70. For an overview of the home economics movement, see Susan Strasser, *Never Done: A History of American Housework* (New York: Pantheon, 1982), 202–23.

71. Mary Stuart Harrison Smith, *Virginia Cookery-Book* (New York: Harper, 1885).

72. *St. Paul's Waco*, 43.

73. *Guild Cook Book*, 145.

74. *St. Paul's Waco*, 82, 15–16, 17–18, 19, 82.

75. Sharpless, *Cooking in Other Women's Kitchens*, xx–xxix.

76. *St. Paul's Waco*, 51, 53, 142, 143.

77. Ibid., 24–25, 26, 86, 89, 91, 99, 145, 158–59, 177, 240; *Guild Cook Book*, 221; *St. Paul's* 1978, 13, 19, 48, 49, 56, 130, 131.

78. *St. Paul's Waco*, 161; *Guild Cook Book*, 211.

79. *St. Paul's* 1978, 18. Since Barnes, an active local historian, was born about 1905 and her sister was two years older, her sister's recipe may be considerably older than 1978, but the praise for her publication was at that point (*Oral Memoirs of Lavonia Jenkins Barnes* [Waco, Tex.: Baylor University Institute for Oral History, 1978], 4).

80. *St. Paul's* 1978, 65, 79, 21.

81. *St. Paul's Waco*, 33.

82. *St. Paul's* 1978, 14.

83. *St. Paul's Waco*, 289–91, 293–95, 301, 309, 310, 312, 328.

84. Ibid., 292, 297, 300, 303, 304, 307, 311, 317, 326.

85. *Guild Cook Book*, unpaged ads.

86. *Out of This World*, 5, 22, 41, 52, 94, 117, 138–39, 168, 170.

CHAPTER 3

Prospecting for Oil

DAVID S. SHIELDS

Of all the quests that early American farmers and horticulturists pursued, none was more enduring and consequential than the pursuit of culinary oils and fats—something less expensive and more suitable for salad dressing than melted lard. From Thomas Jefferson's failed attempts to grow olive trees in Albemarle County, Virginia, to David Wesson's labors in the laboratory to free cottonseed oil of its natural stink, the history of experiments is a fascinating chronicle of popular taste, economic ambition, and food chemistry. It begins in the attempt to acclimatize the best-tasting oil-producing plants of the Old World to the North American landscape and ends with the industrial synthesis of wholly new entities—Crisco and margarine—devised to be inoffensive to taste, even tasteless. These developments played out in a little more than a century, from 1773 to 1890, largely in the American South and were greatly influenced by African American dietary needs.

Italian culinary evangelist Phillip Mazzei settled in the hill country of Virginia in 1773 to establish an American Tuscany of vineyards and olive groves. But the scant three years between the planting of his fields and the outbreak of the American Revolution thwarted both projects. Olive trees take at least ten years to mature and set fruit; muscat vines need five to supply sufficient grapes for a crush. The location of Mazzei's land next to the plantation of Thomas Jefferson, then governor of Virginia, ensured that Mazzei's property would suffer spoilage at the hands of British invaders. The truth is, well before the British came to Charlottesville Mazzei knew that his olive groves would not flourish. He had seen most of the saplings die when the winter temperature dipped below 15 degrees Fahrenheit in 1774. When

Mazzei departed for Europe on a secret mission to secure arms for Virginia in 1779, he left without having fulfilled any of the major ambitions that had brought him to America. Even the vineyard Mazzei's workers had planted for Jefferson at Monticello would never produce a single vintage, falling victim to Virginia's rapacious raccoons, insects, and black rot.[1]

One seed that Mazzei planted did bear fruit—the idea of diversified planting—in Jefferson's imagination. Mazzei's example had turned Jefferson, a rather traditional Virginia staple farmer with an interest in fruit trees, into a horticultural experimentalist inspired by any new plant or animal he encountered.[2] In 1787, during a journey to northern Italy where he witnessed how fruit and oil grounded the diet of the Italian peasantry, Jefferson awoke to the virtues of Mazzei's cherished olive tree. His careful notation in his travel diary of the locales and elevations at which various cultivars flourished revealed that the winter temperatures in most of the United States precluded the olive's cultivation. Yet in the Lowcountry of South Carolina and Georgia, and in the territory of Florida (if and when it came under American control), conditions were roughly comparable to those in Italy. Jefferson contacted the one institution that might oversee the establishment of olives, the South Carolina Agricultural Society, which had organized in 1785. His letter commended olive oil particularly:

> A pound of oil which can be bought for 3d. or 4d. sterling, is equivalent to many pounds of flesh by the quantity of vegetables, it will prepare and render fit and comfortable food. Notwithstanding the great quantity of oil made in France, they have not enough for their own consumption; and, therefore import from other countries. This is an article, of consumption of which, will always keep pace with the production. Raise it, and it begets its own demand. Little is carried to America, because Europe has it not to spare; we, therefore, have not learnt the use of it. But cover the Southern States with it, and every man will become a consumer of it, within whose reach it can be brought, in point of price.[3]

Parts of Jefferson's letter must be explained—for instance, the claim that a pound of oil equaled many pounds of flesh in the preparation of vegetables. He spoke to his countrymen's propensity to fry vegetables in lard or bacon fat. The expense of raising a hog in terms of feed and growth rate, butchering, and processing far exceeded that of collecting and pressing a crop of olives.[4] Jefferson also confronted the question of demand. Since most Americans did not use olive oil, how could the olive become a profitable crop? He reassured planters that European demand, particularly in Revolutionary ally and trading partner France, exceeded supply; furthermore, he suggested that Americans, once familiar with a cheap and available frying medium, would do as southern Europeans had traditionally done—embrace it as the most economical and convenient culinary fat.

Many of the historically minded planters who read Jefferson's letter would have known that the idea of planting olives in the Lowcountry dated from the time of Carolina's founding in 1670. John Locke, the secretary to the Lords Proprietors of Carolina, had composed a prospectus envisioning the colony as a quasi-Mediterranean haven of wine, olive oil, and silk.[5] Olive cuttings from Portugal and Bermuda had been planted along the Ashley and Cooper rivers early in the 1670s; in 1678 colonial agent Richard Blom reported flourishing groves. Mitchell King, the antebellum historian of Carolina olive culture and himself an olive grower, recounted the legend of John Colleton sticking a wand of olive wood into the sandy loam of Charleston and having it sprout.[6] Yet the colonial reports spoke of planting and growing, never of harvesting and pressing oil. Even a 1763 letter quoted by King remarking on olive trees in the city gardens suggests that they were novelties—specimens and conversation pieces. Governor Glen in 1747 did report the winter ice destroying one productive olive tree of a foot and a half girth. But olive oil never appeared on the customs list as an export commodity, and the local crop of olives appears entirely to have been pickled for home consumption.

The South Carolina Agricultural Society never reflected on why these early experiments with the olive had such desultory results. Perhaps the members knew that the obsessive concern with rice, corn, and indigo made the olive beside the point, particularly since the populace loved pork fat when it came to frying. This preference had at times a cultic extremity. In 1822 "Virginiansis Philoporcus" wrote to the *American Farmer*, proclaiming bacon fat ("that precious essence which titillates so exquisitely the papillae of the tongue") to be "far superior to all the oils that ever were discovered."[7]

The disruption of Carolina agriculture wrought by the American Revolution, and the need to establish new commodities for the postwar free trade with all nations, made Carolina's elite planters willing to consider new ideas. Indeed, Henry Laurens, who spent part of the Revolution languishing in the Tower of London, secured an English horticulturist and a shipload of olive cuttings to plant at Mepkin and Charleston on his return; according to John Adams, he harvested fifty to a hundred bushels of fruit a year.[8] Jefferson's shipments to the society did not arrive until 1791. These were allotted to interested members and planted at several locations in the Lowcountry.

Jefferson's olives did not transform the Lowcountry. Nor did Laurens's. Isolated trees (two in Beaufort, six in Charleston)[9] grew to productive maturity and local renown, but Jefferson complained in a letter to James Ronaldson, dated January 12, 1813, "It is now twenty-five years since I sent them two shipments (about 500 plants) of the Olive tree of Aix, the finest Olives in the world. If any of them still exist, it is merely as a curiosity in their gardens; not a single orchard of them has been planted."[10] Cold snaps decimated the inland plantings, while humidity and the moisture of the Lowcountry soil caused most of the trees to fail. Like the colonial plantings, the post-Revolutionary olive experiment resulted in a scatter of hardy trees whose fruits were brined and consumed locally. What was true in Carolina was true in Georgia and Florida. In 1827 a reviewer in the *American Quarterly* of Grant Forbes's utopian *Sketches, Historical and Topographical, of the Floridas* responded to the author's vision of an olive-rich East Florida by observing that "two olive trees, of very large size, and supposed to be of very great age, did grow near St. Augustine, and a few more were raised at New-Smyrna, but from what cause, none of them were fruitful."[11] Not a single cruet of oil came from the South's olive trees until 1831, when John Couper of Cannon's Point, Saint Simons Island, Georgia, produced some from his plantings.

Couper stood foremost among the generation of southern experimentalists who turned to the olive as a possible way out of the soil exhaustion crisis of the 1820s. His letters on olive culture appeared in the first volume of the *Southern Agriculturist*, the journal founded by the South Carolina Agricultural Society to foster exchange among experimentalists in response to the political crisis over the U.S. tariff on cotton and the degradation of the region's topsoil. His name appeared first on the list of endorsers of the

"Report of the Union Agricultural Society of Georgia," proposing the olive as one "substitute for the rapidly depreciating staple, cotton."[12] Couper, along with Robert Chisolm of Beaufort, South Carolina; W. L. Crawford of Darien, Georgia; Mitchell King of Charleston; Thomas Spalding of Sapelo Island, Georgia; J. H. Mey; and Judge Johnson, engaged in large-scale plantings in Beaufort and the Georgia Sea Islands. The most successful olive planter was Louisa Shaw, of Dungeness on Cumberland Island, Georgia, whose grove of six hundred trees produced throughout the nineteenth century and became a tourist attraction.

If Jefferson had known of Shaw's activities, they would have warmed his heart. The youngest daughter of Revolutionary War hero General Nathaniel Greene, she planted the olives the South Carolina Agricultural Society had forwarded to her father. Under her vigilant care they flourished and expanded. Via reports in papers such as the *Darien Gazette* their existence was known throughout the literate South. *American Farmer* in 1828 reprinted one such bulletin: "We are now informed on good authority, that 'olives of a very excellent quality,' have for several years been quite abundant on Cumberland Island, in the vicinity of Port St. Mary's, Geo. And that during the month of August last, many bushels of them were sold at the latter place, at seventy-five cents the bushel."[13] Shaw's grove inspired hope in Couper, Spalding, and Chisolm that the olive could be made a merchantable commodity. Couper secured his two hundred trees from Provence and in May 1825 immediately planted the three- and one-foot-long, branchless stems at Cannon's Point, Saint Simons Island.[14] Eighteen of the plantings died. Surprised at the slow growth, and realizing there would be no return on his land for years to come, Couper intercropped sweet potatoes in the grove, with good result. Although his attempt to expand his grove by cuttings failed, after a false start his experiments with planting from seed succeeded. J. H. Mey also had success growing olive from seed.[15] Thomas Spalding, who secured his olive trees from Leghorn in Italy, complained about the cost, saying that at $2.50 apiece for purchase and transport, the importation of olives on a large scale was "too much for us to afford." He requested that the state "establish nursery grounds for the Olive tree,"[16] but Georgia declined to undertake this public work.

The experiments in olive culture nearly came to naught in 1835, when brutal February cold and ice destroyed most of the trees north of Cumberland Island. Couper was forced to cut his grove to the roots. Old Charleston trees, including a patriarch planted by Laurens on Lamboll Street, died. Yet Couper's roots sprouted shoots, the grove renewed, and the trees began bearing fruit in 1844. Once again planters were reminded that olives were a long-term project, with no expectation of quick returns. James Hamilton Couper, John Couper's son, reflected on the course of his family's efforts in a letter to Charleston olive grower Mitchell King. He did not doubt that the olive could grow in the Lowcountry, regardless of the occasional freezes. Nor did he doubt that pickled olives would enjoy a ready reception.

> The question may be asked by those who have usually regarded olive oil as merely an article of household economy, of very limited use in North America, whether a ready sale of the oil can be depended on? They may believe with the late Abbe Correa, that our country-men have "bacon stomachs," and that it will be very difficult, so far to conquer the obstinacy of established habit, as to induce them to substitute pure oil for rancid bacon. If the only use of this oil were for food, it would undoubtedly require time to introduce it into general consumption; but that time will effect it, there can be no doubt, from the intrinsic value of the commodity.[17]

In 1845, according to the *Report of the Secretary of the Treasury*, 82,655 gallons of olive oil were imported into the United States. Some of this was used in soap manufacture and for machine oil.

Despite the efforts of Mitchell King and J. Hamilton Couper, olive oil would not be produced in the South in more than experimental batches. In a letter to botanist Francis Peyre Porcher, Robert Chisolm of Beaufort (who exhibited sample vials of olive oil at the South Carolina Institute Fair on two occasions in the early 1850s)[18] explained his view of the profitability of olive oil. Chisolm had planted his grove in 1833 with two types of Leghorn olives, a small, round oil olive and an oval-fruited one. He observed, "I do not think that the making of oil from the olive will be likely to prove sufficiently profitable to be pursued in this country for many years, and other crops will necessarily take the lead unless the price of labor or soil in Europe should be increased, when there will, consequently, become a greater demand."[19] Porcher thought poppy seed oil would supply whatever culinary service olive oil might give. But ultimately another common southern plant would provide a more economical culinary oil: benne, or sesame seed.

In 1808, when Thomas Jefferson, now president of the United States, despaired over the adoption of olive trees in the South, Governor John Milledge of Georgia sent him a bottle of benne oil.[20] Jefferson found it equal to olive oil in its delicacy as a salad dressing and resolved to begin its production. The cultivation of benne seed became one of the president's important agricultural experiments of the early 1810s. Jefferson had previously imagined that the olive tree would be, first and foremost, a boon for African slaves in the South, providing them a fat that could be produced with less expense and greater volume than lard or bacon grease. John Couper would echo this sentiment in a letter of 1830, when he remarked, "I am not of the opinion the Olive will be an object of great profit, but if we could introduce oil amongst our slaves, it would add much to their comforts."[21] Yet ironically, the slaves had brought with them the source of oil they needed in their diet, *Sesamum indicum*, or what the West African Mende called benne.

Benne's wealth of oil (almost 50 percent of a seed's makeup) had been noted by agricultural writers repeatedly during the eighteenth century. As early as 1735 a "Mr. Garcia" announced in the *South Carolina Gazette* the establishment of a sesame oil press in Charleston. This press operated until the proprietor's death three years later. John Morel of Savannah in 1769 reported to the American Philosophical Society that "this seed makes oil equal in quality to Florence [olive oil], and some say preferable."[22] Henry Laurens of South Carolina requested that his brother James "procure me as much Sesamum or Bene Seed as you possibly can, & encourage the planting [of] it by all the Negroes at each plantation."[23] Throughout the 1790s the South Carolina Agricultural Society offered premiums to planters who could produce superior oil from sesame, olives, castor beans, sunflowers, cottonseed, or groundnuts (peanuts). Governor John Milledge and his neighbors began field cultivation of sesame around 1800, hoping to supply a native substitute for olive oil. His friend and colleague Colonel William Few moved to New

York City and in 1804 began selling sesame oil pressed commercially in New Jersey. Pressing the sesame in a manner similar to that used to extract flaxseed oil, Milledge enthusiastically reported extracting three quarts of oil from a gallon of seed. Contemporaries observed that this yield was wishful, and that in most cases two quarts of oil could be expected. Thomas Marsh Forman of Maryland tasted the Georgia oil in 1812:

> At the house of my valued friend John McQueen, Esq. of Oatlands, the Bene plant was first made known to me. It was about the last of February, that dining with him, he requested my opinion of a bowl of fine Cabbage Lettuce; it deserved all the praise which I gave to the vegetable, as well as to the dressing, when Mr. McQueen smiling informed me, that the oil was of his own produce, from what made, and the value of the crop.[24]

The West African method of extracting oil was designed for a household level of production and consumption. The seed was pounded by mortar and pestle. After "bruising the seed, and immersing them in boiling water ... the oil rises on the top and is easily skimmed off. Good casks filled, or bottles filled, and well bunged, or corked are proper to preserve this oil which doubtless, will become rancid by heat, time, impurities, and air."[25] Twenty-first-century chemical and nutritional analysis finds that of the culinary oils high in polyunsaturated omega-6, and with high smoke points, sesame oil is least prone to turn rancid, making it the most stable of healthy frying substances.[26]

Benne oil kept as well as olive oil. It could be produced annually and abundantly, without a ten-year wait for productivity, and could be grown as far north as Maryland without much difficulty. It could also be pressed and extracted with less labor and mechanism than olive oil required. A simple iron screw press could do the job.

Many southern farmers grew benne. Indeed, the amount of benne grown cannot be calculated with any certainty, because substantial slave-patch · plantings went unnoted in plantation record books. Judging by surviving documents, planters rarely attempted benne production on a scale to create more than a modest, largely local market for oil (the maximum plantings tended to be fifty acres), yet a number of plantations engaged in artisanal production, using sesame in crop rotations with corn, sweet potatoes, and cowpeas, or with rice and sweet potatoes. A window on the small-scale world of sesame oil production and benne cake livestock feeding is found in the pages of Thomas Walter Peyre's plantation journal (1834–59) at the South Carolina Historical Society. On Peyre's estate the benne press, like the brew house, was first a plantation resource, secondarily a production facility for market goods.

African American farming of benne can be imputed only by anecdotal reports, yet numerous records attest to benne's importance in the slave diet. Indeed, a complex benne cookery adapted from African practices was recorded. In 1820 John S. Skinner, editor of the most important U.S agricultural journal, *American Farmer*, observed that

> The Bene vine or bush, has been produced for some time, in small quantities, in the southern states, from seed imported directly from Africa, and from Asia—It abounds in the former, and in Bengal. Many of the blacks of the Mississippi, have continued the propagation of the seed of the Bene, and make soup of it after parching. The seed may be procured from them and from the blacks in the Carolinas and Georgia.[27]

Skinner's note revealed several things: the African genesis of the plant, the broad geographic range yet relatively low acreage of its cultivation, and the black oversight of seed stock for benne. Skinner also provided a glimpse of its most notable culinary use—as the basis of benne soup.

Rich in oil and nutty in taste, benne can be eaten raw. Because it is highly nutritious (25 percent protein), it could provide sustenance with minimal preparation. But the African American population preferred to intensify the flavorful nuttiness of the seed by browning it in a skillet. Whether hulled or unhulled, seeds could be tossed onto the bottom of an ungreased Dutch oven or iron skillet and stirred until lightly toasted—not scorched in any part.

Parched benne has a host of uses. It could be eaten straight from the skillet, used as a condiment to flavor a pot of stew or greens, or pounded in a mortar or pestle to become a thickening agent or a base for pottage. Every surviving notice of the use of benne mash in cookery indicates that it was mixed with something else. The two basic partnering elements were wheat flour and cornmeal, cooked in salted water or stock.

Benne in the Kitchen

Robert M. Goodwin of Skidaway Island, Georgia, observed in 1824 that for "negroes in this part of the country . . . it [benne] is thought . . . to be much better in soup than okra, and it is used by them in the same manner. I am told it is very good, but I have never tasted it."[28] Calvin Jones noted the extensive use of benne in African American cookery in eastern North Carolina, observing that "among negroes who get little flesh meat, it is a valuable article."[29] Meat rations on plantations tended to be restricted to three and a half pounds of cured pork per week maximum. On small-scale farms there might be no ration, which meant that a slave had to hunt and trap during the off hours of labor to supply meat.[30] Consequently, sesame served as an important dietary protein supplement. The sole surviving recipe for benne soup appeared as a variation of groundnut soup in Sarah Rutledge's 1847 *The Carolina Housewife*. Though attentive to vernacular cookery, Rutledge's collection was intended for a white readership with meat and seafood at its disposal. She added oysters to benne and flour to make a dish that survives in Lowcountry cuisine as Brown Oyster and Benne Stew.

GROUND NUT SOUP

To half a pint of shelled ground nuts, well beaten up, add two spoonsful of flour, and mix well. Put to them a pint of oysters, and a pint and a half of water. While boiling, throw [in] a seed-pepper or two, if small.

BENNIE SOUP

This is made exactly in the same manner except that instead of a half a pint of ground-nuts, a pint and a gill of bennie is mixed with the flour and the oysters.[31]

Rutledge's soup can be considered an evolution of the basic benne soup cooked in the plantation quarters. All the ingredients for that more basic soup were listed in Rutledge's recipe, but the mode of preparation was somewhat different, since she was concerned about preserving the quality of the oysters incorporated into the mix. The foundation soup called for

1 cup benne seed, enough sesame oil to cover the bottom of a cooking vessel, a handful of wheat flour, Salt & Pepper, onions, a quart of water. Toast benne

seed in a dry skillet stirring constantly 2 minutes until browned, but not burnt. Empty contents of the skillet into a mortar and mash the seed into powder. In the same skillet cover the bottom with sesame oil [the African American way of making it is detailed below in the section on oil] and mix in flour. Stir and cook this until you form a brown roux. Fry one large roughly chopped onion. Add finely crushed benne, and then hot water, steadily, stirring constantly. Cook at a constant medium until it is rich and thick and salt to taste. This is a hearty and flavorful soup.[32]

Benne could be kept for winter use at a time when vegetables, apart from root vegetables, could be scarce. Commentators repeatedly remarked on the love of African Americans for onions, whether globe, spring, or wild leek.[33] A chopped onion might be incorporated into the roux and allowed to become translucent before the benne was added, to give a sweet note to the soup and a pleasing texture. A seedpod of hot pepper was also a welcome addition. West Africans added cooked meats to benne soup when available. The foundation soup operated as a canvas for improvisation.

An 1824 article in *American Farmer* stated, "The Negroes in Georgia boil a handful of the seeds with their allowance of Indian Corn."[34] Three years earlier, a North Carolinian had noted, "Mixed in due proportion with their hominy, it heightens its relish, and adds to its nutriment."[35] Because whole seed takes longer to cook than cornmeal, it does not amalgamate well and can stick in one's teeth. The handful of benne cast into the hominy pot most likely had already been parched and pounded.

"Hominy" designated three things: small hominy was ground cornmeal; large hominy meant dried whole kernels of corn; and the word also referred to *posole*, a kind of dried whole-kernel corn soaked in lye to remove the kernel's outer hull. Native Americans throughout the Southeast boiled cornmeal, and English settlers learned to substitute cornmeal for the familiar oat and wheat pottages of their homeland. Because Africans ate millet stews, they too found the substitution of corn acceptable. A West African approach to mixing benne and hominy derives from the traditional practice of serving a groundnut or benne soup over a thick mash of cassava. In the Lowcountry hominy replaced cassava. It was prepared separately, spooned into a bowl, and benne soup was ladled over it. Usually pieces of precooked meat or greens were added to the liquid prior to serving.

In the 1770s Thomas Jefferson wrote that sesame "was brought to S. Carolina from Africa by the negroes. . . . They bake it in their bread, boil it with greens, enrich their broth" with it. His observation about the greens accords with long-collards (the premier cold-weather green), turnip, beet, or white mustard dressed with the favorite European oil, from the olive, standing practice among a number of West African peoples. Casting a handful of whole seed into a cooking pot of mustard greens might be convenient, but it did not release all of the seed's oils. Mashing them beforehand rendered them luscious. In the second decade of the nineteenth century, when oil mills appeared on a number of plantations, the mash cake left after pressing the sesame became a cooking condiment: "The oil cake is very pleasant at table, is eaten freely by horned cattle, swine, &c., and it is often used when fresh to boil with other vegetables, rendering butter unnecessary."[36] The use of benne mash as an oleo in boiling greens and root vegetables resembled North African practices of using tahini (sesame paste) as a condiment in vegetable cookery; it also mimicked the West African habit of adding mashed benne to one-pot preparations. The mixture of benne mash with greens remained a feature of plantation cookery through the antebellum period.

Oily pressed seed cake fit into traditional (i.e., African) cooking practices, yet the demand for sesame oil in the white world of the marketplace was driven by a culinary vogue that nurtured a new taste—a hankering for uncooked greens, vegetables, and fruits. Until the end of the eighteenth century physicians contemplating the nature of human digestion viewed cooking as an externalized form of the digestive process, something that greatly aided the body's efficient uptake of the nutritional elements in food. Uncooked fruits and vegetables were not fully used by the body and, indeed, troubled the stomach and intestines, prompting dyspepsia, a gastrointestinal disorder that led to gas, stomachaches, blockage, and other sorts of internal distress. But in the 1790s old ideas about the function of cooking as a necessary supplement to digestion began to dissolve, as did fears of the dire consequences of dyspepsia. In Europe and, later, in the young United States, the fashion for salads composed of uncooked greens and vegetables spread. Celery rocketed into garden vogue, and lettuces became popular. Uncooked cabbage was shredded into slaws. These salads tasted best when lubricated by an acid (vinegar or lemon juice) and an oil.[37] Melted lard would not do, nor would melted butter. It is no anomaly that the story of Jefferson's discovery of the virtues of benne oil has him eating it on a fresh salad. Jefferson was embracing two novelties simultaneously.

Commercial Production of Oils and Fats

Over the course of the nineteenth century fresh salad grew in popularity. In the 1880s, when Thomas J. Murrey supported himself by selling cookbooks specifically focused on salads and sauces, he believed that salad should be "Cottonseed-oil, Gangilee oil [another name for benne oil], peanut-oil, bene-plant oil, poppy oil, and oil from seeds of the radish and mustard, and, in fact, a hundred other oils which are recommended from time to time for salads by over-enthusiastic writers, are a delusion, and should not be used in salads. They are excellent for frying purposes, and will one day take the place of lard; but never use them on a dainty salad."[38] Murrey was prophetic in his pronouncement of doom on lard. Although Americans would plant olive groves in California and Arizona, it would not be olive oil that filled the fryer vats of restaurants, or displaced lard, or even lubricated the greens of late nineteenth- and twentieth-century Americans. Crisco (the shortening that supplanted lard), Wesson oil, and most "vegetable oil" and "salad oil" used in American salad dressings in the first three quarters of the twentieth century were created from the first named of Murrey's demoted oils: cottonseed oil. The mills of the South pressed only a trickle of olive oil, only a modest stream of sesame oil. They would loose a river of cottonseed oil.

Centuries of culinary practice throughout the Mediterranean and in West Africa stood behind the attempts to incorporate olive oil and benne oil into the North American larder. Not so with cottonseed oil, which was not consumed by humans until the great age of experiments. During the eighteenth century pharmacists had extracted oil from cottonseed in Europe and America as part of the Enlightenment investigation of the medicinal properties of all seed and nut oils, and a patent for the extraction of oil from cottonseed was issued by the United States as early as 1793. C. Whiting's design for a mill to extract the oil from the seed's hull earned a patent on March 2, 1799.[39] Yet the notion that humans might ingest the stuff as an element of common nutrition arose only after (1) the explosive growth of the cotton industry in the southern states after 1800; (2) the rise of a general concern with what to do with surplus seed after the planting stock had been reserved; (3) the observation that livestock had a taste for waste seed, particularly when ground in a mill; and (4) the development of a method for refining the raw oil into something odorless and palatable. It took the entire nineteenth century to meet these four conditions.

Early extractors of oil from cottonseed, like Follett and Smith, who first marketed their popular commercial huller in 1829, noted several things. First, the seed was four-fifths hull and one-fifth oil-bearing kernel. Second, the seed was only 17 to 21 percent oil, less than half that of benne seed and most nuts. Third, the hull had to be stripped on edged stones to get at the seed, followed by cooking the seed meal and then pressing the meal. Captain Benjamin Waring, the pioneer agricultural experimentalist of the South Carolina midlands, had constructed an oil press in Columbia by 1800. The oil extruded from Waring's press flowed cloudy and dark brown and gave off a nutty odor that grew more pronounced and funky as the oil aged. Waring judged that it could not be used for human consumption, and because food concerned him more than producing livestock feed or the ingredients for soap, he turned his press to benne oil, which he produced in marketable quantities until his death.[40]

Eli Whitney's cotton gin, perfected in 1793, separated seeds from the bolls of short-staple cotton efficiently. When the War of 1812 drove cotton prices skyward, a production boom began that led to vast plantings, and so much surplus seed came from the fields that it became a nuisance. Governor David Rogerson Williams of Society Hill, South Carolina, determined to make the waste seed profitable. Already widely known for introducing the mule into southern agriculture, Williams built a commercial oil mill in the late 1820s, intending to manufacture seed cake for cattle and hog feed, lamp oil for home illumination, and cotton fat for soap and lubrication.[41] Throughout the South enterprisers began constructing mills, convinced that processing cotton by-products into saleable commodities would bring a wave of cash. James Hamilton Couper, of the olive-growing Coupers, invested in plants in Natchez, Mississippi, and in Alabama. They bankrupted him in 1836.[42]

Mills sprang up like mushrooms, and they failed in substantial numbers.[43]

The economies of scale did not work, particularly since no human culinary demand drove sales of the product. Whale oil made better soap, linseed oil a better paint base. Still, the ubiquity of cottonseed encouraged regional processors to appear until they consolidated under one administration, the American Cottonseed Oil Trust, in 1880. Monopoly industrialization in and of itself did not fuel the rise of cottonseed oil; chemistry did. Because of the expense of raising hogs, lard proved rather costly as a staple kitchen fat. Chemists managed to refine the oil, hydrogenate it, and mix it with lard into what became known as "compound" lard. At first this was done without public notification, and when the presence of cottonseed oil in lard was revealed, it was perceived as an adulterant. For this reason, and perhaps for cotton's associations with the recently overthrown slave regime in the South, cottonseed oil was not named when it finally emerged as shortening or culinary oil at the end of the nineteenth century. The closest to naming occurred in the brand name, as in the "co" in "Crisco."

Compound lard differed from pure lard in several respects, including a retention of cottonseed oil's distinctive smell. The elimination of this odor became the next focus of research by chemists. In 1884 David Wesson of Chicago's N. K. Fairbanks Company, a producer of animal-based compound fats, began experimenting with compound lard. His success in creating compound lard with the texture of pure lard led to the Oil Trust's absorption of the Fairbanks Company and Wesson's transfer to another subsidiary that explored the chemistry of cottonseed oil exclusively. By 1899 Wesson had developed a process of refining, heating, and vacuum-processing cottonseed oil in such a way that odor and brown tint of the raw oil were entirely removed. (Before 1899 a mitigation of the odor had been achieved by blowing live steam through the oil at atmospheric pressure.) Bankrolled by the trust, Wesson formed a manufacturing company, and from a plant in Savannah, Georgia, he began selling Wesson Oil.[44] In 1903 chemists succeeded in hydrogenating oils into solids, and the Wesson Company marketed Snowdrift, a lard substitute composed entirely of cottonseed oil. Yet it would be Procter and Gamble's chemist Edwin C. Kayser who in 1911 created a shortening of cottonseed oil that did not degrade at room temperature.[45] Crisco would eventually eclipse Snowdrift in the marketplace, fulfilling Murrey's prophecy that lard would be superseded as a frying medium and baking ingredient.

Cottonseed-oil products did not come to dominate the market for culinary oil and shortening because of taste or need. It was because of economy. As a by-product of staple production, cottonseed oil was waste turned to profit. To triumph in the marketplace of food the oil had to lose its objectionable appearance and smell and approximate a palatable blandness on the tongue. It had to be sold under names that did not announce its origin plainly (an attempt to sell shortening as "Cottonlene" failed) and had to be cheap at the point of purchase. The virtues of cottonseed oil lay in the functions it performed, not in its aesthetic quality; indeed, the aesthetics were those of innocuousness. The oil did possess an ethical advantage in the eyes of vegetarians in its provision of a frying medium and baking fat that did not derive from animals. Crisco embraced this constituency warmly. *The Story of Crisco* (1913), in its section on "Vegetarian Dishes," declared proudly, "Crisco is entirely vegetable." When the author asked rhetorically why customers bought Crisco with such enthusiasm, abandoning traditional cooking fats such as butter and lard, she answered her own question: "This was because four classes of people—housewives, chefs, doctors, and dietitians—were glad to be shown a product which at once would make for more digestible, more economical foods, and better tasting foods."[46] Economical? Granted. Digestible? According to whom? Better tasting than butter? Who decided that?

The above quotation reveals who, besides the economy-minded female consumer, matters as an authority in regard to food: chefs, doctors, and dietitians. Only the first member of this trio has a professional interest in taste. Yet at the dawn of the twentieth century the experts on digestion—the nutritionist and the physician—had become the arbiters of good food.

We should not lose sight of the fact that housewives, physicians, dietitians, and chefs had nothing to do with the design, taste profile, or manufacture of Crisco. Food chemists such as David Wesson and Edwin Kayser had created the product and were the new aestheticians of food. If the antebellum agricultural experimentalists mainly pursued the next new saleable taste in creating their varieties, the food chemists at the dawn of the twentieth century made taste subordinate to matters of economy and functionality in inventing their products.

But the reign of the food chemists in twentieth-century American cuisine, though long, was not everlasting. The final quarter of the century witnessed a revival of regional cuisines, traditional foodways, natural taste, and artisanal production. Olives found a home in California, and sesame in Texas, where production served an expanding market for their oils. In 2008 the story told here came full circle. For the first time in a century benne became a crop in Georgia and the Carolinas, reintroduced by the Carolina Gold Rice Foundation and its affiliated growers.[47] Sean Brock, chef of McCrady's restaurant in Charleston, South Carolina, embraced the ingredient and for his renovations of regional cooking won the 2010 James Beard Foundation Award as Best Chef in the Southeast. In Georgia, Dr. Mark L. Hanly and S. L. Davis planted olive groves and organized a group of twenty-four prospective orchardists and producers into the Georgia Olive Growers Association.[48] Groves are now thriving in Blackshear and Appling Counties. The first oil issued from the presses in 2012 and in 2013 enjoys regional distribution.

NOTES

1. John Hailman, *Thomas Jefferson on Wine* (Jackson: University Press of Mississippi, 2006), 371–75.

2. The transformation of his crops can be seen under the 1774 listings in Thomas Jefferson's Garden Book, when a modest range of conventional colonial vegetables are suddenly supplemented by radicchio, Tuscan garlic, *Salvastrella di Pisa*, and other cultivars. "Thomas Jefferson's Garden Book," Thomas Jefferson Papers, an Electronic Archive, at www.thomas jeffersonpapers.org/garden, 2009. My 2009 paper to the Adams/Jefferson Conference in Boston and Monticello, "Green Ink: Thomas Jefferson and the Print World of Transatlantic Agriculture," reflects on the evolution of Jefferson's agricultural philosophy. See www.adams jefferson. com/papers/GreenInk_Shields.pdf, 2010.

3. *Southern Agriculturist* 1, no. 8 (August 1828): 366.

4. The cost of raising a hog varied greatly depending on whether one penned the animals or let them range free. Because of the general destruction that hogs inflict on the landscape, reform-minded farmers were penning hogs with greater frequency during the final decades of the eighteenth century. In a 1792 experiment George Washington raised shoats to maturity, keeping a record of the costs in an attempt to calculate the expense of raising a pig in a compound.

5. Presented to Shaftesbury in manuscript in 1679, it was published as *Observations upon the Growth and Culture of Vines and Olives* (London: W. Sandby, 1766). Two years later it appeared in the seventh edition of Locke's *Works*, the vehicle by which it became widely known in Anglo-America.

6. Mitchell King, *The History and Culture of the Olive: The Anniversary Address of the State Agricultural Society of South Carolina. . . . November 26th, 1846* (Columbia: I. C. Morgan, for the Society, 1846), 20.

7. "More Bacon," *American Farmer* 3, no. 45 (February 1822): 360.

8. David Duncan Wallace, *The Life of Henry Laurens* (New York: G. P. Putnam's Sons, 1915), 64.

9. One of Your Readers, "The Olive," *American Farmer* 8, no. 24 (September 1, 1826): 189.

10. *The Writings of Thomas Jefferson*, ed. Albert Ellery Burgh (Washington, D.C.: Thomas Jefferson Memorial Foundation, 1905), 13:204.

11. "Review," *American Quarterly Review* (September 1827): 227.

12. "Union Agricultural Society," *American Farmer* 6, no. 7 (April 29, 1825): 41–42.

13. "Olives, from the Darien Gazette," *American Farmer* 10, no. 13 (June 27, 1828): 116–17.

14. John Couper, [Letter on Olive Culture], *Southern Agriculturist* 1, no. 7 (July 1828): 304.

15. "On Raising Olive Trees from Seed," *Southern Agriculturist* 6, no. 6 (June 1833): 309.

16. Thomas Spalding, "Olives," *Southern Agriculturist* 1, no. 3 (March 1828): 107–8.

17. King, *History and Culture of the Olive*, 20.

18. "South Carolina Institute Fair," *De Bow's Review of the Southern and Western States* 12 (July 1852): 113.

19. Francis Peyre Porcher, *Resources of the Southern Fields and Forests* (Charleston: Walker, Evans & Cogswell, 1869), 568.

20. Thomas Jefferson, "Letters from Old Trunks," *Virginia Magazine of History and Biography* 48, no. 2 (April 1940): 97–103.

21. John Couper, "Account of an Attempt to Cultivate the Olive—Letter 14th February 1830," *Southern Agriculturist* 4, no. 5 (May 1830): 214.

22. *Transactions*, 1 (Philadelphia, 1789): 309.

23. Letter dated 5 February 1774, in *Papers of Henry Laurens*, vol. 9 (Columbia: University of South Carolina Press), 268.

24. T. M. Forman, *American Farmer* 2, no. 38 (December 15, 1820): 400.

25. Ibid.

26. The American Diabetes Association's findings are epitomized in Lee Ann Holzmeister's "Cooking Oils" at www.diabetesselfmanagement.com/articles/nutrition_meal_planning /cooking_oils/print/ (2010).

27. *American Farmer* 2, no. 17 (July 21, 1820): 135.

28. *American Farmer* 6 (1824): 46.

29. *American Farmer* 3, no. 19 (August 3, 1821): 150.

30. The scholarly debate about the constitution of the slave diet has raged over two decades, troubled in part by the lack of documentary evidence and archaeological findings about slave nutrition from small-scale farms in the South. As Herbert C. Covey and Dwight Eisnach have argued, the widespread practice of pica signals some sort of dietary deficiency. See *What*

the Slaves Ate: Recollections of African American Foods and Foodways from the Slave Narratives (Santa Barbara: ABC-CLIO, 2009), 10–38.

31. Sarah Rutledge, *The Carolina Housewife* (Columbia: University of South Carolina Press, 1979), 45–46.

32. This is my reconstruction of Rutledge's original recipe.

33. "A considerable quantity of Scallions ought to be planted, for they are of easy culture, and to them the negroes are more partial than any other of the alliaceous tribe." *Southern Agriculturalist and Register of Rural Affairs* 3, no. 10 (October 1830): 522.

34. *American Farmer* 6 (1824): 36.

35. Raleigh, June 27, 1821, *American Farmer* 3, no. 19 (August 3, 1821): 150.

36. Skinner, *American Farmer*, 2–17.

37. Early testimonials recommending benne oil repeatedly mention its use as salad oil. Calvin Jones repeats North Carolina congressman William Gaston's observation that he "was particularly fond of the oil with salad, and with fish." John Skinner, editor of the *American Farmer*, prefaced a contributor's letter about benne with an introductory rumination that "the Bene, or Sesamum, produces a very good salad oil, not distinguishable from fine olive oil of France and Italy." See *American Farmer* 2, no. 17 (July 21, 1820): 135.

38. Thomas J. Murrey, *Salads and Sauces* (New York: Frederick A. Stokes, 1884), 21.

39. Benjamin Franklin Taylor, *The Early History of the Cotton Oil Industry in America* (Columbia, S.C.: B. F. Taylor, 1936), 10.

40. Robert Mills, *Statistics of South Carolina* (Columbia, SC, 1826), 212.

41. Harvey Toliver Cook, *The Life and Legacy of David Rogerson Williams* (New York, 1916), 199–204.

42. James E. Bagwell, *Rice Gold: James Hamilton Couper and Plantation Life on the Georgia Coast* (Macon, Ga.: Mercer University Press, 2002), 28–43.

43. For a brief chronicle of the stops and starts of the cottonseed industry in the antebellum period, see Leebert Lloyd Lamborn, *Cotton Seed Products* (New York: D. Van Nostrand, 1904), 18–20.

44. "American Contemporaries—David Wesson," *Industrial and Chemical Engineering* 21, no. 3 (1929): 290–91.

45. A useful summary of the development of hydrogenated oils is contained in the arguments of Procter & Gamble v. Berlin Mills Company, U.S. District Court (Southern District of New York 13–100), printed as an appendix in Carleton Ellis, *The Hydrogenation of Oils* (New York: D. Van Nostrand, 1919), 630–707.

46. Marion Harris Neil, *The Story of Crisco* (Procter & Gamble, 1913), 9.

47. Matt and Ted Lee, "The Next Big (but Tiny) Southern Ingredient," at www.oxford american.org/articles/2010/mar/09/tiny-heirlooms/.

48. See www.georgiaolivegrowers.com/.

CHAPTER 4

Bodies of the Dead

The Wild in Southern Foodways

WILEY C. PREWITT JR.

Among the papers of the Mississippi Game and Fish Commission a worn clipping cries, "Water Valley Hides Bodies Of Its 'Dead!' Merovka Fails to Find Slaughtered Geese Slain on City's Streets." The story goes that on a winter night in 1932, a dense fog forced a flock of wild geese—probably Canada geese—to land in the northern Mississippi town. Citizens reacted with sticks and roasting pans. Effective game laws and enforcement were new to Mississippi at the time, but a citywide goose clubbing drew attention even then. Lawrence Merovka, one of only a handful of federal wardens in the mid-South, investigated but claimed he found no evidence of the incident. "Blinded and helpless, hundreds of the gamest birds in the world, fell defenseless in the streets and were slaughtered by the inhabitants," wrote a local newspaperman. "They are serving wild geese, deliciously baked and properly seasoned, on family tables in scores of homes up at Water Valley."[1]

These days the only clubs most Canada geese encounter are in the hands of golfers. Though still a respected game bird among waterfowlers, the Canada goose has become a "nuisance" in much of the United States. Attracted by the highly fertilized grass of lawns and golf courses, these urban and suburban geese enjoy a more certain food supply and experience less hunting and predation than their ancestors—and their population has risen accordingly. Many of the problem Canadas are resident birds of the giant race *Branta Canadensis maxima,* whose forebears had been restocked by game conservation agencies in an effort to replace dwindling flights of migrating geese during the second half of the twentieth century. It was inconceivable to wildlife biologists attempting to restore some of the glory of waterfowling past that there could ever be too many geese and too little demand. Clearly, when humans pass on ten-pound geese and attack small white balls, things have changed.[2]

For many, the gathering of wild food through hunting and fishing connotes age-old practices and unwavering traditions. But as historian Stuart Marks observed, "Hunting is not a timeless pursuit within a cultural void." Access to game creatures can be ephemeral, and their populations subject to violent cycles. Our perceptions of certain species and their use as game can change drastically over time. The treasure of one era may be the commonplace of the next, and a father's familiar game may be a rarity for his children. This essay approaches the wild in southern foodways from the perspective of changing animal populations, evolving laws, and the fluid human relationship with the land.[3]

The South is a long-settled, long-farmed region where the agricultural use of the land often determined the available game at any particular time. In his hunting stories, William Faulkner described a late nineteenth- and early twentieth-century landscape where hunters traveled to the "Big Bottom," a wild hinterland for large game such as white-tailed deer and black bear. People hunted the "settled country" in Faulkner stories, but they were after small game such as "rabbits and possums" that could endure the hunting pressure of the farming community.[4]

This pattern of small game in farmed areas and large game in nonfarmed wild areas began much earlier than one might suspect. Anthropologist Charles Hudson suggested that the foodways of the South—like many other customs—began with the Native Americans. He paid particular attention to the Mississippian tradition where large populations lived near their agricultural fields for much of the year. By around AD 1200, Mississippian people in the Southeast grew corn, beans, and squash, familiar parts of the traditional southern diet to this day. During the growing and gathering season, they guarded the crop. Although they certainly foraged for available game in the surrounding area, the main hunt took place in the late fall and winter, well away from the settlements in areas where large game was more plentiful.[5]

One of the most interesting illustrations of this pattern is in the accounts of Hernando de Soto's expedition across the Southeast from 1539 to 1543. De Soto and his men traveled from settlement to settlement, in part searching for the precious metal–rich civilizations they believed were there, but also to plunder supplies of native foods, usually corn. As they spent most of their time in the agricultural areas of the Mississippian peoples, they were almost always short of meat. Particularly in the winter, when the Spaniards lived in the towns they had captured, rabbits were some of the only game animals frequently mentioned. Venison was a rarity—not because the Spaniards did not know how to hunt deer, nor because deer were scarce. The native farmers had simply killed most large animals near their fields in the course of defending their crops.[6]

It is possible that de Soto's path of mayhem across the South left Old World pathogens that decimated the Mississippian chiefdoms and helped bring about the collapse of some of the native societies. How Native Americans dealt with the aftermath of the earliest Spanish and French contacts and how the survivors formed the groups and nations that later waves of Europeans met is a subject of continuing debate among anthropologists and archaeologists. With regards to foodways and game, the way of life generally remained a mix of farming, hunting, and gathering, albeit with fewer people.[7]

Increased contact with Europeans and their enviable technologies drew Native Americans and the animals on which they depended into the marketplace. White-tailed deer were the most important food animal for Indians before they adopted livestock. Charles Hudson has estimated that in the South deer made up "50 to 90 per cent of the animal protein eaten." By the late seventeenth century, a trade in deerskins was developing across the Southeast that would grow through most of the eighteenth century. Indians traded skins for all the products they came to need from the Europeans, including whiskey. Made into everything from gloves to bookbindings, deerskins were one of the first lucrative exports from the South, and the volume of the trade could be huge. Traders sent around 80,000 skins a year from Charleston alone in the 1730s. By the middle of the century, the South produced around 500,000 skins a year. Hunting continued, even though both natives and colonists complained about shortages of deer. The alcohol-fueled trade eventually declined through a combination of overhunting, the dispossession of the Native Americans, and the ultimate ascendancy of commercial agriculture.[8]

Nineteenth-century southerners ate wild creatures as a matter of course. Not only subsistence food for the marginal farmer, game and fish were important and familiar commodities bought, sold, and bartered among all parts of society. Farmers hunted when the agricultural cycle allowed, and commercial hunters observed no seasons other than convenience or the demands of the market. Large game from such remote areas as the river bottoms scattered around the South allowed the merchants to offer creatures including deer and turkeys far from where they were killed. While the destruction of the American bison is the best known of the historic commercial hunting ventures, market hunting for eastern game, particularly waterfowl, was relentless and widespread. Wildlife biologists and historians have long held unregulated hunting a major cause of declines for game such as deer and waterfowl during the nineteenth century. Richard and Thomas McCabe called the last half of the century the "exploitation era" and characterized it as the period of the most intense hunting "ever." In his recent work on the food writing of Mark Twain, Andrew Beahrs has noted that many of Twain's culinary dreams were based on wild creatures from specific places, such as canvasbacks and diamondback terrapins from the Chesapeake or black bass from the Mississippi. This regionally "rooted food" that Twain loved relied largely on the accepted commodification of game and its general availability in the marketplace.[9]

The possibility of a sale as well as subsistence added to a general conflict over game among nineteenth-century hunters of varying backgrounds. Upper-class hunters resented competition from poor whites and slaves and at times referenced what they perceived as the unfortunate slaughter of game by the lower orders in the literature of the day. For Alabaman Johnson J. Hooper, "the pot hunter who shoots the bevy . . . murders the whistling cock . . . the clown who nets or traps" was the opposite of the "true sportsmen" who kill in "good style."[10] Historian John Reiger believed that elite nineteenth-century hunters such as Hooper, alarmed at market hunting and the excesses of recreational killing, would ultimately organize and begin the work of wildlife conservation in the United States. His work deals mainly with hunters from the ruling class of the Northeast whose sporting code became the basis of laws restricting the taking of wildlife and establishing refuges, parks, and wilderness areas. This interpretation from Reiger's 1975 work and his recent revision remains the traditional explanation of conservation history, particularly among wildlife professionals. Reiger's research went a long way toward legitimizing hunting and fishing as fit subjects for study, although his sympathetic treatment of wealthy sport hunters remains ill received among historians. The "code of the sportsman" that Reiger described worked its way into mainstream southern hunting culture only very slowly, but by the latter part of the twentieth century, notions of trophy hunting and limiting one's kill would become common themes.[11]

For those on the other side of upper-class resentment and reforming zeal, the emerging body of conservation law meant restrictions on traditional customary rights to the land and its game and fish. Steven Hahn has argued that elites sought to reduce the economic independence of poor whites and freedmen in the postbellum South by instituting game laws that dictated when, where, and how they could hunt. Reducing access to game for subsistence and the market could make for a more tractable work force. Historian Ted Ownby has also suggested that restrictions on certain methods of hunting and especially on excessive killing were as much about reining in the hunters as any concern about the game. Ownby found that the conservation movement of the late nineteenth and early twentieth centuries fit into a broad front of reforms led by evangelical Christians who hoped to bring the virtue of self-control to unruly southern men.[12]

In his work on antebellum hunting, Nicolas Proctor argued that upper-class southerners used the chase to demonstrate a broad mastery over their world. He portrayed the hunt as both training ground and stage for a display of masculine dominion over poor whites, slaves, and nature itself. With so much invested in the pursuit, it is not surprising that the products of the hunt proved to be important tokens of that mastery, tokens that hunters might share or gift to further reflect their own glory.[13]

Proctor noted that for slaves the game itself was the foremost goal of the hunt, and it seems slaves were more active in the field than one might suspect. Through the accounts of former slaves and the archaeological record alongside the hunting narratives of the elites, scholars have created an unexpectedly rich look at hunting and fishing among the enslaved. Masters allowed a surprising amount of hunting, trapping, and fishing, often by a designated huntsman. The wildlife he brought in might offset the costs of provisions for the slaves and provide another saleable commodity for the master. Frequently slaves sold or traded their take for needed items either with or without their master's approval, asserting a measure of independence and resistance through an activity masters had meant for their own benefit. And it is probable that while they were on a serious quest for food, they also enjoyed the recreational aspect of the chase.[14]

After emancipation, hunting and fishing became even more important for African Americans. Evidence shows that many freedmen lived off the land in the uncertain time immediately following the war. The sale of excess game and fish was often the most obvious way to make money. Scott Giltner has described a postbellum South where whites sought to control the labor and recreation of freedmen and where hunting and fishing were part of the broader racial struggle. Giltner offers extensive evidence of elites' dismay with hunting, fishing, and ownership of weapons by African Americans. Upper-class concerns about the independence of freedmen meshed well with the emerging conservation movement, and calls for restrictive game laws that would in effect disarm lower-class hunters were increasingly aimed at blacks. At the same time, in the late nineteenth and early twentieth centuries, wealthy northerners spent part of their winter in the South, often hunting and fishing, making sporting tourism a growing economic concern. Giltner argues that the importance of this new industry helped convince traditionally reluctant southerners that restrictions on hunting could help ensure white supremacy along with plenty of sport for the rich Yankees.[15]

Southern elites certainly wanted to restrict the hunting activities of blacks and poor whites. What is less clear is the efficacy of upper-class anger and the resulting legislation at a time when most southerners lived by farming as share or tenant farmers or on their own land. In the first decades of the twentieth century rural populations generally expanded across the South. Agriculture spread as much of the remaining old-growth timber came under the ax, and large game continued to decline before a well-armed rural populace. When Theodore Roosevelt came south for bear and deer in 1902 and 1907, it was with a certain urgency to experience a kind of hunt already receding into memory. Most people accepted the settling of remote areas as the natural course of events for a growing nation. Farmers would necessarily settle arable areas, producing food and fiber for a wider world. By the time the pioneering wildlife biologist Aldo Leopold surveyed game in Mississippi in the late 1920s, he found only a small deer population and was almost dismissive of preserving a huntable number. Leopold did not even mention the possibility of maintaining a bear population.[16]

The first half of the twentieth century was the age of small game in the South. Deer populations held on in the more remote bottomlands and even supported some hunting, but for the most part small creatures made game for southerners of the time. Some animals, such as possums and squirrels, have two litters of young a year and seem to defy hunting pressure. Others, including rabbits and quail, can reproduce multiple times and created remarkable populations under the right conditions. Weedy fields of the pre-mechanized farm South were the perfect habitat for quail and rabbits, and along with coons, possums, and squirrels, they became the iconic game of the region for decades.[17]

By far the most discussed and worried-over game of this period was the bobwhite quail. The *Bobwhite Thesaurus* claimed that some 2,785 works on quail biology appeared between 1882 and 1982. Since the antebellum period, the upper class had sought to appropriate both the bird and its pursuit. Quail hunting would become for some the American reflection of British grouse shooting with its own estates and customs. The popularity of quail hunting paralleled advancements in shotgun technology. More efficient ignition systems and actions made wing shooting a more reasonable proposition by the late nineteenth century. With breeds of dogs developed specifically for birds, sport hunting for quail became a familiar activity.[18]

Wing shooting quail and, to a lesser extent, waterfowling drove much of the northern sporting tourism in the South of the late nineteenth and early twentieth centuries. Some vacationing hunters bought land primarily in the region of Thomasville, Georgia, and Tallahassee, Florida, creating a cluster of what came to be known as "quail plantations." Eventually there were hunting estates scattered throughout the South, though the most active remain in the south Georgia / north Florida area. Plantation-style hunting was and is a highly ritualized activity involving a number of retainers including wranglers, dog handlers, and wagon drivers, and it was meant to approximate what northern tourists and their local hosts imagined of old southern traditions.[19]

The literature of quail biology and quail hunting overlays a once-vibrant folk tradition that included quail. Quail, generally referred to simply as "birds," were often so common that they were important as sport and commodity across a broad spectrum of society. Jimmy Carter spoke for many when he remembered, "It was inevitable that I would become an avid quail hunter." Of quail hunting, Georgia sporting writer Charles Elliott noted, "Everyone participated from the gallused country lad with a single-barrel shotgun to the affluent citizen." For Mississippi hunter John Bailey, sport blended with work as he became a guide for visiting northern hunters. Bailey's meticulous record keeping offers a glimpse at the astounding numbers of birds the southern farm habitat could produce. From the 1920s to the 1980s Bailey killed around 18,000 wild quail, a number that reflects both his shooting ability and his longevity. However, his average of around three hundred a year was not unusual for active bird hunters at least through the 1950s.[20]

Always in demand as food, quail supported widespread commercial hunting and trapping. Ranging from bartering birds for shotgun shells at the local store to interstate sales, quail trafficking was a well-known part of the rural economy. William Turcotte, an early Mississippi game biologist, estimated in-state quail prices at around one dollar each for live-trapped birds in the 1920s and 1930s. Early game laws turned the trade into a black market but did little to eliminate an exchange ingrained in custom and encouraged by eager consumers. Even in 1957, some 101 years after Johnson Hooper warned his readers about quail trappers, one such South Georgia entrepreneur admitted to retailing around three thousand quail in a little more than a year. Intense sport hunting existed alongside market hunting and trapping supported by an ideal habitat for quail.[21]

The association of wing shooting with white elites lent a racial and economic stigma to the pursuit of other small-game creatures. Sportsmen concerned about quail populations agonized over African Americans straying from "black game" like rabbits and possums and shooting and trapping quail. Of course, small game of all kinds mattered just as much to poor white farmers as it did to blacks. Blacks were easier to blame, and elites might more reasonably hope to restrict their hunting than that of poor whites. The same literature that shows upper-class ire also hints at persistent hunting and trade in game by people on the land. In a 1913 *Field and Stream* article by Memphis writer Nash Buckingham, one of the characters railed against blacks after their group had witnessed a "negro hunter, in behind a fast pointer" make a clean kill on a quail. Though the white character makes it clear that he would not allow such hunting on his own land, the dog work and the good shooting indicate the black man was an accomplished hunter accustomed to quail, let alone "black" game.[22] In 1933 former Mississippi game warden Winchester Jenkins complained, "Any old negro with a $1.00 license under the present law has a right to shoot a covey of quail, on the ground, and that is just what the rabbit-hunting Negro boy does." He advocated a new licensing system based on a social hierarchy of game with permits for birds the most expensive—"to stop the pot hunter"—and those for "rabbits and squirrels" and fur bearers the cheapest. It seems unlikely his plan would have deterred either poor whites or his main targets, the "many negro boys with their pockets stuffed full of quail," during a time when a bird might bring as much cash as hours of hard labor.[23] Access to quail, as well as the quail itself, was part of the many-layered trade in wild food as in Robert Ruark's story of his grandfather securing hunting rights to land in North Carolina. The "Old Man" traded squirrels, coons, and possums, among other favors, for quail hunting on black-owned land in his county. The informal hunting lease gave value to the live birds and reinforced the perceived racial and economic distinctions among game species.[24]

For all the ink spilled over quail, comparatively little has been written about other small game. There is no weighty compilation of rabbit-hunting stories and no "Opposum Thesaurus," although rural folk used almost every creature as food or trade item. Coons and possums offered a substantial amount of meat and marketable pelts, and they became emblematic of the poorer side of southern hunting. The largest coons in the Deep South weigh around twenty pounds, and big possums around ten. The dollar value of their meat was probably less than their pelt until recent years, when fur has gone utterly out of fashion. George Lowery noted that during the 1928–29 season, before the economic collapse, coon pelts in Louisiana averaged more than seven dollars apiece while 518,295 possum skins brought only $570,125. Harder to catch and possessed of a more valuable pelt, coons have always been more prized than possums. As a food animal, the more common—and often quite fat—possum was probably more important for the rural poor. During times when calories mattered, cooks scalded or singed possums before cooking, destroying the pelt but saving the precious fat. By numbers and weight, rabbits probably made up the most common game meal for rural people. Cottontail rabbits weigh around three pounds and the swamp variety may weigh six pounds; both kinds of rabbit can have six litters a year. Rabbits were so common they were often taken for granted, and although their populations fluctuated widely, the farm environment almost always supported a few.[25]

Owners and managers on the quail plantations had long demanded their tenants focus on small game such as coons and possums, which were both unwanted by the elites and were perceived as threats to the ground-nesting quail. On Ichauway Plantation in southwest Georgia, the management instituted bounties as an enticement to residents for what was considered predator control. Around 1930, Ichauway was paying fifty cents for possums and coons, twenty-five cents for crows, and two dollars for stray cats. James Mott, a former worker on Ichauway, remembers the bounties as an important source of cash, and of course, he could eat or sell the food animals. Mott recalled that he and his friends scoured the woods in their spare time, usually at night, amassing ten to fifteen dollars every two weeks—significant money in what he termed the "Hoover Days." For Mott and others, the bounties abetted an already active small game–hunting tradition and directed it toward the advantage of the plantation.[26]

There had long been migration from the rural South toward industrial labor and urban life and away from oppression and failing farms. However, there had always been a demand for enough workers to do the necessary manual work of farming. The coming of World War II offered ever greater opportunities away from the land. Tractors, which were around before the war, became commonplace in the years that followed, diminishing the need for farm labor. Also, agriculturalists innovated and refined equipment until almost every farm operation, including harvest, was mechanized. Government farm policy favored bigger farms and large landowners, and the number of farms decreased as their size steadily increased. Rural folk were in part lured away and in part pushed from the land. Vast areas that had supported the rural population, however poorly, were abandoned. Agricultural activities concentrated in areas conducive to large-scale, clean-field farming, and the number of people actually engaged in farming began a steep decline. Southerners who remained were generally less desperate and less likely to be living directly from the land.[27]

The rural exodus and the mechanization of farming ultimately transformed the landscape. John Bailey noticed some of the changes in north Mississippi as a general thickening. Lands that once contained small weedy fields and made perfect quail range were left to whatever forest cover might regenerate there. Often landowners planted dense stands of loblolly pine. And as people left the countryside, the frequency of fire declined, further encouraging a rank growth that was of little use, at least for quail. Though it was not apparent for a few decades, the new way of life meant the end of widespread quail hunting in the South. By the 1970s quail were in steep decline throughout the region. Parts of Texas and Oklahoma still maintain wild bobwhite populations that are more dependent on weather conditions than farming practices. In the Southeast huntable wild populations remain only on intensively manipulated lands where managers attempt to create the very specific habitat that quail require. Pen-raised birds supply the restaurant trade and some shooting preserves. For the most part, wild quail exist only in remnant populations around the Southeast.[28]

The same conditions that caused the quail decline offered opportunity for game such as deer that had long been scarce. One Tennessee wildlife manager noted that if there had been an endangered species act in the early 1900s, deer surely would have been listed. Georgia forester Leon Neel remembered that his father hunted almost everything in the 1920s and 1930s except "deer, because believe it or not, there were so few around." With smaller human populations in the countryside after World War II, game biologists set about reintroducing deer to the Southeast using innovative scientific restocking methods. It is hardly necessary to point out that the effort succeeded beyond anyone's imagination. By the mid-1950s John Bailey sometimes saw deer on his farm—on land they had not occupied for perhaps a hundred years. By the 1990s Tennessee biologists estimated their whitetail numbers at more than 800,000, up from around 1,000 in the 1940s. From a few thousand in late 1920s Mississippi, the deer population may now number around 1.5 million. Where Leon Neel's father found no deer to shoot in Georgia, the state's annual kill is now around 400,000 animals.[29]

If the bobwhite quail was the iconic game of the South in 1930, then today it is certainly the white-tailed deer. By far most of the material culture of hunting—the weapons, apparel, and gadgetry—is focused on deer. Some hunters still go after squirrels and rabbits. The latter were more adaptable to modern farming practices, and significant populations remain. Much of the interest in rabbits, and, to a lesser degree, in squirrels, involves the dogs used to hunt them. Likewise, most coon hunters today would probably say the experience with their hound is more important than any animals they might take. Many hunters do not even shoot the coons their hounds tree. Fur bearers such as coons and possums are the only truly wild game legally sold today for food, and while there remains a small market for coons, almost no one eats possum in today's South.[30]

Evolving attitudes toward game among southerners are less obvious than changes in land use and the responses of wildlife populations. In the decades following World War II those who remained in the South grew more amenable to the concepts of conservation, notions more understandable on a full stomach. People began to accept game regulations set by the state, in part because the agricultural cycle was no longer the yearly schedule for most people. Wildlife law enforcement also advanced from inconsistent efforts to organized professional departments that were undoubtedly more effective. More people adopted ideas of trophy hunting, and some relegated hunting for food to a somewhat lower status. The old arguments against pothunting seem to resonate as more people were less concerned about actually filling the pot. And most people grew to accept the idea that game was no longer a legal commodity, one of the central tenets of Progressive Era game law reform. Deer hunting has reflected these changes. Consider that even by the 1960s and 1970s deer populations far exceeded healthy levels in much of the South, and biologists urged the killing of females to reduce the numbers. For years, many hunters resisted efforts at doe shooting. Many of these hunters had experienced the incredible resurgence of deer. For them, bucks with their antlers had become coveted trophies, and killing females was out of the question.[31]

Interest in hunting has generally been on the wane. Fewer people hunt, and that population is growing older. Today, even in Mississippi, where in the 1920s Aldo Leopold once remarked on the "intense popular interest in game and hunting," fewer than 15 percent of people actually hunt. For those still in the field, hunting is not as much about food as it once was. Many deer hunters concentrate on trophy hunting. Biologists find it difficult to convince hunters waiting only for a buck to kill the number of females necessary to manage populations. The years when whitetails were almost exterminated and the many seasons of restricted kills may also have eroded the basic folk knowledge of how to properly prepare deer as food. Utterly unlike domestic beef or pork, venison can frustrate cooking efforts, and a few bad experiences can lead to a lifetime of aversion.[32]

Among some hunters, strains of what David Petersen has called "neo-animism" can work to make the hunting experience a more introspective, restrained activity where the actual kill becomes less important. Concerned more with reconnecting to an earlier human existence, such hunters often restrict their lethality using archery gear or other primitive weapons. In part, they seek to slow down the experience, to meditate on the human role as predator. This theme has been a part of some of the best writing on hunting and conservation since World War II. Generally, these writers praise the occasional hard-won kill as the ultimate communion with nature, but they are, as Petersen says, "process-oriented rather than product-driven."[33]

Some of the few people among whom hunting is gaining popularity are those interested in the provenance of the meat they eat and those who seek to own the deaths of the animals they consume. Some of the most thoughtful recent treatments of hunting have been written by people primarily concerned with game as food. Michael Pollan's experiences with feral pigs and Steven Rinella's hunting and gathering projects offer some realistic explorations of what it means to do your own killing. Rinella even has his own series on the Travel Channel where, as a sort of introspective pothunter, he pursues and prepares game in various parts of the world.[34]

An enlightened search for food may be one of the better expressions of modern hunting, but most people do not hunt and probably never will. And American law compels those seriously interested in wild game as food to take to the woods themselves or resort to what remains of an illegal trade in wildlife. Always difficult to quantify, an underground traffic in game and fish in the South remains today. Marc Reisner has documented some of the trade both within the region and among transplanted southerners hungry for a taste of home. Game still has a following on both sides of the law, though access is often the issue. These days it seems reasonable to reconsider the ban on game sales in favor of some type of regulated market. This is in fact what biologist C. Davidson Ankney has already suggested in the case of geese. Some incarnation of commercial hunting as part of a more food-centric wildlife management could address both the overpopulation of some species and the desire for truly wild nonfarmed game. A new legal sustainable trade in wildlife might also reacquaint many southerners with the gift of wild food and reaffirm game as a respected element in a locally and regionally sourced cuisine.[35]

NOTES

1. Official Records Department of Wildlife Conservation, Record group 78, subgroup 2, volume 76, folder "Publicity Sept–Dec 1932," Mississippi Department of Archives and History (hereafter MDAH). Lawrence Merovka does not mention his Water Valley experience in his essay "A Federal Game Warden," in *Flyways: Pioneering Waterfowl Management in North America*, ed. A. S. Hawkins et al. (United States Department of the Interior, Fish and Wildlife Service, 1984), 27–34. However, he does give a vivid picture of the tenacious commercial hunting of the period.

2. Among the many articles on expanding goose populations are Michael R. Conover and Gregory G. Chasko, "Nuisance Canada Goose Problems in the Eastern United States," *Wildlife Society Bulletin* 13, no. 3 (Autumn 1985): 228–33; and C. Davison Ankney, "An Embarrassment of Riches: Too Many Geese," *Journal of Wildlife Management* 60, no. 2 (1996): 217–23.

3. Stuart Marks, *Southern Hunting in Black and White: Nature, History, and Ritual in a Carolina Community* (Princeton, N.J.: Princeton University Press, 1991), 53.

4. William Faulkner, *Big Woods* (New York: Random House, 1955), 124–25. I explored this large game–small game dichotomy in Wiley C. Prewitt Jr., "Return of the Big Woods: Hunting and Habitat in Yoknapatawpha," in *Faulkner and the Natural World: Faulkner and Yoknapatawpha*, ed. Donald M. Kartiganer and Ann J. Abadie (Jackson: University Press of Mississippi, 1996), 198–221.

5. Charles Hudson, *The Southeastern Indians* (Knoxville: University of Tennessee Press, 1976), 80–81, 258–316, 498–501. Hudson reiterates some of these themes, especially with regards to foodways, in the introduction of *The Transformation of the Southeastern Indians, 1540–1760*, ed. Robbie Ethridge and Charles Hudson (Jackson: University Press of Mississippi, 2002), xi–xxxix. Robbie Ethridge claims that Hudson's chapter on subsistence in *The Southeastern Indians* is still the most complete look at Native American foodways in what would

become the South. See Ethridge, *Creek Country: The Creek Indians and Their World* (Chapel Hill: University of North Carolina Press, 2003), 291.

6. Charles Hudson, *Knights of Spain, Warriors of the Sun: Hernando de Soto and the South's Ancient Chiefdoms* (Athens: University of Georgia Press, 1997).

7. Marvin D. Jeter, "From Prehistory through Protohistory to Ethnohistory in and near the Northern Lower Mississippi Valley," in Ethridge and Hudson, *Transformation of the Southeastern Indians*, 177–223. Jeter gives a good look at the complexities of interpreting Native American life from archeological records and European accounts.

8. Hudson, *Knights of Spain*, 274–75. There is a lot of good scholarship on the deerskin trade, such as Timothy Silver, *A New Face on the Countryside: Indians, Colonists, and Slaves in South Atlantic Forests, 1500–1800* (Cambridge: Cambridge University Press, 1990), 86–97; Richard White, *The Roots of Dependency: Subsistence, Environment, and Social Change among the Choctaws, Pawnees, and Navajos* (Lincoln: University of Nebraska Press, 1983), 1–147; Shepard Krech III, *The Ecological Indian: Myth and History* (New York: Norton, 1999), 151–71, deerskin numbers on 160; Ethridge, *Creek Country*, esp. 120–39; and Daniel H. Usner Jr., *Indians, Settlers, and Slaves in a Frontier Exchange Economy: The Lower Mississippi Valley before 1783* (Chapel Hill: University of North Carolina Press, 1992), 24–31, 244–75. For a biological perspective on the hide trade and early deer hunting, see Richard E. McCabe and Thomas R. McCabe, "Of Slings and Arrows: An Historical Retrospection," in *White-Tailed Deer: Ecology and Management*, ed. Lowell K. Hall (Harrisburg, Pa.: Stackpole, 1984), 19–72.

9. McCabe and McCabe, "Slings and Arrows," 60; Andrew Beahrs, *Twain's Feast: Searching for America's Lost Foods in the Footsteps of Samuel Clemens* (New York: Penguin, 2010), 16; Albert E. Cowdrey, *This Land, This South: An Environmental History* (Lexington: University Press of Kentucky, 1983). For more on the long-lived commercial wildfowling trade, see Harry M. Walsh, *The Outlaw Gunner* (Centreville, Md.: Tidewater, 1971).

10. Johnson Jones Hooper, *Dog and Gun: A Few Loose Chapters on Shooting, Among Which Will Be Found Anecdotes and Incidents,* with an introduction by Philip D. Beidler (Tuscaloosa: University of Alabama Press, 1992), 9. This is a facsimile of the 1856 edition originally published by Orange Judd in New York.

11. John F. Reiger, *American Sportsmen and the Origins of Conservation*, 3rd rev. ed. (Corvallis: Oregon State University Press, 2001). The third edition includes a new chapter on antebellum sportsmen, including more on the work of South Carolinian William Elliott.

12. Steven Hahn, "Hunting, Fishing, and Foraging: Common Rights and Class Relations in the Postbellum South," *Radical History Review* 26 (1982): 37–64; Steven Hahn, *The Roots of Southern Populism: Yeoman Farmers and the Transformation of the Georgia Upcountry, 1850–1890* (New York: Oxford University Press, 1984), esp. 240–43. One will almost never find Hahn's view of conservation laws as a power play by the ruling class in traditional conservation literature; see McCabe and McCabe, "Slings and Arrows," 19–72; Hawkins et al., *Flyways*; Keith Sutton, ed., *Arkansas Wildlife: A History* (Fayetteville: University of Arkansas Press, 1998); Ted Ownby, *Subduing Satan: Religion, Recreation, and Manhood in the Rural South,*

1865–1920 (Chapel Hill: University of North Carolina Press, 1990). Though not about the South, three fairly recent works that tell the stories of those on the receiving end of conservation programs are Louis S. Warren, *The Hunter's Game: Poachers and Conservationists in Twentieth-Century America* (New Haven, Conn.: Yale University Press, 1997); Mark David Spence, *Dispossessing the Wilderness: Indian Removal and the Making of the National Parks* (New York: Oxford University Press, 1999); and Karl Jacoby, *Crimes against Nature: Squatters, Poachers, Thieves, and the Hidden History of American Conservation* (Berkeley: University of California Press, 2001).

13. Nicolas W. Proctor, *Bathed in Blood: Hunting and Mastery in the Old South* (Charlottesville: University Press of Virginia, 2002), esp. 55–60 and 144–73. Proctor's chapter "Slave Perceptions of the Hunt" remains a good introduction to the importance of hunting among slaves.

14. Ibid., 144–73; Scott Giltner, "Slave Hunting and Fishing in the Antebellum South," in *"To Love the Wind and Rain": African Americans and Environmental History*, ed. Diane Glave and Mark Stoll (Pittsburgh: University of Pittsburgh Press, 2005), 21–36; Anne L. Bower, ed., *African American Foodways: Explorations of History and Culture* (Chicago: University of Illinois Press, 2007); Herbert C. Covey and Dwight Eisnach, *What the Slaves Ate: Recollections of African American Foods and Foodways from the Slave Narratives* (Santa Barbara: Greenwood Press, 2009).

15. Giltner, "Slave Hunting and Fishing"; Scott E. Giltner, *Hunting and Fishing in the New South: Black Labor and White Leisure after the Civil War* (Baltimore: Johns Hopkins University Press, 2008). Giltner's work affirms the importance of the wild for blacks in the postbellum South and makes an argument that much early twentieth-century game and fish regulation was part of the regionwide effort to dismantle African American freedoms.

16. Wiley Prewitt, "The Best of All Breathing: Hunting and Environmental Change in Mississippi, 1890–1980" (M.A. thesis, University of Mississippi, 1991). The decline of large game at the end of the nineteenth century through the first few decades of the twentieth century is a familiar theme in wildlife conservation literature. See Doug Markham, *Boxes, Rockets, and Pens: A History of Wildlife Recovery in Tennessee* (Knoxville: University Press of Tennessee, 1997); Sutton, *Arkansas Wildlife*. For the changing agricultural South, see Pete Daniel, *Breaking the Land: The Transformation of Cotton, Tobacco, and Rice Cultures since 1880* (Chicago: University of Illinois Press, 1985); Jack Temple Kirby, *Rural Worlds Lost: The American South, 1920–1960* (Baton Rouge: Louisiana State University Press, 1987). Scott Giltner examines Roosevelt's southern bear hunts in *Hunting and Fishing in the New South*, as does Mikko Saikku in *This Delta, This Land: An Environmental History of the Yazoo-Mississippi Flood Plain* (Athens: University of Georgia Press, 2005). See also Theodore Roosevelt, "In the Louisiana Canebrakes," in *American Bears: Selections from the Writings of Theodore Roosevelt*, ed. Paul Schullery (Boulder: Colorado Associated University Press, 1983), 155; Aldo Leopold, "Report on a Game Survey of Mississippi" (Sporting Arms and Ammunition Manufacturers Institute, 1929; digitized reprint, Mississippi Museum of Natural Science, 2010).

17. Prewitt, "Best of All Breathing"; Marks, *Southern Hunting in Black and White*; George A. Feldhamer, Bruce C. Thompson, and Joseph A. Chapman, eds., *Wild Mammals of North America: Biology, Management and Conservation*, 2nd ed. (Baltimore: Johns Hopkins University Press, 2003); Herbert L. Stoddard, *The Bobwhite Quail: Its Habits, Preservation, and Increase* (New York: Charles Scribner's Sons, 1931).

18. Thomas G. Scott, *The Bobwhite Thesaurus* (Edgefield, S.C.: International Quail Foundation, 1985). The hunting literature devoted to quail is enormous. A good anthology that covers many decades is Lamar Underwood, ed., *The Bobwhite Quail Book* (Clinton, N.J.: Amwell, 1980). Stoddard's *The Bobwhite Quail* and Walter Rosene's *The Bobwhite Quail: Its Life and Management* (New Brunswick, N.J.: Rutgers University Press, 1969) are the standard biological texts for quail. However, one more recent example of the continuing research is Gerald A. Cline et al., "Summer Habitat Relationships of Northern Bobwhite in Piedmont Virginia," *Proceedings of the Forty-fifth Conference Southeastern Association of Fish and Wildlife Agencies, November 3–6, 1991, White Sulphur Springs, West Virginia*, 37–48.

19. Clifton Paisley, *From Cotton to Quail: An Agricultural Chronicle of Leon County, Florida, 1860 to 1967* (Gainesville: University of Florida Press, 1968); William R. Brueckheimer, "The Quail Plantations of the Thomasville-Tallahassee-Albany Regions," *Proceedings: Tall Timbers Ecology and Management Conference* 16 (February 22–24, 1979), 144–66; Giltner, *Hunting and Fishing in the New South*; Wayne Capooth, *The Golden Age of Waterfowling* (Germantown, Tenn.: Capooth, 2001); Jimmy Carter, *An Outdoor Journal: Adventures and Reflections* (Fayetteville: University of Arkansas Press, 1994). Carter draws the distinction between plantation hunting and the more common activity. The best recent book on the high side of quail hunting is Guy de la Valdéne, *For a Handful of Feathers* (New York: Atlantic Monthly Press, 1995). Another good sporting writer who has an outsider's take on what remains of southern quail hunting is Jim Fergus in *A Hunter's Road: A Journey with Dog and Gun across the American Uplands* (New York: Holt, 1992). For more on the plantation experience see Jim Fergus, "Tom Wolfe's Quail Tale," *Sports Afield* (March 1999): 46, 48.

20. Carter, *Outdoor Journal*, 166; Charles Elliott, *Prince of Game Birds: The Bobwhite Quail* (Atlanta: Georgia Department of Natural Resources, 1974), 21; George Bird Evans, *Dear John: Nash Buckingham's Letters to John Bailey* (Old Hemlock, 1984), 198–99. Copy of John Bailey's hunting log in possession of author with thanks to Bailey's family.

21. Prewitt, "Best of all Breathing"; transcript of an interview with William Turcotte, Mississippi Museum of Natural Science Library; Hooper, *Dog and Gun*, 60–61; Robert W. Woodruff Papers, Box 159, Folder "Ichauway Plantations, Guy Touchtone, Poaching, Emory Field Station, 1957," Robert Woodruff Library, Special Collections, Emory University. For a more benign use of a quail trap for biological research, see Leon Neel et al., *The Art of Managing Longleaf: A Personal History of the Stoddard Neel Approach* (Athens: University of Georgia Press, 2010), 74.

22. Marks, *Southern Hunting in Black and White*; Giltner, *Hunting and Fishing in the New South*; T. N. Buckingham, "Bob White, Down 'T Aberdeen," *Field and Stream* (September 1913): 453–61, quotes on 460. Earlier in the story, Buckingham and his mates purchase a pitcher of

either home brew or whiskey for some change and one large rabbit from a local black woman. The scene reminded readers of the association of rabbits with the poor, but it should also remind modern readers of the nuanced uses of game in the rural barter system. This story (minus the black bird hunter section) is collected in Lamar Underwood, ed., *Hunting the Southlands* (Clinton, N.J.: Amwell, 1986).

23. Winchester Jenkins, *Wildlife of Mississippi from Forty-Five Years Experience* (Natchez, Miss., 1933), 42–43.

24. Robert Ruark, "Even School Can't Hurt October," in *The Old Man and the Boy* (New York: Holt, 1957), 153–70. This story contains an unusual number of references to southern food both wild and domestic, even for Ruark, who often mentioned food and drink in his work.

25. See Wiley C. Prewitt Jr., "Coons and Possoms" and "Quail," in vol. 7, Foodways, The *New Encyclopedia of Southern Culture*, ed. John T. Edge (Chapel Hill: University of North Carolina Press, 2007); Russell Tinsley, *All About Small Game Hunting in America* (New York: Winchester, 1976); May Jordan, *"Where the Wild Animals Is Plentiful": Diary of an Alabama Fur Trader's Daughter, 1912–1914*, ed. Elisa Moore Baldwin (Tuscaloosa: University of Alabama Press, 1999); George H. Lowery Jr., *The Mammals of Louisiana and Its Adjacent Waters* (Baton Rouge: Louisiana Wildlife and Fisheries Commission, Louisiana State University Press, 1974), 34–35, 159. The very real association of some game with a hard rural life reinforces notions of a hierarchy of game. Years ago I set out to record the story of my great-grandmother and her dogs. It was a well-known tale within my family that she always kept dogs to tree possums for which she had occasional cravings. During the course of an interview when I asked my grandmother to tell about her mother's possum hunting, she looked as if I had lost my mind and went to her grave without admitting anything on tape.

26. James Mott, tape log of interview (IDP-WP-A069 on 1/23/93), in the possession of the author. I was one of four fieldworkers who conducted an ethnographic survey of Ichauway Plantation in Baker County, Georgia, for the Center for the Study of Southern Culture at the University of Mississippi. Two other copies of the audiotapes were made. One copy remains at Ichauway at the Jones Ecological Research Center and one copy at the University of Mississippi. The Ichauway Documentary Project Collection at the University of Mississippi is not open to researchers at the time of this writing. Herbert Stoddard and Ed V. Komarek, "Predator Control in Southeastern Quail Management," reprint of *Transactions of the Sixth North American Wildlife Conference, 1941*, American Wildlife Institute, Washington, D.C., 485–90.

27. Daniel, *Breaking the Land*; Kirby, *Rural Worlds Lost*.

28. John Bailey diary, "Deer"; Prewitt, "Best of All Breathing"; Prewitt, "Quail."

29. Markham, *Boxes, Rockets, and Pens*; Halls, *White-Tailed Deer*; Neel, *Art of Managing Longleaf*, 39; John Bailey diary, "Deer"; Joe Shead, ed., *Deer Hunters' Almanac 2006* (Iola, Wis.: F + W Publications, 2005).

30. Prewitt, "Coons and Possums"; Tinsley, *All About Small Game Hunting in America*; David Hawkins, "Fur, Feathers, Dogs and Fun," *Mississippi Outdoors* 70, no. 6 (November/

December 2007): 14–17; Randy Zellers, "Briar Patch Passion," *Arkansas Wildlife* (January/February 2011): 16–19.

31. Prewitt, "Best of All Breathing"; Marks, *Southern Hunting in Black and White*; Halls, *White-Tailed Deer*.

32. Leopold, "Report on a Game Survey in Mississippi," 11; Randy Spencer, "Reflections on the Past and Thoughts about the Future," *Wildlife Issues* (Fall/Winter 2007): 12–13. The best recent book on deer and the issues that come with them is Richard Nelson, *Heart and Blood: Living with Deer in America* (New York: Knopf, 1997). See also Harold W. Webster Jr., *The Complete Venison Cookbook* (Brandon, Miss.: Quail Ridge, 1996). Webster argues that much of the quality of venison depends on a quick kill performed on an unstressed animal and suggests that this was a more traditional way of killing deer that later hunters had to rediscover.

33. David Petersen, *Heartsblood: Hunting, Spirituality, and Wildness in America* (Washington, D.C.: Island Press, 2000), 99, 181; Ted Kerasote, *Blood Ties: Nature, Culture, and the Hunt* (New York: Random House, 1993). The best recent antihunting work, and one that dissects the many prohunting arguments, is Matt Cartmill, *A View to a Death in the Morning: Hunting and Nature through History* (Cambridge, Mass.: Harvard University Press, 1993). See also Chris McDonald, "Back to Basics: Doe Harvest," *Wildlife Issues* (Fall/Winter 2008): 3.

34. Michael Pollan, *The Omnivore's Dilemma: A Natural History of Four Meals* (New York: Penguin Press, 2006); Steven Rinella, *The Scavenger's Guide to Haute Cuisine* (New York: Miramax Books, 2005), and *Meateater: Adventures from the Life of an American Hunter* (New York: Spiegel and Grau, 2012). Rinella's first TV series was called *The Wild Within*, and more recently, he has a new series called *Meateater* on the Sportsman Channel. Anthony Bourdain and Andrew Zimmern have also explored the mechanics and morality of hunting for food on their programs *No Reservations* and *Bizarre Foods*, respectively. The BBC series *Kill It, Cook It, Eat It* has also dealt with the issue of hunting for food in Britain.

35. Marc Reisner, *Game Wars: The Undercover Pursuit of Wildlife Poachers* (New York: Viking, 1991); Ankney, "An Embarrassment of Riches." A brief but good discussion of game as food and the legal situation in the United States is Mark Kurlansky, "The Wild Ones," *Food & Wine* (November 1997): 92, 94, 98–99. See also Steven Cramer, "Tracking the Wild in 'Wild' Food," in *Wild Food: Proceedings of the Oxford Symposium on Food and Cookery 2004*, ed. Richard Hosking (Totnes, U.K.: Prospect Books, 2006), 184–92. For an introduction to the present-day sale of game and the use of game in upscale British eateries as an example of what we might expect in the United States, see Bruce Palling, "From Game to Flame," *Wall Street Journal*, October 23–25, 2009, W6, W7.

PART 2
People and Communities

IN THIS SECTION, we bring individual and community voices into the conversation. Beth Latshaw, Justin Nystrom, Rayna Green, and Tom Hanchett employ quantitative and qualitative social science survey methods, rigorous oral history project design, labor analyses, demographic observations, and close readings of festivals and celebrations to rethink food studies as community studies. Read together, they make a case that new understandings emerge from a careful analysis of food communities in local and regional settings.

Most recent southern studies anthologies begin with explorations of how the South used to be viewed with a sense of stability and certainty. Next, they point out all the people and places that had to be excluded in order for that certainty to hold. A discussion of the construction of the South, the idea of the South, and the resulting turn away from geography or politics or war as definitional categories often follows. Increasingly, such collections explore the global South. They fully acknowledge and incorporate the global, transnational citizens and commodity chains of today's communities and cultures. Often such collections muster a cautious pessimism that any discussion of a South or Souths will cohere.[1]

Food studies offers insights on this global and transnational South conversation. Southern food studies provides data that confirms networks of global and transnational people, capital, and cultures. One of the early book-length treatments of American foodways, Donna Gabaccia's *We Are What We Eat*, used the colonial South to argue that southern foodways were Creolized, hybridized, and immigrant inflected.

Southern food studies also dispenses with strict borders between the U.S. South and other global communities. A number of recent books, including Frederick Douglass Opie's *Hog and Hominy*, set the invention of southern food traditions in the diasporas and migrations that challenged the boundaries between such communities, framing soul food as an invented tradition, useful to diverse communities in different ways at different times.

Amplifying that argument, commodity chain and transnational scholars have carefully documented configurations of labor, capital, goods, and cultures in the Caribbean and elsewhere, grounding the U.S. South in global communities.[2] Contributors in this section add sociological data and individual stories through which such configurations can be clearly seen.

In "The Soul of the South: Race, Food, and Identity in the American South," Beth A. Latshaw takes on slippery conceptions of identity, ethnicity, and region. Through food and responses to food, she makes sense of the simultaneity and flexibility of tradition, taste, and belonging. Analyzing the results of a telephone survey, Latshaw shows the changing valences of identity in terms of race, length of residence in a place, political affiliation, and class. She cross-analyzes those identities with fondness for specific foods, food practices, and foodways rituals. Latshaw challenges us to see a new definition of "southern" emerge, as diverse citizens reject older, no longer useful identities and build newer, more flexible, more expansive regional selves. Identification with southern food holds, but in the process, white-black hierarchies fall away.

A story of Italian grocers proves crucial to understanding New Orleans foodways as a complementary mix of European, African, and Caribbean cooking practices. In Justin Nystrom's essay, "Italian New Orleans and the Business of Food in the Immigrant City: There's More to the Muffuletta Than Meets the Eye," Italian merchants tell their family stories in an oral history project. Nystrom substantiates the origin story of the quintessential New Orleans working-class sandwich, the muffuletta, and demonstrates how Italian grocers provided basic ingredients to chefs and home cooks of varied races and ethnicities. As he documents family stories in oral histories, Nystrom discovers a dockworker-run port city, now largely erased by rail- and truck-driven corporate supply chains and grocery store consolidations.

Even as scholarly and popular attention has turned in recent years to hybrid foods, overlapping cultures, and the interactions of cooking styles across the southern states, the influence of Native American foodways has remained largely undertheorized. Rayna Green puts Native foods and cooking practices at the center in "Mother Corn and the Dixie Pig: Native Food in the Native South." Studying crops, oral recipes, menus from community festivals, and formal cookbooks, Green examines Native foods of our historical past and Native foods of our present. She discards the evidentially false assertion that all Native peoples were largely removed from the South by the era of the Trail of Tears.[3] Instead, she looks at the food networks created and sustained by Native Americans throughout the history of the U.S. South and concludes that cherished ingredients such as pork and corn, for which many wax nostalgic, are unimaginable without the original and ongoing presence of Native American southerners.

Tom Hanchett, historian at the Levine Museum of the New South, focuses on a quintessential New South question. In "A Salad Bowl City: The Food Geography of Charlotte, North Carolina," he employs labor-demographic analysis and participant observation to outline the foodways of immigrant, mill, and plantation-inheritance foodways of the Piedmont South. With that data in hand, he asks us to think about how communities feed themselves in a sprawling suburban region. Hanchett also challenges us to study how new communities are forged in a twenty-first-century South that is rapidly diversifying.

NOTES

1. See, for instance, Anthony Stanonis, ed., *Dixie Emporium: Tourism, Foodways, and Consumer Culture in the American South* (Athens: University of Georgia Press, 2008); Tara McPherson, *Reconstructing Dixie: Race, Gender, and Nostalgia in the Imagined South* (Durham, N.C.: Duke University Press, 2003); James L. Peacock et al., eds., *The American South in a Global World* (Chapel Hill: University of North Carolina Press, 2005); Jennifer Greeson, *Our South: Geographic Fantasy and the Rise of National Literature* (Cambridge, Mass.: Harvard University Press, 2010); and Kathryn McKee and Annette Trefzer, "Local Literatures, Global Contexts: The New Southern Studies," *American Literature* 78, no. 4 (2006): 677–90.

2. Donna Gabaccia, *We Are What We Eat: Ethnic Food and the Making of Americans* (Cambridge, Mass.: Harvard University Press, 2000); Frederick Douglass Opie, *Hog and Hominy: Soul Food from America to Africa* (New York: Columbia University Press, 2008); Steven Topnik et al., eds., *From Silver to Cocaine: Latin American Commodity Chains and the Build-*

ing of the World Economy, 1500–2000 (Durham, N.C.: Duke University Press, 2006); Richard Wilk, ed., *Fast Food/Slow Food: The Cultural Economy of the Global Food System* (Lanham, Md.: AltaMira, 2006).

3. As Philip DeLoria has called it, the "dead Indian syndrome." See, for instance, his *Playing Indian* (New Haven, Conn.: Yale University Press, 1999).

CHAPTER 5

The Soul of the South

Race, Food, and Identity in the American South

BETH A. LATSHAW

Introduction

When I bring up my research on southern foodways, I am consistently asked two central questions: first, why study food, and second, why study food in relation to the American South? To begin, in the twenty-first century, it seems nearly impossible to ignore the omnipresence of food in American popular culture, illuminating an association between eating habits, food preferences, and culture—an association presumed to be ubiquitous and deep, but often taken for granted.[1] Furthermore, food is inevitably intertwined and intimately related to numerous aspects of social life and more "traditional" topics of social investigation.[2] For instance, poverty, unemployment, homelessness, and the general lack of nourishment demonstrate close ties to social inequality. Research on eating disorders, body image, and food habits often links these concepts to social-psychological theories of social identity, self-esteem, and beauty norms presented in the media.[3] In contrast, the overconsumption of food forms a central concern of both the sociology of medicine and education subfields.

Moreover, what and when one eats are tied to one's ethnicity, family structure, neighborhood context, and socioeconomic status, all topics of concern to sociologists of the family and stratification.[4] In addition, sociologists would also certainly take notice of how the dynamics of gender roles, domestic labor, and the family meal have shifted since the 1970s. An increasing number of mothers work full-time but are still expected to prepare meals for their families, presenting yet another link between food and the research of gender sociologists.[5] Finally, food is closely related to the socio-logical subfields of religion, culture, and race/ethnicity, as it plays a central role in building social cohesion/solidarity for spiritual and ethnic groups, confirmed by the persistent presence and usage of food in religious rituals, celebrations, gatherings, festivals, and ethnic enclaves.[6]

These premises provide ample support for the notion that sociologists should pay attention to food because of its inescapable ties to countless building blocks of social life. Despite this apparent reality, as Ferguson and Zukin correctly point out, the "material and symbolic richness" of the pro-vision, distribution, and production of food, as well as the role food plays in marking boundaries around social groups, has been largely ignored by the discipline.[7] Alex McIntosh maintains that while a number of social the-orists have indeed alluded to the human need for food, food preference and consumption is "frequently taken for granted" both as a vital element of social life and as a basis for collective identity.[8] Critics have also said that the "sociology of food" subfield suffers from the lack of a central, defining paradigm.[9] Despite sociologists' distance from the study of food and society, anthropologists have long studied how foodways aid in the generation and maintenance of symbolic, cultural meanings and boundaries.[10]

The term "foodways" itself can be defined as the "the customs, beliefs, and practices surrounding the production, presentation, and consumption of food" or, more simply, as "the intersection of food and culture."[11] Within foodways studies, the *cultural* approach sees food as a significant social con-struct imbued with symbolic meaning.[12] A "food culture," like a language, is a form of communication and a "prime domain for conveying and encoding meaning."[13] Thus, food can reinforce a group's distinctiveness—as in Chris-tians drinking grape juice/wine and consuming bread during Communion and Jews consuming matzo during Passover—thereby fortifying the group's symbolic boundaries and marking its uniqueness from outsiders.[14] More-over, while consuming a sandwich is certainly not intended to transmit so-cial information, signify group membership, or provide information about the self (thereby serving only a "utilitarian function"), eating a "punnet of sheeps' eyeballs" (or, perhaps, eating chitterlings in the South) is far more significant, fulfilling what Shavitt and Nelson call a "social identity func-tion."[15] This essay draws on this important social psychological distinction and adopts a cultural approach to interpreting foodways in the southern region.

This leads to the second important question regarding the intent of this piece: why bother studying food in relation to the American South? First, as sociologist Larry J. Griffin remarks, no other region in the United States "has been more intensively analyzed and interpreted than the American South,"[16] making it an interesting and important site of sociological and empirical investigation. Furthermore, the belief that the South is somehow qualitatively "different" from the rest of America in its history, its values, and its culture has led scores of scholars to "search for the origins, expressions, and consequences of 'southern distinctiveness'" and to ponder what it means to be a "southerner" in twenty-first-century America.[17] As Griffin, Evenson, and Thompson highlight, "what it means to be a southerner and how people are to act on these understandings are now very much in flux."[18] Thus, just "who" is a southerner or who has a right to claim a southern identity is not only "highly uncertain" today; it also justifies a revisiting and inquiry into the interplays of race, region, identity, and, I argue, foodways.

Southern writer John Egerton has called food "central to the region's image, its personality, and its character," naming it "an esthetic wonder, a sensory delight, [and even a] mystical experience."[19] It is said to be innovative, artistic, and inspiring; it has been described as everything from diverse, distinctive, and delectable to proud, persistent, and, at times, even controversial. Most certainly, its sights, sounds, tastes, smells, and touch are thought to evoke childhood, stir up emotions from the past, and aid southerners in creating new memories around the modern dining table. In the hearts and minds of southerners from the past and present, only one thing could possibly embody such traits and induce such sentiment: *southern food.*

Indeed, it takes little more than a glance around a local bookstore or a short drive across any state in this vast region to witness just how central southern food is to southern culture in the twenty-first century. From barbecue joints to soul kitchens to country cookeries and church picnics, food certainly appears to lie at the heart of southern hospitality, tradition, and heritage. Moreover, this food is said to possess meaning and symbolism far surpassing what some view as simply a tasty meal. Just as Griffin notes that the southern region has been "celebrated and vilified with a fervor absent from meditations about other sections of this country,"[20] so too has its food, making it a frequent subject of contemplation, fascination, and inquiry. Moreover, in a time when what it means to be a "southerner" is increasingly ambiguous,[21] and vast industrialization, commercialization, and in-migration reshape the southern landscape, the preparation, consumption, and celebration of southern food is looked on as a cultural medium one turns to when expressing a regional identity today.

While scholars and writers intricately detail the rich history of southern foodways, black and white southerners also explicitly reference the present-day link between southern food, culture, and identity in a hefty collection of cookbooks.[22] These works, housing detailed passages on the origins, meanings, and memory-making utility of foods, clearly propose a direct connection between southern food and regional identity. For instance, one author states that southern food is "intricately woven into the fabric of Southern culture," while another asserts that "food is part of [southerners'] cultural identity."[23] This is consistent with the work of John Shelton Reed, Kenan Professor Emeritus of Sociology at the University of North Carolina and an authority on southern culture, who states that when seeking to define the "cultural South" today, one plausible strategy involves simply finding those people who, for example, eat grits, listen to country music, and attend Baptist churches more often than other Americans. According to Reed, southerners often see themselves as different, distinctive, and possessing "shared ethical understandings about what is good . . . true . . . beautiful . . . and even what is edible," culminating in a common "cultural style" that defines and delineates the boundaries of what he calls a southern "ethnic group."[24] Following Reed's notion, the consumption of southern foodways, like ethnic foodways, might be interpreted as a modern-day expression of one's southern identity.

This idea that foodways are the modern vehicle through which one's "southernness" is expressed is particularly pertinent because, as John Egerton explains, in a time of declining regional identity, when southern accents and lifestyles become increasingly rare, southern food is one of the few authentic southern artifacts that "survives." As Susan Kalcik's "Ethnic Foodways in America" similarly illustrates, foodways in general are "particularly resistant to change." Even when confronted with a plethora of national food chains and mass-marketed brand-name products, southern foods remain one of the "earliest-formed layers of [southern] culture" and, simultaneously, one of the "last to erode."[25] Thus, this love of regional cuisine might be one of the few things that southerners of all races, ages, and classes lay claim to, have shared in the past, and still find commonality in today. In other words, at a time when southern identity is fragile and the South is becoming increasingly "Americanized," its traditional foodways have the potential to bind southerners and to be an accessible medium to use in finding cohesion or creating a context for the celebration and performance of southern identity.

While scholarly and culinary works assert that a definite link exists between food and southern identity, what about everyday, common southern folks? Do they truly prefer, consume, and attach meaning to this food? Moreover, if they do, in a region scarred by racial division, is it possible that foodways are a potential site of social, racial, and regional unity? Southern foods are certainly framed in this light by several southern authors and regional groups. John Egerton calls this cuisine "the most positive element of our collective character, an inspiring symbol of reconciliation, healing, and union," claiming it might "unlock the rusty gates of race and class, age and sex."[26] Similarly, in 2004 the Southern Foodways Alliance held a symposium in Oxford, Mississippi, titled "Southern Foodways in Black and White." The symposium overview stated: "We believe that food is our region's greatest shared creation. And we see food as a unifier in a diverse region, as a means by which we may address the issues that have long vexed our homeland."[27] In essence, by framing southern foods as something southerners of all races, classes, and religions claim and share, it seems natural that they could be used to find a sense of commonality or to ease into discussions of a difficult past.

Still, African American cookbook authors and scholars sometimes frame and define southern food in a slightly different way, interpreting it not as distinctively "southern" per se but as "soul food" or "Black food," asserting that this cuisine symbolizes "the persistent presence of an African worldview in [their] customs, beliefs and practices."[28] In this sense, foods such as greens and grits are not necessarily connected to a communal southern identity but to an enduring African American identity, serving as a reflection of not only the stamina, survival, and inventiveness used to persevere through the experience of slavery but also their cultural separateness, or at least difference, from white southerners. In fact, soul food cookbook author Bob Jeffries states, "Soul . . . is a quality that is more accurately said to inhere not in the food but instead in the cook and the eater," asserting that "while all soul food is Southern, not all Southern food is soul."[29] In this light, a white southerner could never actually cook or eat authentic "soul food" as an African American southerner could.

In all, when considering the heavy claims cookbook authors and food-ways scholars make about both the power and meaning of southern food, the question of whether regional food preferences are in fact an expression of cultural hybridity versus contestation takes center stage. However, commentators and celebrators of southern foodways have lacked the systematic empirical data to examine such assertions. Hence, it seems crucial to address whether *everyday* southerners themselves do, in fact, celebrate, prefer, and consume southern foods and thereby gain a sense of regional commonality on doing so. Moreover, is it one's place of residence, one's race, one's expressed/articulated regional identity, or the interplay between these factors that best explains this phenomenon?

Data and Method

The University of North Carolina's Southern Focus Polls are especially appropriate data for assessing the foodways preferences of a representative sample of southerners. The Southern Focus Polls, nineteen in total, were conducted by the Center for the Study of the American South (CSAS) and the Odum Institute for Research in Social Science (IRSS) at the University of North Carolina between 1991 and 2001. These surveys were intended to acquire a representative sample of southerners (as many national surveys fail to do) and to ask questions relevant to the region. The polls, typically administered twice yearly (spring and fall), used a telephone survey to gather a random sample of 800 to 1,200 southerners and 400 to 500 nonsoutherners. For all of the polls, the target survey population was adults aged eighteen or older, residing in houses with telephones in the United States. In general, geographic southerners were oversampled in the polls (relative to their proportions in the nation's population) to assure that the group was adequately represented in the survey, and African American respondents were occasionally oversampled. Each survey is statistically representative of residents living in the two regions of the nation (the South and the non-South), but not of the United States as a whole until the regional samples are weighted to compensate for the oversampling of southerners.

Drawing from these nineteen possible polls, I primarily use information on regional residence, race, southern identity, food salience, and the consumption of southern foods to answer this essay's guiding questions. My independent variables, the survey questions they are based on, and their response alternatives/coding are listed in the appendix to this chapter.

Turning to my measures of a preference for or consumption of southern food, I isolate a series of foods that southern cookbooks and food histories have highlighted as being among the foods considered most emblematic of the cuisine found in, associated with, or consumed around the region. In the Spring 1995 Southern Focus Poll, pollsters asked the following question: "Now I'm going to list some unusual foods. For each one tell me whether you eat it often, sometimes, seldom, or never. If you've never heard of it, tell me that too." The complete list of southern foodways items asked about includes okra, chitterlings, fried tomatoes, pork rind, sweet potato pie, catfish, boiled peanuts, and moon pie. I recoded responses as "Often (3), Sometimes (2), Seldom (1), and Never/Never heard of/Don't know (0)" and then summed the eight foods into a southern foodways scale. The scale ranges from 0 to 24, with lower values signifying low consumption, middle-range values representing moderate to considerable consumption, and higher values symbolizing very frequent consumption.

Southern Foodways Scale

	Low Consumption	Moderate Consumption	High Consumption
0	8	16	24
Never Eats	Seldom Eats	Sometimes Eats	Often Eats

If food is emblematic of culture in the way I hypothesize, the findings should result in a hierarchy of differences in food practice and preference. First, there should be a quite apparent non-South versus South difference, so that those who simply live in the South prefer and consume southern food more often than those who live outside the South. Moreover, among geographic southerners, a number of differences should emerge: those between black and white respondents in patterned ways (following the southern vs. soul food divide), between those who identify as southern versus those who do not, between those who have lived in the South all of their lives versus those who have not, and between those who reside in the Deep South versus the more peripheral southern territories or the non-South. Moreover, ordinary least squares (OLS) regression on a southern foodways scale will aid in identifying, when controlling for exogenous variables, whether either claiming a southern identity or having high food salience mediates the relationship between (1) region and food preference and (2) race and food preference.

What Southerners Think About Southern Food

BIVARIATE TRENDS

When aiming to understand what ordinary, everyday southerners really think about southern food, one logical strategy simply would be to ask them. The Spring 1992 Southern Focus Poll did just that, offering an open-ended question that states: "What do you think about southern food?" Not surprisingly, responses were overwhelmingly positive. One respondent reflected, "[I've] eaten good food, but nothing is as good as southern cooking," while another said, "It's the best in the world." While some southerners commented on its unhealthy nature, joking, "[I've] eaten it all my life and I'm not dead yet," several linked it to their childhood and family memories, claiming to be "raised on it." While the most common responses were "I love it," "I like it," "It's good," "It's wonderful," or "It's great," some respondents moved beyond taste to provide slightly deeper responses, calling it part of a "unique heritage" and claiming it was an "important cuisine to study." In all, 62 percent of southerners gave extremely positive adjectives/descriptions ("love it," "very good," "fantastic"), another 24 percent provided positive but somewhat less emotive responses ("good," "pretty good," "fine") and, most

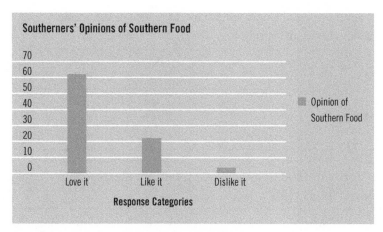

FIGURE 3. Southerners' Opinions of Southern Food.

importantly, only 4 percent expressed an outright distaste for or negative description of southern food (see fig. 3).

Having established a general sense that southern residents have a positive opinion of their regional cuisine, the next question is whether southerners not only say they like southern food but actually *consume* it more often than people who reside outside the region. Turning to tables 1 and 2, the evidence is quite transparent. People who live in the South are more likely to eat southern food often and less likely to never eat it than people who live outside the South (table 1). In fact, only 13 percent of those living in southern states report never eating southern food, as opposed to almost half of those residing in the Northeast, Midwest, or the West (table 2).

The context and timing of one's southern residence appears to be an important factor as well. As shown in table 3A, even for people who presently reside in a nonsouthern state, having *ever lived* in the South makes them more likely than those who never lived in the South to eat southern food occasionally (and less likely than strangers to the region to say they've never eaten it). In fact, as shown in table 3B, as time lived in the South increases, southern food consumption tends to increase as well, making those who have lived in the South their entire lives the least likely to never eat southern cuisine and the most likely to eat it often.

TABLE 1. Southern Food Consumption by Residence in the South versus outside the South (Spring 1995)

	Never Eat It	Seldom Eat It	Sometimes Eat It	Often Eat It	N
Lives In South	13%	36%	35%	16%	1,268
Lives Outside South	45%	35%	16%	4%	507
				Total	1,775

TABLE 2. Southern Food Consumption by Residence in Regions of United States (Spring 1995)

	Never Eat It	Seldom Eat It	Sometimes Eat It	Often Eat It	N
South	13%	36%	35%	16%	1,268
Northeast	45%	34%	17%	4%	288
Midwest	41%	39%	15%	5%	130
West Coast	49%	35%	14%	2%	89
				Total	1,775

Southern food consumption also varies by one's location within the region and during his or her formative years. As shown in table 4A, residents of the Deep South (Georgia, South Carolina, Alabama, Mississippi, Louisiana), when compared to those living in the Peripheral South (North Carolina, Virginia, Texas, Florida, Oklahoma, Tennessee, Kentucky, Arkansas) or in nonsouthern states, are more likely to consume southern food often and less likely to never eat it. Similarly, more than three times as many people who grew up/were socialized in the South (table 4B), when compared to those raised outside the South, eat southern food often. This trend is paralleled at the other extreme, as the number of those living in the South at age sixteen who never eat southern foods is one-fourth the size of those who live outside the South and never eat it.

When shifting the definition of a "southerner" from meaning one's current residence in the South to reflecting one's self-expressed identity as "a southerner," these differences in consumption patterns become even more striking. As shown in table 5, nearly four times as many people who identify

TABLE 3A. Southern Food Consumption by Ever Lived in South (Spring 1995): Nonsouthern Residents

	Never Eat It	Seldom Eat It	Sometimes Eat It	Often Eat It	N
Ever lived in South	33%	42%	20%	5%	95
Never lived in South	51%	34%	12%	3%	370
				Total	465

TABLE 3B. Southern Food Consumption by Time Spent/Lived in South (Spring 1995): Southern Residents.

	Never Eat It	Seldom Eat It	Sometimes Eat It	Often Eat It	N
Less than five years	23%	50%	22%	5%	60
Six to ten years	25%	40%	18%	17%	60
More than ten years	16%	38%	31%	15%	251
All my life	9%	32%	41%	18%	795
				Total	1,166

with the South "often" eat the food as those who do not claim that identity, and one-fifth the number of identifiers, compared to nonidentifiers, "never eats" southern delicacies.

Not surprisingly, southern food consumption also varies by religious affiliation, socioeconomic status, educational attainment, and one's attitude toward the role food plays in defining today's South. As shown below, Protestants in the United States as a whole (table 6A) and living exclusively in the southern region (table 6B) are more likely to eat southern food often and less likely to never eat it than non-Protestant affiliates. This is not particularly surprising, as when reading southern cookbooks and food histories, it becomes quite clear that southern food has a dominant presence at southern church picnics and gatherings. Thus, while southern food plays a quite important role in regional religious faith generally, it tends to be linked to Protestantism more often than to other groups and religious minorities.[30]

Southern food is also unavoidably tied to issues of social class and ed-

TABLE 4A. Southern Food Consumption by Part of South Lived In
(Spring 1995): All Respondents

	Never Eat It	Seldom Eat It	Sometimes Eat It	Often Eat It	N
Lives in Deep South	12%	36%	36%	16%	442
Lives in Peripheral South	21%	37%	35%	7%	826
Lives outside South	47%	35%	14%	4%	507
				Total	1,775

TABLE 4B. Southern Food Consumption by Spending One's Formative
Years in the South (Spring 1995)

	Never Eat It	Seldom Eat It	Sometimes Eat It	Often Eat It	N
Lived in South at age 16	10%	34%	39%	17%	1,094
Outside South at age 16	41%	38%	16%	5%	633
				Total	1,727

ucational attainment. As the next table illustrates, members of the lowest income bracket are more likely to eat southern food often and less likely to never eat it when compared to members of all other income groups in the United States (table 7A) and within the South (table 7B). This association between regional foodways and poverty is in alignment with C. Vann Woodward's prominent mid-twentieth-century essay "The Search for Southern Identity," which rooted southern distinctiveness in three main "historical experiences" (white) southerners shared: guilt over the institution of slavery, immense economic hardship and impoverishment, and military defeat. Indeed, when reflecting on the severe economic hardships that the majority of the region's residents experienced, black and white southerners often interpret southern food in a metaphorical sense, as symbolizing the perseverance of "the southerner" and his/her homeland or the ability to create an artful cuisine out of mere scraps. As John T. Edge, director of the Southern Foodways Alliance, observes, southern foods are "totemic to white and black Southerners" because "both see it as reaching back to the tough times they

TABLE 5. Southern Food Consumption by Identification as a Southerner (Spring 1995)

	Never Eat It	Seldom Eat It	Sometimes Eat It	Often Eat It	N
Yes, a southerner	8%	33%	40%	19%	996
No, not a southerner	40%	38%	17%	5%	741
				Total	1,737

TABLE 6A. Southern Food Consumption by Religious Affiliation in the United States (Spring 1995)

	Never Eat It	Seldom Eat It	Sometimes Eat It	Often Eat It	N
Protestant	13%	34%	37%	16%	1,040
Non-Protestant	34%	39%	19%	8%	735
				Total	1,775

TABLE 6B. Southern Food Consumption by Religious Affiliation in the Southern Region (Spring 1995)

	Never Eat It	Seldom Eat It	Sometimes Eat It	Often Eat It	N
Protestant	8%	33%	41%	18%	846
Non-Protestant	21%	41%	25%	13%	422
				Total	1,268

TABLE 7A. Southern Food Consumption by Income Level in the United States (Spring 1995)

	Never Eat It	Seldom Eat It	Sometimes Eat It	Often Eat It	N
Less than $10,000	13%	32%	32%	23%	167
$10,000–30,000	23%	34%	30%	13%	533
$30,000–60,000	21%	37%	30%	12%	548
More than $60,000	26%	39%	27%	8%	275
				Total	1,523

TABLE 7B. Southern Food Consumption by Income Level in the Southern Region (Spring 1995)

	Never Eat It	Seldom Eat It	Sometimes Eat It	Often Eat It	N
Less than $10,000	7%	32%	34%	27%	131
$10,000–30,000	14%	34%	36%	16%	383
$30,000–60,000	10%	37%	38%	15%	382
More than $60,000	15%	40%	34%	11%	180
				Total	1,076

survived."[31] Furthermore, southerners of all races and classes are said to share an appreciation and pride for "home cooking" or "country cooking," part of the appeal of which is that it is essentially "common food" that is "simply and flavorfully prepared."[32] And while some writers maintain that southerners of all classes share equally in their penchant for southern food, it appears that lower-income groups do consume it more often.

This association between southern food consumption and socioeconomic status is replicated when using one's educational level as a proxy for social class. When examining the U.S. population (table 8A) and solely the southern population (table 8B), we see that those with lower levels of education are more likely to consume southern food often and less likely to never consume it than are those with higher attainment levels. In both cases, those with more than a college degree are the least likely to report consuming southern foods often. When taken together, these income and educational

TABLE 8A. Southern Food Consumption by Education Level in the United States (Spring 1995)

	Never Eat It	Seldom Eat It	Sometimes Eat It	Often Eat It	N
Less than High School	17%	30%	37%	16%	197
High School Graduate	21%	34%	30%	15%	569
Some College	23%	33%	31%	13%	429
More than College	23%	41%	27%	9%	575
				Total	1,770

TABLE 8B. Southern Food Consumption by Education Level in the Southern Region (Spring 1995)

	Never Eat It	Seldom Eat It	Sometimes Eat It	Often Eat It	N
Less than High School	11%	31%	39%	19%	160
High School Graduate	10%	34%	37%	19%	404
Some College	15%	33%	36%	16%	311
More than College	13%	42%	33%	12%	389
				Total	1,264

differences in food consumption disclose that while southerners as a whole are more likely to consume southern food than nonsoutherners, southerners in lower income and educational brackets are likely to do it more often than their more privileged southern counterparts, revealing a persistent association between the affordability/humbleness of southern food items and economic or social disadvantage in the region.

Not only does knowing one's residential location and history, religious affiliation, and income/education level aid us in predicting his or her southern food consumption, but knowing a person's attitudes about foodways does as well. When asked how important "eating black-eyed peas on New Year's Day" is in defining today's South, those who rank the food as very important (or people having "high food salience") are more likely to eat southern foods often and far less likely to never eat them. The results remain consistent when examining the full sample (table 9A) as well as the southern sample

TABLE 9A. Southern Food Consumption by Food Salience in the
United States (Spring 1995)

	Never Eat It	Seldom Eat It	Sometimes Eat It	Often Eat It	N
Food very important	9%	34%	35%	22%	548
Food not as important	30%	38%	24%	8%	1,055
				Total	1,603

TABLE 9B. Southern Food Consumption by Food Salience in the
Southern Region (Spring 1995)

	Never Eat It	Seldom Eat It	Sometimes Eat It	Often Eat It	N
Food very important	6%	31%	37%	26%	450
Food not as important	17%	40%	32%	11%	646

alone (table 9B), showing that thinking southern food is important is associated with consuming more of the food both in and outside the region.
This observation speaks to the suggestion that those who think southern
food is important but no longer reside in the South might turn to this cultural medium when wishing to celebrate their southern identity today.

The next question is whether it is indeed possible, as southern food writers and scholars have claimed, that southern food is the one thing southerners of all races have shared in the past and can find commonality in today.
When examining the evidence presented in tables 10A and 10B, several
conclusions about racial differences in southern food consumption or preference emerge. First, when examining blacks and whites who reside in the
South (table 10A), we see that African American southerners (compared to
white southerners) are less likely to never eat southern food and more likely
to eat it often. However, it is too simple to examine the effects of regional
residence and race alone without considering how one's identification as a
southerner comes into play. Thus, in table 10B, race and region are examined simultaneously, comparing blacks and whites who live in the South to
nonsoutherners. Here we notice that black southerners (when compared to

TABLE 10A. Southern Food Consumption by Race in the Southern Region
(Spring 1995)

	Never Eat It	Seldom Eat It	Sometimes Eat It	Often Eat It	N
Black	3%	34%	40%	23%	248
White	15%	36%	35%	14%	948
				Total	1,196

TABLE 10B. Southern Food Consumption by Race and Region
(Spring 1995)

	Never Eat It	Seldom Eat It	Sometimes Eat It	Often Eat It	N
Nonsoutherner	45%	35%	16%	4%	507
Black southerner	3%	34%	40%	23%	635
White southerner	15%	36%	34%	15%	1,020
				Total	1,775

white southerners and nonsoutherners) are still more likely to eat southern food often and least likely to never eat it, but the rates of consumption between white and black southerners are clearly more *alike than different* when compared to the *dissimilar* food habits of nonsoutherners.

To examine this notion with greater precision, the southern foodways scale can be broken down to assess each food item contained within it. As shown in the six bar graphs (figs. 4–9), a general trend becomes quite apparent. In essence, black and white southerners show quite comparable (and at times nearly identical) consumption patterns, while diverging quite markedly from nonsoutherners. Evidence of this finding appears for the following southern food items: okra, catfish, moon pie, boiled peanuts, pork rind, and fried tomatoes.

Still, this pattern does not hold when examining two of the eight food items that are incorporated in the foodways scale. In Figures 10 and 11, we notice quite different consumption patterns among white southerners, black southerners, and nonsoutherners for both sweet potato pie and chitterlings.

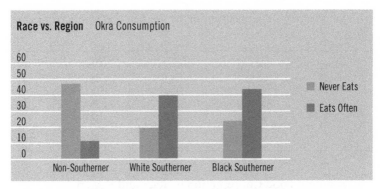

FIGURE 4. Race vs. Region—Okra Consumption.

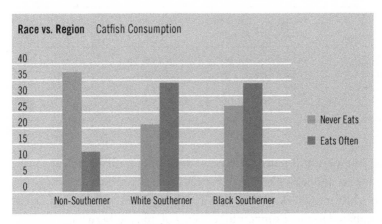

FIGURE 5. Race vs. Region—Catfish Consumption.

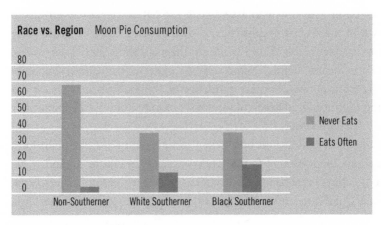

FIGURE 6. Race vs. Region—Moon Pie Consumption.

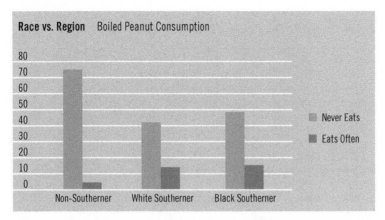

FIGURE 7. Race vs. Region—Boiled Peanut Consumption.

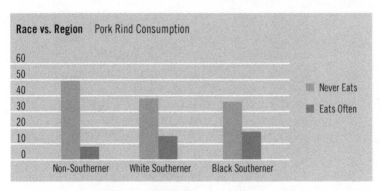

FIGURE 8. Race vs. Region—Pork Rind Consumption.

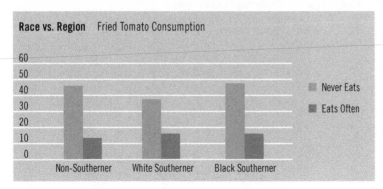

FIGURE 9. Race vs. Region—Fried Tomato Consumption.

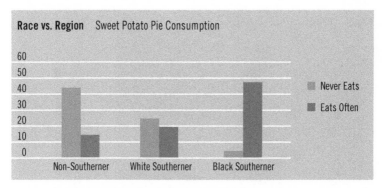

FIGURE 10. Race vs. Region—Sweet Potato Pie Consumption.

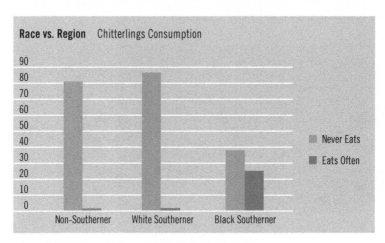

FIGURE 11. Race vs. Region—Chitterlings Consumption.

Viewing these graphs suggests that a common southern identity cannot explain the consumption of *all* foods that would be considered "southern." In other words, some other social phenomenon or factor is likely operating that might better explain the higher consumption of these particular southern foods among African Americans.

MULTIVARIATE REGRESSION ANALYSIS

Having established these bivariate trends, I ran a series of additive OLS regression models, positing the dependence of the southern foodways scale on race, region, regional identity, food salience, and a number of control variables. The results, summarized in table 11, led me to three general con-

TABLE 11. Metric and Standardized OLS Regression Coefficients for Models of Southern Food Consumption on Independent Variables (Complete Sample; Spring 1995)

	Model 1		Model 2		Model 3	
	Metric	Standardized	Metric	Standardized	Metric	Standardized
Lives in Deep South	2.163**	.193**	1.609**	.143**	1.873**	.156**
	(0.595)		(0.604)		(0.611)	
Lives in Peripheral South	0.435	.044	−0.014	−.001	0.101	.010
	(0.557)		(0.564)		(0.559)	
Black	1.608**	.123**	1.735**	.133**	1.504**	.118**
	(0.327)		(0.329)		(0.333)	
Hispanic	0.284	.008	0.131	.003	0.363	.009
	(0.794)		(0.815)		(0.871)	
Female	−0.387	−.039	−0.396	−.040	−0.456	−.046
	(0.235)		(0.235)		(0.242)	
Age	0.194**	.653**	0.163**	.545**	0.159**	.520**
	(0.041)		(0.042)		(0.043)	
Age Sq.	−0.002**	−.580**	−0.001**	−.488**	−0.001**	−.479**
	(0.000)		(0.000)		(0.000)	
Income						
$10,000–30,000	−1.151**	−.112**	−1.119**	−.109**	−0.648	−.063
	(0.401)		(0.403)		(0.425)	
$30,000–60,000	−0.876*	−.086*	−0.862*	−.085*	−0.560	−.055
	(0.424)		(0.425)		(0.444)	
More than $60,000	−1.399**	−.111**	−1.276**	−.102**	−1.039*	−.083*
	(0.486)		(0.487)		(0.507)	

(*continued*)

TABLE 11. *Continued*

	Model 1		Model 2		Model 3	
	Metric	Standardized	Metric	Standardized	Metric	Standardized
Education						
High School Graduate	−0.564	−.054	−0.535	−.051	−0.584	−.056
	(0.426)		(0.427)		(0.448)	
Some College	−0.429	−.038	−0.533	−.047	−0.512	−.045
	(0.444)		(0.446)		(0.467)	
More than College	−1.010*	−.097*	−0.958*	−.092*	−0.786	−.075
	(0.456)		(0.457)		(0.477)	
Protestant	1.231**	.122**	1.202**	.119**	1.014**	.100**
	(0.253)		(0.254)		(0.263)	
Lived in South at Age 16	1.533**	.151**	0.646	.064	0.672	.067
	(0.363)		(0.402)		(0.409)	
Rural Residence	0.548	.044	0.500	.041	0.566	.045
	(0.295)		(0.295)		(0.310)	
Church Attendance						
High Attendance	0.504	.036	0.506	.036	0.641	.044
	(0.421)		(0.420)		(0.441)	
Moderate Attendance	0.584	.053	0.545	.049	0.515	.046
	(0.360)		(0.360)		(0.372)	
Low Attendance	0.568	.057	0.562	.057	0.459	.046
	(0.326)		(0.325)		(0.335)	
Ever Lived in South	1.117*	.106*	1.093*	.103*	0.822	.078
	(0.546)		(0.544)		(0.536)	
Lived in South All Life	1.818**	.185**	1.451*	.148*	1.446*	.145*
	(0.638)		(0.648)		(0.644)	
Claims Southern Identity			1.886**	.190**	1.499**	.151**
			(0.394)		(0.404)	
Food Salience					1.810**	.175**
					(0.258)	
Constant	1.502	—	2.254	—	1.963	—
	(1.033)		(1.041)*		(1.088)	
Observations	1352	1352	1325	1325	1189	1189
F-test	$F_{(21, 1330)} = 26.77^{**}$		$F_{(22, 1302)} = 26.73^{**}$		$F_{(23, 1165)} = 27.51^{**}$	

Standard errors in parentheses; * significant at $p < .05$; ** significant at $p < .01$

clusions. First, both claiming a southern identity and seeing food as "salient" significantly stimulate southern food consumption. Second, the findings give little support to my hypothesis that the impact of region is mediated by southern identity and food salience, as residence in the Deep South continues to increase southern food consumption, but residence in the Peripheral South had no significant effect. Third, southern identity and food salience do not mediate the effect of race at all: models 2 and 3 simply cannot account for why blacks have a greater consumption of southern foods. Thus, something not easily measured about southern and/or black culture continues to apply. These persistent effects of both race and region on southern food consumption say something, independent of this investigation, about both living in the Deep South and being black, and about what it means to be a southerner. In other words, if consuming southern foods often is one alternative way of celebrating or expressing one's southernness, as cookbook authorities and scholars claim, southerners from the Deep South and African Americans may be the most "southern" of them all. Moreover, the fact that race, region, age, Protestantism, and living in the South one's whole life *persistently* affect foods eaten, despite controlling for identity and southern food salience, hints at the presence of unknown factors that might better explain southern food consumption and are not accounted for here.

It is possible that these findings reflect anthropologist Maria Franklin's notion that southern foodways were "one of the earliest vehicles for the expression of culture and identity" in this country, particularly for enslaved blacks living in the American South.[33] According to Franklin, in the antebellum South, black women found a sense of empowerment and control (even amid atrocious conditions) when working in plantation kitchens, often teaching white mistresses cooking techniques and sharing recipes utilizing African ingredients such as okra.[34] In this vein of thought, many southern food traditions emerged during enslavement, persisted over time, and ultimately came to signify a sense of "blackness" or cultural identity and heritage for African Americans, becoming a "core diet" even for southern blacks who migrated north.[35] As John Egerton notes, many plantation mistresses and white southern housewives likely followed the instruction of black women in southern kitchens, and thus it has been claimed that such lessons culminated in the recipes that serve as a foundation for southern cooking today.

Conclusions

In all, the Southern Focus Polls reveal a great deal about what southerners think about southern food, how often they eat it, and what kinds of southerners are consuming it. The variations in food consumption across income/educational groups, religious affiliations, localities, and residential histories accurately reflect the rich literature on southern foodways, emphasizing its association with a humble, simple life, Protestantism and church picnics, living in the Deep South, and being raised in or living one's entire life in the region. As cookbook author Damon Lee Fowler states in Edge's *A Gracious Plenty*, "Each time a Southern cook hefts a skillet to the stovetop, he or she is not alone. Trapped within the iron confines of these skillets and stewpots are the scents and secrets of a family's culinary history."[36] This connection between the southern past and present, as reflected in the data, seems omnipresent in the persistent celebration and consumption of southern food today.

However, when attempting to sort out the relationships among regional residence, race, and southern identity, the findings are not as clear cut. In other words, the suggestion that by gathering around a table, southern foods might serve as a potential site of social, racial, and regional reconciliation and cohesion that, as Egerton says, now "unlocks the rusty gates of race and class, age and sex" is still open to debate.[37] Certainly, the data point out how important these foods are to African American and white southerners today, and to a certain extent, that they do show some commonality in their food preference. Still, as many southern food historians and scholars point out, southern food might be *particularly* meaningful to African Americans because of its association with times of enslavement.

As shown in table 12A, in the United States as a whole, African Americans are more likely than whites to think southern food is very important in defining today's South. However, as shown in table 12B, when looking solely at residents of the South, black and white southerners are *equally* likely to think southern food is important in today's South, suggesting that for blacks, residence is less important in influencing whether or not southern food is important, perhaps because for African Americans in and outside the South, southern food might be important due to its connection to a cultural legacy and southern past. In comparison, for whites, it appears that current southern residence is associated with a higher likelihood of think-

TABLE 12A. Food Salience by Race in the United States (Spring 1995)

	Black	White	N
Food very important	41%	33%	516
Food not as important	59%	67%	964
		Total	1,480

Significant at the .05 level.

TABLE 12B. Food Salience by Race in the South (Spring 1995)

	Black	White	N
Food very important	42%	42%	430
Food not as important	58%	58%	594
			1,024

Not significant at the .05 level

ing the food is important. As John T. Edge aptly points out, "Jim Crow laws may have dictated where blacks could go to school and with whom they could consort, but in the kitchen the black cook was able to express a sort of subversive creativity. . . . In the kitchen, freedom of expression was tolerated, even encouraged."[38] This fact might aid us in explaining why African Americans, perhaps by honoring and celebrating this heritage, might be so much more likely to think southern food is important, regardless of their current regional residence.

Still, Edge is quick to point out that if southerners do intend to use southern foodways to establish a sense of community, cohesion, and unity in today's South, to battle over what is a southern food versus a soul food, or debate to whom this food belongs, could represent a step in the wrong direction. According to Edge, "Answers are as numerous, and as various, as recipes for fried chicken. . . . The wisest among us look not for differences but similarities."[39] Thus, perhaps it is not the divergences but parallels in consumption tendencies and food salience among African American and white southerners that should be remembered and emphasized here. In essence, if a taste for and pride in these foods—regardless of differences in their meaning and symbolism to groups—is shared, the possibility of food being a healer, unifier, and road to progress should not be overlooked.

Appendix

MEASUREMENT OF INDEPENDENT VARIABLES

Variable	Question	Responses Alternatives
Region of Residence	"Which state am I calling?"	South (S.C., Ala., Ga., Miss., La., Ark., Fla., Ky., N.C., Okla., Tenn., Tex., Va.); Non-South (all other contiguous states)
Southern Identity	Respondents (South): "Do you consider yourself a southerner, or not?" Respondents (Non-South): "Do you consider yourself or anyone in your family a southerner?"	Yes; No Yes (Self; Self/Family); No (Family; Self/Family)
Food Salience	"For each of the following, please tell me whether you think it is very important, somewhat important, not very important, or not at all important in your definition of today's South: *Black-Eyed Peas on New Year's*"	Very Important; Less Important (Somewhat, Not Very or Not Important)
Race	"What race do you consider yourself?"	Black; White*
Time Spent in the South	Respondents (South): "Not counting time spent away from school and for other temporary reasons, have you lived in the South all your life or not?" Respondents (Non-South): "Have you ever lived in a Southern state?"	Less than 5 yrs; 6 to 10 yrs; More than 10 yrs; All my life Ever Lived; Never Lived
Income	"Please stop me when a group best describes your total household income before taxes."	Less than $10,000; $10,000–29,999; $30,000–59,999; More than $60,000
Religion	"What is your religious affiliation?"	Protestant; Catholic/Other
Socialization in the South	"Which state did you live in when you were 16?"	Lived in Southern State at Age 16; Lived in Non-Southern State at Age 16
Education	"How many years of school have you completed?"	Less than HS; HS Graduate; Some College; More than College

*Note: Respondents in the sample who identified "Hispanic" or "Other" as their racial/ethnic background were eliminated from the analysis due to the small number of them present in the sample and my driving research question of whether black and white southerners, in particular, shared a penchant for southern foodways.

NOTES

1. Wm. Alex McIntosh, *Sociologies of Food and Nutrition* (New York: Plenum, 1996); Carole Counihan and Penny Van Esterik, eds., *Food and Culture: A Reader* (New York: Routledge, 1997); Linda Civitello, *Cuisine and Culture: A History of Food and People* (New York: Wiley, 2003).

2. Stephen Mennel, Anne Murcott, and Anneke H. van Otterloo, *The Sociology of Food: Eating, Diet, and Culture* (London: Sage, 1992); Anne Murcott, ed., *The Sociology of Food and Eating* (Croft, U.K.: Gower, 1983).

3. Susan Bordo, "Anorexia Nervosa: Psychopathology as Crystallization of Culture," and Emily Massara, "Que Gordita," in Counihan and Van Esterik, *Food and Culture*.

4. Jeffery Sobal and Albert J. Stunkard, "Socioeconomic Status and Obesity: A Review of the Literature," *Psychological Bulletin* 105, no. 2 (March 1989): 260–75; Leann Lipps Birch and Kirsten Krahnstoever Davidson, "Family Environmental Factors Influencing the Developing Behavioral Controls of Food Intake and Childhood Overweight," *Pediatric Clinics of North America* 48, no. 4 (August 1, 2001): 893–907.

5. Arlie Hochschild, *The Second Shift* (New York: Penguin, 1989); Shelly Coverman, "Explaining Husbands' Participation in Domestic Labor," *Sociological Quarterly* 26, no. 1 (Spring 1985): 81–97; Beth Anne Shelton and Daphne John, "The Division of Household Labor," *Annual Review of Sociology* 22, no. 1 (1996): 299–322.

6. Donna R. Gabaccia, *We Are What We Eat: Ethnic Food and the Making of Americans* (Cambridge, Mass.: Harvard University Press, 1998); Linda Keller Brown and Linda Mussel, eds., *Ethnic and Regional Foodways in the United States* (Knoxville: University of Tennessee Press, 1984); Richard D. Alba, *Ethnic Identity: The Transformation of White America* (New Haven, Conn.: Yale University Press, 1992).

7. Priscilla P. Ferguson and Sharon Zukin, "What's Cooking?" *Theory and Society* 24 (1995): 193.

8. McIntosh, *Sociologies of Food*, 1.

9. Ferguson and Zukin, "What's Cooking?" 193.

10. Counihan and Van Esterik, *Food and Culture*; Mennell et al., *Sociology of Food*; Pamela Goyan Kittler and Kathryn P. Sucher, *Food and Culture*, 3rd ed. (Belmont, CA: Wadsworth/Thompson Learning, 2001); Mary Douglas, "Deciphering a Meal," *Daedalus* 10 (1972): 61–81.

11. Gwenda Beed Davey, "Foodways," in *The Oxford Companion to Australian Folklore*, ed. Gwenda Beed Davey and Graham Seal (Melbourne: Oxford University Press, 1993); Charles Camp, "Foodways" in *American Folklore: An Encyclopedia*, ed. Jan Harold Brunvand (New York: Garland, 1996).

12. Benjamin Orlove and Ella Schmidt, "Swallowing Their Pride: Indigenous and Industrial Beer in Peru and Bolivia," *Theory and Society* 24 (1995): 271–98.

13. Carole M. Counihan, *The Anthropology of Food and Body: Gender, Meaning and Power* (New York: Routledge, 1999), 19; Orlove and Schmidt, "Swallowing Their Pride."

14. Simon R. Charsley, *Wedding Cakes and Cultural History* (London: Routledge, 1992);

Marcie Cohen Ferris, "Feeding the Jewish Soul in the Delta Diaspora," *Southern Cultures* 10, no. 3 (2004): 52–85.

15. Sharon Shavitt and Michelle R. Nelson, "The Social Identity Function in Person Perception: Communicated Meanings of Product Preferences," in *Why We Evaluate: Function of Attitudes,* ed. Gregory R. Maio and James M. Olson (Mahwah, N.J.: Erlbaum, 1999), 37–57. For additional information on social-psychological approaches to foodways, see Mark Conner and Christopher J. Armitage, *The Social Psychology of Food* (Buckingham, U.K.: Open University Press, 2002).

16. Larry J. Griffin, "Why Was the South a Problem to America?" in *The South as an American Problem* (Athens: University of Georgia Press, 1995), 10.

17. Larry J. Griffin, "Southern Distinctiveness, Yet Again; or, Why America Still Needs the South," *Southern Cultures* 6, no. 3 (Fall 2000): 47–72.

18. Larry J. Griffin, Ranae J. Evenson, and Ashley B. Thompson, "Southerners All?" *Southern Cultures* 11, no. 1 (Spring 2005): 6–25.

19. John Egerton, *Southern Food: At Home, on the Road, in History* (Chapel Hill: University of North Carolina Press, 1987), 2–3.

20. Griffin, "Why Was the South a Problem to America?" 10.

21. See Griffin et al., "Southerners All?"

22. See Egerton, *Southern Food*; Martha McCullough-Williams, *Dishes and Beverages of the Old South* (Knoxville: University of Tennessee Press, 1988 [originally published 1913]); and Joe Gray Taylor, *Eating, Drinking, and Visiting the South: An Informal History* (Baton Rouge: Louisiana State University Press, 1982).

23. Patricia Mitchell, *Good Food, Good Folks, Good Times: Just Being Southern* (self-published, 1998), 3; Bill Neal, *Bill Neal's Southern Cooking* (Chapel Hill: University of North Carolina Press, 1985), 3; for an elaborate description of how Jewish southerners merged their own culinary traditions and ethnic identity with southern foodways, see also Marcie Cohen Ferris, *Matzoh Ball Gumbo: Culinary Tales of the Jewish South* (Chapel Hill: University of North Carolina Press, 2005).

24. John Shelton Reed, *My Tears Spoiled My Aim and Other Reflections on Southern Culture* (Columbia: University of Missouri Press, 1993), 15, 29, 39, 50–52; see also George Tindall, "Beyond the Mainstream: The Ethnic Southerner," in *Southerners* (Baton Rouge: Louisiana State University Press, 1976), 1–21; Lewis M. Killian, *White Southerners* (Amherst: University of Massachusetts Press, 1985). While Reed's usage of the concept "ethnic" has been criticized for characterizing mainly white southerners and ignoring the "very different, possibly contrary" meanings of southernness for African Americans (see Larry J. Griffin, "The Promise of a Sociology of the South," *Southern Cultures* 7, no. 1 [Spring 2001]: 68), his analogy is still useful here because race is a main variable of consideration within this essay. Moreover, this criticism of Reed points to a dire need to look at ethnic variations in southernness, another key goal of this piece. Thus, following Reed's notion, southern foodways, like ethnic foodways, might be interpreted as an expression of this southern ethnic/regional identity.

25. Egerton, *Southern Food*, 2–3; Susan Kalcik, "Ethnic Foodways in America: Symbol and the Performance of Identity," in Brown and Mussel, *Ethnic and Regional Foodways*, 38–39.

26. Egerton, *Southern Food*, 4; see also John T. Edge, *A Gracious Plenty* (New York: Putnam, 1999); Mitchell, *Good Food, Good Folks, Good Times*; Taylor, *Eating, Drinking, and Visiting the South*.

27. For more information, see http://www.southernfoodways.com/sym_04.shtml.

28. Jessica B. Harris, *African-American Heritage Cookbook* (New York: Simon & Schuster, 1995), introduction.

29. Bob Jeffries, *Soul Food Cookbook* (Indianapolis: Bobbs-Merrill, 1969), 1–2; see also Doris Witt, *Black Hunger* (Minneapolis: University of Minnesota Press, 2004).

30. Marcie Cohen Ferris, "Feeding the Jewish Soul in the Delta Diaspora," *Southern Cultures* 10, no. 3 (Fall 2004): 52–85; see also Griffin et al., "Southerners All?"

31. Warren St. John, "Greens in Black and White," *New York Times*, October 6, 2004.

32. Mitchell, *Good Food, Good Folks, Good Times*, 8.

33. Maria Franklin, "The Archaeological Dimension of Soul Food: Interpreting Race, Culture, and Afro-Virginian Identity," in *Race and the Archaeology of Identity*, ed. Charles E. Orser Jr. (Salt Lake City: University of Utah Press, 2001), 91.

34. Ibid. See also Elaine N. McIntosh, *American Food Habits in Historical Perspective* (Westport, Conn.: Praeger, 1995); Janet Theophano, *Eat My Words: Reading Women's Lives through the Cookbooks They Wrote* (New York: Palgrave, 2002).

35. Franklin, "Archeological Dimension," 91; see also Brown and Mussel, *Ethnic and Regional Foodways*.

36. Quoted in Edge, *A Gracious Plenty*, 129.

37. Egerton, *Southern Food*, 4.

38. Edge, *A Gracious Plenty*, 209.

39. Ibid.

CHAPTER 6

Italian New Orleans and the Business of Food in the Immigrant City

There's More to the Muffuletta than Meets the Eye

JUSTIN A. NYSTROM

"I was just a kid back then," recalled John Gendusa. "My father had a route down in St. Bernard, so I would go with him down in St. Bernard. And we'd go down to the sugar refinery. . . . All these places had restaurants, [lots] of places up and down the river." He remembered an old lady at the refinery's lunchroom who would always give him a pork chop to eat, because she thought he was too skinny. Perched in the passenger seat with pork chop in hand, he and his father would make the rounds. "[We] took hundreds of loaves of bread, early in the morning, and all of the dockworkers, they'd come eat one, two sandwiches to get started . . . big, big, heavy . . . you know, *big guys*. They'd get two sandwiches . . . because they worked hard." Gendusa's was a memory of the late 1950s and 1960s, when a set of shipping patterns that had been in place since the age of sail still governed life in the port city of New Orleans.[1]

His father's delivery route supplied Gendusa with a front-row seat to a world that was about to disappear. The countless sandwich shops that once dotted the neighborhoods of the city's busy riverfront became victims in the 1970s and 1980s of a global transition to "intermodal transportation," when cranes and container ships rapidly replaced the miles of wharves that once lined the New Orleans riverfront—along with the thousands of hungry stevedores that worked there. "Oh, yes, there's nothing like that going on at all," lamented Gendusa, "but back in the old days, we sold a lot of bread up and down the river."[2]

Like a lot of New Orleans families whose ancestors emigrated from the Mediterranean island of Sicily, the fortunes of the Gendusa family have always been tied closely to the business of food. John Gendusa's great-grandfather left Palermo in 1903 to become a sharecropper in Patterson, Louisiana. His grandparents moved to Morgan City and briefly operated a grocery there before coming to New Orleans after World War I and establishing the bakery that today still bears the family name. In 1929 the business carved out its place in culinary history when, in the midst of a transit strike, the John Gendusa bakery partnered with Martin Brothers' Restaurant to develop what most people consider to be the city's first poor boy loaf. In the 1990s John Gendusa moved the bakery out of its declining neighborhood to Gentilly, where today his thirty-one-year-old son, Jason, is in the process of taking over the daily operations of the bakery. Now in its fourth generation, the business must navigate the shifting market for bread in post-Katrina New Orleans in order to secure a viable future.[3]

Observant writers have long identified the correlation between the immigrant legacy in New Orleans and the development of its unique food culture. In fact, one need look no further than the opening sentence of Lafcadio Hearn's iconic *La Cuisine Creole* for late nineteenth-century perceptions of the influence of ethnic mingling on not just foodways but also the fundamental identity of the Crescent City. "Creole cookery," notes Hearn, "partakes of the nature of its birthplace—New Orleans—which is cosmopolitan in its nature, blending the characteristics of the American, French, Spanish, Italian, West Indian, and Mexican." Hearn's ability to discern Italian influences as early as 1885, when the Sicilian migration had really only begun, reveals the depth of their cultural imprint. A hundred and twenty-five years later, authors such as Elsa Hahne continue to document the inexorable link between the immigrant experience and New Orleans's evolution as a food town. In *You Are Where You Eat*, a work that is equal parts photo essay, ethnohistory, and cookbook, Hahne implores her oral history subjects to pass the distinctly New Orleanian concept of the "Holy Trinity" through their own ethnic and historical lens. For Camille Joanne Cieuatat, who despite her French familial name boasts strong Sicilian roots, this trinity is "olive oil, onion, [and] garlic."[4]

There can be no mistake of the influence of Italian foodways on the greater culinary traditions of New Orleans, and one might find any number of fine restaurants today that offer what is billed as "Creole Italian" food. Yet for Sicilians in New Orleans, food was not only an expression of their home-land and its cultural heritage; it also served as the vehicle by which many of the immigrant generation achieved what they perceived as the American dream. Whether it had been a corner grocery, a truck farm, a barroom, or a major operation such as Standard Fruit, Italians, and specifically Sicilians, had been extensively involved in the producing, preparing, and marketing of food.

The business of food has also shaped the culture and economy of New Orleans for perhaps no other reason than for the last century and a half, the port city has straddled one of the world's great cultural and commercial crossroads. On one hand, it imports commodities as diverse as Jamaican and African coffee, bananas from Central America, and olives and citrus from the Mediterranean. At the same time, it serves as the marketplace for the rich bounty of the Gulf of Mexico and the agricultural production of the Mississippi Valley. The nature of the port's day-to-day operation, as well as the types of commodities that flow through it, may have undergone a dra-matic change in the last four decades, but food-related commerce remains an important ingredient in the city's financial lifeblood.[5]

It is in this food business—in operations both large and small—where Italian immigrants and their descendants, such as the Gendusas, have been most influential in the region. Yet the centrality of foodways remains a discussion not often emphasized in the wider historiography of Italians in the Gulf South. Most academics have observed the Italian immigrant experience in the context of racial violence and try to answer the ques-tion of whether or not they were "white" in the eyes of turn-of-the-century southerners. Related to this issue, but directed more to a popular audience, are those publications that revolve around the Hennessy murder of 1890, the subsequent lynching of Sicilians in New Orleans, and to what de-gree the genesis of the American mafia can be attributed to the Crescent City.[6]

Only a handful of scholarly works address the importance of agricul-ture and international trade, thereby grounding the Italian experience in the broader economic trends of the Gulf South. The oral histories of Ital-ian immigrants and their descendants conducted by Vincenzia Scarpaci in

Louisiana's sugar parishes during the mid-1960s offer a rare and valuable insight into the motivations of laborers who plied the Atlantic to take part in the annual *zuccarata*, or cane harvest season. If more tangentially, Thomas Karnes's work on the Standard Fruit Company chronicles the key role that the comparatively small population of Italians in mid-nineteenth-century New Orleans played in developing one of the Gulf South's most powerful corporations before the rise of big oil. As these works show, whether through the importation of produce or the harvesting of cane, the global trade in food-based commodities was a primary reason why so many Italians migrated to the Gulf South in the first place. Moreover, whether due to active turn-of-the-century recruiting campaigns of the Louisiana Sugar Growers Association, or the trade routes in Mediterranean citrus that linked the ports of New Orleans and Palermo, more than 90 percent of the Italian-speaking immigrants that disembarked at the Governor Nicholls Wharf hailed from Sicily.[7]

While much of the literature exploring the relationship between food and Italian immigration in New Orleans falls into the category of coffee table–style books or focuses narrowly on cultural celebration and culinary traditions, food writing as a field in general has begun to mature. As a consequence, we are beginning to see an increasing amount of work that considers the value of foodways as a serious interpretive framework for studying social and cultural history. No longer do savvy food writers rhapsodize *only* about sauces, presentation, and aromas, but they have also begun to consider the historical origins and social impact of their culinary subjects. In this manner, Sara Roahen's insightful work on the cultural influence of Italian foodways on New Orleans straddles the line between popular and academic audiences. And Joel Denkler's *The World on a Plate* has encouraged historians of immigration and ethnicity to consider the medium of food. Although all of these works are still firmly grounded in the food itself, they reflect a deeper appreciation of the intellectual possibilities of foodways scholarship.[8]

The study of Sicilian immigrants and their descendants in New Orleans's food industry presents a particular methodological challenge for the cultural historian. This is especially true for the immigrant generation itself—a people who came to America at a time when they belonged to a marginal segment of society and, as a consequence, attracted little attention from textual contemporary accounts, unless for suspected criminal or subversive behavior. As a class, most Sicilian immigrants who came to New Orleans were poor, which, along with marginal literacy rates, means that few traditional archival sources are available. As a historian of nineteenth-century America, I am accustomed to piecing together fragmentary evidence from the public record and periodicals in order to sketch out a rough portrait of people who left few firsthand accounts of their own time on earth. Yet while we can learn much from sifting through immigration and census records, court documents, and newspaper reports, they seldom offer the deep insight into personal motivation that all historians seek.[9]

Luckily, I benefited from an oral history program conducted between 1977 and 1988 by Joseph Maselli, a man whose efforts resulted in the establishment of the American Italian Cultural Center in New Orleans. A wholesale liquor distributor and real estate developer by profession, Maselli was not trained in oral history, yet he possessed a keen appreciation for what was actively being lost as the immigrant generation began to die off in the 1970s. Maselli was widely respected by his peers and knowledgeable of his subject and, as a consequence, was able to encourage several dozen individuals to share their reflections on the meaning of the Italian experience in New Orleans. Without this resource, much of what we know would have been consigned to the unknowable past.[10]

My own ongoing oral history project has helped me identify how trends in the culture and business of food have paralleled broader transformations that have taken place in New Orleans since the 1930s—and in particular since World War II. Moreover, the ability to interview the descendants of Maselli's subjects has been particularly useful with regard to evaluating memory and the degree to which successive generations retain historical consciousness through oral tradition. Yet what has emerged most starkly from this comparison is the realization that the relationship between the Italian families of New Orleans and the business of food continues to evolve—that it is part of a greater continuum that began when the immigrant generation reached the Mississippi River levee.

The Immigrant Generation and the Business of Food

Perhaps the near impossibility of buying land on the island of Sicily led immigrants from that place to embrace so fully the idea of enterprise in America. Outside of New Orleans, Sicilian immigrants—who lived incredibly bare existences while laboring on sugar plantations—managed to accumulate savings and buy property. Within fifteen years of their first arriving, most Sicilian immigrants had moved away from tenant housing and low-paying jobs in the cane fields to independent operations. Entrepreneurial activity, whether in New Orleans or elsewhere, offered one of the few avenues for true economic advancement for these immigrants, whose broken English meant that they would only be able to secure low-paying, menial work in the wage marketplace. As it is today with other immigrant groups, the food business offered non-English-speaking Italians a viable opportunity to run a profitable establishment—one that can be conducted in the international languages of cuisine and prices. Once the first wave of immigrants had secured a foothold in Louisiana, they could sponsor the migration of relatives still in Sicily where, if anything, economic conditions only continued to deteriorate.[11]

Discussing how it seemed like every Italian that came to New Orleans somehow managed to open a grocery or barroom of some kind, Niccolino "Peter" Compagno recounted how his grandfather always joked that immigrants would walk straight from the riverfront to Magazine Street and open an establishment selling food in the first vacant place they came across. "They used to get a kick out of it," noted Compagno of this story, because they all knew that it was not true. His grandfather, Antonio Compagno, came to New Orleans in 1861 from Ustica, a tiny island only sixty kilometers north of the Sicilian port of Palermo. After working on the riverfront for some years, he saved up enough money to open a grocery and barroom on the corner of Magazine and Felicity Streets in the city's Irish Channel neighborhood. Like many thriving Italian businessmen, he sent for and sponsored family members to join him. His eldest grandson, Peter, came in 1883, followed shortly thereafter by Peter's brothers, Frank, Anthony, and Charles. When grandfather Antonio died in 1902, the business went to his son, who had been born in New Orleans. Eventually Peter and his brothers bought out their uncle and helped each other establish their own bars and restaurants in different parts of Uptown.[12]

While the combination restaurant, grocery, and bar that Compagno's father ran at Felicity and Magazine was operated by an Italian family, its fare could hardly be called distinctly Italian. They were known mainly for their oysters. Compagno described working the delivery counter there in the 1920s and 1930s—an era so enlightened that somebody living within eight blocks of the bar could phone in an order for oysters on the half shell and cold beer. "They would have the tray that you would have four, five dozen oysters on it, and they'd open them up, and I'd take it on my hand, and I'd deliver it to those people." A dozen oysters on the half shell cost a quarter back then, where the fried variety ran thirty-five cents. The wholesale cost of a hundred-pound sack of oysters was ninety cents, and Compagno could remember Martina and Martina Oysters, another Italian company, delivering a hundred sacks a week, piling them onto the sidewalk on Magazine Street.[13]

Many Italian-speaking immigrants found work even nearer the spot where they disembarked. In 1907 a twenty-one-year-old Bartolomeo Perrone took the *Il Piemonte* from Palermo to the port of New Orleans. When he arrived, he had ten dollars in his pocket and the name of a sponsor living on Decatur Street in the French Quarter. By the time he registered for the draft during World War I, he was living on Bourbon Street and working as a canner at the Southern Canning Company. At some point he became a food salesman, and in 1924 he entered into a partnership with another Italian to open Progress Grocery on Decatur Street. "He had a lot of spunk," remembered his grandson, John Perrone Jr. "A fella came into the store and was going to rob the store and he pulled out a knife . . . which was kinda like the Italian style at the time. . . . My grandfather picked up a stock fish, they called it 'stockafish,' and it was a cod that was from Norway, it was air dried and they were usually about three feet long, and it looked like a piece of driftwood. It was hard as a rock." Bartolomeo Perrone, wielding the baccalà menacingly by its tail, began to threaten the would-be robber: "The first thing I'm gonna do is knock that knife outta your hand," he says. "The next thing I'm gonna do is beat you on the head with this." It did not take long for the robber to flee in the face of a probable beating with a piece of salt cod. While stories of the immigrant generation in oral histories often tend toward hagiography, it is undeniable that it took significant grit to succeed.[14]

The French Quarter between the turn of the century and World War II could be a tough place and by that time had become overwhelmingly an Italian neighborhood. Unlike Compagno's bar and restaurant in the Irish Channel, businesses such as Progress Grocery served a much more familiar clientele made up of the many Sicilian immigrants who either worked at the nearby French Market or who operated businesses in the Quarter. Like Central Grocery, another Sicilian-run store that opened in 1906 and remains in business today, the fare one might expect to find was international, with a distinctly Italian character. "I'd go in the back," remembered John Gendusa as he stretched his arms wide apart, "and he had this big ol' barrel, and that's where he'd mix his olive salad." Like many of the customers who frequented these traditional Italian groceries, Joe Pacaccio most remembers the aroma—so much so that when he opened Carmine's, his restaurant in Metairie, he bought and hung nearly two hundred pounds of baccalà from the rafters just so the place would acquire the same sensory quality. "Codfish, garlic, salami, cheeses, all the cheeses that you could want to eat," were the aromas Pacaccio recalled. "We would take [a twelve-pound piece of Romano cheese] out in the morning," added Perrone, "and we would put it into a glass case that was not refrigerated on purpose. . . . You wanted it to warm up so you could cut it without it crumbling. It had so much oil and butterfat in it that we literally had a block of wood that we would use to elevate it on inside its tray so that the butterfat could drip down below the cheese and not . . . not have it swimming in oil when you picked it up to make a cut from it. Well, the aroma from that cheese was incredible."[15]

The corner or neighborhood grocery was also a function of living patterns in an urban setting such as the French Quarter or many of the other densely populated neighborhoods of New Orleans. Sitting in the dining room of the Napoleon House, a popular French Quarter restaurant and bar that he runs with his sister Maria, Sal Impastato pointed to an old photograph on the wall in order to underscore this point. "I don't know if you saw the picture on our wall. . . . It's my uncle, standing in the grocery store . . . and my dad is the one who is the small boy in the picture." It was taken from a time before he was born, but it spoke to a family memory about the tradition he continues, even if today he serves a substantially different clientele. "That's a bygone era. All the little . . . grocery stores that everybody I guess had the same thing . . . but they were all two or three blocks away from the house and it's where everybody shopped. There were no big box stores as they call them now."[16]

Pressed to identify an Italian food that was emblematic of both the culinary traditions of Sicily and the nature of the family business—not to mention the very identity of the French Quarter for much of the twentieth century—one would have to pick the muffuletta sandwich. Well known across the country today, the muffulettas served at Central Grocery attract a devoted clientele of tourists and locals alike. Despite the Central's plausible claim as its inventor, others point to another establishment as its possible progenitor. Biaggio Montalbano, who came to New Orleans in 1912 and who had by 1920 had opened a sandwich shop at 724 Saint Philip Street, certainly produced an early rendition of the muffuletta, although according to gelateria owners and French Quarter natives Rosario and Joseph Brocato, it may have been actually called the "Roma" sandwich.[17]

Even today, a discussion of Montalbano's elicits colorful stories from people who grew up in the French Quarter between the 1920s and 1960s, its memory still resonating with the last generation who remembered a French Quarter that was overwhelmingly Italian and Roman Catholic. Lyle Saxon's homage to New Orleans culture, *Gumbo Ya-Ya*, described a glimpse through the door of Montalbano's Grocery circa 1940, as remembered by Joe Pacaccio:

> You find yourself in a narrow room, furnished with a long counter, shelves and a glass showcase, and . . . among jars of antipasto and anchovies, cheeses and sausages imported from Italy, are numerous statues of saints, crucifixes and holy pictures. Statues, too, occupy half of the counter, and at the far end is an altar in which burn crimson vigil lights and on which repose statues of the Holy Family. . . . He had all the saints . . . on the walls, pictures and statues of all the saints and he had a thousand candles burning at one time. . . . While you were waiting for your muffuletta sandwich he'd push the candles to you so you had to come up with a buck and burn one, you know, for your family.[18]

Maria Impastato observed, "It was a shrine, actually. All the saints' pictures and statues and candles were lit all the time." Not only did Montalbano hand cut all of his meat with a long and undoubtedly razor-sharp knife, he sold his muffulettas by the pound. "I've seen him sell muffulettas for over seventy-five dollars a sandwich. . . . Of course they were huge," explained Pacaccio as he held his hands sixteen inches apart. "Let me put it to you this way—it'll put any corned beef sandwich from New York to shame as far as height and volume. That's how big he used to make his muffulettas."[19]

John Gendusa pointed out during a tour of his bakery that the name "muffuletta" actually refers to the type of bread on which one makes the sandwich. On it goes all of the sorts of toppings we generally associate with Sicilian antipasti, including a variety of cold cuts and cheeses. Yet what sets the muffuletta apart, other than its distinctive bread, is the application of a thick layer of New Orleans–style olive salad—a mixture of black and green olives, giardiniera, capers, spices, and olive oil. Both Central and Progress Groceries sold the muffuletta, at least at first, to the army of Italian workers who made a living either on the docks opposite Decatur Street or vending produce and seafood at the French Market. It is likely, however, that Montalbano's was probably the first to reach a significant audience outside of New Orleans—not for any particular marketing reason but because the crew that filmed Elvis Presley in *King Creole* across the street at McDonough School 15 could be found lining up outside of his door in the first three months of 1958.[20]

Individuals who are old enough to remember the French Quarter in the years right after World War II witnessed a culture in its twilight. The immigrant generation who came to New Orleans embraced the food business and conducted their affairs in a manner that would have been far more familiar to merchants in the nineteenth century than they would be to their children twenty years later. Technologies that revolutionized the transportation of people and things were just beginning to have an impact on New Orleans, a city whose commercial and social patterns had been founded on the concept of being able to find what one needed within walking distance. For those Italian kids who called the French Quarter home in the 1940s and 1950s, eating flavored ice at Brocato's, plundering the sample tray at Solari's, or enjoying a muffuletta from Montalbano's while sitting on the stoop in front of their home, it would truly be a paradise lost. Indeed, whether they knew it or not, the forces that had built their world had already changed direction.

World War II and Generational Change in Italian New Orleans

Many of the immigrant generation who started food businesses in the first two decades of the twentieth century slowly ceded the enterprises to their children during the years leading up to and after World War II. It was a time of change not only for these families but also for New Orleans and the nation as a whole. The nature of the French Quarter began to change during the 1950s. So too did the food business, as corner groceries yielded to a new concept in efficiency: the supermarket. As in the rest of America, the automobile drew residents of the inner city farther into the suburbs, and with this change disappeared the need for the urban street peddler—a job that had supplied countless Sicilian immigrants with their first entrepreneurial experience. Also numbered were the days of the French Market and other similar facilities in the city, such as the St. Roch market in the Eighth Ward. Yet the Sicilian families who established a toehold in the city's thriving food culture found ways to adapt in the years following World War II, enabling them to continue their traditions while strengthening their influence in the industry.

Probably the biggest change to take place in the day-to-day foodways of New Orleans after World War II was the way in which everyday people "made groceries." Even in the 1930s, an astute observer could see the transition materializing as chains like H. G. Hill and A & P began opening larger stores in the city. The Poydras Market, which had served the Faubourg St. Mary since the middle of the nineteenth century much as the French Market had served the Quarter, had been demolished in the 1930s. Meanwhile, a German immigrant grocer's son by the name of John Schwegmann set into motion a plan to modernize the store that would make his name synonymous with self-service groceries in New Orleans. Among the earliest Sicilians to do the same thing would be the Zuppardo brothers.[21]

Anthony and Joseph Zuppardo's father, Peter, actually came to America twice. The first time was as a young teen in 1903, when he worked on the railroad alongside his father and uncle, a job that exposed him to the cold Wyoming winter. When he returned in 1913 after a stint in the Italian army, family ties and a deepened appreciation for tropical weather kept him in New Orleans. As his son later explained, Peter Zuppardo went into business for himself during World War I. Looking for work on the docks that fronted the French Quarter, Zuppardo met Luca Vaccaro, one of the brothers who ran the powerful Standard Fruit and Steamship Company. "Lukie Vaccaro gave him a couple of cars of bananas and made him sell them to the peddlers to keep the peddlers off the wharf," noted his son. "And he started selling to peddlers with these two cars of bananas.... My dad was afraid to take them because he didn't have any money to pay for them. Lukie said, 'you go ahead and sell them, when you get done,' he said, 'you bring me the money.'" By the start of World War II, Peter Zuppardo had become the largest wholesaler of bananas in the country.[22]

Although Peter Zuppardo supported his sons' ambitions, their route to success was not directly through their father's business—though it would involve the business of food. The brothers started at the bottom, peddling fruits and vegetables in the French Quarter and surrounding neighborhoods. "We used to peddle together, and I'd get out of school, he'd take me," remembered Joseph of Anthony, who was eleven years his senior. "I was always with my brother." Like many Italian entrepreneurs, their father invested a substantial portion of his savings in real property. Peter Zuppardo made a gift of two adjacent lots to his sons on old U.S. 90, or Gentilly Boulevard, where it intersected Elysian Fields Avenue. In 1932, at the age of eighteen, Anthony Zuppardo began constructing a permanent open-air fruit stand to serve customers heading in and out of town on U.S. 90, the main east-west artery at the time. "We used to hop cars, open oysters . . . sell stuff right there," explained Joseph. In the 1930s Gentilly was still the country, with cow pastures and open spaces, but that began to change quickly. When H. G. Hill, an early Nashville-based grocery chain, started building a store right across the street in 1937, Tony Zuppardo realized the necessity of progress and began enclosing the fruit stand, transforming it into Economical Supermarket. He had patterned his store on what he considered the first true "supermarket" in New Orleans, George Puglia's place on St. Claude Avenue. As friends with shared cultural and business ties, Puglia encouraged the Zuppardos and offered tips that helped the new enterprise become a success.[23]

Despite their closeness, it was not entirely clear that Joseph Zuppardo would follow in his brother's footsteps when Economical Supermarket first appeared, yet the fact that half of the store rested on his property certainly gave him a stake in the operation. Between 1939 and 1943, Joseph attended a seminary on the north shore of Lake Pontchartrain with an eye toward becoming a Catholic priest. Changing his plans, he enrolled at Louisiana State University in 1943 but was almost immediately drafted into the U.S. Army. "When I got out of the service," he remembered, "I came over [to the store]. . . . It was a Good Friday when I got discharged, Easter Saturday I came over here and worked in my uniform. I didn't have any clothes that would fit me." Shortly thereafter he formed a formal partnership with his brother, got married, and never returned to his studies at LSU. For the next sixty years, the brothers operated the Economical Supermarket as the neighborhood of Gentilly built up around them, finally closing in 2005 after levee failures that followed in the wake of Katrina drowned the store and the homes of its customers in the surrounding area.[24]

John Perrone Jr.'s father also returned to the workforce after World War II when he took over the day-to-day operations of Progress Grocery. Just as it had for many American families, the war had broken down a small part of patriarchic authority that was such an intrinsic quality of Sicilian immigrant culture. Perrone told a story that was emblematic of this transformation: "My uncle beat my dad home from World War II. . . . My father was twenty-six years old coming back, my uncle was twenty-four. . . . My uncle gets my dad on the side and says, 'You're not going to believe this, John.' He says, 'What?' He says, 'Papa let me drive the car. He gave me the keys and let me drive his car.' . . . Twenty-four years old . . . had never driven his father's car. But he figured since he was twenty-four and he fought in the war, he had the privilege of being able to drive the family car." In some ways, John Perrone Jr.'s father did not change much about the way the grocery functioned except that he put in air conditioning in the 1950s and periodically added to the selection of merchandise in the store to reflect the changing shopping habits of the French Quarter.[25]

John Perrone was different in an important respect from his immigrant father—he had been to college, graduating from Loyola University in New Orleans in 1941. Bartolomeo Perrone and Progress Grocery had always been in both the wholesale and retail grocery business. Wholesale sales to restaurants had been a small part of the total picture in those days, but that would eventually change in a dramatic way. Perhaps John Perrone's accounting degree played a role in helping him identify what would be the future of the family business.[26]

Even as Zuppardo's store and its Gentilly neighborhood grew, John Perrone Jr. witnessed the opposite trend unfolding as he grew up in his family's grocery in the French Quarter. The changes were both cultural and economic, and neither aspect was very encouraging. "I could see it happening," remembered Perrone. "There were those days when all you heard spoken in the store was Italian. . . . I was twelve years old, and more [at the grocery] just to hang around than to work. . . . My grandfather would be speaking, my dad spoke fluent Italian, and a lot of the customer base that came in [did too]." Yet by the time he turned fifteen, as the 1960s wore on, things changed very quickly. As Perrone observed, "They started to get older, and started to die off, now you're looking at your second generation of Americans. . . . It didn't translate anymore. It was supermarket time. The supermarkets also started carrying a lot of the products that we did, and our business dropped off." Tourists had not discovered the muffuletta sandwich as they have today (indeed, the French Quarter as a whole had not yet become the tourist attraction that we see now), and the economic realities of running an old-fashioned grocery in the Quarter began to set in. "It was very difficult to get into the French Quarter. . . . You couldn't park. . . . Everybody got [parking] tickets. You had to have a real good reason to come down. And I just . . . I said to myself, 'I wouldn't do it.' And people didn't."[27]

Peter Impastato was already in his thirties and had three children when he got out of the army after World War II. He had been born in 1912 and had grown up in the French Quarter, in the historic house that former New Orleans mayor Nicholas Girod had once dreamed could give shelter to an exiled Napoleon Bonaparte. Impastato's uncle and father had bought the spacious building during the 1910s from money earned through peddling fruits from a cart and laboring in one of the Quarter's "macaroni" factories.

By 1930 the extended family lived in its several apartments. On the ground floor the Napoleon House Grocery was like many smaller corner groceries throughout the city, which meant that by the late 1940s it was quickly becoming obsolete. Knowing that the family business needed to adjust in order to continue, Peter Impastato expanded the bar operation of the Napoleon House, or "Nap House," as locals knew it, and it soon became a rather bohemian establishment where local artists and college students from Tulane and Loyola came to hang out, drink, and listen to Caruso playing on an old Victrola in the bar's inner room.[28]

Peter Impastato's children grew up with one foot in the past and one in the future. Though he still worked in the French Quarter and the older generation still made its home in the apartments above the bar, Impastato raised his family in what today is called "Old Gentilly," in the area behind the fairgrounds. In some ways, life in Gentilly continued in a familiar pattern, not only because many Sicilians who had once lived in places that adjoined the riverfront like the French Quarter or Faubourg Marigny migrated to the suburb of Gentilly, but because the Impastato children lived in one half of a shotgun double, only a wall away from their maternal grandparents. Yet they also bought groceries at Zuppardo's Economical Grocery, despite the fact that they all enjoyed going to the French Market to buy vegetables. "He knew a lot of the people that had the produce there," Maria Impastato remembered of trips to the French Market. "He'd after work a lot of times go get a crate of whatever was in season and go deliver it to my aunt on Dumaine, bring some over here, and then bring the rest to us at home." But at the same time, he loved going to Zuppardo's: "Daddy took a bus to go there . . . to go shopping there, oh yeah, because we all knew them, and they had great vegetables, they had great meat." It was a dilemma faced by other families. The French Market might have offered the best seasonal produce and freshest seafood, but the supermarket, unlike the Quarter, was conveniently located and had an accommodating parking lot.[29]

For the children of the Sicilian immigrant generation, the move from the French Quarter and older parts of town to Gentilly and other suburbs was pronounced. Roy Zuppardo described a pattern of real estate investment that many Sicilian-descended families shared: "My grandfather would not misspend a nickel. Anytime he had any money saved he would go and buy a house. And so he would buy a house in his area, and so he'd put his kids there, so everybody lived on the same block and it was a great way to grow up. [Gentilly] was . . . was a community of Italians and Zuppardos and family and cousins and we all lived in a two or three block area." In the case of the Zuppardos, the family followed the path of the family business, and that path led to Gentilly. In the 1950s the gravitational center of Italian New Orleans began heading away from the French Quarter, and it was a change one could measure through the food business.[30]

In 1950 food writer Clementine Paddleford visited the famous Solari's grocery store in the French Quarter and shared her experiences in the pages of *Gourmet* magazine. By then, the establishment had cultivated a reputation as one of the nation's most exquisite retailers and mail-order houses for gourmet items. If Paddleford recognized that she was in not only an Italian neighborhood but a grocery founded in 1863 by a Genoese immigrant, J. B. Solari, she left no indication. To Paddleford everything was "Creole," but for the kids living in the Quarter of the same era, it was decidedly *Italian*. "Solari's? Oh, we *lived* at Solari's. That's where all the kids in the French Quarter got their snacks," recalled Joe Pacaccio with great fondness. It was located on the corner of Iberville and Royal, where today the Brennan's Mr. B's Bistro now stands. "And they always had samples out. Samples of olives, samples of spreads, samples of crackers, so as kids, we knew we could go to Solari's and get a sample. . . . We'd eat!" Maria Impastato, who would shop at Solari's with her aunt who lived above the Napoleon House bar, remembered that "they baked their own bread. . . . You could smell all the smells, it was very fresh. All the bins full of either beans or rice or nuts . . . truly like an old-time . . . Sicilian market."[31]

In 1959 the owner of the Solari Company, Omar M. Cheer, died. Thirty-five years earlier, he had bought the enterprise from the Solari family and in the intervening years had done much to build its reputation as a nationally known gourmet store. Cheer lived in an upper floor of the building, and in a routine belonging to a bygone era, he would eat breakfast every morning at his reserved spot at Solari's fabled lunch counter. Yet his heirs saw less value in running the business and more in the worth of its real estate. A group of investors from Texas bought the building in 1961 and promptly razed the structure that had housed Solari's since 1873. Though another investor built a new building in the same location and allowed the store to operate there for another four years, it never regained its old magic. The same company later bulldozed the Regal Brewery and the Vieux Carré Inn and replaced them with a Hilton hotel, as the Canal side of the Quarter began to assume its modern appearance. "That was a loss, I think, in the French Quarter," observed Maria Impastato. "People in the French Quarter *really* miss that. When that changed, I remember daddy talking about it, because all my aunts, that lived in the Quarter, and their families . . . that was their market, and that was a big loss for them. They didn't have to go out, way out to the suburbs, you know, to get groceries. That was a big, big change."[32]

The Third Generation Comes of Age

When Sal Impastato took over daily operation of the Napoleon House from his father in 1971, it was clear that more changes were necessary if the business were to stay afloat. "We were open . . . late morning," recounted Impastato, "and a lot of people would come in, get a drink, and would also bring lunch from somewhere else. So, after some thought, I decided to open up a sandwich shop." One of his bartenders was Nick Montalbano, who was of an older generation and had been a close friend of Sal's father. Montalbano's Grocery had since closed and Nick's brother, Martin, who had unsuccessfully tried to operate the business after his father's passing, was in need of work. (As Joe Pacaccio observed, their father had always run the place by himself, and in a very un-Sicilian fashion he did not bring his sons up to learn the business.) Martin Montalbano already had a good recipe for olive salad and knew how to prepare the sandwiches, so it was a natural for Impastato to begin serving the iconic muffuletta at the Napoleon House. The change coincided with what Impastato characterized as a steady increase in the amount of tourism in the French Quarter. When Sal and Maria's aunt passed, they converted the upstairs of the historic building, a place that for almost the entirety of the twentieth century had been a private family residence, into a banquet hall that customers could rent for special events.[33]

Impastato was undoubtedly right about the gains in foot traffic, but the tourist scene in the Quarter, along with the food business in the rest of the city, was about to round an even more momentous corner. "I joined my dad in about 1976 and just right after that I remember my good friend, an attorney, Larry Layman, says, 'John, you gotta check out this little restaurant right down the street,'" recalled John Perrone about his first trip to K-Paul's Louisiana Kitchen. "At that time, Paul Prudhomme used to come in and he would buy his ingredients for his fettuccini and Reggiano parmesan, things like this, for his restaurant. Nobody knew who he was at the time, and all of a sudden he hit with his blackened redfish." Writers such as Brett Anderson and Tom Fitzmorris have identified the opening of Prudhomme's quirky French Quarter restaurant as the moment when literally everything changed about the food scene in New Orleans, and its advent was equally important for those families, such as the Perrones and the Impastatos, who continued to sell food in the French Quarter.[34]

John Perrone shared a story about Prudhomme that reflects both the excitement of those days and the newly found audience for all things New Orleans once people around the nation discovered Louisiana's unique cuisine:

> One year in the early eighties, I mean at the very epicenter of his popularity, during JazzFest, which was our absolute best time of the year ... he ordered up about fifty muffulettas for his staff on a Saturday to feed them lunch.... So we got it ready and they were going to send somebody to pick it up. Well, Paul had a three-wheeler ... and he had about a twelve foot long antenna with a whip antenna with a flag on it to let people know he was coming so he wouldn't get run over on the street.... And he came to pick up the sandwiches, on his three-wheeler, which he did not get off of.... Our store was only around twenty feet wide with an aisle down the center, so that tells you how much room we had. And at the time we had about thirty people in the store, which was just about as many as you could put in. He had somebody open that front door for him, he popped that three-wheeler into the store, came up on to the counter, [and] he says, "I'm going to pick up the sandwiches for my staff." ... And while all of this was going on people were crowding around getting his autograph, and I had to get one too, for the signing of the bill for the sandwiches. And then he turned that thing around and went out the store. And one guy is saying, he says, "Look, I got Paul Prudhomme's autograph." I said, "Yeah, so do I, but mine's worth a little bit more than yours."

On the face of things, most businesses would be ecstatic to have such foot traffic coming through their doors, but there was an unseen side to Perrone's business that was undergoing a transformation even more dramatic than this spike in the sale of muffuletta sandwiches. "I saw my restaurant base go from . . . like, let's say, ten percent to a hundred percent in a few years' time," explained Perrone, "so restaurants were opening left and right in the late seventies through the eighties which was . . . we were all of a sudden had a base of restaurants in the French Quarter that we didn't have before. So my business in the wholesale end started to snowball at that time. And my dad said the same thing." The store, which had originated as a neighborhood grocery but had fallen onto hard times when the old Italians left the Quarter in the 1960s, had by the 1980s become primarily a tourist attraction. Perrone eventually closed Progress Grocery in 2001, selling the building at 915 Decatur Street to a group of investors who failed in their attempt to replicate the business that the Perrone family had operated for the last seventy-seven years. As the sons of Biaggio Montalbano discovered decades before, the new owners of Progress Grocery found that there was more to serving a legendary muffuletta than meets the eye.[35]

Today, John Perrone operates a wholesale food company with his sons in Jefferson Parish, selling imported goods to restaurants throughout Louisiana and Mississippi. Even in this modern business, the family has been unable to escape change. The port's conversion to "containerization" in the 1980s, the same global economic force that had taken away so many of John Gendusa's bread customers, had even more direct ramifications for an importer such as Perrone. It meant that his imported goods had to be ordered in far greater quantity. "My dad used to bring in sixty cases of twenty-four ounce anchovies—just sixty cases, that's unheard of today. You wouldn't even think about bringing in something that . . . that small amount." In some respects, the changes at the port forced his business to grow in order to handle the volumes necessary to be profitable. Nowadays, everything comes in twenty- and forty-foot containers, which to Perrone's way of thinking was an "incredible improvement." The days of longshoremen hauling pallets of goods onto busy wharves along the riverfront of New Orleans might paint a romantic image in the imagination, but as Perrone points out, it was not only inefficient; it led to a lot of damaged goods that had to be discarded. On the hot August day that I visited the warehouse of Perrone and Sons to conduct my interview, employees were busy grinding down a giant fifty-pound wheel of imported Romano cheese for resale to restaurant customers. When John Perrone let me peer into the specially built room that housed the grinding equipment, I caught the aroma and thought about Progress Grocery and a block of cheese under a glass dome oozing oil on a warm summer afternoon.[36]

In the same year that a Dallas-based investment group decided to demolish the old Solari's building in the French Quarter, the Zuppardo family broke ground on its second supermarket. Its location was indicative of both the next generation taking over the business and the broader demographic trends in the New Orleans metropolitan area. As their Gentilly location had once appeared thirty years before, the new Economical Grocery located on Veteran's Highway near Transcontinental Boulevard might have seemed to the untrained eye to be located in an unnecessarily rural area. "One of my earliest recollections," said Roy Zuppardo, the son of Joseph Zuppardo, "was that I was a young teenager, and one of the cashiers was in the warehouse and I heard her screaming, and I ran upstairs, and there was a snake in the warehouse. . . . That was not unusual because that was the woods. There was nothing behind the store, there was nothing across the street from the store." This Metairie location anticipated the surge of suburban expansion that took place after 1960 as thousands of New Orleanians left Orleans Parish. To describe the exodus entirely in terms of "white flight" would be an oversimplification, but the real and perceived threats of a city in the midst of serious racial discord certainly played a role in the demographic shift. By the 1980s the family's suburban foresight had proven prescient.[37]

The grocery business had undergone significant changes since 1980, when Joseph Maselli had interviewed Roy Zuppardo's father, and they were a continuation of the modernizing trends that the family business had done so much to foster. Like other supermarkets in the 1940s, Economical Grocery introduced innovations that streamlined the supply and lowered the price of wholesale groceries to their stores. They created the first cooperative in the city, known as the Bell Stores, in order to pool their purchasing power and advertising reach, a move that lowered their costs to below what an individual family-run corner grocery could match. At that time, the grocery industry tried to enforce a "fair trade price" in order to govern the market and protect the thousands of small retailers that dotted the landscape from being undercut by larger competitors. As early as 1932, the New Orleans Retail Grocers' Association began to fight against the modernizing trend toward larger aggregations of buyers, sermonizing in the pages of its annual that "financially sound price cutters are few and far between." Some undoubtedly saw the handwriting on the wall, if only in the desperate rhetoric of the Grocers' Association in its plea to turn back the hands of time.[38]

The same move to containerization that had enabled Perrone and Sons to more efficiently import goods for its wholesale food business had also affected the Zuppardo stores in several crucial ways. "How we get our merchandise ... at this particular point in time," noted Roy Zuppardo, "it's changed dramatically. We used to spend a lot of time purchasing directly from food companies like Kraft. . . . Progresso would deliver to us no matter what . . . but some companies . . . Procter and Gamble would deliver directly to the stores. . . . So that has changed. . . . Now there are fewer and fewer warehouses from which we can buy groceries from [sic]. So we are pretty much married to one or two suppliers, whereas before we had an unlimited amount of suppliers, anyone that would sell to independents would get our business." Fortunately for the remaining Zuppardo store, they continue to sell a sufficient volume to stay competitive, even without the old Gentilly location. The family had plans to rebuild after Katrina, but a convergence of factors, including an inability to get city government approval of construction plans in a timely fashion, kept that from happening. Eventually, the Walgreens chain "made an offer [the Zuppardos] couldn't refuse" and leased the site where Anthony Zuppardo had built his all-night produce stand in 1932. There is some small irony in the construction of a Walgreens there, as it, along with cvs Pharmacy, has become ubiquitous in New Orleans today, serving many of the same functions that little Italian corner groceries did a century ago.[39]

One of the downsides to the grocery business consolidation of the last twenty years is that stores, whether a big chain such as Rouse's, which dominates the New Orleans market, or independents such as Zuppardo's or Dorignac's, cannot offer their customers the same sort of variety that they once could. "If Mrs. Jones wanted a particular item that the warehouse didn't carry because the movement wasn't there, Zuppardo's . . . and even

Dorignac's . . . I knew that we were two stores that would get whatever our customers asked us for because we valued their business. Today it's like if you don't want one of the sixteen brands that I have . . . you got . . . just go shop someplace else. That's that Walmart mentality, that's what I have—buy it or go someplace else," explained Zuppardo. But he also sees opportunity in the impersonality of the big chain stores, created by the laws of the market. To wit, there will always be a niche for better customer service.[40]

In recent decades, the Zuppardos benefited from their early embrace of prepared foods. "When we opened the store," noted Zuppardo, "my father put a kitchen at the Veteran's store. Now, it wasn't much of a kitchen, but it was a small little kitchen. And his idea was, 'you know what, I'll get my wife to come in, she'll make meatballs, stuffed artichokes . . . stuff that she knows how to do, and we can make a few bucks selling that sort of . . . cooked food.'" The move was perfectly timed to meet the needs of households where both parents worked, not to mention the invention of the microwave oven. Today, prepared or semiprepared foods make up a significant portion of the floor space and sales of higher-end groceries such as the Greensboro, North Carolina–based Fresh Market, and Whole Foods, which started in Austin, Texas, in the 1980s. As Zuppardo proudly noted, "for a small grocery store like ours . . . there's at least seventeen or eighteen different kinds of soup you can buy on a daily basis, at least twelve to fifteen different entrees served on a daily basis." That the quality of the food itself still lies at the heart of the matter at Zuppardo's Economical Grocery seems reflective of how important food culture remains to the descendants of Sicilian immigrants and New Orleanians alike.[41]

Legacies

When I interviewed John Perrone and Joseph Pacaccio, I visited with Perrone's kindergarten-aged grandson, the fifth generation of the Perrone family in the United States. He will likely someday join what is a thriving wholesale food business, keeping the family tradition alive just as Perrone's own sons have done. Roy Zuppardo was guardedly optimistic about the future of the business that his father started and is today being run mostly by his children's generation. "There will always be a niche for the Zuppardo family," he suggested, "especially in this market where you've got almost a hundred years of service and people who know you and good will built up. So I believe that, at least for the next generation we'll be around."[42]

The Gendusas are already bringing the next generation into the business. My brief visit to their bakery on Mirabeau Avenue in August 2010 gave me only a glimpse of the scope of work involved in running such a business. Jason Gendusa worked alongside his employees in the unairconditioned heat, making dough, forming loaves, and proofing for the next baking. Growing up in the bakery, he certainly knew what he was getting into, and there was no pressure from his father, John: "So he made up his own mind, and when he did, I said, 'you're sure that's what you want to do,' and I questioned it, and he's here now, and he's doing it, so, I guess that's what he wanted to do." The only real stipulation that John Gendusa placed on his son was that he had to get a college degree. Asked about his reasoning for continuing the trade, despite all of the obstacles the bakery faces, Jason Gendusa looked back on the rich history of the family business. "We are kind of a legacy in New Orleans. . . . My great-grandfather originated the first po-boy . . . my grandfather did and my father's done it. It's been . . . it's how we supported the family. . . . It's . . . hard to let go, you know? After Katrina there were those times where you would think, well, no more bakery." Today, father and son work together to seek out new markets for the bread that defines an important part of the city's history and culture.[43]

Yet other interviewees were less sanguine about the future, cognizant of the hard work and endless challenges faced by anyone working in the constantly evolving food industry. When asked about the future of the Napoleon House, Sal Impastato reflected,

> Yeah, I don't know . . . maybe before Katrina I could have answered it, but I really can't tell you. . . . This is a tough business, and . . . we have a lot of family doing everything that it takes to keep it going . . . and we're all getting to retirement age, or past. So, like myself, I was the only one to say, "I want to take it over," . . . when I did in seventy-one . . . not knowing how it was going to be or how it was going to turn out. I don't know if anybody really wants to do that, and it would be really hard to do it by yourself. You really need . . . need a lot of family helping out . . . if you are going to do this type of business.

As he and other interviewees have observed, families are smaller today than they were in the time of his grandparents. Only time will tell what lies in store for the future of the Napoleon House.[44]

The vignettes in this essay focus on a small number of the food businesses owned and operated by Sicilian immigrants and their descendants over the years, yet they reveal transformations that span what historians more recently have termed "the long twentieth century." Those descendants living today, who carry on family traditions in the food industry, do so consciously aware of their business's strong ties to the city's history. In many ways, this was true even in the 1950s as the first college-educated generation chose the continuation of the family business over seizing opportunities in the then-booming oil and gas industry. In our own time, with the omnipresent chain restaurant and "Walmart mentality," we find a new generation setting out with renewed enthusiasm to preserve what is culturally important about both their city and ethnic heritage. If the experiences of their forefathers are any indication, we might look to the fates of this new generation for clues to the fate of all that is unique about the foodways of New Orleans.

NOTES

This essay is part of a larger project on the relationship between Sicilian immigrants to New Orleans and the business of food titled "Making Groceries: Corner Markets, Food Culture, and the Creation of Italian New Orleans."

1. Interview of John Gendusa and Jason Gendusa by Justin Nystrom, August 19, 2010, video recording and transcript in possession of author.

2. There has been a significant amount of academic scholarship on the emergence of intermodal transit in the last two decades. See Edna Bonacich and Jake B. Wilson, *Getting the Goods: Ports, Labor, and the Logistics Revolution* (Ithaca, N.Y.: Cornell University Press, 2007); Marc Levinson, *The Box: How the Shipping Container Made the World Smaller and the World Economy Bigger* (Princeton, N.J.: Princeton University Press, 2008); John and Jason Gendusa interview.

3. John and Jason Gendusa interview; 1910 United States Census, Police Jury Ward 8, St. Mary, Louisiana. Roll T624_531, Page 29A, Ennum. Dist. 99, Image 909 (this and all subsequent census records were accessed via Ancestry.com); John T. Edge, "Saving New Orleans Culture, One Sandwich at a Time," *New York Times*, November 11, 2009.

4. Lafcadio Hearn, *La Cuisine Creole: A Collection of Culinary Recipes* (New Orleans: F. F. Hansell, 1885), frontispiece; Elsa Hahne, *You Are Where You Eat: Stories and Recipes from the Neighborhoods of New Orleans* (Jackson: University Press of Mississippi, 2008), 15.

5. For a brief background on the activities of the Port of New Orleans, see Richard Campanella, *Bienville's Dilemma: A Historical Geography of New Orleans* (Lafayette: Center for Louisiana Studies, 2008), 229–32.

6. For an example of scholarly work dealing with lynching and whiteness, see Clive Webb, "The Lynching of Sicilian Immigrants in the American South, 1886–1910," *American Nineteenth Century History* 3, no. 1 (March 2002): 45–76. More popular pieces on the Hennessy murder, lynching, and questions of mafia activity include Richard Gambino, *Vendetta: A True Story of the Worst Lynching in America* (New York: Doubleday, 1977); Thomas Hunt and Martha Sheldon, *Deep Water: Joseph P. Macheca and the Birth of the American Mafia* (Lincoln, Nebr.: iUniverse, 2007).

7. Jean Ann (Vincenzia) Scarpaci, "Immigrants in the New South: Italians in Louisiana's Sugar Parishes, 1880–1910," *Labor History* 16, no. 2 (Spring 1975): 165–83; Thomas L. Karnes, *Tropical Enterprise: The Standard Fruit and Steamship Company in Latin America* (Baton Rouge: Louisiana State University Press, 1978). Another work, while scholarly in some respects, offers an otherwise deeply nostalgic look at the Italian immigrant experience in the Gulf South. See Anthony V. Margavio and Jerome J. Salomone, *Bread and Respect: The Italians of Louisiana* (Gretna, La.: Pelican, 2002).

8. Typical representations of the popular literature on the Sicilian food tradition in New Orleans include Nancy Tregre Wilson, *Louisiana's Italians, Food, Recipes, & Folkways* (Gretna, La.: Pelican, 2005). See also Kerri McCaffety, *St. Joseph Altars* (Gretna, La.: Pelican, 2003); Sara Roahen, "Red Gravy," *Gastronomica* 8, no. 1 (Winter 2008): 56–65; Joel Denkler, *The World on a Plate: A Tour through the History of America's Ethnic Cuisine* (Lincoln, Nebr.: Bison Books, 2007); John F. Mariani, *How Italian Food Conquered the World* (New York: Palgrave Macmillan, 2011).

9. The author's other field of study is the social, cultural, and political history of the American Civil War era. See Justin A. Nystrom, *New Orleans after the Civil War: Race, Politics, and a New Birth of Freedom* (Baltimore: Johns Hopkins University Press, 2010).

10. The American Italian Cultural Center and Library are located at 537 South Peters Street in New Orleans.

11. Interview of Paul Leslie by Justin Nystrom, July 17, 2010, videorecording in possession of author. Leslie, emeritus faculty at Nicholls State University, is executive director at the Laurel Valley Plantation historic site.

12. Interview of Niccolino "Peter" Compagno by Joseph Maselli, November 14, 1977. American Italian Research Library, American Italian Cultural Center, New Orleans (Hereafter cited as AICC); *New Orleans Daily Picayune*, January 12, 1902. The original barroom and grocery was located at 1601 Magazine Street, the present location of Harkins Florist. See *New Orleans Daily Picayune*, August 4, 1904. His brothers established bars at 900 Washington Avenue (no longer standing), 4605 Magazine, and the corner of Fern and St. Charles Avenue, the present location of Vincent's restaurant.

13. Niccolino Compagno interview.

14. Today the family uses the spelling "Perrone," but in all records prior to 1930, the name is spelled "Pirrone"; Bartolomé Pirrone arrived March 10, 1907. Passenger Lists Arriving at New Orleans, Louisiana, 1820–1902; World War I Draft Registration Database; 1920 United States Census, New Orleans, Louisiana, Ward 6, Roll T625_620, Page 7B, Ennum. Dist. 96, Img. 307 (all accessed via Ancestry.com); interview with John Perrone Jr. and Joseph Pacaccio by Justin Nystrom, August 2, 2010, videorecording and transcript in possession of author.

15. John Gendusa interview; Perrone and Pacaccio interview.

16. Interview of Maria Impastato and Sal Impastato by Justin Nystrom, August 18, 2010, videorecording and transcript in possession of author.

17. Interview of Rosario and Joseph Brocato by Joseph Maselli, April 5, 1988, AICC; Biaggio Montalbano first appears in the public record in New Orleans as living and operating a grocery at 724 Saint Philip Street, a property he owned. By 1930 he declared his property to be worth a substantial $12,000. He immigrated to New Orleans in 1912, where Central Grocery had opened for business in 1906. The question of who "invented" the muffuletta sandwich thus depends entirely on which establishment first served them—a fact not resolvable by any evidence discovered by the author. See 1920 United States Census, New Orleans, Ward 5, Orleans, Louisiana, Roll T625_620, Page 15B, Ennum. Dist. 78, Img. 713; 1930 United States Census, New Orleans, Louisiana, Roll 803, Page 5A, Ennum. Dist. 80, Img. 831.0.

18. Lyle Saxon, Edward Dreyer, and Robert Tallant, *Gumbo Ya-Ya: A Collection of Louisiana Folk Tales* (Boston: Houghton Mifflin, 1945), 102–3. Saxon misspells Montalbano's first name as "Biaccio."

19. Perrone and Pacaccio interview; Sal and Maria Impastato interview.

20. Roahen, "Red Gravy," 59; Perrone and Pacaccio interview.

21. For a geographical perspective of mid-century suburbanization see Campanella, *Bienville's Dilemma*, 188–90.

22. Interview of Joseph Zuppardo by Joseph Maselli, May 13, 1980, AICC.

23. Ibid.; H. G. Hill still operates today in middle Tennessee but was once a chain with more than five hundred stores. See a brief history at www.hghills.com. A McDonald's fast-food restaurant had replaced the Hill grocery by 1980.

24. Joseph Zuppardo interview.

25. Perrone and Pacaccio interview.

26. Ibid.

27. Ibid.

28. *New Orleans City Guide* (Washington, D.C.: Federal Writers Project of the Works Progress Administration, 1938), 33; Maria and Sal Impastato interview; 1920 United States Census, New Orleans Ward 5, Louisiana, Roll T625_20, Page 1B, Ennum. Dist. 76, Img. 611; 1930 United States Census, New Orleans, Louisiana, Roll 803, Page 9A, Ennum. Dist. 84, Img. 917.0.

29. Maria and Sal Impastato interview.

30. Interview of Rosario Zuppardo by Justin Nystrom, July 14, 2010, video recording and transcript in possession of author.

31. Clementine Paddleford, "Food Flashes," *Gourmet*, May 1950 (accessed via archive at www.gourmet.com); *New Orleans Daily Picayune*, June 22, 1890; Perrone and Pacaccio interview; Maria and Sal Impastato interview.

32. *New Orleans Times-Picayune*, January 20, 1959, September 1, 1965; Maria and Sal Impastato interview.

33. Ibid.

34. Brett Anderson, "The Natural," in *Cornbread Nation 4: The Best of Southern Food Writing*, ed. Dale Volberg Reed and John Shelton Reed (Athens: University of Georgia Press, 2008), 53–66; Tom Fitzmorris, *Hungry Town: A Culinary History of New Orleans, The City Where Food Is Almost Everything* (New York: Steward, Tabori & Chang, 2010), 49–54.

35. Perrone and Pacaccio interview; Brett Anderson, "Changing Scenes: Culinary Institute Grad Opens Restaurant in Hotel; Progresso Deli Occupies Former Progress Grocery Space," *New Orleans Times-Picayune*, April 24, 2001.

36. Ibid.

37. Rosario Zuppardo interview.

38. Joseph Zuppardo interview; "The Inevitable End of Price Cutting," *New Orleans Retail Grocers' Annual*, August 1932, 9. Louisiana Collection, Howard-Tilton Memorial Library, Tulane University, New Orleans.

39. Rosario Zuppardo interview.

40. Ibid.

41. Ibid.

42. Ibid.; Roy Zuppardo interview.

43. John and Jason Gendusa interview.

44. Sal and Maria Impastato interview.

CHAPTER 7

Mother Corn and the Dixie Pig

Native Food in the Native South

RAYNA GREEN

Native food is in the news. Every day. All over the country, except in the South, farmers, chefs, environmentalists, and food writers are excited about Native food and foodways. That excitement usually comes from a "discovery" (or rediscovery) of the many virtues of old "slow" foods in the now hip vernacular—local, fresh, and seasonal foods that are good for you, good for the land, and good for the small food producer. Often, these rediscovered foods come from "Native" varieties that seed savers, naturalists, nutritionists, and Indians have propped up, from animals that regulators, commercial producers, and advocates have brought back from the brink of extinction, and from habitats redeemed from under middens of waste and neglect.[1]

Some Native communities, in revitalizing their own cultural histories and economies, have begun again to raise, catch, and market crops and critters long associated with them but just as long ago replaced. Hopis and other Pueblos farm and market native varieties of corn, beans, and other vegetables to provide a better diet and income for their people, while Ojibwas do the same with wild rice in the Great Lakes. In the Plains, where once the death of bison was synonymous with the defeat and death of Indians themselves, buffalo herds now thrive on tribal and public lands. Northwest Coastal people fish for salmon, pack and ship it to an audience eager for it, and serve it at salmon feasts, some for the communities, some for the income generated by cultural tourism.

In spite of the good press, Native food and foodways are, as ever, subject to massive assaults on their maintenance and survival. What hunters, hatmakers, the cavalry, miners, and trains didn't deplete or destroy in the eighteenth and nineteenth centuries, industrial and domestic polluters, ranchers, big farmers, dams, cities, and roads rolled over in the twentieth century. Modern tribal efforts at resource revitalization still meet resistance because they interfere—as Indians always have—with large non-Indian economic and cultural interests. Native people and park rangers in the Plains fight ranchers over the renewed presence of brucellosis-carrying buffalo in proximity to the huge cattle herds that graze, subsidized by federal money, on public lands. Northwest Coastal people struggle against international agency regulators, Japanese fish factories, and sport fishers for the right to catch the fish emblematic of their survival as a people. Always, Native Alaskans battle with the state and federal governments and with animal rights activists to continue their traditional subsistence diet and thus maintain cultural skills and legal rights. They all know, out there in Indian country, that the loss of traditional diet and the cultural skills needed to maintain it has killed more Indians than Andy Jackson. And they all know that the food fights, like the struggles to restore language and ceremony, are modern fights for survival. Where they are known to be central to the economies and cultural histories of the entire region, Native food and the politics that govern Native resources are at the top of regional discussion.

Native food and foodways in the South, however, attract neither the rabid enthusiasms nor wild resistances of other parts of the country. Four hundred years ago, the settler-saving "gifts" of Indian food and food production technologies, along with the salvation of an English adventurer by the Indian chief's beautiful daughter, anchored colonial mythology; three hundred years ago Indian corn and tobacco centered the new growth economy; two hundred years ago Indian food resources still constituted, in essence, the base diet of the region. Yet this history seems nearly irrelevant today—as do Indians themselves—to popular conceptions of the South.

It was not always thus. Native food was once the only food story. Early travelers and colonists of the Americas spoke at length of the abundance and richness of the natural environment, the good that Indians made of it, and the absolute dependence of the would-be colonists on Indian mastery of that environment. Archaeologists of Jamestown and other southern sites echo and reinforce these early accounts, confirming that Natives in precolonial Virginia and North Carolina, the Upland South, coastal Mississippi,

Florida, and Alabama ate well and often from a huge and diverse larder.[2] In most instances, they cultivated appropriately and well, renewing their resources by methods of complementary planting, crop rotation, nutritional enhancement, and resource-restorative rules for the gathering of plants and hunting of animals. Meat, fish, shellfish, vegetables, fruits, and nuts made for a better, richer, more abundant, and more nutritious diet than available to most of the Anglo-Europeans that journeyed to the South and a more dependable, consistent, diverse diet than most Indians elsewhere (except those in the Southwest and Pacific Northwest).[3]

From their indigenous relatives in Mexico, Southeastern (and Southwestern) Indians had centuries ago learned the knowledge and skills associated with cultivating corn, which they shared with receptive settlers.[4] Essential Native practices included combining corn and beans to create protein- and amino acid–rich meals; consuming hominy, corn breads, soups, drinks, and mushes (grits, tamales) made from limed corn (nixtamalization); using nitrogen-enriching leguminous ash in various corn dishes; interplanting corn with nitrogen-replacing or nitrogen-enriching varieties (e.g., legumes); and rotating nutritionally exhausted croplands with alternate crops.[5] It didn't take the Spanish very long at all, merely twenty years into their sixteenth-century invasions, to substitute many of their own imports for Native food resources. But well into the seventeenth century—in the remainder of the British-occupied Southeast—Native diet and Native knowledge formed the core of the new southern foodways even as the British process for amending and replacing that diet, Native knowledge and skills, and Indians themselves escalated. It took nearly a hundred years for the agriculturally and hunting-challenged British, in particular (at least the classes of Brits who first came to the Southeast), to begin amending the Native larder and food technologies for their own foods and technologies from home. It took two centuries more of dismantling Indian food technologies and land management skills to understand the errors of doing so, with once good agricultural lands farmed out and eroded by 1900, the population plagued by niacin deficiency, and pellagra reaching epidemic proportions.[6]

By the eighteenth century, when most colonists had succeeded in breaking the exclusive hold that the Native diet had on their survival, the "new" foods from Europe (Spain, France, the British Isles), Africa, and the Caribbean merged with native staples to create the complex mélange that is today's southern cuisine. These changes affected Indian and non-Indian alike. From Indians the new southerners had developed the taste for and habit of eating more vegetables, particularly greens (fresh and cooked), than did other Americans. These native vegetables, both gathered and cultivated, joined Spanish-imported produce such as melons, peaches, and peppers. African food tastes and habits reinforced the Indian vegetable/greens complex and brought in new and healthful crops such as sesame and okra, and legumes such as black-eyed peas and peanuts thrived in the Lowland and southeastern climate.[7] From Africans many also acquired the taste for hot peppers and spices and for the technique of frying. Later, all would adopt dairy products—as they were able to raise the dairy cattle—wheat flour, and sugar when they could afford them, and more liquor when they could make it. Pigs, introduced in the sixteenth century, rooted their way into Indian communities in the late eighteenth century. Women, the primary farmers of the southern Indian world, first resisted the feral beasts that ravaged their fields and crops, but they eventually accepted the domesticated (and wild) food source that meant meat on the Indian table.[8] And Indians, like other southerners, learned to use pigs not only as their main meat source but also a source of cooking grease, side meat, and flavoring. They "nativized" the once-alien animal, just as the newcomers once normalized and accepted the American animals and plants new to them, and incorporated pig into dishes featuring Mother Corn alone. These foods remain some of those most beloved by southern Indians.

Indian removal in the 1830s was supposed to settle the resource battles first begun in the seventeenth century. Cherokees, Choctaws, Creeks, and Chickasaws stood in the way of land-grabbers, gold seekers, and farmer/landowners with cash crops based in a slave economy. The forced land cessions accompanying Indian removal did indeed take most of the prime farming, hunting, and fishing lands held by Indians in the South, leaving behind many small communities with little but the weakened cultural skills essential to their survival. Those removed retained something of the skills and knowledge regarding the basic foods and foodways, which they tried, only partially successfully, to restore in Oklahoma. Indian losses would be the miner's canary, as they always were, for the environmental and economic disasters that were yet to unhinge large parts of the agrarian South.

The small group of Choctaws, once stellar farmers, who managed to stay in Mississippi were eventually reduced to the poorest of sharecroppers by the turn of the twentieth century. Their hunter-fisher-gatherer Houma relatives, in the Louisiana bayous since the late seventeenth century, would become French-speaking, forced to take protective cover in the ways and manners of their neighbors. They and the Seminoles and Miccosukees, who had fled to Florida before removal, had become masters of their environments, subsisting on food sourcing from small farms and watery habitats into the twenty-first century. But Houmas, unlike the Seminoles who resisted assimilation in any visible way, would remain unrecognized and relatively obscured as Indians to the world around them. Cherokees who avoided removal in North Carolina remained in the hills, as poor and isolated as their Appalachian neighbors but able to continue a reasonably successful survival exploitation of the environment left to them. The menu from a 1949 feast given for anthropologists suggests not only how deeply Cherokee foodways had burrowed into the now all-but-Native diet of the Upland South but also how natural, how unexotic, how southern that diet was.

Other remaining Indians in the South—in South Carolina, Virginia, and North Carolina, in particular—faced a fate different from their removed relatives. Fragmented into small isolated communities, impoverished, collectively landless for the most part, with no federal treaties and a continuing lack of federal recognition, they most often "disappeared" as Indians. They kept what they could of the old ways and blended through intermarriage and interaction, as they always had done, with white and black folks, with Christians, with English-speakers. They ate more and more like the people with whom they lived, just as their neighbors had once learned to eat like them. But they remained at the edges of that society, further and further segregated into smaller units, with their identity as Indians virtually erased after the Civil War, the end of slavery, and Reconstruction by the South's primal obsession with black and white. Indian extinction had not succeeded; marginalization had.

Virginia's Indians, for example, so essential to the founding identity of the place and so embedded in its historical memory, found themselves without any viable social niche. In 1924, via the Racial Integrity Act, they found themselves in a state that declared most Indians nonexistent or illegal entities. This declaration of their legal nonexistence drove Virginia Indians to rise up and insist on repeal of the invidious law that separated them from their historic identity. One of the ways in which they did that was to reenact the historic relationship, forged in Native food, between them and the colonists. In the colonial era, "Powhatans" (a collective term for all Virginia Indians of the day) had delivered tribute deer to the governor of Virginia every year in lieu of taxes on lands held by Indians. Continuing this practice into the late twentieth century reinforced the survival and continuity of Virginia's Indians, several groups of which eventually obtained state recognition. Relatively recently, that recognition resulted in the restoration of their right to use the lands' more abundant larder so praised by early colonists for more than 350 of the last 400 years. By 2005 Pamunkeys and Mattaponi could again hunt deer and fish for shad off their state reservations and collect oysters from the bay without a state license. Still, the Mattaponi in Virginia currently are trying to stop a proposed reservoir that would divert water from the Mattaponi River, endangering their shad fisheries and the shreds of the traditional life they have remaining. Still, much-loved Virginia spring shad feasts, like those offered the colonists four hundred years ago by Virginia's Indians, have come to be reserved for Virginia political events that exclude Indians (and women). In many ways the complex relationship of Virginia's citizens to Indians, as expressed through the acceptance and rejection of Native food and foodways—as well as Virginia natives' persistence toward their food and foodways—may act as a paradigm for the southern Indian story.

A few Native dishes never passed into the mainstream southern culinary repertoire and remain distinctly and exclusively Indian, very much a part of native identity, cherished and propped up in a public way, served to strangers and friends and certainly in revitalized Green Corn or stomp dance communal dinners. Bean bread and *so-chan* among the North Carolina Cherokees are dishes likely not found elsewhere in Appalachia. Choctaws and Chickasaws in Oklahoma eat *banaha*, a tamale-like corn mush with field peas and/or pea shell ash, and hominy in every form it comes in, including *tamfula* (often pronounced "tomfuller"), a hominy and hickory nut soup/cream unlikely to be on a restaurant menu even in Oklahoma. *Sofkee*, a soup or drink of soured cornmeal, links Seminoles and Miccosukees in Florida to Seminoles, Yuchis, and Creeks in Oklahoma and is never found outside Indian communities.[9] Many of these precious foods listed above may indeed have been the staples of the long-ago diet. Others, such as the various corn-and-pig dishes or berry dumplings (often "cobblers" or "pies") that have characterized Indian cooking since the late eighteenth century, represent the beginnings of dietary change long ago, yet they became enshrined within their communities as uniquely Cherokee, uniquely Choctaw, uniquely Indian. Today these foods and foodways belong to the communities that cook and serve them, in spite of the profound changes they represented when first introduced. Some foods maintain the ancient Indian relationships with and responsibilities to plants and animals, and most native communities worry about passing on their skills and tastes, just as they worry about the death of language. Even when they can get canned hominy, frozen corn, bottled grape juice, and four different kinds of greens at the grocery store, they still organize cultural camps and plant native gardens where younger Indians can learn traditions that now represent physical and cultural survival.

In the late 1970s the United States began to look with favor on marginalized cuisines. Ethnic pride and cultural rights movements of the 1960s demanded acknowledgment for the cultural contributions of those once repressed. The long tradition of African American foodways became a distinctive and redemptive badge of cultural pride, and the new term "soul food" became synonymous with both traditional African American cuisine and the best of "southern cooking." Thus, soul food, Cajun food, so-called white trash cooking, and good old country cooking started to have their day alongside plantation (antebellum) food, French-Creole traditions, and Lowcountry haute cuisine. The new southern food historians, a multivocal collection of people of good faith, mind, and heart, respectfully acknowledge the many peoples and ethnicities that have created and amended the delightful fusion that is southern cuisine. But discussions based solely on black and white relationships still dominate, and roiling underneath the civilities of new acknowledgments remains the intensely southern spat over which group really gave the most to this beloved food, planting old and ever volatile claims to the kingdom right in the middle of a plate of barbecue.

No Indian claims to a rightful place within southern foodways surfaced in these tangles, and no one has made any claims on Indians' behalf. Indians have not established restaurants that serve up ethnic pride along with the foods that underpin the southern diet. No public relations campaign, protest, or demand for respect has accompanied the recent elevation of grits and greens to nearly sanctified status in New South cuisine. Some might say southern Indians have been too busy putting their cultural and physical survival, their very existence, on the agenda to pursue a more substantive acknowledgment of their historic contributions. But could the focus on Native food provide more than simply some suggestions for what historical curiosities might be served to interested patrons at the casino restaurant or for what might amount to just a little more political correctness regarding Native people by the next cookbook writer? Just what might a little attention to Native food history in the South be worth, and to whom might that worth be manifest?

It is true that southern Indians and their foods do not have the competitive edge granted Indians in the West with their national attachments to the charismatic megafauna—buffalo, whales, seals—so emblematic of Native place and history in the West and Far North. But a different kind of repatriation might do us all good, and we could start by bringing back those native varieties that appear lost, to say nothing of showing interest in the reasons that certain foods were not lost to Native communities. The new small farms and farmer's markets, the new chefs that care so deeply about the restoration of southern food, might want to join forces with the oldest farmers to their mutual benefit. We could start in Mississippi where a Choctaw woman recently sold Mason jars filled with a kind of shoepeg hominy she had raised and processed without a subsidy. Getting her grits on the menu somewhere would do more than simply lend chic credibility to this revitalized southern cult food. We might all find ways to support and extend the kinds of *so-chan* and ramp gardens that the Eastern Band of Cherokee Indians has started in North Carolina. The story (and the action that needs to follow a good story) is missing in the South, where Native food might bring good news. And with that news could come a cultural construct that might be surprisingly useful—a region of the mind called Native South—a good name, perhaps, for the chain of restaurants that could appear in Indian casinos. The food served there would be shockingly familiar, albeit a tad underseasoned, to all good southerners, and once again Indians will welcome everyone to eat. Come on in where you see the neon cornstalk flashing over the smiling Dixie pig.

NOTES

1. For the best account of the need for study and restoration of Native habitats, plants, and animals and Euro-American/African American heritage plants and animals, as well as the agricultural and animal management technologies necessary for restoration, see Gary Nabhan, ed., *Renewing America's Food Traditions: Saving and Savoring the Continent's Most Endangered Foods* (White River Junction, Vt.: Chelsea Green, 2008). This volume includes a red list of endangered foods, as well as descriptions of foods thus far restored. See also Gary Paul Nabhan, *Enduring Seeds: Native American Agriculture and Wild Plant Conservation* (Berkeley, Calif.: North Point Press, 1989). For generalist accounts of Native food and foodways, see Rayna Green, "Native American Food," in *Smithsonian Folklife Cookbook*, ed. Katherine and Thomas Kirlin (Washington, D.C.: Smithsonian Institution Press, 1991), and Linda Murray Berzok, *American Indian Food* (Westport, Conn.: Greenwood, 2005). Quite a number of glossy Native cookbooks, good on highly modernized Indian recipes but generally thin on cultural history, have appeared in the last ten years. These books are mostly devoted to the popular modern Southwestern style but may include a few "classics" from the Native Northwest and Northeast. Rare is the mention of Native food in the South. For a modern Indian cookbook that does contain a section on southeastern foods, see Beverley Cox and Martin Jacobs, *Spirit of the Harvest: North American Indian Cooking* (New York: Stewart, Tabori & Chang, 1991). Some small cookbooks—issued within and often by Indian communities and cooks—document Native cooking in the "old days" of the nineteenth century and include some mid-twentieth-century variations on older foodways. These do not, in general, offer much about the historical contexts of and changes in these foods and food technologies, though the recipes themselves note changes in ingredients and cooking technologies. Most include only Cherokee and Choctaw recipes, with occasional mentions of Seminole and Creek foods; see Frances Gwaltney, comp., *Corn Recipes from the Indians*, intro. Mary Frances Chiltoskey (Cherokee, N.C.: Cherokee Publications, 1988, 1991); Frances Lambet Whisler, *Indian Cookin'* (Nowega Press, 1973); Mary Ulmer and Samuel E. Beck, *Cherokee Cooklore: Preparing Cherokee Foods*, published by Mary and Goingback Chiltoskey, in cooperation with Stephens Press, Inc. (Cherokee, N.C.: Museum of the Cherokee Indian, 1951), which contains an interview and demonstration of traditional foodways with Aggie Lossiah and others, a reprint of William Bartram's 1789 account of the foods of Cherokee and Creek Indians, and a newspaper

account and menu of a 1949 feast given by North Carolina Cherokees for the North Carolina Anthropological Society. Some Oklahoma Indian publications from the 1930s to the 1970s also contain recipes and information about southern Indian foodways; see Eula Doonkeen, ed., *Indian Cookbook* (Oklahoma City: Alco, 1975); Nettie Wheeler, *Indian Recipes from Cherokee Indians of Eastern Oklahoma* (Hoffman, n.d.); and for a rare (not Cherokee, Choctaw, etc.) commentary on foodways in a contemporary southern Indian group, see Karen I. Blu, "Lumbee," in *Handbook of North American Indians* 14 (Washington, D.C.: Smithsonian Institution Press, 2004), 314.

2. William Bartram, *Travels through North & South Carolina, Georgia, East & West Florida, the Cherokee Country, the Extensive Territories of the Muscogulges, or Creek Confederacy, and the Country of the Chactaws; Containing an Account of the Soil and Natural Productions of Those Regions, Together with Observations on the Manners of the Indians* (James & Johnson, 1791; repr. Charlottesville: University of Virginia Press, 1980); Thomas Hariot, *A Briefe and True Report of the New Found Land of Virginia, Part 1*, trans. Richard Hakluyt, illust. John White (Theodore de Bry, 1588, 1590; J. Sabin & Sons, 1871); Samuel Cole Williams, ed., *Adair's History of the American Indians* (1775; repr. Promontory Press, 1930); David Stick, ed., *Indian Food and Cooking in Coastal North Carolina 400 Years Ago*, expanded by Lebame Houston and Wynne Dough (Harpers Ferry, W.Va.: National Park Service, n.d.); Jane Buikstra, "The Lower Illinois River Region: A Prehistoric Context for the Study of Ancient Diet and Health," in *Paleopathology at the Origins of Agriculture*, ed. Mark Nathan Cohen and George Armelagos (Burlington, Mass.: Academic Press, 1984).

3. Some, like the Chickasaws, who were frequently in conflict with the new settlers, whose lands and stability were rarely threatened, and who were not as committed to agriculture as their neighbors, were not always so successful at feeding themselves. Their Choctaw neighbors, who were prolific farmers, often shared or traded enough with them to fill the gaps.

4. For a readable general history of corn, including information about the Native science of growing and preparing corn and the demise of serious corn agriculture in the South, see Betty Fussell, *The Story of Corn: The Myths and History, the Culture and Agriculture, the Art and Science of America's Quintessential Crop* (New York: Knopf, 1994). See also Muriel H. Wright, "American Indian Corn Dishes," *Chronicles of Oklahoma* 36, no. 2 (1958): 155–66.

5. Contemporary commentators, Indian and non-Indian, often use the term "the Three Sisters" in referring to the common Native method of interplanting corn, beans, and squash. While this popularized poetic reference comes from and is applicable to actual Iroquoian usage, no other Indian group ever referred to these foods or to interplanting in this manner.

6. Pellagra is a disease of malnutrition and poverty, long associated with folks who were dependent on a nutritionally inadequate diet of corn and little else. Research also suggests that pellagra was further exacerbated, or rather, the epidemic triggered, by turn-of-the-century changes in milling corn that left it degerminated. See A. J. Bollet, "Politics and Pellagra: The Epidemic of Pellagra in the U.S. in the Early Twentieth Century," *Yale Journal of Biological Medicine* (May/June 1992): 211–21. Scientists continue to offer even more support for the ef-

ficacy of Native agricultural and food preparation technologies and for the restoration of technologies that produce the same conditions in food products, that is, whole grains in the instance of corn.

7. Peanuts came to the Americas via the slave trade. From the Incas (Peru), the Spanish brought peanuts to Africa, where they were grown to support the slave trade, eventually making their way to the Americas on slave ships. Corn had a similar role in the slave trade in Africa, where, like peanuts, it was introduced from outside and formed an easily and cheaply grown and stored commodity for the feeding of slaves on their journey to enslavement, where they would, in turn, grow corn and peanuts for their masters in the New World.

8. Theda Perdue, *Cherokee Women: Gender and Culture Change, 1700–1835* (Lincoln: University of Nebraska Press, 1998); Wilma A. Dunaway, "Rethinking Cherokee Acculturation: Women's Resistance to Agrarian Capitalism and Cultural Change, 1800–1838," *American Indian Culture and Research Journal* 21, no. 1 (1997): 128–49; Margaret C. Scarry, "Native American 'Garden Agriculture' in Southeastern North America," *World Archaeology* 27, no. 2 (June 2005): 259–74; Thomas M. Hatley, "Cherokee Women Farmers Hold Their Ground," in *Appalachian Frontier Settlement, Society, and Development in the Preindustrial Era*, ed. Robert Mitchell (Lexington: University Press of Kentucky, 1991), 37–51; Robert Newman, "The Acceptance of European Domestic Animals by the Eighteenth Century Cherokee," *Tennessee Anthropologist* 4, no. 1 (Spring 1979): 102–5. To further explore gender role changes and cultural and environmental shift and their connections to foodways and food technologies in Cherokee history, see Sarah H. Hill, *Weaving New Worlds: Southeastern Cherokee Women and Their Basketry* (Chapel Hill: University of North Carolina Press, 1996).

9. Regarding Choctaw/Chickasaw *tamfula*, some settlers ate these dishes early on in their settlements but most certainly gave them up after the Indians who shared them were removed from their former co-residence with settlers. Joseph Dabney recounts in *Smokehouse Ham* (Nashville: Cumberland House, 1998) that the early southern Appalachian settlers liked the *sofkee* that the Creek Indians (and possibly Chickasaws) made, though they called it "Tom Fuller," and the author was never able to learn why.

CHAPTER 8

A Salad Bowl City

The Food Geography of Charlotte, North Carolina

TOM HANCHETT

Exploring foodways can open up fresh perspectives on wider society. In my neighborhood along Central Avenue in Charlotte, North Carolina, ethnic restaurants and grocery stores started popping up in the 1990s. Today at the corner of Central and Rosehaven, you can park your car amid a jumble of little shopping plazas and walk to a Vietnamese grocery and two Vietnamese restaurants, a Mexican grocery and a taqueria, a Salvadoran deli and two Salvadoran eateries, a Somali restaurant and grocery, an Ethiopian bar-restaurant-nightclub, and a Lebanese grocery-restaurant. It's a delightful place to sample unfamiliar cuisines. It turns out also to be an exciting window on a whole new urban geography. In fast-growing southern metropolitan areas such as Charlotte, and less visibly in older cities as well, people are creating what might be called "salad bowl suburbs"—a new, mixed-up, tossed salad of cultures.

Not Melting Pot, not Chinatown, but a Salad Bowl

For generations, a couple of mental models dominated discussion of ethnicity in U.S. cities. One was the melting pot. The other was the image of ethnic enclave—Chinatown, Little Italy, and the like—which scholars elaborated into the notion of urban ecology, a narrative of inevitable "invasion and succession." Let's look first at those ideas before moving on to what is actually happening today.

The melting pot is one of the most cherished metaphors of American culture. It harks back to the steel mills of the late nineteenth and early twentieth centuries where iron ore, coke, and other raw inputs came together at intense temperatures in giant cauldrons called crucibles. Poured out and cooled, the resulting steel was a new material, stronger than any of its components. What a wonderful image for this nation whose motto is "one from many," *e pluribus unum*. Hector Crèvecoeur, a French writer visiting America, called attention to the melting effect as early as 1782: "Here individuals of all nations are melted into a new race of men."[1] The melting pot seems to have become the dominant metaphor around 1900 as photographs of white-hot crucibles in the rolling mills of Pittsburgh appeared in the era's new illustrated magazines and photogravure sections of newspapers.

Implicit in the melting pot image was the notion that immigrants must lose the cultures they brought with them and create a new uniformly American culture. "Understand that America is God's Crucible, the great Melting-Pot where all the races of Europe are melting and re-forming! Here you stand ... in your fifty groups, your fifty languages, and histories, and your fifty blood hatreds and rivalries. But you won't be long like that, brothers. . . . Germans and Frenchmen, Irishmen and Englishmen, Jews and Russians— into the Crucible with you all! God is making the American." So wrote Israel Zangwill in his play *The Melting Pot* in 1909.[2]

That date coincided with America's largest immigrant wave. Beginning in the 1850s and gathering momentum into the 1910s, the United States experienced a growing tide of new arrivals that defined the nation we know today. It also generated intense fear. Would existing American culture be drowned out? The new profession of social work, the increased push for universal public education, and the rise of scholarly fields such as urban sociology were just a few of the responses as people sought to understand what was going on and help Americanize the newcomers. Ultimately, in 1917 and 1924, strict laws halted most immigration except from areas deemed culturally safe such as England.

The arrivals who streamed into American cities in the late nineteenth and early twentieth centuries tended to settle in distinct neighborhoods. Some of that resulted from natural tendencies for people of like language and foodways to cluster and help each other out. But the dominant society also played a huge role. Real estate professionals united to refuse to sell or rent to particular ethnic groups. Restrictive covenants, a legal tool inserted into deeds to limit who could buy or occupy the land, became commonplace by the 1890s. The practice of zoning, which spread during the 1920s, reinforced those boundaries. The upshot was a pattern of ethnic enclaves. Chinatown, Little Italy, Greektown, the Barrio, and also African American districts all became accepted and expected in big cities.

Scholars in the emerging fields of sociology and urban geography unconsciously reinforced those assumptions. Robert Park and Earnest Burgess at the University of Chicago sketched out a concentric ring theory of urban growth.[3] Immigrants settled first in inner-city tenement neighborhoods. Then as they moved up economically, they moved outward physically, farther and farther into the suburbs. Colleague Roderick McKenzie elaborated on this model, noting that in highly segregated Chicago, groups seemed to "invade" a neighborhood, crowding out all other ethnic groups much in the way that a new plant species can crowd out others as grassland matures into a forest.[4] He coined the term "invasion and succession," which not only matched what people were indeed seeing but also had an attractive air of scientific inevitability that came from nature's ecology—a natural law of cities.

The image of invasion and succession became a self-fulfilling prophecy. If people thought that "once strangers move in, we will be forced out," then they became likely to flee at the first sight of ethnic neighbors. The federal government threw its weight behind the idea when it wrote regulations for the new Federal Housing Administration in 1938. This hugely influential program insured banks that made long-term loans to homeowners— something that sounds boring and esoteric but defined the shape of American cities. FHA regulations required that neighborhoods must be protected against "being invaded" by "incompatible racial and social groups."[5] The result in every U.S. city was a landscape of tightly defined neighborhoods set apart by race, ethnicity, and income.

The odd thing about the melting pot metaphor, though, was that on closer observation it did not actually describe what was happening. Immigrants' children and grandchildren did indeed give up much of their old culture, but they kept some things—food, for example. Italians continued cooking pasta and making spaghetti sauce for dinner, even if they might munch on an all-American hotdog for lunch. And to continue the Italian example, some exotic ethnic foods such as pizza and lasagna were adopted by their neighbors and came to seem thoroughly American.

As early as the 1950s, scholars struggling with this reality began searching for a better metaphor. What if, instead of a melting pot, we talked about America as a salad bowl? Carl Degler, one of the era's foremost U.S. historians, coined the term in a 1959 book.[6] In a salad many ingredients come together to create a new dish, each bite mingling different flavors. Other excellent ideas have been suggested along this line. Perhaps a stewpot is more accurate than a salad bowl, since the process of "cooking together" over time in this new land does indeed change each of us. Or maybe a potluck would be a useful image, since we each bring something different to the table but tend to take onto our own plates what we choose based on our preexisting notions of what might taste good. I like all of those, but the salad bowl seems to have caught on most widely, so we'll use that here. And it does sound good next to "suburb."

Charlotte's East Side—from Lily White to Racially and Economically Mixed

In the description of Central Avenue at the start of this essay, you may have caught a bit of wonder in my voice. The multiethnic concept is new to Charlotte. Like most cities in the southeastern United States, Charlotte had very few foreign-born residents a generation ago. In that last immigrant wave a century earlier, newcomers gravitated to the big industrial cities of the Northeast and Midwest and to the wide-open farmland of the Great Plains. The South, in contrast, struggled with poverty in the aftermath of the Civil War. New cotton mills did string like beads along the main line of the Southern Railway, with Charlotte as a major trading hub for the emerging textile region by the 1920s. But in comparison to the vast steel plants of Pittsburgh or stockyards of Chicago, the South's cotton mills were small and able to pull all the labor they needed from southern hills and mountains without seeking immigrants from abroad. In other words, this was a region of native-born white people and native-born black people, with hardly any

Asians or Italians or eastern Europeans. When I first came to Charlotte in 1981 it was difficult for this Chicago boy to find an acceptable slice of pizza, much less something as exotic as a bagel.

Obviously things have changed drastically, setting the stage for the intermingling I have hinted at. Before we delve into that, though, we need to go back into the deeper history of Central Avenue. What I did not realize until I began this research was how the Central Avenue corridor had evolved before I first saw it in 1981. Like nearly all of urban America, no one planned Central Avenue. The way it developed over many decades made it an especially welcoming place for newcomers seeking a better life.

In 1899 developers George Stephens and F. C. Abbott laid out the first suburb on Charlotte's east side, Piedmont Park, straddling an old farm lane.[7] They grandly renamed the road Central Avenue, since it ran through the center of their subdivision, and they made it wide to hold the track of the streetcar line that would carry commuters back and forth to downtown. They inserted restrictive covenants in the lot deeds, stipulating a minimum house cost and residence by Caucasians only. A few big houses went up in the first blocks of Central Avenue during the 1900s, and a few more followed in the 1910s along The Plaza, the heart of the next suburb to the east. But other sectors of town proved more attractive to Charlotte's leading families, and by the 1920s the city's East Side along Central Avenue was a middling residential area, neither rich nor poor.

In addition to these early white-collar subdivisions, another neighborhood helped define Charlotte's East Side. Belmont–Villa Heights, a blue-collar district, sprang up just off Central Avenue around the Louise cotton mill in the years around 1900. As America moved into the prosperous post–World War II decades of the mid-twentieth century, textile workers and their descendants began moving away from the mills. The East Side was often where they went.

From the 1950s through the 1970s, dozens of new suburban subdivisions strung outward along Central Avenue for its entire four-mile length. Small one-story houses, usually well under a thousand square feet at the beginning of the era, intermingled with duplexes and other modest rental properties. Over time, houses in each new subdivision became a little bigger. The upward economic fortunes of the initial families, plus Charlotte's general growth, which attracted transplants from all over the nation, pushed dwellings toward the two-thousand-square-foot range by the 1970s.

By that time the Central Avenue corridor was attracting major multifamily development. A vogue for "apartment communities" took hold nationwide between the 1960s and 1980s. Groupings of two- and three-story buildings set in attractive landscaping, often with swimming pools and clubhouses, were advertised to young professionals. Central Avenue and its vicinity got more of these than perhaps any other part of town.

Businesses followed the general suburban trend. Central Avenue's initial stores clustered near where the Central Avenue streetcar turned onto The Plaza in the 1920s. During the 1950s and 1960s, small strip plazas marched farther out Central, groups of two or three stores facing a parking lot. In 1975 the East Side unexpectedly gained a grand regional shopping center, Eastland Mall. Three major department stores anchored two levels of specialty shops plus an ice-skating rink and a new adventure in dining, Charlotte's first food court. Some observers wondered how this big facility could compete with just-opened Southpark Mall in Charlotte's rich southeastern sector. But to most people Eastland Mall gave comfortable assurance that this once humble side of town had really arrived.

Charlotteans regarded the East Side in general, and Central Avenue in particular, as a very good place to live and do business. Its mix of housing choices welcomed young families and people moving up economically into the middle class. By no means was it Charlotte's elite district; that was the southeast, out beyond the mill owners' 1910s garden suburb of Myers Park. Nor was it the black side of town. Real estate practices and deed restrictions pushed African Americans to the north and west of Charlotte from the 1900s into the 1960s. Indeed, as late as 1960, census data showed that all the neighborhoods along Central Avenue were nearly 100 percent white.

The East Side felt tremors of racial change in the late 1960s. As federally funded "urban renewal" demolished black neighborhoods near downtown, landlords decided that Belmont–Villa Heights would house many of the displaced families. The old mill district abruptly switched from all white to nearly all black. It seemed a classic case of the natural law of invasion and succession, just as scholars had laid out. Would all of the Central Avenue corridor soon become African American?

Attitudes toward race were changing in the 1960s, however. The Civil
Rights Act of 1964, which forbade discrimination in public places, is well
known. Less familiar is the Fair Housing Act of 1968, which mandated
"equal housing opportunity" in all rentals and sales. In 1977 the Community
Reinvestment Act required banks to lend to home buyers in every neighborhood without regard to race. None of these laws were magic potions, and
much inequality remained, but in retrospect it is now clear that the overall effect was to chip away at age-old segregation patterns. Racially mixed
neighborhoods began to come into existence and enjoy a fair amount of
stability over time. The old urban ecology of white flight, invasion and succession, no longer automatically applied.

In Charlotte civic leaders made a point of welcoming integration, especially after the local schools became the national test case for court-ordered
busing, the 1971 Supreme Court case *Swann v. Charlotte-Mecklenburg*. In
1970 Charlotte ranked as the fifth most segregated U.S. city.[8] By 2000 it had
become the nation's second *least* segregated urban place. Given the reputation of the American South as the nation's hotbed of racial apartheid, this
turnabout was indeed remarkable.[9]

You could see that racial transformation up close on the East Side.[10] Data
for the six census tracts that lined Central Avenue counted them nearly
100 percent white in 1960. By 1970 Belmont–Villa Heights was on its way
to being all black, but other neighborhoods had not budged. In 1980 the
data showed the Plaza-Midwood neighborhood adjacent to Belmont–Villa
Heights now 77 percent white, 29 percent black. Was it tipping? No, there
it froze. Through the 1990s and beyond, Plaza-Midwood remained close
to the citywide ratio of 79 percent white, 20 percent black, as did the other
tracts along Central. Except for Belmont–Villa Heights, every neighborhood
was between 71 percent and 86 percent white by 1990.

As the 1990s dawned, the East Side remained a sought-after swath of suburbia. All of Central Avenue was now technically inside the city; state laws
throughout much of the South make it easy for cities to annex outlying territory, so unlike in metro areas such as New York or Chicago, suburbs here
seldom became separate incorporated municipalities. In terms of the built
environment, however, the East Side looked exactly like suburbia anywhere.
The car was king, residential sidewalks were rare, and strip shopping plazas

lined the main streets. By the 1990s storefronts sometimes went vacant and Eastland Mall struggled in the face of massive modernization at competing Southpark Mall. Small houses and older duplexes sometimes struggled to find tenants, reflecting the rising aspirations of Charlotte citizens. Yet even with the arrival of upwardly mobile African Americans since the 1970s, the East Side remained solidly middle-class and desirable, exactly the sort of *Leave It to Beaver* or *Brady Bunch* suburbia celebrated on TV sitcoms.

Foreign Immigrants Arrive

José Hernández-Paris still vividly remembers when he saw Charlotte's first Mexican restaurant run by actual Mexicans. José's parents had emigrated in the 1970s from Colombia, rare foreigners in this overwhelmingly native-born town. Driving down South Boulevard one day in the 1980s, the family glimpsed a sign for an eatery called El Cancun about to open in a disused fast-food building. Mexicans were at work upfitting the interior. Excited to see fellow Spanish speakers, the Hernández-Paris clan stopped the car and pitched in.

Unbeknownst to Hernández and his family, the United States was poised on the brink of a massive new immigration. Scholars are still unraveling the causes. Changes in immigrant laws beginning in 1965 ended the 1920s quotas that had favored northern Europeans. Newcomers first spilled into traditional gateways such as New York, Florida, Texas, and California. Further legal developments in those states during the 1990s made them less welcoming. A new national law aimed at curtailing border crossings unexpectedly pushed migrants who were already in the United States to find more permanent jobs. Together all the various developments spurred a flow of immigrants into states where foreign-born had once been rare. Wrote the Brookings Institution in a study titled *The Rise of New Immigrant Gateways*: "The U.S. foreign-born population grew 57.4 percent in the 1990s; by 2000 nearly one-third of U.S. immigrants resided outside established settlement states. Thirteen states primarily in the West and Southeast—including many that had not previously been major destinations for immigrants—saw foreign-born growth rates more than double the national average."[11]

North Carolina emerged as one of the top states, with Charlotte particularly affected. Banks in the city led the national trend toward interstate banking starting in the 1980s, making Charlotte the country's second-biggest bank center by 2000, behind only New York City. Economic euphoria sparked employment opportunities at every level from highly paid office work to entry-level service positions landscaping lawns, washing dishes, and building new houses. Arrivals flooded in, both from across the United States and around the globe. Brookings Institution ranked Charlotte as the fourth-fastest growing Latino metro area in the United States during the 1990s, one of four "Hispanic hypergrowth cities" alongside Atlanta, Georgia, and Raleigh and Greensboro, North Carolina. By 2005, Brookings observed, Charlotte moved up to second fastest. Mexicans were most visible, but Latinos arrived from every Central American and South American country. Vietnamese also came in large numbers, along with other Asians from India and Pakistan, Korea and Cambodia. Still more newcomers arrived from Eastern Europe, North and West Africa, and the Middle East. In 1990 people born outside the United States made up barely 1 percent of Charlotte's population. By 2010 the number zoomed above 13 percent.

Charlotte's new foreign-born headed straight for the suburbs. A century earlier, inner-city tenement districts of tightly packed old apartments had been synonymous with immigrant life, places such as the Lower East Side of New York. Charlotte had no such areas. Back when tenements rose in major cities, Charlotte had been little more than a village of twenty thousand souls. Immigrants arriving in the 1990s looked around Charlotte for neighborhoods with good, but not expensive, rental housing. For many people that meant the East Side, those worn-in but still attractive post–World War II suburban apartment complexes and small houses along Central Avenue.

Central Avenue at Rosehaven: The Salad Bowl Up Close

Slide into a blue vinyl booth at El Pulgarcito de Americas on a Saturday or Sunday afternoon. Burly construction foremen in *tejano* cowboy hats, their big pickup trucks parked outside, hunch over plates of steak, refried beans, plantains, and lettuce. Families ring tables—parents, young children, and maybe an *abuela* (grandmother). TVs show Mexican *telenovelas* with on-screen subtitles in Spanish, necessary because someone is happily playing *banda sinaloa* pop hits, tuba-driven polkas, loudly on the jukebox.

Back in 1981 when I first arrived in Charlotte, myself a young newcomer settling into a worn-in duplex off Central Avenue, this spot was drab middle-American retail. The Rainbo Bakery Thrift Outlet sold day-old bread out of this shop. Next door a strip of tiny storefronts included Frame It Yourself, Modeler's Hobby Shop, Hairport Wigs, and Fancy Pup Dog Grooming. On the other side were Party Palace Novelties and Sugar Shack Deli.[12] The plain, boxy, one-story buildings constructed in the 1960s and 1970s looked out on an unadorned asphalt parking lot. Behind the shopping strip stood some late 1950s duplexes, looking like regular suburban ranch houses until you saw the two front doors and two street numbers, then a block of single-family split-levels. Across Central Avenue was Glen Hollow Apartments, a huddle of yellow-brick, two-story garden apartments developed in the late 1960s or 1970s. All of that unremarkable built environment is still there today but filled with an entirely different mix of people.

I'm sitting with Henry Chirinos, asking how he came to start this bustling restaurant.[13] "I come to the U.S. in 1990, following my brother, who knew a job for me at a country club on Long Island," he recalls. "I was dishwasher, bus-boy. I tell the guy, 'I want to be cook.' I learn to cook American food, Italian, Greek, Jewish, anything. That's my school here." After ten years of cooking, Chirinos's wife suggested they visit Charlotte, where some of her family already lived. "I see it growing. I see no Salvadoran restaurant." The old Rainbo Bread store, which had been upfitted for a restaurant that later failed, was available to rent.

Chirinos modestly called his new spot El Pulgarcito, "the little flea," in honor of the little countries he and his wife came from: Honduras and adjacent El Salvador. Most of Charlotte's Spanish speakers were Mexican, however, and any American customers would also be expecting Mexican tacos rather than unfamiliar Salvadoran *papusas*, the thick corn pancakes stuffed with minced pork or beans and cheese. So if you open El Pulgarito's menu today you may choose from a page each of *platos typicos* from Mexico, Honduras, and El Salvador.

It takes me a while, but I gradually realize that the menu reflects what is going on among Spanish speakers in the United States. People who have grown up in separate countries with separate cultures are now coming together to form a new "Latino" community. Flavors are coming together, too—not melting into an indistinguishable new thing but instead retaining their individual savor. Or, I should say, *sabor.*

Where did Chirinos live while he built his business? A garden apartment complex. Not right here on Central Avenue, but not far away in a slightly newer area near the University of North Carolina at Charlotte. As soon as he could afford it, he moved farther out and bought a house of his own. Today Chirinos lives with his wife and two daughters, ages nine and seventeen, just east of Charlotte in the suburban town of Harrisburg—an outward journey exactly like those that earlier generations of East Side residents took as they moved from the rental housing around Louise Mill out to the single-family houses in the then-new Central Avenue subdivisions.

So if he did not live right here, why did he choose Central Avenue for his restaurant? "Central is a good business road," he says: lots of cars, lots of potential customers. Spanish speakers are thick on the ground, renting in the many duplexes and apartment communities. Charlotte's Latin American Coalition, the highly regarded nonprofit agency that helps newcomers get acclimated, recently moved its headquarters into this block. On weekends in harvest season fruit sellers set up impromptu stands where they can find bits of shade, and *paleta* vendors wheel past pushing carts filled with cool Mexican fruit popsicles.

If we stop there, it would be easy to label Central Avenue the *barrio*, the Latino district, but a short stroll around the parking lot that Henry Chirinos shares shows a much different reality. Next door to the east is Cedarland grocery and deli, which serves shoppers from the Middle East. Just beyond that you'll find a Mexican *tienda* (general store) called La Luna, and then Pho an Hoa, a Vietnamese soup parlor. Going in the other direction there is a Vietnamese grocery, Queen of Sheba Ethiopian nightclub, a competitor of Chirinos's called Pan Salvadoreno, and the newest addition, Jamile's International Cuisine, where two African refugee women cook *suqaar* stew and *anjera* griddle bread from their native Somalia. All of these food traditions share this single parking lot, within a space no longer than a baseball outfielder's long throw to home plate.

Each place functions as a cultural center for its ethnic group. Unlike the old-line Chinatown or Little Italy, Central Avenue sees very little food tourism. When I go into these spots, I see few people who look like me, a white, native-born American. Instead, these are places where physically dispersed people find each other and build community. At Jamile's, for instance, Hamsa Hashi and Jamile Sheikh seem to be always busy even when there are no customers in the dining room. "Oh, we are cooking for the Africans who cannot come here, who work at the airport and in factories," said Hamsa when I asked.[14] Indeed, there is often a taxi outside, a Somali driver taking a meal break himself then heading away with takeout for others.

"Community without propinquity is the overall trend among all new immigrants," writes cultural geographer Elizabeth Chacko in a careful study of Ethiopians in suburban Washington, D.C. "In a setting characterized by residential scattering, Ethiopians stay connected and flourish as a society through activities that bring them to centralized places."[15] First of those are usually restaurants, grocery stores, and faith centers. In Charlotte, Hamsa and Jamile worship at the new Islamic Center mosque three blocks from their restaurant, its prayer minaret sprouting from what was once a suburban ranch house. The last time I visited their restaurant, construction was going on next door. "We are making a grocery," said Jamile's husband with shy pride, "for our Somali community."

Will cultural interchange increase over time? It is already taking place in some respects, though it is hard for an outsider to see. At the Cedarland deli everyone looks "Middle Eastern" to me. But ask the men behind the cash register where they are from and they say Lebanon, Egypt, and Morocco—ethnically distinct countries separated by thousands of miles. The same process that is melding traditions to forge a "Latino" identity also seems to be happening here. And merchants from the different cultures are collaborating behind the scenes. "Out of lemons, need some kind of equipment, we can go next door, glad to help," says Chirinos of his neighbors. Will physical intermingling eventually lead to new food hybrids, maybe a *papusa* stuffed not with chopped pork but with savory chicken *suqaar*? I'd love to stick around and find out.

An effort is afoot to bridge the East Side's many cultures and forge links

with the native-born white and black Americans who—despite all the ethnic storefronts—remain the majority of residents. Nancy Plummer, born on
Central Avenue eighty years ago, and Nini Bautista, a Filipino newcomer,
came together to create Taste of the World in 2005. They wanted to call attention to their district's vitality despite the shadow of just-closed Eastland
Mall; indeed, it is rare to see more than one or two vacant stores over the
four miles of Central Avenue. Once a year Plummer, Bautista, and a team of
volunteers organize a fleet of minibuses to take visitors on East Side eating
tours. In partnership with Charlotte's citywide Crossroads Project, which
aims to integrate immigrants and longtime residents, Taste of the World
publishes a handsome guide to more than twenty East Side eateries and the
families who operate them, available both as a booklet and online.[16]

A New Urban Geography

The salad bowl suburb phenomenon extends far beyond Central Avenue.
On Saturdays and Sundays—the two busiest days for most immigrant businesses—I've taken to searching for "four-continent shopping centers," spots
where you can park once and walk to food establishments from at least
four completely different geographies.[17] Five miles east from Central Avenue, out in suburban Matthews, there's a 1970s strip plaza with a Ukrainian
deli (Europe), a Mexican bakery, and also an old-line southern restaurant
(North America), a South African butcher (Africa), and a Korean/Japanese
grocery (Asia). At least three other similarly diverse clusters exist at different
compass points around the metropolitan area. Each location includes a busy
street, underused shopping plazas, and nearby housing that is not expensive
but at the same time not run-down.

Salad bowl suburbs exist in other southern cities. In Atlanta, for example,
Buford Highway has gained fame for its miles-long mélange of strip malls
inhabited by entrepreneurs of every ethnicity.[18] The Southern Foodways
Alliance published a history of the street that pointed out how good, inexpensive housing came available as a huge General Motors assembly plant
shut down. SFA asked one of the area's Korean pioneers, Harold Shin, how
he decided to open his vast Buford Highway Farmers Market, a mega-
supermarket with departments targeting Latino, Korean, Russian, and other

immigrants. "Heavy, heavy traffic," he said simply, "warehousing, manufacturing, everything.... Busyness, you know, that dynamic, people just doing business."[19]

It is tempting, given the high visibility of particular streets such as Buford Highway or Central Avenue, to assume that what is coming into being are "international corridors." But actually immigrants are going wherever housing fits their price range. Spanish speakers live at every point of the compass in metro Atlanta, according to a geographer's survey of spots for hiring Latino day laborers.[20] Likewise with Muslims: Zabihah.com, an online resource that bills itself as "the world's largest guide to Halal restaurants and products," shows mosques in all sections of the city.[21] Out on Buford Highway, Harold Shin agrees:

> Older cities, you know Chicago, New York, maybe even LA, there's the distinct—this is the Korea Town. This is Chinatown. This is the Polish area. This is East LA. You really don't have that here. You have areas of concentration of businesses but you kind of—it's almost like somebody took a handful of your ethnic groups and just did a little shake and just [laughs] threw it down and scattered it all over the place.[22]

Having begun this essay looking at food around a single suburban intersection, we can now see the outlines of something much larger. Foodways studies helps us discern a social landscape in which what you can afford—rather than your ethnicity—defines where you can live. That's remarkable in the American South, known for so long as a hotbed of racial segregation. If you had predicted fifty years ago that the region would become an immigrant destination, few would have listened to you. That those newcomers might live intermingled in the land once marked by "white" and "colored" water fountains—such a vision would have met total disbelief.

The South's historic racial patterns and previous paucity of immigrants make the salad bowl phenomenon stand out here, but I am starting to suspect that the pattern is nationwide.[23] "Immigrants Make Paths to Suburbia, Not Cities," headlined the *New York Times* in a report on 2010 census findings. Racial and ethnic segregation seem to be on the decline, observes Brookings Institution demographer William Frey. "Nationally we are moving toward greater integration."[24] His analysis shows that racial separation declined in sixty-one of the top hundred U.S. metro areas during the decade 2000–2010. Immigrants now are just as likely to locate in suburbia as elsewhere, Frey and other Brookings researchers report, producing "a dappled map in which foreign born and native born, poor and non-poor, are scattered and intermingled across the entire metropolitan landscape."

In Columbus, Ohio, professor David Walker at Ohio Wesleyan University is working with geography students to explore how Somali, Latino, and other immigrants are bringing new life to the failing Northland Mall area.[25] In Boise, Idaho, "there are more ethnic food markets than meet the eye around town," reports James Patrick Kelly in the *Idaho Statesman*. "Many of them are tucked away in strip malls and off-the-beaten-path neighborhoods throughout the Valley."[26] Anchorage, Alaska, experiencing a "dizzying" influx of new immigrants, is no melting pot, marvels the *Anchorage Daily News*. "Instead it's a mosaic" where "immigrant owned businesses stud strip malls."[27]

Recently Southern Foodways Alliance director John T. Edge and I visited Indianapolis to see if the pattern played out there. Along Lafayette Road in the northwest suburbs we first hit pay dirt. Same unexciting strip plazas, same worn-in apartment complexes as along Central Avenue—even a failing mall, here called Lafayette Square, and empty big-box stores. "What people do not see right away is that new small businesses are moving in to fill those vacancies," says Mary Clark of the Lafayette Square Coalition. "You can eat your way around the world here. And you can learn about others while doing it."[28]

Just as in Charlotte and Atlanta, Lafayette Road is beginning to be known as an international corridor, but the salad bowl effect occurs elsewhere throughout the metro area. Immigrants have brought Russian groceries to the north side, halal Pakistani pizza to the west side, Burmese breakfast specialties to the far south suburbs—and like in Latino Charlotte, foods are beginning to intermingle. At Havana Café, proprietor Flora Shutt sells Cuban favorites that her American customers expect, along with *papusas* from her own native El Salvador plus soup from Honduras. "El Salvador is my home but here we have the food of many places," she told us. "Reinforcement for Ms. Shutt's point came by way of her own lunch," Edge observed, "a Hawaiian-style pineapple and ham pizza from a nearby Domino's."[29]

People who expect old-style ethnic enclaves often fail to grasp the new vitality. A Chinatown, that's what Indianapolis needs, Mayor Greg Ballard proposed in 2008. "I'd like Indianapolis to be looked on as a welcoming, international city. You go around the world—San Francisco or London—and Chinatowns are some of the best places."[30] The 2010 census shows that it already is welcoming and international. Immigration to the Indianapolis metro zoomed 124 percent between 2000 and 2010, topping 114,000 people.[31]

Instead of pining for a Chinatown, Drew Appleby built a website. IndyEthnicFood.com maps cuisines and introduces the faces behind the flavors. Like Taste of the World in Charlotte, it aims to connect adventurous eaters with ethnic entrepreneurs. And as in Charlotte, there's a bigger mission. Appleby and his team of volunteer explorer/writers want to "educate Indianapolis about diversity through food."[32]

Indeed, that is the value of studying foodways. Looking at who is eating what, where, and why, we get to know our neighbors and see our community and ourselves more clearly.

NOTES

1. Hector St. John de Crèvecoeur, "What Is an American?" *Letters from an American Farmer* (New York: Fox, Duffield & Company, reprint 1904), 51–56.

2. Quoted in Isaac B. Berkson, *Theories of Americanization, A Critical Study* (New York: Teachers College, Columbia University, 1920), 73.

3. Robert E. Park, Ernest W. Burgess, and Roderick D. McKenzie, eds., *The City* (Chicago: University of Chicago Press, 1925). On current opinions of the models proposed by Park, Burgess, and their Chicago colleagues, see, for instance, Wilbur Zelinsky, *Enigma of Ethnicity: Another American Dilemma* (Iowa City: University of Iowa Press, 2001).

4. McKenzie, R.D. "The Ecological Approach to the Study of the Human Community." *American Journal of Sociology* 30 (1924): 287–301.

5. FHA *Underwriters Manual*, quoted in Kenneth Jackson, *Crabgrass Frontier: The Suburbanization of the United States* (New York: Oxford University Press, 1985), 208.

6. Carl N. Degler, *Out of Our Past: The Forces That Shaped Modern America*, 3rd ed. (1959; New York: Harper Perennial, 1984), 332.

7. For more on Charlotte growth history, see Thomas Hanchett, *Sorting Out the New South City: Race, Class, and Urban Development in Charlotte, 1870s–1970s* (Chapel Hill: University of North Carolina Press, 1998); Thomas Hanchett, "Salad Bowl Suburbs: A History of Charlotte's East Side and South Boulevard Immigrant Corridors," in *Charlotte, N.C.: The Global Evolution*

of a New South City, ed. William Graves and Heather Smith (Athens: University of Georgia Press, 2010), 246–62.

8. Annemette Soresen, Karl E. Taeuber, and Leslie J. Hollingsworth, *Indexes of Racial Segregation for 109 Cities in the United States, 1940 to 1970, with Methodological Appendix* (Madison: University of Wisconsin, Institute for Research on Poverty, 1974), table 1.

9. Lois M. Quinn and John Pawasarat, "Racial Integration in Urban America: A Block Level Analysis of African American and White Housing Patterns," www.uwm.edu/Dept/ETI /integration/integration.htm. See also John Woestendeik and Ted Mellnik, "Fewer People Living in Racial Isolation, Mecklenburg More Diverse, More Integrated," *Charlotte Observer*, April 5, 2001.

10. U.S. Bureau of the Census, Census of Population and Housing: 1960 Census Tracts PHC (1)-24, Charlotte, N.C. SMSA (Washington, D.C.: U.S. Government Printing Office, 1961), 13–46; U.S. Bureau of the Census, Census of Housing: 1960 City Blocks HC (3)-293, Charlotte, N.C. SMSA (Washington, D.C.: U.S. Government Printing Office, 1961), 1–28; U.S. Bureau of the Census, Census of Population and Housing: 1970 City Blocks HC (3)-165, Charlotte, N.C. Urbanized Area SMSA (Washington, D.C.: U.S. Government Printing Office, 1971), 2–42; U.S. Bureau of the Census, Census of Population and Housing: 1980 Block Statistics PHC80 1–116, Charlotte-Gastonia, N.C. SMSA (Washington, D.C.: U.S. Government Printing Office, 1911), 30–76; U.S. Bureau of the Census, Census of Population and Housing: 1990 Block Group Statistics, Charlotte-Gastonia, N.C.; U.S. Bureau of the Census, Census of Population and Housing: 2000 Block Group Statistics, Charlotte-Gastonia, N.C. See also Elise C. Richards, "Residential Segregation in Charlotte, N.C.: Federal Policies, Urban Renewal and the Role of the North Carolina Fund" (Terry Sanford Institute of Public Policy, Duke University, 2002), 29.

11. Audrey Singer, *The Rise of New Immigrant Gateways* (Washington, D.C.: Brookings Institution, 2004), 1.

12. *1981 Charlotte (Mecklenburg County, N.C.) Directory*, vol. 1 (Richmond, Va.: Hill Directory Company, 1981), street directory section, 61.

13. Author's interview with Henry Chirinos, March 13, 2012.

14. Author interview with Hamsa Hashi and Jamile Sheikh, June 12, 2010. See also Hanchett, "Somali Food, History's in the Side Dishes," at http://www.historysouth.org/foodfromhome .html.

15. Elizabeth Chacko, "Ethiopian Ethos and the Creation of Ethiopian Places in Suburban Washington, D.C.," *Journal of Cultural Geography* (Spring/Summer 2003): 21–42.

16. http://www.charlotteeast.com/totw/.

17. On Charlotte's widely scattered ethnic eateries see, for instance, Hanchett, "World of Flavor: Be a Food Tourist in Charlotte," *Charlotte Observer*, September 13, 2011, and the "Food from Home" *Charlotte Observer* column series collected at http://www.historysouth.org/food fromhome.html.

18. Torre Olson, "A Short History of Buford Highway," *City Guide Atlanta / Buford Highway* (Southern Foodways Alliance, 2010).

19. Harold Shinn, Buford Highway Farmers Market (SFA Oral History, 2010), http://southernfoodways.org/documentary/oh/buford_hwy/harold_shinn.shtml.

20. Terry Easton, "Geographies of Hope and Despair: Atlanta's African American, Latino, and White Day Laborers," published in the online journal *SouthernSpaces.org*, December 2007. See also http://www.atlantaregional.com/about-us/public-involvement/global-atlanta-works /global-atlanta-snapshots.

21. Zabihah is just one of several food resource guides on the web that can be used to explore and map cultural geography across many cites. See also "Japanese Grocery Stores in the United States and Territories" at http://www.justhungry.com/handbook/just-hungry-handbooks /japanese-grocery-store-list and http://xuvn.com/foodofvietnam/grocer%20search.htm. Finding a specialty store for any one of these ethnicities will likely point you to a cluster of stores of many ethnicities.

22. Harold Shinn, Buford Highway Farmers Market (SFA Oral History, 2010), http://southernfoodways.org/documentary/oh/buford_hwy/harold_shinn.shtml.

23. A variety of scholars are describing ethnic suburbanization, using a variety of names. Wei Li points to concentrations of Chinese in certain California suburbs, which she calls ethnoburbs: "Ethnoburb Versus Chinatown: Two Types of Urban Ethnic Communities in Los Angeles," *Cybergeo* 10 (1998): 1–12. See also Wei Li, *Ethnoburb: The New Ethnic Community in Suburban America* (Honolulu: University of Hawaii Press, 2009). Wilbur Zelinsky discusses a pattern he calls heterolocalism in *The Enigma of Ethnicity: Another American Dilemma* (Iowa City: University of Iowa Press, 2001), 124–54. William Frey falls back on the old melting pot metaphor: "Melting Pot Suburbs," in *Redefining Urban and Suburban America: Evidence from Census 2000*, ed. Bruce Katz and Robert Lang (Washington, D.C.: Brookings Institution, 2003).

24. Sabrina Tavenise and Robert Gebeloff, "Immigrants Make Paths to Suburbia, Not Cities," *New York Times*, December 14, 2010.

25. Carrie Ghose, "Ethnic Businesses Ending Vacancies," *Business First of Columbus*, August 20, 2010.

26. James Patrick Kelly, "Ethnic Markets, Treasure Valley Locations," *Idaho Statesman*, August 28, 2006.

27. "New Faces, New City," *Anchorage Daily News*, 2006.

28. John T. Edge, "In Indianapolis, the World Comes to Eat," *New York Times*, February 22, 2011.

29. Ibid.

30. Ibid.

31. Jill H. Wilson and Audrey Singer, *Immigrants in 2010: Metropolitan America, A Decade of Change* (Washington, D.C.: Brookings Institution, 2011).

32. Quoted in Edge, "In Indianapolis."

PART 3

Spaces and Technologies

SCIENCE, TECHNOLOGY, GEOGRAPHY, and social constructions frame this section. When humanities scholars of food studies first looked to kindred disciplines for methodological inspiration, we learned from our colleagues in the fields of nutrition and family and consumer sciences. Historians such as Harvey Levenstein, Laura Shapiro, and Mary Hoffeschelle traced Progressive Era cooking school curricula. They examined the standardization of measurements, nutritional guidelines, and taste in home economics programs. And they explored the gendered and racialized expectations reflected in medical language of daintiness, pungency, and healthiness.

Such efforts helped clarify the social construction of medicine and science that resulted in recommended daily vitamin allowances, as well as various pyramids, pie charts, and other oddly shaped diagrams of healthy eating. They helped tease out the hierarchies of race, class, and gender latent in our definitions of values and demeaned foodstuffs, whether those definitions came from early epidemiology or government extension efforts. They helped us understand twentieth-century fascinations with purity, efficiency, transparency, and whiteness in both our food and our eating spaces.[1]

However, early efforts to study overarching national themes in medicine, nutrition, and social activism sometimes sacrificed the particular. Carolyn de la Peña, Katie Rawson, and Angela Jill Cooley move forward the methods learned from our more technologically and scientifically minded colleagues. They return us to clearly outlined technological rhetoric, specific places, and sharply defined (even if virtual) spaces.

In "Eating Technology at Krispy Kreme," Carolyn de la Peña studies business plans, architectural blueprints, and machinery patents to understand consumer loyalty to Krispy Kreme doughnuts. Situating the company in its Piedmont mill-town home, de la Peña broadens our view beyond the fried round of yeasted dough to encompass a midcentury faith in technology and efficiency, wrapped in a nostalgic scrim of comfort, family, and southern mornings. She explains how a processed food that advertises assembly-line standardization came to be considered an authentic southern food.

Continuing the theme of business and technology in southern food studies, Katie Rawson offers "'America's Place for Inclusion': Stories of Food, Labor, and Equality at the Waffle House." Rawson moves the investigation to cyberspace as she catalogs the relationship between physical spaces in Waffle House restaurants and the language of nostalgia employed in the virtual spaces of discussion boards and corporate websites. Rawson reinvigorates the analysis of class through the material and social geographies of restaurant layouts.

"'The Customer Is Always White': Food, Race, and Contested Eating Space in the South," by Angela Jill Cooley, demonstrates intersections of race and class in public eating spaces. Her searches of legal documents, especially court records and food and liquor licenses, appear at first glance to have little in common with the technologies and geographies employed by de la Peña and Rawson. Yet Cooley shows how the rhetorics of technology, cleanliness, purity, and sanitation illuminate underlying Jim Crow racial structures. By pairing geographical analysis with close textual readings of citations, inspections, and licenses, Cooley shows the slow incorporation of nonwhite restaurateurs into the white-black racial order of the mid-twentieth-century South.

Read together, these scholars dismantle some of the most cherished tropes of southern food. They argue that comfort can be the antithesis of handmade. They help us see that loyalty can be unmoored from direct, intimate physical interaction. They make clear how the common table can be the most racially policed location in a given city or town. They replace the shorthand of nostalgia with careful insights into the social constructions that buttress ideas of comfort, loyalty, and invitation.

NOTE

1. Harvey Levenstein, *Revolution at the Table* (Berkeley: University of California Press, 2003); Harvey Levenstein, *The Paradox of Plenty: A Social History of Eating in Modern America* (Berkeley: University of California Press, 2003); Laura Shapiro, *Perfection Salad: Women and Cooking at the Turn of the Century* (New York: Farrar, Strauss & Giroux, 1986); Mary Hoffeschelle, "'Better Homes on Better Farms': Domestic Reform in Rural Tennessee," *Frontiers: A Journal of Women's Studies* 22, no. 1 (2001): 51–73.

CHAPTER 9

Eating Technology at Krispy Kreme

CAROLYN DE LA PEÑA

These doughnuts touch people to the core of their being.
LINCOLN SPOOR, Krispy Kreme franchisee, in *Esquire*, September 1998

Eating Technology at Krispy Kreme

The social historian E. P. Thompson has argued that food should be understood not as a solid material for consumption but rather as a process within which every point offers "radiating complexities."[1] Thompson's analysis concerns the dynamics of a working-class food revolt, yet his metaphor remains useful in considering how the act of eating engages an individual with the social processes embedded in production, labor, and consumption. We can easily think of food as a taste or unit of energy dissemination; yet when we eat we also ingest, literally, the cultural practices of how food is produced. Our decision, then, to eat or not to eat is driven not by an abstracted "neutral" preference of texture, taste, or environment. It is based on our willingness to embrace particular people, practices, and places and reject others. In this essay I argue that Krispy Kreme doughnuts have radiated a particular set of cultural complexities about the place of machines in the South. By analyzing the consumer experience of Krispy Kreme from its inception in 1937 to its transsouthern turn of the 1990s, paying particular attention to the visible mechanization of Krispy Kreme stores and product, I argue that the doughnut has attained its cult status because of its environment as much as its taste.[2] Since the 1930s, Krispy Kreme has embedded intimate visual access to complex machines within its consumer experience. This has been particularly advantageous for a product native to a region that has, since the postbellum period, actively sought to realize particular industrial dreams. This essay considers three periods in Krispy Kreme's development: the company's inception and initial growth as a labor-driven "factory" between 1937 and 1958, the chain's redesign and expansion as a labor-free mechanized system between 1958 and 1973, and its reconfiguration into a retail-oriented "doughnut theater" from the late 1980s to the present. By resituating this food product in its original regional and visual context, we illuminate the important role that technological production has played in creating and sustaining its consumer appeal.

Krispy Kreme and the Promise of Southern Industry, 1937–1958

Krispy Kreme is a curious southern tradition. Unlike biscuits or black-eyed peas, doughnuts claim no lengthy lineage in the South. Doughnuts, or "fast nach kuchen," were introduced to Pennsylvania by German immigrants and, with the exception of the French beignets of New Orleans, appear to have made few inroads in the South prior to 1937.[3] In spite of the region's lack of doughnut tradition, several food practices accommodated the snack's successful transplantation. First, food is essential to southerners' sense of place, tradition, and memory.[4] Ritual events and festivals depend on food for their performance, such as the hoppin' John, collard greens, fried okra, cornbread, and stewed tomatoes that mark New Year's for many southerners. The region was therefore well suited for a food that evoked a sense of place and could be connected with significant events. Second, many southerners possess a prominent sweet tooth. According to historian John Egerton, "southerners of every class and calling have coveted sweets since the Virginia colony was in its prime."[5] This desire intensified after the commercial production of baking powder and baking soda in the 1880s, making sweets cheaper to make and purchase. For a century, baked goods have been frequent indulgences for most classes of southerners and an expected component of a hospitable southern meal. Third, the ubiquitous craft of biscuit making inclined southerners to become connoisseurs of yeast-based sweets, skilled in judging minute distinctions in ingredient ratios, oven temperature, and makers' skills. Finally, fried foods such as hush puppies—cornbread balls fried in grease—regularly appeared in southern diets, thus easing acceptance for a food item that is, primarily, a sweet, fried ball of potato and flour.[6]

The idea of Krispy Kreme began in 1933 and took four years to come to fruition in Winston-Salem, North Carolina. That was the year that eighteen-year-old Vernon Rudolph's uncle purchased a doughnut recipe from New Orleans chef Joe LeBeau. According to company lore, the younger Rudolph decided to base his business in Winston-Salem only after the uncle and nephew had a failed store in Paducah, Kentucky. Vernon drove around the South and Midwest for four years looking for another town to make a go of it—with about $200, some doughnut-making equipment, and his Pontiac. After ruling out Nashville, Atlanta, Charleston, and Peoria, Illinois, Vernon found the answer on a package of Camel cigarettes. "A town with a company producing a nationally advertised product has to be a good bet," he purportedly said before driving to Winston-Salem to open his first Krispy Kreme shop.[7]

Historians tend to focus on the northern states when telling the story of American industrialization. Mill work in Pennsylvania in the 1850s, stock-yard labor in late nineteenth-century Chicago, early twentieth-century immigrant labor in New York City—these are the stories used to detail the frenetic pace of industrial expansion in American urban centers and the social and cultural impact of industrial life on workers. Within these narratives it is easy to overlook the Piedmont area of North Carolina, where cities such as Charlotte and Winston-Salem stood among the fastest-growing cities in the South between 1880 and 1910.[8] Winston-Salem itself emerged as a model city of southern industrial progress, one of the few to live up to the halcyon dreams of southern industrial promoters after Reconstruction.

In the wake of the Civil War, many southerners saw industrialization as the solution to the region's problems.[9] A consensus appeared among capitalists, legislators, and members of the popular press: industrial development could ensure progress and decrease the region's reliance on the North as a provider of finished goods. As the *Greensboro Patriot* explained to readers in 1883, "the next census" would show that "counties living on one crop carried only to the first stage are stagnant and lifeless—the land worn out and the population gone to more congenial climes. . . . Agriculture, manufacturers, mining, and commerce must unite to make a state prosperous."[10] For many southerners, the early twentieth century was a period when, given the right set of circumstances, technology could create boomtowns across the region. All one needed to turn a rural hamlet into a profitable urban center, it seemed, were efficient machines and a bit of imagination. Furniture, cigar, cigarette, flour, iron, and steel factories were among the most common investments, their future profits touted to potential investors in expensive brochures. Most of these industrial investment schemes failed, yet even the "spectacular" failures barely eased the fever. In 1890 George Thomas, trying to justify his own reluctance to invest in a new industrial town, asked incredulously, "Do you think they can make a city out of every village in the south?"[11]

Between the Civil War and World War I, many southern cities undertook major technological projects. Large cities such as Montgomery, Alabama, led the nation in investments in electrification and transportation technology. Factories emerged in small towns and large; many resulted from civic boosters who sought to create another Birmingham, Alabama—a city that had risen from ruin in the depression-plagued 1870s to become, by 1910, the "dreamed of southern industrial city." In its vicinity, alone between 1885 and 1892, according to historian Edward Ayers, "hopeful capitalists built twenty-five blast furnaces in Alabama, many of them in remote places."[12] As a result, many southerners came to equate proximity to urbanity (and its attendant technologies) with success, current or pending; and life on the farm could appear retrograde in comparison.[13] For rural southerners such as Arthur Hudson, who recalled as a child traveling into town on "frosty" Mississippi mornings and "smell[ing] the exciting train smoke," this sense of progress and activity was embedded in their assessment of industrial sites.[14] Southern "technological exuberance" also showed up in popular press discourse, as evidenced by one Arkansas reporter's choice of metaphor to explain his town's sluggish rate of growth: "A great many business men, even in towns the size of Harrison are content with being nickel-in-the-slot machines when they might be electric motors."[15]

In 1937 Winston-Salem was one of these technological regions. Forty-five miles away lay Greensboro, a town that in the early 1880s established new factories that converted raw materials into finished goods. By the 1890s Greensboro had become the home of North Carolina Steel and Iron and its newly prosperous investors. "I do not believe there is any possibility of failure," said one citizen of Greensboro industries. "It is like reading the tales in *Arabian Nights*, fortunes are made so easily."[16] Rudolph tapped the similar optimism about opportunities in Winston-Salem. Arguably, the affiliation between Krispy Kreme and Winston-Salem accomplished several things. First, the city assured Rudolph that his business would have plenty of industrial employees and industry leaders as customers. Second, the location suggested that Krispy Kreme itself would become associated with an economically successful part of the region, a valuable asset for a man with an eye toward wholesale expansion.

The third asset was a consumer base likely to take note of his machines. When Rudolph opened his first Krispy Kreme shop downtown, he sold wholesale only. According to company records, he began marketing doughnuts to the public only after people smelled them cooking and knocked on the door. To meet demand, Rudolph installed a window in the wall through which customers not only purchased doughnuts but also saw directly into the production area. Whether Rudolph thought it was important for customers to see his doughnut machines or whether opening the window onto the production process was simply the most efficient means for direct sales remains uncertain. Nevertheless, between 1937 and 1958 Rudolph opened roughly thirty shops across twelve states in the Southeast; all were designed with windows providing easy visual access to the production floor. According to training materials, Rudolph's employees received instructions to "cut [doughnuts] directly inside the front plate glass window" in order "to attract attention."[17]

It is unclear whether Rudolph consciously set out to make his stores similar to factories.[18] At grand openings, he published flyers encouraging citizens to come for "factory tours" where they could sample doughnuts and walk through what he characterized as a "modern, wide open kitchen" (figure 12). And Rudolph and his eventual franchise owners did refer to their doughnut stores as "plants."[19] Yet Rudolph seems to have been more interested in giving customers a way to see doughnuts being made than he was in featuring his doughnut-making machines specifically. This may have been an attempt to address concerns about cleanliness, especially after the well-publicized reforms following the Pure Food and Drug Act of 1906 and following with a

The Most Modern Retail Doughnut Shop in the South

18 Delicious Varieties to Choose from!
"Made Light and Krispy the Krispy Kreme way"

★ Glazed ★ Jelly Filled ★ Cream Filled
★ Cinnamon Twists
★ Cake Doughnuts with Chocolate
★ Vanilla and Maple Icing ★ Peanuts
★ Cocoanut ★ Glazed ★ Sugared
★ Cinnamon and Other Combinations

*See them made continuously in
our Modern, Wide Open Kitchen*

ACRES OF FREE PARKING

ISPY KREME Doughnut Co.

FIGURE 12. A Krispy Kreme advertisement, circa 1950, inviting customers to see doughnuts made "continuously in our Modern, Wide Open Kitchen." Krispy Kreme Doughnut Corporation Records, circa 1937–97, #594, Box 7, Folder 7, Archives Center, National Museum of American History, Behring Center, Smithsonian Institution, Washington, D.C.

host of reforms in food and drug marketing, packaging, and labeling during the Progressive Era.[20]

Early photographs of Krispy Kreme stores suggest hybrid environments that combined technological innovation and old-fashioned craftsmanship. Customers may have been drawn with calls to see the "plants" or view the "most modern kitchen" around, but once inside the store, they saw a combination of mechanized and traditional labor: employees operated automated mixing and frying equipment alongside bakers who blended mixes, rolled dough, and cut doughnuts by hand (figure 13). By the late 1940s the main spectacle became the Ring King Junior, Rudolph's newly patented device capable of producing up to seventy-five dozen doughnuts an hour by fully automating the extruding and frying process.[21] Even this machine—as

FIGURE 13. Employees combine hand and machine labor at a Birmingham, Alabama, Krispy Kreme in 1958. Krispy Kreme Doughnut Corporation Records, circa 1937–97, #594, Box 19, Folder 2, Archives Center, National Museum of American History, Behring Center, Smithsonian Institution, Washington, D.C.

attention-drawing as its continuous frying process could be—was dwarfed by its operators, who constantly monitored the mix and ensured the removal of doughnuts from the lower baskets to the upper cooling trays. It is possible that this mixture of craft and technology appealed to customers, many of whom had begun to frequent the stores to watch the doughnut-making process. As environments, Krispy Kreme stores in this early era fit with contemporary debates that played out in the media (and on the street corner) about whether industry and modernity invited an era of progress or destroyed the nostalgic traditions of rural southern life. Robert Winston commented that the growing urban center of Durham, North Carolina, was "sucking the very life-blood from the slow, old-fashioned towns nearby."[22] With the erosion of small towns and "slow, old-fashioned" habits came the erosion of what made the South unique. Ambivalence permeated the modernization process: while boosters welcomed growth and profit, others lamented the loss of tradition and place that industry represented. As historian Edward Ayers has diagnosed, "the growing southern cities were not so much signs of urban opportunity as of rural sickness."[23] This was, after all, only a decade or so after the Agrarians, a vociferous if small group of intellectuals loosely affiliated with Vanderbilt University, had published *I'll Take My Stand*, a 1930 collective anti-industry manifesto.[24] Southern workers may have had their own reasons to feel ambivalent toward mechanization. The overproduction of cotton during the 1920s depressed cotton prices and heightened competition, economically ravaging the region. Between 1920 and 1930 the urban population of the South increased 25 percent as southerners sought opportunities away from farms and mill towns. Yet low wages, lack of job security, stretch-outs, and layoffs meant stable industrial employment was hard to come by.[25] The onset of the Great Depression worsened conditions, resulting in strikes and high unemployment that revealed the precariousness of a southern industrial economy.

Customers who frequented Rudolph's Winston-Salem store were perhaps unaware of these broader issues when they came in search of a doughnut. My assertion here is not that machine dreams or industrial volatility in some way "caused" the success of Krispy Kreme. Rather, I suggest that this dialectic produced a climate particularly well suited for the success of Krispy Kreme. LeBeau, the French chef from whom Rudolph's uncle had purchased that original recipe, had failed in New Orleans. The Rudolphs encountered similar difficulties after opening their first shop and scouting other sites. Even Alfred Levitt, the "doughnut king" who created the Automatic Doughnut machine and promoted it heavily in his New York City store, enjoyed limited success. Only in the southern belt of textile and tobacco mill towns—beginning in Winston-Salem and stretching across the region—did machine-made doughnuts generate fevered demand, suggesting something unique was at work.[26]

Circular Soldiers: Visible Machines and Synchronized Consumers, 1955–1973

Between the 1950s and the late 1960s Krispy Kreme expanded its stores within and beyond its home region. This brought significant profits, enabling Rudolph to improve his machine systems so as to craft a fully uniform doughnut. To this end he gradually eliminated hand cutting from stores in the 1950s and replaced these employees with automatic cutting machines. He also centralized machine production facilities in a separate machine shop in Winston-Salem. There, engineers created the most advanced machines for doughnut production at the time, including automatic proofing, cooking, glazing, and loading machines. Arguably, Rudolph emerged in this period as more engineer than doughnut maker: one employee remembered his boss's insistence on pursuing innovation, even at the cost of profit and efficiency. In the mid-1960s Rudolph insisted on installing a computerized batching system in store mixing departments and refused to give up on the system even when its faulty card-reading system necessitated frequent production stoppages.[27]

Customers experienced this march toward automation through a standardization of taste and an automated visual experience. The first change was slight; the second, dramatic. While the Krispy Kreme wholesale business remained a vital contributor to company profits, Rudolph increasingly saw the stores themselves as important sources of consumer desire and brand identification. With roughly thirty shops across six southeastern states and a growing base of loyal customers, he recognized the necessity of constructing stores easily identifiable from nearby interstates and products that delivered a uniform taste across disparate localities. My attention here, however, is on another motivation: that of providing customers an unobstructed view of an intensely automated production process.

Krispy Kreme's mechanized redesign took two forms in the late 1950s and 1960s. The first can be seen in the Birmingham, Alabama, store beginning in 1959. Here customers experienced a retail space similar to earlier stores; the difference was in the windows behind the cash register that looked onto a new, more automated production center. The design effectively separated retail from production. The view into the back area, however, captivated customers' attention. Over the next few years Rudolph spearheaded efforts to completely redesign store interiors with the single goal of expanding this industrial view to customers sitting or standing in the retail space.[28]

On one hand, the appeal of this design is obvious. Watching the doughnuts move across assembly lines to be dipped and glazed and eventually emerge in the retail space was simply entertaining. Rather than looking at a blank wall, the customer was able to see something happening, and to eat the result of that marvelous process for very little money. Yet the particular context of the postwar South demands a closer view—when people were watching the doughnuts in motion, what connections might they have made? What was it that made this process particularly appealing at the time? One answer can be found in the television program *Industry on Parade*. Sponsored by the National Association of Manufacturers, these 13.5-minute episodes were designed to communicate the importance of the free market, investment in business, and the symbiotic relationship between maximum machine production and a high American standard of living.[29] From 1952 through the mid-1960s, these episodes entered Americans' living rooms and classrooms with the simple message that "better living comes from machines."[30]

Although not a southern program, *IOP* appeared across the nation to generally enthusiastic reviews in most cities. Yet southern cities proved particularly receptive to the material. Commentators suggested that the series served not merely as good entertainment but also as an important educational tool. "We find this to be an excellent, informative show . . . [and] wish there were more shows like it," reported the film director of WBTV in Charlotte and Greensboro, North Carolina, to the show's producers in 1952. Norfolk, Virginia, viewers purportedly considered the shows "very interesting," wrote one station manager in his program evaluation. In Huntington, West Virginia, the programs proved popular enough that one station manager sought to "make arrangements with the schools in this area to use the film in their weekly assemblies." A manager at the public broadcasting station in Richmond, Virginia, declared *IOP* "the finest [material] of its kind offered to television stations."[31] This enthusiasm facilitated a context in which Krispy Kreme's extensive renovations were understood. At least one reporter who covered the opening of one of these new stores included a photo of doughnuts conveying behind consumers in the retail area. The caption describes them as "circular soldiers marching off to market."[32]

Within this environment, Krispy Kreme transformed its interior production view from one of homegrown mechanics to one of large-scale industrial science. According to a company brochure, the uniform redesign of all Krispy Kreme stores included "enhanced" viewing windows "to show conveyor belts moving fresh-made doughnuts past the eyes of hungry consumers."[33] Company newsletters reveal the concerted effort to improve consumer access to doughnut machines. In 1965 the Tuscaloosa, Alabama, shop installed plate-glass windows "allowing customers to see activity in the production room." In 1963 the third Nashville, Tennessee, store opened with "a back wall with windows looking into the production area." Some stores opened additional areas to consumer inspection. In the Fort Walton, Florida, store, from 1959 on, customers could observe the packaging room while purchasing doughnuts. The franchise owner believed this innovation increased business by allowing people to see "doughnuts packaged under sanitary and efficient conditions with a minimum of confusion."[34] Company architects and executives, according to internal documents, served as standard-bearers, bringing the message of visible production to the hundred stores across the South. "Possibly accent tile could be introduced to make the production area more interesting to the viewer," suggests a company executive to one store owner in 1965, as it would better "exploit the feature you have of seeing your products produced."[35]

By 1965 Krispy Kreme realized its ideal store design with the Ponce de Leon franchise in Atlanta. Archival photographs reveal a new seamlessness between the retail and production areas and a significant increase in the size and number of automated machines in use. To understand how this environment functioned as a "regime of sense" whereby consumers experienced a relationship to machines as beneficial, it is helpful to consider "seeing" Krispy Kreme in this era as a three-stage process. The exterior (much like the image of this store in Mobile, Alabama) rendered the interior transparent and fully visible from the parking lot and surrounding streetscape (figure 14). Designed to attract attention from surrounding boulevards and highways, the design presented two primary symbols to alert drivers to Krispy Kreme: a large sign emblazoned with the standard crowned "KK" and a view that passed directly through the retail space and into the mechanized production area in the back of the building. Once inside the store, customers found themselves invited to sit at a rectangular counter where an all-female, primarily white staff accepted their orders (figure 15). Taking a seat at the counter afforded a view of windows: one could look out onto the

FIGURE 14. The new Krispy Kreme store design in the early 1970s at the store on Government Street in Mobile, Alabama. Krispy Kreme Doughnut Corporation Records, circa 1937–97, #594, Box 19, Folder 2, Archives Center, National Museum of American History, Behring Center, Smithsonian Institution, Washington, D.C.

parking lots or, more likely, look behind the menu boards through the wide windows at the conveyor system carrying an endless stream of hot dough-nuts. Were one to press her nose to the glass, she could glimpse the produc-tion area itself, a 6,000-square-foot space where doughnuts whisked from machine to machine without, it seemed, the aid of human labor (figure 16).[36] One company brochure aptly described the production facility as a "modern laboratory" where the "completely automated" process had "revolutionized the industry."[37] Arguably, the uniforms of female attendants strengthened the signification of a high-tech space. Dressed in white shoes, dresses, and triangular caps, they looked more like nurses than doughnut packagers. The expansive space, hygienic environment, and sparse, "white-coated" machine attendants make "laboratory" a particularly effective descriptor. The pro-

FIGURE 15. The Ponce de Leon Avenue store in Atlanta, circa 1965. Krispy Kreme Doughnut Corporation Records, circa 1937–97, #594, Box 19, Folder 38, Archives Center, National Museum of American History, Behring Center, Smithsonian Institution, Washington, D.C.

FIGURE 16. The back production area at Atlanta's Ponce de Leon Avenue Krispy Kreme, circa 1965. Krispy Kreme Doughnut Corporation Records, circa 1937–97, #594, Box 19, Folder 38, Archives Center, National Museum of American History, Behring Center, Smithsonian Institution, Washington, D.C.

duction area appeared to be an environment where actual laboring bodies impeded rather than assisted in the production of goods. Over the next decade most Krispy Kremes were redesigned with this same three-part formula, although stores frequently differed in the size and complexity of their automated machines depending on the demand of their wholesale markets.

In this new visual world of doughnut production, very few human hands touched Krispy Kreme doughnuts. They were necessary, in fact, only in the final stages of the process, and even then they did not touch the product directly: sanitary "sticks" wielded by workers actually caught the finished doughnuts by the holes.[38] On one hand, this was not new. As Jeffrey Meikle and Joel Dinerstein have argued, the 1930s in general was a time of popular machine aesthetics that privileged the pace and sound of the machine over the presence of its human operator or creator.[39] Yet southerners had not celebrated machines in the 1930s in the same way. Southerners had a more ambivalent view, particularly in regard to questions of human labor. This may help explain why Rudolph, in spite of his engineering abilities, opted to restrict mechanization to his Ring King Junior until the mid-1950s.[40] In this context, the visual impact of the 1963 Ponce de Leon store is striking. How are we to understand southern consumers' eagerness, arguably even more so than their northern counterparts, to buy from the doughnut factory these products untouched by human hands?

One clue may be found in wartime industrial expansion, much of it fueled by federal dollars, which produced both a boom in southern factory employment and a sense of dislocation and disorder on the part of many who experienced it.[41] The South, in the words of historian David Goldfield, "transformed itself into the epitome of the urbanized, postindustrial sunbelt," but the transformation may have come too much too fast. In Mississippi alone income rose by 100 percent during the war years, yet, without the accompanying infrastructure support, even secure income failed to guarantee housing or a viable mode of transportation to or from a factory job. In 1943 a *Washington Post* reporter toured the urbanizing South and encountered cities overflowing with war workers who lacked basic services. The article was titled "Journey through Chaos." Continued government sponsorship of the military-industrial complex during the Cold War perpetuated the growing pains experienced by southerners.[42]

Krispy Kreme was the antithesis of a journey through chaos, and customers could taste it. Their testimonies from this period reveal that they inextricably linked the visual pleasure of watching doughnuts precisely and efficiently produced with the sensual pleasure of consuming those produced doughnuts. Lisa McNary recounted, from her vantage point in the early 1990s, memories induced twenty-five years prior when she first experienced Krispy Kreme. She characterized it as "the first shop I ever saw" that "mechanically showed the flipping of doughnuts into that pool of luscious icing." Wes Eisenberg of Jacksonville, Florida, recalled equally vivid memories of going to Krispy Kreme as a child and watching "the machines for the longest time" while his father, "mesmerized by the mechanics," stood nearby. Tim Boyer, in an account of visiting an "original" store in the 1990s, described what pleased him about the encounter in terms that could well have been written in the 1960s: there was, he declared, "something very special about following the doughnut's life cycle all the way to my mouth."[43]

These visceral descriptions of machines "flipping" doughnuts into a "pool" of icing, machines mesmerizing and revealing a doughnut's "life cycle," suggest that an immediacy was achieved between the machine and the consumer in these redesigned spaces. This concept is notable because the machines were behind glass, well beyond the reach of consumers; even their sound was muted. Possibly, however, this distance actually created a sense of intimacy. Watching the machines required one's attention—you had to look through the window to follow the process. Looking away meant easily losing track of a doughnut. Paying careful attention pulled consumers into the mechanized process and involved them in the creation of their doughnuts. The lack of apparent operators likely facilitated patrons' interest; they were made to feel responsible for ensuring that the doughnuts in fact reached the desired destinations of their mouths.

Good Krispy Kremes were, and are, hot Krispy Kremes. In order to procure a hot doughnut, customers in the 1960s synchronized their desires to the rhythm of machines. Krispy Kreme officials waited until the late 1980s to schedule production times to coincide with retail demand. Prior to that point, shops geared hot production toward wholesale customers, ensuring a system in which production times varied from store to store and customers remained uncertain as to the availability of hot doughnuts. Since stores eyed

wholesale markets, machines typically operated late in the evening and ir-
regularly during the day, depending on demand. Stewart Deck recalled how,
as a child, he had enjoyed what he called "the whole experience" of seeing
doughnuts made. Part of this experience was "standing in the parking lot,
waiting in the car for the hot light to come on."[44] According to former CEO
Scott Livengood, customers often waited deliberately for the production
machines to run before entering the store. Frequently the pursuit of a Krispy
Kreme necessitated looking for doughnuts at times one might not otherwise
desire them.[45]

Photographs from the Ponce de Leon store can be deceiving. If we look
on the "laboratory" as a region devoid of workers, the space appears alien-
ating and cold. Such a system seems far removed from the blended space
where hand labor and machine technique combined to produce Rudolph's
early products. Yet the complexity of Krispy Kreme's machines drew in
eyes and ears. By erasing labor and emphasizing machines, the new physical space encouraged an intimate experience of industrial production that
produced pleasure. The exchange elevated customers' importance within
the automated system and syncopated production and consumption needs
between man and machine.

Doughnut Theater: Reading the Postindustrial
Krispy Kreme, 1973–2006

In 1985 prospective Krispy Kreme employees received job training via a
pamphlet titled "The Krispy Kreme Way." "As you look into the retail area
and into the production area," explained the employee manual *Becoming a
Production Professional*, "you quickly see that windows allow our customers
to watch us make their doughnuts. Krispy Kreme is on display and you, as
the person who actually makes the doughnuts, are the star of our show."
Once employees learned to master the craft and performance of production,
the brochure explained, they were invited to "take a bow."[46]

Shortly after Vernon Rudolph died in 1973, Beatrice Foods purchased
the company. It introduced numerous changes to the product and space of
Krispy Kreme, most notably by adding soups and sandwiches to the menu
and changing the doughnut recipe. Between 1976 and 1988, Krispy Kreme

ended its forty-year period of store expansion. In 1988 several franchise owners united to buy back the company. They followed their successful bid with a strategic expansion plan intended to increase profits and resurrect brand equity. The grand scheme emerged after the new owners concluded a series of focus group discussions with loyal customers in an effort to sketch more clearly the core attraction of Krispy Kreme. The answer appeared in a set of general adjectives including "wholesome, positive, and fun family times." Each of these adjectives encompassed something the company called "the hot doughnut experience."[47]

Beginning in 1989, Krispy Kreme consciously set out to "capitalize" on this experience. The company adjusted the production times in existing stores in order to ensure that the doughnut machines ran at times of peak consumer demand. All franchise owners received instructions to "take [a] large block of time in the morning and evening and dedicate it to the retail customer and the hot doughnut experience."[48] Krispy Kreme became, in the words of corporate biographers, "a true retail company" by moving the focus from wholesale to in-store consumption. Since consumer research clearly showed that patrons visited Krispy Kreme because of the mechanized pro- duction system *and* its great-tasting doughnuts, the best strategy for the company's post-Beatrice revitalization lay in retiring production processes that befit "a wholesaler that just happened to do some retail sales."[49]

Between the late 1980s and the late 1990s Krispy Kreme expanded beyond the South, opening high-profile stores in Las Vegas, Manhattan, and Los An- geles. Each of these new retail centers was designed as a "doughnut theater." Instead of doughnuts being made behind glass walls removed from the re- tail area, doughnut production now moved into the retail space. Customers who entered "theater" stores confronted the conveyor system as they lined up to buy at the counter: it was difficult to overlook the constant stream of doughnuts flowing into the retail area, oftentimes making a wide 180-degree arc outward from the counter before heading back behind the counter to be boxed or sold directly to waiting customers. To draw customers into the theater, stores illuminated the HOT NOW light from 5:30 a.m. to 11 a.m. and 5:30 p.m. to 11 p.m. To ensure that customers realized they were part of the "show," many stores incorporated participatory elements including the distribution of paper "production" hats to children and occasional invitations to take customers "backstage" to see the machines positioned out of sight.

According to Mac McAleer, a franchisee in Texas and former member of Krispy Kreme's board of directors, promoters of the reorganization aimed to find a "multi-sensory" method of retailing so customers associated Krispy Kreme with fun times. Given the continued emphasis customers placed on the importance of the doughnut machine in their letters to the company, McAleer and Livengood decided to center the "experience" on production by moving the machines from behind the glass to a more interactive position in retail design. "One thing that we are very intentional about is making sure that the doughnut-making process is visible and that the Krispy Kreme experience is a multi-sensory experience," Livengood wrote in the company's official corporate biography in 2004. "There are certain elements of our brand that are captivating. Once in the store, we have our doughnut-making theater. We have that glass wall where you can see the entire doughnut-making process going on."[50]

This strategy has been a success in many respects. Store openings in Las Vegas and Los Angeles drew lines that stretched around the buildings as customers eagerly waited to receive "hot doughnuts now." The Manhattan store produced a literal feeding frenzy with hour-long lines and extensive press coverage that included Nora Ephron declaring in the *New Yorker* that "the sight of all those doughnuts marching solemnly to their fate makes me proud to be an American."[51] Throughout the late 1990s Krispy Kreme expansions enjoyed visible displays of consumer exuberance. And while some of this must be attributed to the company's savvy promotional techniques (which included sending dozens of free doughnuts to newspaper and television news agencies before store openings as well as to television personalities who might mention the product on the air), they also suggest that the theater appeals to Krispy Kreme buyers in the South and beyond. The theater concept has proved a successful mantra if one counts expansions as key indicators of brand health. In March 2006 the chain had expanded to 360 stores in 45 states as well as outlets in Canada and the United Kingdom.

If we assume that Krispy Kreme's success has been, to some degree, the result of a "regime of sense" in which customers experience machines in ways they find pleasurable, we can theorize that these new "theaters" may have something to tell us about the place of machines, labor, and consumer pleasure in the twenty-first century. The interior spaces of these retail environments leave little doubt that machines at Krispy Kreme have changed dramatically from the 1940s and 1960s. There is no hand labor here, not even a laboratory with scientific tenders. Employees are instructed that their primary responsibility is to help put on the show for consumers, a job description that can only be followed if their attention is not actually required to operate the machines. Customers no longer tour the Ring King Junior in the "factory" of the 1940s, or look through the small windows of the 1950s, or watch the production process from their barstool as in the 1960s. Today Krispy Kreme machines, with their curving conveyor belts, literally embrace customers, pushing out into the consumer space rather than pulling consumers into the space of production. What one sees is the final moment of conveyed consumption and the retail worker delivering the "show." And the old "serendipity" required to connect consumers with hot doughnuts has disappeared. Today, doughnuts always seem to be "hot now."

If "doughnut theater" is now how Americans want to taste their Krispy Kremes, the current place of industry in everyday life helps us understand this preference. In the postindustrial era, when the promise of factory work has proven illusory for most Americans, we may indeed desire to experience Krispy Kreme machines as something other than mirrors of the factory experience. While the nostalgic photos of old Krispy Kreme stores in the South hanging on the walls of today's stores continue to connect the store experience with mechanized labor and factory views, the production machines themselves tell a much different story. They are now scaled down, friendly, and even performative. At today's Krispy Kreme, even the machines work in customer service.

From this angle, Scott Livengood's suggestion several years ago that, for Krispy Kreme customers, experiencing the store's new retail environments is like "standing on the ocean front and watching the tide come in" warrants some analysis. The key element in producing this analogous experience, he explained, was the conveyors that offered "that same consistent, relaxing motion that is really positive to people who may or may not understand what is happening to them."[52] The description of the store as ocean and the conveyor belts as "tide com[ing] in" reflects a dramatic shift from the iconology of machines in earlier stores. In the 1930s and 1940s customers experienced directly the combination of hand and machine labor involved in doughnut production. In the 1960s a more automated environment facilitated a synchronicity between consumers and machines; the view may have been "mesmerizing," but it was a mesmerization achieved through the act of viewing the actual production process. Livengood's rhetoric suggests that technology now happens *to* rather than happens *for* consumers at Krispy Kreme. No longer participatory "laboratories" of innovation, stores of the 1990s turned production machines into another element of the interior décor.[53]

Recent evidence suggests that customers are finding something lacking at Krispy Kreme. Sales began to drop after 2000, a fact that some attributed to Krispy Kreme's rapid expansion. We might also attribute it to the "hot doughnut machine." In 2001, after three years of research, the company introduced a dramatically different doughnut production technique in several stores. Requiring only a thousand square feet to operate instead of the six thousand afforded a typical "factory store," the new machine facilitated brand expansion in urban areas or smaller suburban markets where retail space was prohibitive or customer base limited. Doughnuts could not be made in such limited space, but they could be reheated. The hot doughnut machine brings doughnuts into the store already made, often from a "commissary" or off-site factory production area not open for viewing. In the store they are placed in the machine, reheated, and then "conveyed" and glazed in front of retail customers. "I was amazed," commented one executive who experienced the system at the Charlotte store, "just amazed and proud. Every customer who came through picked up a hot doughnut, ate the doughnut, and was happy. They never noticed the piece of missing equipment, the fryer." "We've gone to great measures," he continued, "to make sure the experience is the same."[54] The decline in sales, however, suggests otherwise.

Numerous reasons could explain Krispy Kreme's recent plunge in profits. Possibly, the recent expansion of the chain translates into too many stores making it too easy to get a doughnut. In time demand may rise to meet supply. Or the decline in sales might stem from the fact that Krispy Kreme no longer delivers the same "experience" that built passionate connections to this product over its first half century. Krispy Kreme certainly understands that customers come for its machines. But in their rush to create a multi-sensory experience, they likely failed to sufficiently probe the ways in which consumers desired to see machines.

By crafting an experience that emphasizes performance over production, Krispy Kreme has departed from a formula they created without trying, one that succeeded precisely because customers wanted to know what was happening to them because of machines. What held this together, I have argued, was an echoing effect whereby Krispy Kreme functioned not only as a doughnut "factory" but also as a factory closely connected to "real" factories either in its self-conscious presentation or in its visible iconology. In the twenty-first century, discerning what a Krispy Kreme "factory" might mirror even if it tried is difficult—as difficult as defining the postmodern South. With few factory jobs and the decline of viable unions to ensure fair industrial wages for those that remain, we can no longer easily frame Krispy Kreme as one of many "industrial" processes in the landscape. Factory jobs failed to create viable "cities of every village," as southerners once hoped. And many factory towns continue, along with their inhabitants, to struggle in the wake of outsourcing and plant closures facilitated by cheaper land and cheaper labor in the global marketplace. Perhaps in this regard, people do understand what is happening to them at Krispy Kreme. Standing in the center of the retail theater, customers look into a mirror of our stepped-down industrial expectations. As with increasingly packaged "factory tours" where consumers watch premade videos of "industrial production" before being routed quickly to the gift shop, we happily celebrate machine-made products. But such happiness depends on keeping a safe distance from the actual process of production where we might ask where, by whom, and with what costs our goods are produced. Krispy Kreme once manufactured pleasure by visually embedding consumers within the signifiers of their industrial dreams. For southerners raised in a culture long haunted by a sense of inferiority to northern industrial power, the pursuit of such dreams continues to make an occasional nostalgic, if lengthy, road trip worthwhile. But the current troubles faced by Krispy Kreme suggest that, because of its attempt to appeal to a national market or simply changes within the South itself, the store has lost much of its meaning both in the chain's home region and among descendants of the southern diaspora of the twentieth century. Indeed, given fears of corporate outsourcing, the machines central to the production of Krispy Kreme doughnuts might trigger more angst than comfort. Krispy Kreme's recent decline may simply be the result of overextension or the popularity of low-carb diets. It may also be that our problem with the doughnut is actually one with the view.

NOTES

1. E. P. Thompson, "The Moral Economy of the English Crowd in the Eighteenth Century," from *Customs in Common*, reprinted in *The Essential E. P. Thompson*, ed. Dorothy Thompson (New York: New Press, 2001), 321. My thanks to Amy Bentley for bringing this essay to my attention.

2. Krispy Kreme spends roughly $100,000 a year on advertising and promotion. In 2004 it was the third strongest brand after Target and Apple. Both of these brands spend "tens of millions of dollars" on advertisements and promotions. Kirk Kazanjian and Amy Joyner, *Making Dough: The 12 Secret Ingredients of Krispy Kreme's Sweet Success* (Hoboken, N.J.: Wiley, 2004), 82.

3. The notable exception here is New Orleans beignets, doughnuts from a French tradition. A. Monroe Aurand Jr., ed., *Cooking with the Pennsylvania Dutch* (Harrisburg, Pa.: Aurand Press, 1946), 7.

4. Southerners typically connect food experiences to particular memories. "When I think of home . . . I think of food like this," commented Matalie Grant of Alabama during a "southerners" feast for ex-patriots living in Manhattan. John Egerton, *Southern Food: At Home, on the Road, in History* (New York: Knopf, 1987), 2.

5. Ibid., 28.

6. It is important to note that Rudolph's decision to give away doughnuts in the evening suggests that Krispy Kreme doughnuts were not originally intended for breakfast. This may explain why there is little evidence of resistance to the product, in spite of the fact that the southern breakfast was seen as an essential social and familial event and played an important role in the performance of patriarchy across classes into the twentieth century. For more information, see Anthony J. Stanonis, "Just Like Mammy Used to Make: Foodways in the Jim Crow South," in *Dixie Emporium: Tourism, Foodways, and Consumer Culture in the American South*, ed. Anthony J. Stanonis (Athens: University of Georgia Press, 2008), 208–33.

7. Krispy Kreme Doughnut Corporation finding aid, National Museum of American History (NMAH), 2. See also Kazanjian and Joyner, *Making Dough*, xv.

8. Edward Ayers, *The Promise of the New South: Life after Reconstruction* (New York: Oxford University Press, 1992), 322¬–24.

9. Followers of Booker T. Washington could see in industrial growth an opportunity for

blacks and whites to achieve social coexistence rather than integration. With additional training in the trades and industrial labor, blacks would find valued employment and gradually
move up the economic ladder, creating economic collaboration while protecting racial separation, a process Washington described as like "separate fingers on a hand of mutual progress."
Ibid., 55.

10. Ibid.

11. Ibid., 62. For studies of southern attitudes toward industrialization, see David Carlton,
Mill and Town in South Carolina, 1880–1920 (Baton Rouge: Louisiana State University Press,
1982); Robert Dorman, *Revolt of the Provinces: The Regionalist Movement in America, 1920–
1945* (Chapel Hill: University of North Carolina Press, 1993); Douglas Flamming, *Creating the
Modern South: Millhands and Managers in Dalton, Georgia, 1884–1984* (Chapel Hill: University of North Carolina Press, 1992); Paul Gaston, *The New South Creed: A Study in Southern
Mythmaking* (Baton Rouge: Louisiana State University Press, 1976). According to W. J. Cash,
the mission in the South of the late nineteenth century was to build "more than a thousand
mills." *The Mind of the South* (New York: Vintage Books, 1941, 1991), 192.

12. Ayers, *New South*, 59. Such sentiments were supported by the reaction of one journalist in Greenville, Alabama, who, on the arrival of streetcars in 1892, predicted that "the next
things will be electric lights, then will come factories, etc. Let the good things come." See the
Greenville Advocate (October 26, 1892), quoted in Ayers, *New South*, 72.

13. According to Ted Ownby, factory workers were "associated with consumption in the
minds of all Southerners" in the late nineteenth century because of their higher rates of dis-
posable income than rural workers and the high wages and cash payment system in factories.
Ted Ownby, *American Dreams in Mississippi: Consumers, Poverty, and Culture, 1830–1998*
(Chapel Hill: University of North Carolina Press, 1999), 85. For more information see Joe
Gray Taylor, *Eating, Drinking, and Visiting in the South: An Informal History* (Baton Rouge:
Louisiana State University Press, 1982), 107. It is important to note some contradictions in the
ways in which middle- and upper-class southerners viewed factory workers, particularly in
the nineteenth century. While factory workers may have been associated with higher wages
than agricultural laborers during this period, they were not generally afforded more respect
than those who worked outside of the factory. According to W. J. Cash, the common epithets
of "factory rats" and "lint heads," used to refer to cotton mill workers, demonstrated the "social
contempt" for industrial workers that had developed by 1900. *Mind of the South*, 201–2.

14. Arthur Palmer Hudson, "An Attala Boyhood," *Journal of Mississippi History* 4 (July
1942): 151, quoted in Ayers, *New South*, 59.

15. *Harrison Times* (March 6, 1897), quoted in Ayers, *New South*, 59. Cecelia Tichi argues
that during this era mechanical metaphors frequently described the workings of the human
body. See *Shifting Gears: Technology, Literature, and Culture in Modernist America* (Chapel
Hill: University of North Carolina Press, 1987).

16. Ayers, *New South*, 62.

17. Louise Skillman, "A Brief Outline of the History of Krispy Kreme," Krispy Kreme

Collection, series 2, box 1, folder 1, NMAH, Smithsonian. Rudolph opened his second shop in Charlotte, North Carolina, in 1938 and another in Charleston, West Virginia, in 1941; by 1946 he had incorporated the assets of other shops he converted into Krispy Kreme. By 1947 a "number" of new stores were licensed to franchisees. By 1952 Krispy Kreme expanded to Tampa, Florida. Information on store openings comes from the timeline featured in Kazanjian and Joyner, *Making Dough*, 196¬–99.

18. Customers may have been more likely to associate doughnut machines with "factories" than they would have with other similarly simple machines, given the presentation of doughnut fryers in popular culture. In the Homer Price story "The Doughnuts," Robert McCloskey has his hero do battle with an overzealous Ring King look-alike in his uncle's diner. See *Homer Price* (New York: Puffin Books, 1943), 50–68. Eddie Cantor's *Palmy Days* from 1931 is set in a doughnut factory where the machines provide the syncopation for the female dancers/operators. And the 1933–34 Chicago World's Fair featured an automatic doughnut fryer among its modern inventions.

19. Kazanjian and Joyner, *Making Dough*, 11.

20. Prospective customers likely connected the offer to "tour the factory" with better-known factory tours such as that at Heinz, where, since the late nineteenth century, members of the consuming public saw for themselves that Heinz's catsup was the product of clean young women in clean white aprons using hygienic funneling techniques. For more information see Laura Shapiro, *Perfection Salad: Women and Cooking at the Turn of the Century* (New York: Modern Library, 2001).

21. Kazanjian and Joyner, *Making Dough*, 103. Krispy Kreme did not develop the first automatic doughnut machine in the United States. Adolph Levitt built a machine in 1920 that he displayed in his Manhattan bakery window. By 1930 his success enabled him to open a large store featuring his machines at the corner of 45th and Broadway. It appears likely that Rudolph purchased a similar machine before developing his own Ring King Junior. According to Levitt's granddaughter, Levitt sold 128 of these machines—which bear a striking resemblance to the Ring King—the first year. See Sally Levitt Steinberg, *The Donut Book* (New York: Knopf, 1987), 23.

22. Quoted in Jean Bradley Anderson, *Durham County: A History of Durham County, North Carolina* (Durham, N.C.: Duke University Press, 2011), 166.

23. Ayers, *New South*, 63.

24. The Agrarians argued that southerners had, in their rush to reenter the union, cast aside entrenched southern values in what they characterized as a "rush to industrialize." Many urged that only the South's agrarian roots could preserve a tranquil, spiritually focused life able to rescue the nation from its reckless march toward industrial progress—and social disintegration. Arguably such verdicts could only be reached by individuals in positions of privilege who remained largely unaware of the difficulties of agricultural labor that had driven many to industrial jobs in the first place. For information on the Agrarians see *I'll Take My Stand: The South and the Agrarian Tradition* (1930; Baton Rouge: Louisiana State University

Press, 1970), xxv–xxvi; Paul Conkin, *The Southern Agrarians* (Knoxville: University of Tennessee Press, 1988), 57–88; Dorman, *Revolt of the Provinces*, 105–44; Grace Elizabeth Hale, *Making Whiteness: The Culture of Segregation in the South, 1890–1940* (New York: Pantheon, 1998), 138–45. For contemporary perceptions of labor conditions in the 1920s and 1930s see Cash, *Mind of the South* (257–62, 271–72, 345).

25. A privileging of rural practices on the part of certain elites lent a nostalgic patina to traditional "homespun" ways of life. At the same time, it could cast those individuals who desired the goods produced by industry as dangerous colluders. Elvis Presley's mother, Gladys Smith, was considered a rebel in rural Mississippi in the 1920s and 1930s because she spent too much free time "shopping" for pleasure. William Faulkner's and Eudora Welty's novels from this period similarly reveal the tension caused by southerners who challenged the traditional restraint of rural values through their "frivolous" purchases of modern products. Welty's *Ponder Heart*, for example, characterizes the transgressive consumption of one female character by referencing her relationship to an industrial machine: "Bonnie Dee kept the washing machine on the front porch, just like any Peacock." Ownby, *American Dreams*, 98–99, quotations of Faulkner and Welty on 147.

26. Terry Smith, *Making the Modern: Industry, Art, and Design in America* (Chicago: University of Chicago Press, 1993), 7.

27. Information on the company's automation can be found on the corporate website and in Charles Fishman, "The King of Kreme," *Fast Company* 28 (October 1999): 262.

28. It would be fruitful to research the ways in which the American Doughnut Manufacturers Association encouraged mechanization of their product after World War II. One ad produced by the association featured a serviceman in military uniform speaking with a white-collar executive while standing over an automated doughnut machine. The accompanying text, "So you want to go into the Doughnut Business," suggests that servicemen were a particular target for franchise ownership and that machines were viewed as important draws for this demographic. See Steinberg, *Donut Book*, 100. The doughnut industry also may have sought to mechanize doughnuts explicitly to change the product's reputation as an inefficient or injurious food. This appears to have been a probable impact of educational materials produced during World War II in order to improve the American diet. One poster explicitly informed workers that eating "only a cake or doughnut for lunch" was akin to "helping Hitler." See Clive McCay et al., "Eat Well to Work Well: The Lunch Box Should Carry a Hearty Meal," in *War Emergency Bulletin* 38; *Cornell Bulletin for Homemakers* 524 (1942).

29. *Industry on Parade*, episode #119, National Museum of American History Collection, Smithsonian. "In America," one segment begins, "we are likely to wake up to the music of a radio clock, arrive at work in a precision-built train or a mass-produced automobile, sit at a desk or stand at a machine in a centrally heated and air-conditioned building, come home to a delicious meal made with frozen foods, telephone friends and family anywhere in the country, enjoy an evening of television, and go to sleep in pajamas made of synthetic fabrics under an electric blanket." The series ceased production in 1960. An undated brochure on the series,

published sometime in the mid- to late 1960s, reports that "despite the fact that NAM ceased producing new programs for this series at the beginning of 1960, re-issues are still being played one of more times a week over about 250 stations in this country, as well as the foreign and military outlets." Individuals have told me they remember seeing the series during their childhoods in the mid- to late 1960s. Brochure, NAM collection, Hagley Museum and Library.

30. Children were an especially captive audience for NAM's lessons. As early as 1945 the IIC had sent, by their estimate, study materials to more than a million children in three thousand schools across the country. Titles such as "You and Industry," "What Makes Opportunity," "American Dream," and "About Machines" became school texts for a generation of young children eager to learn the ropes of postwar economic success. Brochures in the NAM collection, Hagley Museum and Library. For information on the education campaign of NAM/IIC, see Henry E. Abt, "Review of the group relations department activities and recommendations for 1945," unpublished, in "group relations review," 1944, box 844; weekly report, p. 10, National Information Committee administrative files, box 842; and untitled report on "advertising," November 8, 1942, in 1943 folder, box 843. All sources from the NAM collection, Hagley Museum and Library. "You and Machines" brochure from the NAM collection 1411, Series 16, box 221, "You and Machines" folder. For more information on the shift to "consumer" citizenship and NAM's role in this process, see Lizabeth Cohen, *A Consumer's Republic: The Politics of Mass Consumption in Postwar America* (New York: Vintage, 2003). The Industry on Parade television archive is available at the National Museum of American History, Smithsonian Institution.

31. All evaluations were written between 1950 and 1952 and can be found in Industry on Parade, box 158, series 1, NAM Collection, Hagley Museum and Library.

32. Henry Lamb, "Doughnuts Cover USA," *Forsyth Suburbanite Progress*, Krispy Kreme Collection, NMAH, B14, F5.

33. Company brochure, Krispy Kreme Collection #594, NMAH.

34. See Krispy Kreme newsletter, v. 7, n. 2 (November 1963) and v. 8, n. 5 (March 1965), NMAH.

35. "Franchise review and recommendation," 23, ca. 1965, NMAH.

36. Photographs of the Savannah, Georgia, store from 1968 offer a better look at what sorts of views were afforded to customers in the retail area. Here the retail windows look directly onto the conveyor system, with the beginning of the automated production area visible on the other side. See NMAH, B19, F44.

37. One photograph in the Krispy Kreme archive features a group of white-collar business men examining a conveyor machine at the Ponce de Leon store in 1965. Their intent expressions as they study the machine (tended by a female packer) suggests that they found the system revolutionary and worth visiting. See NMAH, B19, F38.

38. Human hands were still responsible for mixing Krispy Kreme batter—typically black hands rather than the white ones featured in visible production areas. It is unclear from company records whether the company's retail environment was segregated in the 1960s.

Newsletters and photographs suggest that very few blacks worked in the retail area (one photograph appears to feature a light-skinned female employee from the early 1960s). It is possible that race may have contributed to the decision to move mixing out of customer view in the 1960s; photographs showing "mixing" employees from the 1940s overwhelmingly feature whites, yet by the 1960s this department appears to have been predominantly black. According to historian Anthony J. Stanonis, food has long functioned for southerners as a means for conveying "messages that affirmed the racial and patriarchal status quo." "Just Like Mammy Used to Make: Foodways in the Jim Crow South," in *Dixie Emporium*, pp. 208–33. Krispy Kreme's 1960s redesign occurs squarely within the civil rights area when blacks resisted whites' long-standing separation of dining facilities on the grounds that blacks were, as Stanonis explains, lacked "cleanliness." In light of such tensions, the act of moving the mixing room out of view should be understood as an act of rendering invisible black labor. The act may have allowed customers to understand the "expertise" of doughnut production as emerging entirely from white male engineers and white female attendants rather than the cooperative process of black hand labor and white mechanized systems. Stanonis, "Just Like Mammy," 209, 210.

39. See, for example, Jeffrey L. Meikle, *Twentieth Century Limited: Industrial Design in America, 1925–1939* (Philadelphia: Temple University Press, 1979), 199, 207; Joel Dinerstein, *Swinging the Machine: Modernity, Technology, and African American Culture between the World Wars* (Amherst: University of Massachusetts Press, 2003), 141, 148.

40. Interestingly, trade show photographs reveal that well into the 1960s Krispy Kreme used their Ring King Junior fryer and not their conveyor systems when presenting at local industrial events. See, for example, photographs from trade shows in Atlanta (1951) and St. Louis (1958). In 1951 no machine was visible; by 1958 only the Ring King Junior was on display. NMAH, Krispy Kreme Collection, B23, F20.

41. Southern cities had grown by 36 percent in the 1940s, leading the nation in urban growth, much of it spurred by government investment in military centers. See David Goldfield, *Promised Land: The South since 1945* (Arlington Heights, Ill.: H. Davidson, 1987), 21–39.

42. Ibid., 8–9.

43. Letters from 11/12/96, B15, F10; 2/25/97, B6, F10; 11/12/96, B6, F13, #594, Krispy Kreme Collection, NMAH.

44. Kazanjian and Joyner, *Making Dough*, 180.

45. Scott Livengood, "Krispy Kreme Doughnuts," *Uncommon Practice*, ed. Andy Milligan and Shaun Smith (New York: FT Prentice Hall, 2002), 83.

46. "Becoming a production professional using 150 equipment," p. 3, ca. 1985, collection #594, series 2, sub 3, folder 3, box 6.

47. Scott Livengood refers to this in Kazanjian and Joyner, *Making Dough*, xvii. The customer research is discussed on 9–11.

48. Ibid., 11.

49. Ibid.

50. Ibid., 10, 12.

51. Nora Ephron, "Sugar Babies," *New Yorker* (February 1997): 31–32. See also Roy Blount Jr., "Southern Comfort," *New York Times Magazine* (September 8, 1996), 67.

52. Kazanjian and Joyner, *Making Dough*, 12.

53. Evidence suggests that the visual presentation of machines has, in fact, become more important than the use of machines to efficiently produce doughnuts. In 2004 Krispy Kreme stock plunged when reports revealed that they had miscounted expenditures as revenue. Several articles appeared documenting the company's questionable accounting practice of recording the money acquired from the purchase of production machinery by new franchisees as profit for the company as a whole. That amount, roughly $770,000 by 2004, which should have appeared as a liability against the parent corporation, was instead appearing as a gain. Interpreted one way, the machines had then become far more profitable products than even the doughnuts. By developing costly "performative" machines and insisting that all franchisees purchase that equipment from the company, Krispy Kreme guaranteed a profit each time they opened a store even before baking a single doughnut. The brand had become so caught up in the experience of its machines—or what they interpreted to be the experience of its machines—that they overextended franchises financially in order to produce a doughnut experience rather than a doughnut. Rick Brooks and Mark Maremont, "Sticky Situation: Ovens Are Cooling at Krispy Kreme as Woes Multiply," *Wall Street Journal* (September 3, 2004).

54. Quoted in Kazanjian and Joyner, *Making Dough*, 111.

CHAPTER 10

"America's Place for Inclusion"

Stories of Food, Labor, and Equality at the Waffle House

KATIE RAWSON

"Love it. Martin Luther King had a dream, and I think Waffle House was in it," declares singer-songwriter John Mayer.[1] According to Waffle House's chairman Joe Rogers Jr., in the introduction of *Inc*, Waffle House's corporate magazine, Waffle House is not simply "Good Food, Fast" or even "America's Place to Work, America's Place to Eat" but also "America's Place for Inclusion."[2] While the claims Mayer and Rogers made about the profound national position of the Waffle House may be hyperbolic and even off-putting, these statements reflect the way Waffle House fans and Waffle House Incorporated consistently present the all-night diner as a diverse and egalitarian American place.

Waffle House is a Georgia-based diner that has done more than survive into the twenty-first century; it has explosively franchised. It is an all-night diner with inexpensive food, and, as a diner instead of a fast-food restaurant, it has waiters and waitresses. The chain is popularly presented as having a southern and working-class identity, but these traits are alternately rarified, criticized, camped, and simply experienced. The company's crafted and maintained brand oscillates between recognition of its retro appeal and attempts to claim varying elements of the contemporary market (for example, in the "light corner menu" and "dollar menu," both adopted in 2010). Waffle House usually represents itself as fostering interpersonal relationships and a "local" identity that places such as McDonalds or Applebee's do not. It is a restaurant with a concerned corporate structure, a cult following, and a customer base of mixed class, age, and race.

This essay is a critical exploration of the notion of inclusion and of the ways in which different kinds of narrative are used to constitute it within a particular site. Waffle House serves as a case study to understand how and why ideals of inclusion are produced at certain sites and how this relates to the realities of these sites. This essay focuses on corporate and cultural narratives as sites of value-driven authorship, and on the impact of spatial construction as a way to understand these narratives and evaluate them in an experiential context. Particularly, it explores how these corporate and cultural narratives of inclusion deal with or elide issues of race and class.

Defining Inclusion

The notion of inclusion is central to how Waffle House sees itself. But what does Joe Rogers Jr. actually mean when he says that Waffle House is "America's Place for Inclusion"? Before seeking to examine how inclusion is put to work in narratives about Waffle House, I want to clarify the concept of inclusion itself. In her introduction to *Inc*, Waffle House editor Julie London inversely (and vaguely) defines the term, saying, "Diversity is about inclusion and respect."[3] Though not especially insightful, this sentence provides a foundation to begin thinking about inclusion. First, London situates the notion of inclusion within social structures: differentiated people and the way they interact are the focus of her letter as well as the focus of the magazine. Second, she brings into play two important concepts: diversity and respect.

Working out from the suggestions Waffle House Inc. makes relating diversity, respect, and inclusion, this essay draws on political theorist Iris Marion Young's ideas of inclusion. In *Inclusion and Democracy*, Young posits that inclusive democracy allows everyone involved to have an influential voice. Maintaining the importance of difference, she calls for an open forum where various people with various positions and rhetorical styles could be heard.[4] Like London's assertion, Young's definition of inclusion requires people to recognize diversity and then respectfully communicate without effacing difference. Her definition, designed for political forums, can be used as a critical tool to examine the commercial and social space of a Waffle House by finding the correlative for constituencies and for voice. In Young's terms, who would need to be included to make Waffle House "America's Place for Inclusion"? Workers, customers (or people who desire to be customers), and corporate personnel—and depending on the situation, it may also include members of communities near Waffle Houses. And what does Waffle House have to say? As a place that serves meals, Waffle House employs mouths for more than just speaking. The access would need to be physical as well as social or political. Issues of inclusion would address who can enter a Waffle House and who can eat or work there. An inclusive Waffle House would be physically accessible. It would also be respectful to the persons who enter. For a Waffle House to be fully inclusive, the waiters would not only have to serve all customers; the customers must also be accepting of the waiters. As "America's Place for Inclusion," Waffle House would be a space where a variety of discourses are acceptable. However, one need not embody the ideal to talk about it or think toward it.[5]

This essay examines two major bodies of work: corporate narratives and cultural narratives. Narratives, in this essay, are defined as the stories that are circulated about a site, and narratives of inclusion are stories that address the realities or fantasies of diverse people having access and meaningful interaction. These stories simultaneously reflect experience and demonstrate the desires of the tellers, and, in turn, they influence the decisions of customers, the general public, and the company. This essay, then, analyzes how these groups talk or think toward inclusion and then discusses how these corporate and cultural narratives intersect and what this talk may omit or obscure.

The corporate narratives are significant because they form and influence company discourse and decisions, both of which affect customer and worker interests as well as experiences of inclusion. Corporate narratives also respond to a broad range of cultural pressures, particularly ones that relate to profitability. In the case of Waffle House, the corporate narratives are the backbone of a strategy of intense and closely governed branding. This essay attempts to discern what shapes these stories, how they affect realities, and especially how they maneuver tense issues such as race and class—recurring concerns both in American discussions of inclusion and in the identity of Waffle House.

To analyze these narratives, this essay relies heavily on the corporate-produced media—Waffle House Inc.'s website, magazine, museum, menus, and publicity materials—in conjunction with articles from other sources.

Waffle House Inc. materials reflect branding practices and investment in company image. Rhetorical analysis of these materials, particularly in comparison with external sources, reveals what they are protecting: the concepts they value and the threats to their corporate image.

While corporate narratives can help us understand the conditions and decisions of an atmosphere and presentation of inclusion, cultural narratives give us access to experience. Understanding how the public sees and interprets Waffle House is at the center of seeing why and how certain narratives of inclusion develop. Waffle House narratives emerge in a wide array of media forms (films, newspaper and magazine articles, television news spots, albums and music videos), telling stories that shape Waffle House's public image. This essay focuses on a grassroots form of storytelling: the Internet communities that emerged around Waffle House in the 2000s.[6]

The Internet provides a great deal of access to public materials about private experiences. Of course, direct observation and reading online postings are far different tasks. Understanding online communities involves being attentive to both who is posting and who is governing a site. What are these spaces, and how do they affect what stories are being told? Can they be places of insight as much as limitation? Online social resources provide participatory access to public discourse about a corporate entity.[7]

In these online narratives, I examine what stories are told, how they are told, who the key characters of these stories are and how they interact, and who is doing the telling, in order to better understand how people who participate in (and even love) Waffle House discourse engage with ideas of inclusion. I have limited my examination to narratives of inclusion, as opposed to narratives of exclusion. It is also significant that online work is a constantly changing terrain. What is at one time a central site for a particular movement may not exist several years later. A corporate entity may have a complete transformation, as Waffle House did in its 2010 website redesign, which shifted the site from a focus on workers to a focus on customers. Currently, the site provides tools not only to deal with the shifts but also to be able to view them more clearly, such as the Way Back Machine, an online archive that provides access to previous iterations of the Waffle House website as well as sites that no longer exist (the Waffle House Shrine).

Waffle House, a Diner

When Joe Rogers Sr. and Tom Forkner opened Waffle House in 1955 in Avondale Estates, Georgia, a white suburban Atlanta neighborhood, it was part of a rising and shifting postwar diner culture in America.[8] Diners began as places where factory workers went to eat after work or during breaks and moved fairly quickly to include roadside establishments where men who worked on the road—truckers, traveling salesmen—could get a hot meal. However, in the 1940s and 1950s, changes in labor and consumer culture, particularly the upsurge of families dining out, changed diner culture. In order to gain women customers, restaurateurs made the buildings more inviting, added booths, and began using female waitresses as the main workforce. The industry, made up primarily of independent owners, worked to "broaden their constituency, making inroads into the largely untapped market of businessmen, high school kids, young couples, and middle-income families." Simultaneously, diners transformed from solidly working-class restaurants to middle- and working-class establishments.[9]

Historian Andrew Hurley argues that the cross-class work of diners "paved the way for the triumph of national chains," forming "the transition from a localized, socially fragmented culture of consumption to a more homogenized mass culture dominated by national and multinational corporations."[10] However, he says diners, as a restaurant form, could not get away from their blue-collar past; they maintained cross-class anxiety and generally faded into the background. In fact, Waffle House did not disappear in the rise of franchises but became one of them (opening their second restaurant in 1957) while keeping its identity as a diner.[11] Yet Waffle House does continue to deal with "a working-class heritage."[12]

As a national chain that still works on the formula of a diner, Waffle House tends to have cross-genre and cross-class anxiety. Waffle House's reputation for personal attachments stems from its diner aspects such as its open floor plan and its continuous hours, but these features are also what makes it different and why it is often classed below a family restaurant chain. Yet with its ceramic plates and waitresses, it is not a fast-food restaurant, either. A chain diner, Waffle House thwarts the diner/chain distinction cultural historian Joseph T. Manzo makes in his observation that "there may still be a diner on down the road for the [person] who cannot find or does not want to find a pair of golden arches."[13] As a diner, Waffle House invokes the appeal of earlier diners to factory workers, teenagers, and middle-class women, and at the same time it invokes some of the nostalgia of the concept of a diner as a historic place—a consumer icon of the 1950s—and of notions of inclusive class mobility.

The current demographics of Waffle House, with working-class adults and middle-class youth dominating the customer base, reflect cross-class inclusion, but these demographics also suggest that the diner did not maintain its hold as a middle-class eatery. Instead, more than 1,500 yellow and black Waffle House signs dot the landscape, as far west as Arizona and as far north as Illinois, making these restaurants seem simultaneously retro, working class, and inclusive.

Corporate Narratives

In 2007 Waffle House Incorporated launched *Inc* magazine. The title, according to editor Julie London, stands not for "incorporated" but for "inclusion."[14] Perhaps the most interesting aspect of *Inc* is that it is an in-house magazine. It is not presenting an image of diversity for the public (in fact, attaining copies of the publication can be quite difficult). The pages of *Inc* are filled with descriptions of Waffle House community initiatives (ranging from sponsoring a hip-hop film festival to working with an international volunteer program) as well as biographical articles and interviews with employees who worked their way into management. The publication is one element in an array of media produced by the company to craft and promote narratives that demonstrate and praise corporate diversity and success. It is accompanied by glossy articles on NFL stars turned Waffle House management, tour guides' stories of coveted and claimed manager's jackets at the Waffle House Museum, and photographs of smiling, interracial work forces on the Waffle House website.

Waffle House Inc. is vocal about the company's ownership and management structure, which in theory promotes meritocracy and inclusion. On every Waffle House menu, wall, and advertisement is the company's slogan: "America's Place to Work, America's Place to Eat." The phrase tells a different story than Burger King's "Have it your way" by linguistically putting workers first. In addition to promoting the company's program of benefits (health insurance and paid leave), Waffle House focuses on two aspects of its corporate system: stock in the company and an in-house management recruitment program.[15]

Waffle House is privately held, so only company employees may become stockholders. This allows employees at any level to have a stake in—and earn a profit from—the company beyond their waged job, thereby including workers in a larger financial framework. As a company, the incentive to have invested workers is earnings driven: corporations with employee-owned stock plans are statistically more profitable and receive tax benefits.[16] As a worker, particularly a low-wage hourly worker, the opportunity to invest is rare, and the returns are usually beneficial.[17]

Waffle House's in-house management creation system, which allows both hourly workers and managers to climb into higher positions, is also framed as a system of employee and diversity investment. Within the corporate structure, the Waffle House Inc. operations managers must begin as managers of individual stores. While this means Waffle House management is familiar with different aspects of the business and breeds a sense of brand loyalty, it also promotes the notion that people within the company work their way up and that the system is open for those who serve. According to company representative Ann Parker, this in-house promotion formula has helped Waffle House build a management system that "includes men and women of various cultures, races, educational backgrounds and ages," although a more comprehensive statistical study would be necessary to prove this assessment.[18]

Touting worker stock programs and the successes of an internal management system, Waffle House Inc. frames itself as a place where employees are offered equal opportunity and access to decision making; however, in an ideally inclusive setting, *all* employees' voices and concerns would need to be heard and deliberated on. The Waffle House corporate system allows some opportunity, while at times overlooking other problems of labor conditions. For example, a series of workers' rights lawsuits concerning disability and medical benefits have been filed against the company. In 1998 Northlake Regional Medical Center sued the Waffle House System Employee Benefit Plan over nonpayment for employee care. Northlake won the suit.[19] In 2000 the Equal Employment Opportunity Commission (EEOC) sued Waffle House Inc. because a worker was fired after having a seizure. The termination was in violation of the Americans with Disabilities Act, and Waffle House lost the suit.[20] In both of these instances, Waffle House, attempting to act in its own financial favor, denied rights to workers. While these cases do not negate other systematic elements of inclusion within the company, these counterexamples show how corporate narratives can sidestep the realities of unequal access and experience.

Most of the company materials—from internal publications to publicity pieces to the restaurant menus and décor—present workers as a feel-good center of the enterprise. In these stories workers are "valued and appreciated," and they are usually represented as empowered and able to move up in power, position, and income. While some employees have moved through the ranks of Waffle House, their stories can belie the difficulty of many workers' lives. However, in a 2004 interview, founder Joe Rogers Sr. said, "Most of our waitresses have hard lives. . . . A lot of them have a bunch of kids at home and maybe their husbands don't have good jobs. We can't solve all their problems, but we can listen to them."[21] He does not elaborate about what this listening means, whether it is an informal counselor position (like many popular representations of Waffle House waitresses) or part of a larger company governance structure that listens to the voices of workers. The statement also does not address the low wages that Waffle House waitresses make and the ways those low wages may add to difficult lives, nor does it address the role of childcare in the lives of Waffle House workers beyond acknowledging that they may have children. However, Rogers's statement does recognize the humanity of waitresses, including negative aspects of their experiences, and defines them outside of their roles as servers.

Cultural Narratives

For a decade, Waffle House experiences were chronicled in first-person posts on a website called Waffle House Shrine, begun in 1999 by then-student Kamran Sajadi.[22] Until its closure around 2009, Sajadi posted the Waffle House–centric writings of customers and fans, artists, and occasionally workers. In 2010, when Waffle House redesigned its website, it added a "Regulars" section that echoes Sajadi's work; however, it does not include workers' voices, and since it is maintained by the corporation, it does not have the same feel (or sometimes strangeness) that the Waffle House Shrine did.[23]

The Shrine is, as the name implies, a place for fans and therefore does not include the large body of anti–Waffle House material circulating on the Internet and in the cultural ether. However, because the narratives are overwhelmingly ones of inclusion, the site is a rich source for understanding how and why those narratives are constructed. The array of voices and positions on the site thwarts any notion of a cohesive Waffle House narrative. The posts, which overwhelmingly focus on worker-customer interaction, vacillate between romanticizing workers and creating space for a complex and inclusive democratic discourse, reflecting what Sajadi says of Waffle House itself: "it's just America at it's [sic] purest."[24]

Most of the posts are undated, and many are unsigned. The site itself is simple; drawing on Waffle House's motifs, it has black script on a yellow background. The site is almost exclusively text, with one photograph of a night-lit Waffle House at the top of the page. The Shrine is as much a product of late twentieth-century, user-generated online content as it is a representation of Waffle House. Still, it is rich with individual voices and discursive nuance in a way that differs from "official" cultural productions such as films or articles and even single-user-generated content after a decade of blogging experience.

Workers are often at the center of stories about Waffle House, but the narratives cut in two directions. The first, in which the waitress is reified as friend and counselor, builds on the narrative of inclusion but often ignores the realities of customers' and waiters' positions. The second, where the Waffle House waiter is denigrated, often through humor, is particularly related to class, illuminating how the narratives of inclusion are derailed by classist beliefs. The narrative of the transcendent customer-waitress relationship is the most common post type on the Waffle House Shrine (even more common than celebrations of the food itself). Analyzing two examples, from Joyce and from Mike, will demonstrate some of the ideals, nuances, and complications of crafting stories of meaningful interaction, particularly between working-class employees and middle-class customers. In 2007 Joyce wrote:

> I love Waffle house. Always have. They are so friendly. Here is my story. My husband and I were trapped in New Orleans for Katrina. . . . I am a nurse, he is a paramedic. After days of working nonstop in a city hospital we were finally flown over the flood to a bus and evacuated to Lafayette, where we got off at 4 a.m. filthy, sweaty and tired, dragging what was left of our belongings with us.
>
> We saw Waffle House and went in to use their bathroom to sponge off and have a hot meal. The waitress saw us, and asked if we'd been evacuated. We told her our story. With tears in her eyes, as she served our meal, she told us of losing her own home and job there . . . that she was working temporarily after being evacuated herself . . . and paid for our meals!
>
> Our hearts were so touched by that after the ordeal in the city . . . that this Waffle House employee who had also lost so much would do that for us . . . that of course we cried.
>
> It has been two years since the storm, but the memory of that waitress still brings tears to our eyes.
>
> And yes, it was wonderful to see a familiar site open in the middle of the night where we could have a meal and try to figure out how to get to our son's house. That sign brings good memories to us both.

This scene, while it may seem melodramatic, traffics in several Waffle House Shrine tropes of inclusion. The author notes the familiarity of the chain, the middle-of-night refuge, and the ways that those experiences become associated with the brand through its sign. More significant, though, is the waitress, who is presented as selfless despite being in upheaval and need herself. This narrative is clearly of a particular moment, not only in a Waffle House, but of the post-Katrina Gulf region; however, it presents the frequently stated sentiment of Waffle House waitresses as people invested in those who come into the restaurant in ways that extend beyond food service.

An example of a more common (and in some ways more problematic) narrative is from Mike of Miami, Florida. He says:

> Just ate with wife and kids at Waffle House just outside Atlanta GA. I think store #638, at any rate I loved the chef's visor hat which was red and had Waffle House spelled out and Grill Master on the brim. I asked her if I could buy a

hat like that, she said no way you have to earn this hat after 18 years of working there. WOW that's a lot of eggs and waffles I thought. Then I saw a black visor with WH on the front and a black plastic brim. This hat was really cool too. Just think, a new cult of WH hats for all types of people to wear. You know a cool club, young, rich, poor, old, whatever an elite club. So I asked if that one was available to buy and she said no. About two minutes later another waitress came out and gave me her hat. WOW a cool WH hat. I then realized it was used and had waffle batter on the brim and in on the inside head band was crusty old hair gel. I was too proud to give it back so I have washed it and now wear it well to our yacht club. People have loved the story of the hat. LETS GET WH CORPORATE TO SELL THIS [SIC] HATS.

Several interesting moves occur in this story. First, the speaker discusses how the Waffle House hats could be used to create "a cool club, young, rich, poor, old, whatever an elite club." This statement is strange because it includes categories of the nonelite into what is posited as an elite club. The exclusive nature of the club comes not from social position but from the choice to identify with Waffle House. Moreover, it comes from buying: convincing the company to sell hats the employees currently wear. The narrative is also an inconsistent invocation of class. The Waffle House workers are admired for their hats, their work, and their kindness, but at the same time the story includes this honest moment of a gap between himself and the worker, where her work and her body becomes physically manifest. A waitress gives him a hat, and his response is "WOW a cool WH hat"—until he is confronted with waffle batter and "crusty old hair gel." The next three sentences reinforce all of Mike's conflicting narrative constructions. He is "too proud" to give the hat back. Does this mean he thinks getting the hat is an accomplishment? that he does not want to seem ungrateful? that he does not want to insult the waitress's pride? The emotion is quite ambiguous, but the action is concrete: he washes the hat, removing the labor and body of the waitress, but he keeps the hat and story, which are shown off at "the yacht club," an actual social elite club that distances him significantly from his waitress. Is his post a narrative of kindness and gratitude, about a human interaction, or is it about the dehumanization of a waitress through claiming the bounty of her hat? The contrast of the last two lines highlights the confusion between personal interaction and commercial enterprise. While the story is central to his hat, he believes Waffle House should sell them to the public. Does this imply that his story is, in a sense, the story of Waffle House and thus can be commoditized as well? I do not want to discount the genuine relationships that can and have been created in Waffle Houses. I do, however, think this story illuminates how the belief in customer-waiter friendship can elide the reality of systemic labor inequalities in these situations.

While the Waffle House Shrine also gives voice to workers, several of whom talk about the importance of tipping and the low pay scale of being a Waffle House employee, it also includes the recurring construction of workers who seem to fall into customers' fantasies of service. In these testimonies, the writers' experiences and understandings, presented through their narratives, are not false. However, in returning repeatedly to the image of waitress as counselor or mother, they may ignore the material conditions of many Waffle House workers and deny the inherent inequality of their positions.[25]

Shifting Social Narratives

While class is a central category for thinking about discourses of inclusion and exclusion surrounding Waffle House, nostalgia for classless or cross-class 1950s diner culture can gloss over the racial exclusion inherent in these dining establishments.[26] This is especially true in the context of the American South. Focusing on the racial integration of Waffle House during the 1960s, we can see how representations both conflict and shift with the realities and expectations of society.

While Waffle House presents itself as American ("America's Place to Work, America's Place to Eat," "America's Place for Inclusion"), it also presents itself as southern.[27] Its distinct building and bright yellow and black sign is part of American southern iconography: on Hootie and the Blowfish's album *Scattered, Smothered, Covered* and in rap group 112's video "It's Over Now," in *Tin Cup* and *Crossroads*. In articles and on websites, it is defined as "Southern as sweet tea" and placed at the top of "Things Southern."[28]

As Leigh Anne Duck argues in *The Nation's Region*, cultural narratives about the American South simultaneously act to create the South as other and to create the South as a microcosm of the United States.[29] Because of the history of racial exclusion in southern restaurants, and the national narrative of racism as a southern problem (the structure of national-regional imaginaries), people are more likely to assess southern eateries in terms of race relations, which may account, in part, for Waffle House Inc.'s use of racially inclusive narratives.

Pop star John Mayer's statement that "Martin Luther King had a dream, and I think Waffle House was in it" seems to be a shortcut to say that Waffle House is racially diverse.[30] If we return to Dr. King's speech (which I imagine Mayer did not), perhaps the most salient statement of this dream is:

> I have a dream that one day on the red hills of Georgia, the sons of former slaves and the sons of former slave owners will be able to sit down together at the table of brotherhood.[31]

In this dream of racial inclusion, where does Waffle House stand? In "the red hills of Georgia," two stories are told about the integration of Waffle House, which somewhat but not completely coincide. A 2004 *Atlanta Journal-Constitution* article about Rogers, the cofounder of Waffle House, says,

> All were welcome at Waffle House, even during the years of racial conflict over integration. In 1961, Rogers said, there were sit-in demonstrations at whites-only restaurants. At that point, no black person had asked to be seated at a Waffle House, he said. When demonstrators approached the Waffle House at Peachtree and 10th Street in Atlanta, Rogers defused the protest by inviting everyone inside who wished to eat.[32]

This statement comes forty years after another newspaper, the *Atlanta Daily World*, reported a different story on the same subject. The January 16, 1964, article reads,

> a demonstration at a restaurant Thursday evening resulted in [12 people] being served. The sit-in demonstration took place at the Waffle House at 972 Peachtree St. NW. The demonstrators sat without service for about an hour before the manager, Randolph Chavers, entered his restaurant and told his head waiter to serve the young people.
>
> Up until this time the head waiter stated that the establishment was closed and he wasn't serving anyone. He said he was sending for the manager who would have to make a decision. . . . When asked if it was policy to serve every-

one, the manager replied, "as long as they come in orderly and not cause any disturbance, they will be served."[33]

Though both of these incidents could have occurred, the 1964 article is likely more accurate, for a few reasons. First, it does not have forty years of history, powerful social change, and shifting memory between the incident and the telling. Second, the 1964 story is not from a party who is invested in having a particular story of integration told. (In fact, the *Atlanta Daily World* was criticized for not supporting restaurant sit-ins.[34]) Third, the 1964 article tells a fairly complicated story of integration.

The twelve protesters sat without service, which is consistent with many sit-ins; however, instead of serving some people and not serving others, the head waiter refused all service and closed the restaurant until he received word from management. The manager affirmed that the restaurant was open to orderly customers regardless of race (which of course does allow for some exclusion, but fulfills the mission of the protest).

More significant is why the cofounder of Waffle House tells the story he tells in 2004. While it is easy to conclude that Rogers wants to present Waffle House as an integrationist instead of segregationist space, the changes in the story are more complex. Rogers is at the center of the 2004 story. In the 1964 article the manager who invited everyone to eat is Randolph Chavers, but Rogers puts himself on the scene. The head waiter and the protestors are, to some extent, excluded from the 2004 retelling. The head waiter (and the acting manager, and really all labor) disappears and is replaced by the corporate boss. The protestors, meanwhile, are kept outside until invited in as customers. In the 1964 telling, the protest takes place and momentarily takes over Waffle House. In the 2004 refiguring, the cofounder keeps conflict at bay, safely outside his establishment and outside his representation of this historical interaction.

These stories have the same general outcome: when asked, all people would be served. However, refiguring the placement and players in the incident (not to mention the three-year gap between 1961 and 1964) shifts the power of this incident dramatically. It removes the struggle and waiting from the Civil Rights protest, the local variation in the struggle (the waiter deciding to close entirely), and the lower-level labor and management, replacing them with the ownership. It places Waffle House squarely on the side of social progress, instead of addressing the contentious negotiations of public space in Atlanta restaurants in the 1960s. Developing from the theory that social and individual memory is formed around contemporary needs, we can look at how Waffle House's current relationship to charges of discrimination provides some impetus for positively repositioning its relationship to integration. This is not to say that Rogers's story is a deliberate fabrication; rather, it offers a response to changing social contexts (i.e., attitudes toward integration and race in America).

These changing contexts are even more significant for Waffle House in the early twenty-first century: since the 1990s Waffle House has had more than twenty cases of racial discrimination filed against the company. The majority of these cases involve white employees refusing to serve or harassing minority customers. In several of the trials, the defendants were found not guilty; in others, Waffle House Inc. settled with the plaintiffs.[35] These charges and trials set the stage for Waffle House to actively develop a corporate image of racial equality and inclusion, which includes making the right choices concerning civil rights. The 2004 integrationist story is reiterated by a second story told by and about Waffle House: when Dr. King was assassinated and other businesses closed their doors for fear of riots, Waffle House left theirs open.[36]

From sit-ins to staying open, these narratives of racial inclusion are structured around how space functions, especially in terms of access—who can be in a particular place. The next section further considers ideas and experiences of inclusion by analyzing how restaurant space is structured and used.

Open Doors

A popular claim about Waffle House, which the company itself encourages, is that these always-open restaurants do not have locks.[37] At least fourteen posts at the Waffle House Shrine weigh in on the issue. While Waffle Houses are open 24 hours a day, 365 days a year, they do indeed have locks. The story, though, taps into the concept of constant access and the illusion of safety. A place where people do not lock the doors does not just mean customers can come in anytime; it also implies people are trusted. These stories, then, present Waffle House as a refuge. The corporate 365/24 operating decision that leads to the myth of lockless doors also affects the narrative and reality of Waffle House spaces. Because it is open late and does not serve alcohol, it can become a haven for a wider group of people. Diners, strip clubs, dance clubs, and bars are the key late-night venues: these places primarily target a specific age demographic (and are highly gendered spaces). Waffle House is a place where people go at night for a variety of reasons, from college students (pulling all-nighters or post-partying) and late-shift workers to evacuees and weary travelers.[38]

The night hours shift social frameworks within the restaurant. Sociologist Murray Melbin compares late-night experience to a geographical frontier, positing that late at night, interaction changes, creating a space with fewer social constraints, more lawlessness and violence, but also more frequent positive social interaction.[39] The lower population density of late-night hours disrupts hierarchies, giving marginalized people more freedom with fewer people present to enforce both organizational rules and social norms. Putting more power into individuals' hands, with less of a guarantee of authoritative involvement, leads to several outcomes. First, it widens acceptable patterns of behavior. Second, because there are fewer people, individuals are more likely to engage in human interaction—to converse with a stranger, for example. Finally, because social pressures are changed by lower population density, people are more likely to engage in longer, less direct conversation.[40] These changes in interaction correlate to ideas of inclusion: a greater diversity is accepted, and people are more likely to interact outside of their normal sphere.

Of course, this theory of night behavior also posits higher rates of lawlessness, so that while behavioral differences can support feelings of inclusion, Waffle House also sees its share of violence and crime. The most common citation of Waffle House in newspapers is crime reports. This image is so prevalent that when WBTV, the CBS affiliate in Charlotte, North Carolina, broadcast a segment on American Idol stars eating at a local Waffle House, journalist Trent Faris begins his report saying, "Any other morning this might look like police responding to a robbery at a Waffle House."[41] The affiliation between Waffle House and crime is not surprising given that it is open twenty-four hours; the same criteria that lead to the openness and exchange of late-night hours also lead to violence. In addition, for many years Waffle House was a cash-only establishment, making it a target for robberies. This reputation of violence has been historically ignored in Waffle House corporate materials. However, in 2007 the singer Kid Rock started a violent fight in an Atlanta Waffle House, garnering a flurry of negative publicity for himself and the chain (much of it through jokes about violence and class position). Waffle House later joined with Kid Rock in a fund-raiser for an Atlanta homeless shelter: he signed autographs in the diner (instead of serving food, as he was originally scheduled to do) in an attempt to repair and reframe the association between celebrity violence and the restaurant.[42]

These realities of violence are seldom represented on fan pages such as the Waffle House Shrine. The rare posts that discuss violence and crime do so in ways that elide the disruption of positive narratives. For example, a Waffle House Shrine post says, at the Waffle House in Statesville, North Carolina, "there was a sign with a .357 Magnum circled in red with a line through it, I guess it's the international anti–domestic violence symbol." While the brief nature of these comments does not tell the reader if this reading of the sign is ironic or sincere, the comment underscores the ways that narrative gets constructed to overlook the presence of violence. A "no guns" sign inherently implies that the threat of guns, and thus the threat of violence, is present, yet the sign is presented as negating that violence. In fact, this description, with its reference to domestic violence, also transforms the sign into a marker of refuge. The tone of the posting (which is notoriously difficult to discern online) may also suggest that the writer does not engage with violence on a regular basis (illuminating the untroubled view of many of the clearly middle-class Shrine posters). The person who hung the sign may have been being funny, or may have been worried about firearms in the workplace, or both. The two references to robbery on the Waffle House Shrine work in similar ways: they are both embedded in the discussions of whether or not Waffle Houses have locks on their doors. One person states that in the event of a robbery, the staff is supposed to lock the doors until the police arrive, and thus Waffle Houses do have locks. The other says that they do not lock their doors after a robbery and upholds the myth that Waffle Houses do not have locks at all. While these statements allow for the possibility of violence, they only discuss it in terms of temporarily disrupting—or not disrupting at all—the pattern of openness.

Open Kitchens

Though the stories do not directly address the fact, perhaps the most significant aspect of the Waffle House that leads to its perception as a place of inclusion is the placement of the kitchen. According to Hurley, "the most dramatic change" in diners was creating a separate kitchen away from customers. This change was meant to appeal to diners' sense of class, of not dining at a "greasy-spoon."[43] As other diners moved their cooks into kitchens, Waffle House maintained its open griddle, leaving no separation between the front and back of the house. This lack of distinction creates an image of availability and equality, particularly breaking down barriers between customers and workers.

As kitchens moved out of the sight of diners in restaurants, so did the personal actions of servers. Anthropologist Greta Foff Paules writes, "Much as domestic servants in the nineteenth century did not dine with or in the presence of masters, so today waitresses are forbidden to take breaks, sit, smoke, eat, or drink in the presence of customers." The restrictions against functioning as a person in front of customers create distance between the server and the served and "fortify status lines."[44] In Waffle House, though, those lines are blurred, as Waffle House waiters do take breaks, sit, eat, drink, and smoke around and with customers. By removing these boundaries, the personhood of the staff is reinforced, even without direct interaction.

Of course, the dissolution of boundaries between server and customer is far from absolute and far from unproblematic. The architecture in some ways simply hides the hierarchy of the restaurant. Waiters are not dehumanized, but the power dynamics of the space of most restaurants are also disrupted. Sociologist Karla A. Erickson says that in typical American restaurants (where the kitchen and dining room are separated—not the open diner construction of Waffle House), customers are confined to the vantage point where they are seated, while servers, because they have greater access and mobility to areas of the restaurant, may "feel a sense of ownership and view the restaurant as their space."[45] Because the layout of Waffle House gives all constituencies equal visual access, workers' and customers' feelings of ownership shift. Customers can also feel as if they possess the restaurant, and workers may not experience or be perceived as having inside knowledge in the same way.

Waffle House language reflects this idea of special knowledge. On the menus, "scattered," "smothered," and "covered" are defined explicitly—the hash browns are spread out, grilled onions are added, and a slice of cheese is melted on top. While other ordering language is not printed on the menus, the open kitchen layout allows customers to listen and learn the language of the staff. The customers get to be included in a special linguistic code, a mode of belonging that blurs established modes of interaction between customers and workers.

On one level shared experience and knowledge leads to a greater sense of equality, but while this open geography does change interactions between patrons and servers, the implicit hierarchy remains. Workers spend most of their time on their feet, while customers sit. Although customers have a visual and auditory entrée to the kitchen area, they are (for the most part) still not physically allowed in the space.[46]

Trends in Corporate and Customer Narratives

If we look at these corporate and customer narratives of Waffle House, several trends emerge. First, the corporate and customer narratives frequently present Waffle House as a place that is open to all and a place where the workers are central symbolic figures. If we return to Young's notion of inclusion, we can see how these narratives may ignore some central elements of a truly inclusive space.

Especially in the American South, equal access to restaurants is a significant source of interest. Stories of lockless doors and strifeless integration feed the contemporary American desire for Dr. King's "table of brotherhood." The notion of interracial and cross-class experience—in both the customer and employee base—that we see in corporate and customer narratives reinforces the fantasy of a place that fulfills American promises and hopes for inclusion. The fact that Waffle House is also accessible by its volume of availability as a national chain mixes fantasies of capitalist growth with democratic ideals. The capitalist/inclusive fantasies are then further reified through corporate narratives of rags-to-riches managers and customer narratives about personal ties to Waffle House experiences and products.

In addition to an accessible space, Waffle House (unlike Ruby Tuesday or Applebee's, which may also have a diverse clientele) fosters the idea of relationships between workers and customers. This relationship is created not only by the design of the restaurant building but also by the corporate rhetoric, for example, putting "America's Place to Work" in the same phrase as "America's Place to Eat" or putting special ordering lingo on the menu so that everyone can say "scattered, smothered, covered." Because restaurants are places of distinct hierarchy, shifting the experience—exposing the kitchen, creating an atmosphere where back-of-the-house and front-of-the-house exchanges are shared—can appear to be an egalitarian move. Because people see and hear workers, they see themselves as less separated from labor. Waffle House Inc. materials reinforce this lack of separation by constantly representing their employees, by celebrating them publicly and declaring them central elements in the company's construction. By acknowledging labor, they appear to be more inclusive of the experience of workers.

Unfortunately, these narratives often overlook real material and structural differences. They often replace the voice or input of workers with talk *about* workers. This shift leads to the inconsistencies with worker's rights in relation to the company and a romanticization of workers that overlooks the structural economic and social differences, normalizes them in a frame of inclusion, and therefore no longer sees or acknowledges practices (such as wage disparity or working conditions) that may need change.

While based in experience, these narratives are stories about promise. They are not the only stories out there: a quick search for online references to Waffle House reveals many narratives that disparage the working class. I end this essay with one of the prevailing counternarratives of Waffle House. Comedian Bill Hicks tells the following joke in a 1989 routine:

I was in Nashville, Tennessee, last year. After the show I went to a Waffle
House. I'm not proud of it, I was hungry. And I'm alone, I'm eating, and I'm
reading a book, right?

Waitress walks over to me [*sounds of chewing gum*], "Hey, whatcha readin'
for?" Isn't that the weirdest fuckin' question you've ever heard? Not what am
I reading, but what am I reading *for*? Well, goddammit, ya stumped me! Why
do I read? Well ... hmmm ... I dunno ... I guess I read for a lot of reasons, and
the main one is so I don't end up being a fuckin' waffle waitress. Yeah, that'd be
real high on the list.

First, Hicks dispels the notion of Waffle House as a place for community: he
goes there late at night because he is hungry. Then he sets up two positions:
one where people read, and the other where they work at Waffle House.
The joke brings to the forefront class difference, but it does not do so with
constructive ends. Instead, it traffics in exclusion: the audience is expected
to laugh with Hicks because they are expected to be readers and not Waffle
House waitresses. Hicks not only refuses to romanticize the waitress; he goes
so far as to dehumanize her and in doing so creates an all-encompassing
image of the Waffle House waitress as illiterate (an unfounded claim). His
humor brings out divisions that the narratives of inclusion, perhaps para-
doxically, both hide and attempt to bridge. He continues, shifting from the
workers to the clientele:

So then this trucker in the next booth gets up, stands over me, and goes,
"Wellll ... Looks like we got ourselves a reader. ..." What the fuck's going on?
Like I walked into a Klan rally with a Boy George costume on or something.
Am I stepping out of some intellectual closet here? I read. There, I said it. I feel
better. ... Some serious humanity, man, some serious pockets of humanity out
there.[47]

The joke maintains its problematic relationship to class and throws in
stereotypes of southern regionalism. In Hicks' joke, the term "humanity"
is, in fact, dehumanizing: the idea is that one *cannot believe these people*, is
appalled by them. This exchange, with its antagonism and ultimate procla-
mation of gaping difference, is the antithesis of the inclusion narrative. It
posits that a trucker, a waitress, and a middle-class reading comedian do
not (and potentially cannot ever) engage in meaningful positive interac-

tion. While Hicks creates meaning, the creation makes distance and involves monologue, as opposed to a potential for dialogue.

While the narratives of inclusion surrounding Waffle House may not accurately reflect the practices at Waffle House or the power dynamics within those practices, they do attempt to create a space where the humanity of a diverse group of people is sincerely acknowledged. Though these narratives may hide important elements of injustice and ignorance, they are attempting to see the interactions within this twenty-four hour southern diner as real "pockets of humanity." In turn, they become interesting pockets themselves.

NOTES

1. "John Mayer on Waffle House," *Inc: A Waffle House Diversity Magazine*, October 2006, 6.

2. Julie London, "A Letter from the Editor," *Inc: A Waffle House Diversity Magazine*, October 2006, 1.

3. Ibid.

4. Iris Marion Young, *Inclusion and Democracy* (New York: Oxford University Press, 2000).

5. Ibid., 17–18.

6. The role of Facebook and Twitter in narratives about Waffle House may contribute further insights to this discussion; however, Waffle House's foray into these forms has really only emerged in the past year.

7. Looking at online communities has different constraints and openings from on-site observation. In the case of Waffle House, one gets a greater range of access to different locations; however, the conversation is limited to people with Internet access who choose to speak publicly online.

8. "The Waffle House Story," accessed April 28, 2008, http://www.wafflehouse.com/wh history.asp.

9. Andrew Hurley, "From Hash House to Family Restaurant: The Transformation of the Diner and Post–World War II Consumer Culture," *Journal of American History* 84, no. 3 (1997): 1284, 1287, 1288, 1290.

10. Ibid., 1284.

11. "The Waffle House Story."

12. Hurley, "Hash House," 1302.

13. Joseph T. Manzo, "From Pushcart to Modular Restaurant: The Diner on the Landscape," *Journal of American Culture* 13, no. 3 (1990): 21.

14. London, "Letter from the Editor," 1.

15. "Hourly Careers," Waffle House Careers, accessed April 26, 2008, http://www.whcareers .com/hour_career.asp.

16. "A Statistical Profile of Employee Ownership" and "Employee Ownership and Corporate Performance," National Center for Employee Ownership, accessed April 26, 2008, http://www .nceo.org/library/eo_stat.html.

17. "Employee Ownership and Corporate Performance."

18. Ann Parker, "What Could Be More Inclusive than Homegrown Management?" *Inc: A Waffle House Diversity Magazine*, October 2006, 10.

19. ERISA, "Benefit Claim Thwarted by Limitation in SPD Alone," ERISA *Litigation Alert*. 4.10: 1, 8–9.

20. "Equal Employment Opportunity Commission v. Waffle House, Inc.: Certiorari to the United States Court of Appeals for the Fourth Circuit," *Supreme Court Cases: The Twenty-First Century (2000–Present)*. EbscoHost.

21. Bill Osinski, "The Cornerstone of Waffle House: At 50, Chain Still Reflects Co-founder's People Skills," *Atlanta Journal-Constitution*, December 24, 2004.

22. Kamran Sajadi, Waffle House Shrine, accessed April 8, 2008, http://www.geocities .com/waffleshrine (site discontinued). When Sajadi began the page, he was a student at Duke University. It seems he is now a urologist. See Yvonne Zipp, "Southern Hospitality, 24 Hours a Day," *Christian Science Monitor*, August 13, 1999, cover story, Academic Search Complete; "Things Southern: The Waffle House," Overstated, accessed April 26, 2008, http://overstated .net/2003/08/28/things-southern-waffle-house; Kamran's student website, http://www.duke .edu/~kps1/; http://www.ohsu.edu/xd/health/services/providers/sajadi.cfm.

23. "Regulars' Page," accessed February 12, 2011. http://www.wafflehouse.com/welcome /your-house/regulars-page.

24. Waffle House Shrine.

25. It is important to note that Waffle House also draws customers from people who work low-wage jobs. The relationship between working-class customers and servers and middle-class customers and servers may be different. This element of Waffle House relationships should be explored in order to have a more complex and comprehensive analysis of narrative and realities of Waffle House. I have primarily focused on middle-class customers.

26. Hurley, "Hash House," 1308.

27. "John Mayer on Waffle House."

28. Zipp, "Southern Hospitality," and "Things Southern: The Waffle House."

29. Leigh Anne Duck, *The Nation's Region: Southern Modernism, Segregation, and U.S. Nationalism* (Athens: University of Georgia Press, 2006).

30. "John Mayer on Waffle House."

31. Martin Luther King, *I Have a Dream: Writing and Speeches that Changed the World, Special 75th Anniversary Edition* (New York: HarperOne, 1992).

32. Osinski, "Cornerstone of Waffle House."

33. "12 Are Served at Restaurant," *Atlanta Daily World*, January 16, 1964, 5. Proquest Historical Newspapers.

34. Michelle Hallsell, "Newspapers: The *Atlanta Daily World*," The Black Press: Soldiers with-

out Swords (website), PBS, accessed February 22, 2011, http://www.pbs.org/blackpress/news _bios/newbios/nwsppr/atlnta/atlnta.html.

35. "Waffle House Chain Accused of Racial Basis [*sic*]," *Atlanta Business Chronicle*, June 23, 1999; Walter Woods, "Suits Claim Waffle House Discriminated Against Black Customers," *Atlanta Business Chronicle*, September 17, 2003; "Waffle House Hit with Discrimination Suits," *Atlanta Business Chronicle*, January 18, 2005; "Northlake Foods Settles Discrimination Suits," *Atlanta Business Chronicle*, August 2, 2005.

36. Osinski, "Cornerstone of Waffle House."

37. "The Waffle House Story."

38. Waffle House Shrine.

39. Murray Melbin, "Night as Frontier," *American Sociological Review* 43, no. 1 (February 1978): 3–22.

40. Ibid., 9–13.

41. "Idols at Waffle House," accessed April 26, 2008, http://www.youtube.com/watch?v=dV _RlQVHNxw.

42. Associated Press, "Kid Rock Causes Scene at Waffle House: Entertainer Slings Hash for Homeless in Dekalb County," accessed February 12, 2011, http://www.msnbc.msn.com /id/23593629/ns/us_news-giving/.

43. Hurley, "Hash House," 1297.

44. Greta Foff Paules, *Dishing It Out: Power and Resistance among Waitresses in a New Jersey Restaurant* (Philadelphia: Temple University Press, 1991), 132–33.

45. Karla A. Erickson, "Tight Spaces and Salsa-Stained Aprons: Bodies at Work in American Restaurants," in *The Restaurants Book: Ethnographies of Where We Eat*, ed. David Beriss and David Sutton (New York: Berg, 2007), 21.

46. One phenomenon of note is that at many Waffle Houses, some patrons—regulars— have access behind the counter. Usually this involves getting their own coffee or other beverage, which still separates them from food preparation. Self-service beverages are now commonplace in fast-food restaurants and some independent family restaurants, so this practice is part of certain mores of dining out; however, being behind the counter is spatially unusual.

47. Bill Hicks, "Waffle House," video from 1989 routine, accessed April 27, 2008, http://www .youtube.com/watch?v=YcPQhS8W8g4.

CHAPTER 11

"The Customer Is Always White"

Food, Race, and Contested Eating Space in the South

ANGELA JILL COOLEY

In 1964 Ollie's Barbecue sat at the intersection of Ninth Street and Seventh Avenue South in Birmingham, Alabama. Ollie's was a white-owned restaurant that offered table seating to white-collar businessmen and white families. Barbecue, nonalcoholic beverages, and homemade pies made up the majority of the restaurant's sales. After almost forty years in business, the restaurant had been passed down through three generations of the McClung family. The current proprietors, Ollie McClung Sr. and his son, professed to run a business guided by their religious and family-oriented principles. They did not serve alcohol, they did not open on Sundays, and they placed a sign on every table that read, "No profanity please. Ladies and children are usually present. We appreciate your cooperation." On the restaurant's walls, the McClungs displayed religious verses and a picture of Barry Goldwater. The McClungs considered most of their white customers to be "regulars" and recognized them by face if not by name.

Although Ollie's Barbecue catered to a white customer base, it was located in an African American neighborhood and served black customers takeout at the end of the service counter. Until 1963 the Birmingham City Code required the racial segregation of eating places. After the city repealed this law, Ollie's still refused to seat African Americans. In fact, Ollie's continued to refuse service to African Americans in the dining room even after the U.S. Congress required restaurant desegregation. The McClungs made legal history by unsuccessfully challenging the constitutionality of the federal law in court. This action and similar suits brought by other white southern restaurateurs represented the culmination of around four years of direct action struggle to desegregate southern eating space since the Greensboro sit-ins started in February 1960.[1]

The civil rights movement exposed the contested nature of public eating space in the South as activists and white supremacists vied to have their interpretation of the appropriate use of southern space respected and accepted. Civil rights activists challenged the inferior status of African Americans in southern consumer culture as well as the representation of blacks as subservient in public spaces and images devoted to the preparation, consumption, and service of food. For their part, white supremacists identified direct action protests in eating places as a threat to the carefully constructed images of blackness as servile and inferior that white Americans had spent generations cultivating. Both sides of the highly publicized civil rights campaigns to desegregate public eating places recognized the intimate associations that existed among food, consumption, race, body, and identity. They also comprehended the necessary and pervasive nature of food and the ramifications that desegregated eating space might have for other aspects of society, both public and private.

Although the struggle for civil rights epitomized the concept of public eating places as contested space in the southern urban environment, the movement only made evident a process that had been taking place for many decades. The development of public eating spaces starting in the early twentieth century reveals an increasingly urban and mobile South attempting to accommodate more concentrated, diverse populations and an increasingly consumption-oriented culture. The leisure experience of dining out, which at one time had been limited primarily to a privileged elite feasting in carefully prescribed environments, gave way to a more motley assortment of lower-class establishments that hosted assorted crowds who ate out for necessity, convenience, or entertainment and often partook of a variety of less wholesome activities of urban indulgence. Scholars have offered little analysis of the development of southern eating places, the role such spaces played in the development of consumer culture, or the effect of such establishments on the construction of racial, class, ethnic, and gender identities. This essay is intended to uncover the genesis of civil rights conflicts in public eating places by exploring the contested nature of these consumer spaces in the early twentieth century.

Decades before the sit-ins and desegregation court cases, public eating places in southern urban areas reflected the broader cultural conflicts among middle-class white authorities and various lower-class elements, each attempting to mold public urban space to meet their own desires, needs, and anxieties. Public eating establishments, because they simultaneously represented home and quintessential urban space, played a key role in new urban identities. The public consumption of food predated the widespread consumer culture of the twentieth century. Taverns, inns, brothels, saloons, hotels, and restaurants, to name a few, existed to feed the many different appetites of nineteenth-century southerners.

But public dining spaces changed quantitatively and qualitatively in the early twentieth century. As urban areas grew, such spaces became more numerous and more public by catering to a wider range of urban personalities. The pervasive and visual nature of modern media made the existence of small stands, cafés, diners, and lunchrooms, among other types of establishments, better known by communicating location to strangers through urban directories, advertisements, signs, and other modes of identification. Public establishments lost the regulating influence of family and community mores, which engendered cultural conformity through a combination of communal values, experiences, and censure. Instead, the assortment of races, socioeconomic classes, ethnicities, and genders that gathered in southern urban areas projected their own identities into public eating places. The resulting conflict, which played out in city councils, local courts, and media as well as within the public dining spaces themselves, saw the politically and economically empowered class of white urban professionals attempt to exercise control over these places.

This essay raises many issues that are informed by traditional southern historiography as well as food studies more generally. In southern history, this study considers the construction of racial identity within a particular feature of twentieth-century consumer culture—that is, the consumption of food in the urban public environment. In this respect, this examination stems from the work of the historian Grace Elizabeth Hale, who explores how segregation culture served to define whiteness in the early twentieth century, primarily through the vehicles of racialized images and spectacle within the consumer sphere. "Segregation remained vulnerable at its muddled middle," Hale writes, "where mixed-race people moved through mixed-race spaces." She identifies the South as the space where this "muddled middle" became most perceptible.[2] This essay fashions Hale's analysis more narrowly and explores southern urban spaces where food consumption took place as a significant site within this "muddled middle" where various combinations of race, class, ethnicity, and gender challenged the ability of white southern urban authorities to define racial identity and maintain social control.

The connections between food, gender, and sexuality in public spaces are especially important for this essay. Many scholars connect foodways to gender and sexuality because all three categories interconnect with power, economics, politics, globalism, and colonialism. In her influential work *Carnal Appetites: FoodSexIdentities*, Elspeth Probyn suggests that examining the various manifestations of everyday eating, specifically "what, how, and with whom we eat," can help us reconnect with these other issues on a fundamental level.[3] Although this essay is much less theoretical than Probyn's profound analysis, it is nonetheless concerned with the relationships among food, sexuality, power, economics, and politics. Twentieth-century southerners recognized the intimate associations of both food and sexuality to the human body, to what goes into and out of the human body, and to what becomes a constituent part of individual bodies. For hegemonic white southerners, the constitution of the body that emerged as the result of both nourishment and sex related directly to constructions of whiteness and racial purity. For this reason, the white power structure often interpreted public eating places to represent gendered space, and any sexual expression considered to be inappropriate, much like inappropriate forms of nourishment, affected negotiations of power within such spaces.

Finally, a key area of scholarly literature underlying this work involves explorations of public spaces in which food is prepared, served, and consumed. Public eating places involve a broad range of establishments, from the fine-dining restaurants and private clubs offering privileged leisure experiences to the elite to the hot-dog stands providing quick, inexpensive lunches to the laboring classes. Many important social and cultural characteristics emerge and are negotiated within and around these spaces. Distinctions between the private and the public become particularly magnified in establishments where such a personal and intimate activity takes place in a public forum. Scholars are beginning to explore these public spaces as sites of cultural interaction that signify various manners of production and consumption within a particular society. David Beriss and David Sutton edited a collection called *The Restaurants Book: Ethnographies of Where We Eat*, which examines restaurants as sites of cultural power and identification within society on a global and local context.[4] This essay looks at public eating places as spaces of conflict, social control, and resistance within the twentieth-century South as newly urban populations strove to shape public space to fit their own images of amusement and respectability.

Dining Out in the Old and New South

Before the Civil War, the leisure experience of dining out tended to be limited to the planter elite. The port cities of New Orleans and Charleston, among others, boasted fine-dining establishments that offered lavish environments in which the wealthy could wine and dine on foods prepared in the French tradition. James Silk Buckingham, a British visitor to New Orleans in the 1830s, raved about the city's dining rooms. Often established in the city's fine hotels, New Orleans's dining rooms served at times hundreds of patrons, featured delicate chandeliers and columned ballrooms, and hosted the wealthiest Louisiana natives and visitors. Guests dined together at long, decorative tables that separated men and women.[5] Antebellum Richmond, too, boasted fine-dining accommodations usually named after well-known local proprietors such as Tom Griffin and Charles Thompson. These establishments offered excellent fare obtained from the local countryside. "When a gentleman entered a restaurant and ordered a piece of roast beef," Thomas Joseph Macon recalls, "he got home-killed beef, fat, tender and rich in flavor, and when he called for oysters they were set before him cooked with pure country butter, or genuine fresh hog's lard."[6] In Charleston, South Carolina, Mary Chesnut's family regarded the restaurants so highly they sent their enslaved black cook Romeo there to train.[7]

In the Gilded Age, fine dining continued to be a standard practice among the South's business and political elite. These establishments allowed the New South cadre of wealthy politicians, businessmen, and merchants to dine in the manner to which the antebellum planter class had been accustomed. Restaurants represented male bastions where fine dining, drinking, and smoking took place, and they separated women from eating space frequented by men. Ladies' cafés allowed the wives of the New South elite to participate in the consumer experience of dining out without exposure to a predominantly male environment that might subject them to activities considered inappropriate. In 1882 the fine-dining establishment Thompson's Restaurant promised "neatly furnished . . . quiet, retired [dining rooms] . . . with every home comfort" for his ladies' café in Atlanta. Thompson allowed male companions to accompany women to his café, but other establishments, such as Allen's Palace Restaurant's Ladies Dining Room and Ice Cream Saloon, insisted that it was "for ladies only." Both proprietors put these facilities under the charge of their wives.[8] Female stewardship helped assure potential patrons that these spaces would be "safe" urban venues for white women.

A myriad of activities took women of these newly urban populations into the city at mealtimes, including shopping, club work, and other activities considered to be gender appropriate for women of a higher socioeconomic station. In 1868 Atlanta restaurateur O. L. Pease and his wife solicited patronage from women desiring a respite "after fatiguing walks" or "shopping" trips. He promised a "safe and pleasant retreat" for women to "refresh . . . with oysters or any other delicacies."[9] Ladies' cafés tended to offer lighter fare considered to be appropriate for a woman's more delicate tastes. They offered pleasant amenities, such as piano playing during lunch and supper hours.[10] Most importantly, however, they offered space in which it was considered appropriate for white women to dine alone or with appropriate companions. In late nineteenth-century dining establishments, no specific guidelines regulated these spaces other than community and class cohesion. Proprietors and patrons determined what was proper and appropriate within urban dining space without infringement from public authorities.

Lower-class patrons frequented neither restaurants nor ladies' cafés. Most black and white laborers and former farmers who encountered southern cities did not possess the funds or social status to take meals among such luxury. Yet they were not precluded from taking their meals in public spaces. Many such persons lived in boardinghouses or hotels where meals were included as part of the room rate under the "American plan" of service. Others took advantage of the free lunches lavishly furnished by local saloons. For the price of a glass of beer or whiskey, patrons devoured impressive spreads for their midday repast.[11] Saloons generally allowed patrons to help themselves to buffets that started simply enough, serving "a cracker and a slice of cheap sausage." By the turn of the century, buffets reportedly offered "a first-class lunch in every respect" with hot turtle soup, roast beef, potato salad, olives, pork and beans, or barbecued pork—the same fare served at many of the city's fine restaurants.[12] Saloon keepers competed to attract customers and often used up their profits to provide the best fare.[13] Because many southern cities did not allow women to patronize bars, such spaces represented male preserves where eating, drinking, gambling, smoking, and other legal and illegal activities took place.

Dining Out in the Early Twentieth Century

The turn of the twentieth century saw a dramatic change to public dining culture. Starting around 1900, several factors coalesced, resulting in the emergence of public eating spaces that catered to a variety of clientele. First, saloon proprietors, with support from restaurateurs and temperance advocates, lobbied local legislators to end the free lunch. In June 1897 a group of Atlanta saloon keepers petitioned the city council for legislation prohibiting the practice. They resented the expense involved and the lowly status of those attracted to the buffets. The Kimball House Hotel's saloon reportedly abolished the custom and, as a result, experienced an increase in the class and behavior of their lunch patrons. Although he did not halt the practice, John P. Buckalew lamented the cost and "the lower classes of trade" free lunches attracted to his saloon called Buck's Place. Other proprietors defended the practice as an aid to digestion or charity. "The lunches attract a poorer class of trade," Ernest Naylor of the Opera Saloon agreed, "but it does me good to see the hungry ones eat." Naylor represented a minority opinion among Atlanta's saloon community. Most barkeepers operated open buffets only because they feared losing business. By 1898 the anti–free lunch forces prevailed, and the city council limited bar food service to pretzels and crackers.[14]

The free lunch controversy galvanized urban areas across the South at the turn of the twentieth century. In 1901 a group of saloon operators in Macon, Georgia, petitioned their city council to abolish the practice. As in Atlanta, Macon proprietors differed on the issue. One barkeeper vowed to continue the practice even if the legislation prevailed: "They say that if council should grant the petition and forbid the serving of free lunch they will sell lunch for 5 [cents] and give away a glass of beer with each purchase of lunch." Although patrons insisted that they saved money and made strong friendships "over the bar rails," Macon, like many other southern communities, banned the practice.[15] By the second decade of the twentieth century, temperance advocates threatened the existence of the saloons themselves. The end to the free lunch and to saloons more generally meant that many lower-class men lost access to an inexpensive regular midday meal.

Corresponding with the end of the free lunch, southern hotels adopted the "European plan" of service, by which meals were not included in the cost of the room. Under this new scheme, patrons purchased meals separately either at the hotel dining room or another eating place. Hotels across the South advertised the European plan as one of their many new modern and upscale accommodations. At the turn of the century the Arlington, the newest hotel in Montgomery, Alabama, advertised the European plan along with its "new and fresh" architecture and furniture. In Norfolk, Virginia, the Lynnhaven, touted as the city's "latest and largest fire-proof hotel," noted its use of the European plan. As another modern amenity, the Lynnhaven encouraged visitors to book reservations via telegraph. By 1913 Louisville had only one hotel, the Willard, which solely used the American plan. The Willard Hotel, an older establishment that catered to in-state travelers, promised "Best in the City for the Money," but no modern conveniences or advancements.[16] For the modern, upscale southern hotel at the turn of the twentieth century, the European plan prevailed.[17] Again, this left a significant portion of the South's urban population, including residents who lived permanently at hotels as well as transients, without an affordable, convenient, and reliable source of sustenance.

An important demographic trend helped fill the void left by saloons and hotels for inexpensive everyday food service. Around the turn of the twentieth century Greek natives immigrated in significant numbers to southern cities where they found a niche in the food-service industry. Although the percentage of immigrants in southern cities was quite small, especially compared to national trends, this ethnic group had a significant influence on the southern food service industry. Greek immigrants operated a variety of different food-related businesses, such as dairies, fish markets, food-service stands, confectionaries, cafés, lunchrooms, and restaurants, in southern towns and cities. As entrepreneurs, they came to dominate the retail food service industry, monopolizing the quick-order segment of the industry and opening higher-class establishments as well.

From roughly 1890 to 1920, Greeks immigrated to the United States in large numbers to escape financial and political difficulties in the Balkans. Greek immigrants primarily settled in northern cities. According to one estimate, only one in fifteen Greeks who immigrated to the United States prior to 1920 settled in a southern state.[18] In 1908 the Greek population of Atlanta, Birmingham, and Savannah was estimated to be 500 each (compared with an estimated Greek population of 15,000 and 20,000 in Chicago and New York, respectively).[19] These estimates may be slightly exaggerated: the federal census lists 104 Greek immigrants in Birmingham in 1900 and only 298 in 1910.[20] Nevertheless, it is clear that a significantly smaller percentage of Greek immigrants moved south. Despite the small number of Greeks in the South, and because a significant portion of them entered the food service industry, the Greek immigrant community had a disproportionate influence on public food culture in the twentieth-century South. They opened and operated "quick service" stands, cafés, and lunchrooms catering to less affluent patrons. Their proprietorship signaled the popularity of such establishments among non-Greek southerners as well.

Greek immigrants generally did not come to America in large groups. Usually individual men joined a brother, cousin, or fellow villager who was already established in business.[21] Those who ended up in the South often took a circuitous route. Birmingham restaurateur Nicholas Christu originally emigrated from Castelrelorigon, Greece, to Ellis Island on October 30, 1910. He immediately traveled to Ashland, Ohio, where an immigrant from his home village hired him to work at a candy store and soda fountain. Christu moved around Ohio working for friends in various different cities until he could afford to open his own business. After World War I, Christu's new wife, also a Greek immigrant, heard that many people from their home village had settled in Birmingham, Alabama. The couple moved to Birmingham, where Christu worked at a restaurant until he could afford to purchase his own small sandwich shop.[22]

Christu's story resembles that of many other Greeks in southern food service. They moved around to gain experience, make contacts, and earn money before opening their own businesses. As a community, Greek immigrants valued the camaraderie of their extended family and compatriots as well as the personal independence of owning their own businesses. Dino Thompson's father was moving his family south to Florida looking for new opportunities when he stopped at a small café in Myrtle Beach, South Carolina, for lunch and ended up buying the entire restaurant. Thompson's father agreed to stay in Myrtle Beach when he learned that the small southern beach town already had a Greek community, many of whom worked in food service.[23] In Birmingham, Christu, too, found a vibrant Greek community made up, to a significant extent, of restaurateurs, lunch-stand operators, and café proprietors. He recalls that approximately 90 percent of the city's restaurants in the 1920s were owned by Greek immigrants.[24]

Even if Christu exaggerated this estimation, Greeks certainly owned a significant portion of eating places in Birmingham and across the South. Wherever they settled, Greeks opened their own businesses because it provided more financial and personal independence than wage work.[25] In establishing eateries, the Greek colonies helped build southern urban areas. More specifically, they helped define how food would be prepared and served in the public sphere, irrespective of the designs of the predominantly native-born, middle-class urban authorities. Their presence ensured that public spaces where food was served, regardless of the exact nature of the establishment, would represent more diverse venues where people of different backgrounds and life experiences would meet and intermingle.

As a result of these concurrent developments, the number of public eating places advertising their services in southern cities increased dramatically at the turn of the twentieth century. In the years 1900, 1901, and 1902, for example, the Atlanta City Directory listed around forty eateries, mostly high-end restaurants. Starting in 1903, the number of establishments rose to 144 and continued to rise in the years that followed, revealing the operation of a number of quick lunch places such as cafés and lunchrooms. Perhaps many of these eating places had existed previously but had just decided to advertise or list their names in the city directory in that year. However, even this possibility describes a significant shift in the way that southerners knew about and thought about public eating space. Previously unlisted eateries might attract a local neighborhood crowd or close associates of the proprietor, but they would not be easily available to strangers looking for a quick lunch in the city. In this way, even if they were not all entirely new, the approximate hundred additional public eating places located in Atlanta in 1903 were at the very least newly "public."

Public Eating Places as Contested Space

This dramatic increase had significant consequences for the process of urbanization in the twentieth-century South. The vast majority of these "new" public eating places represented establishments owned by immigrants, African Americans, or lower-class whites and patronized by the lower socioeconomic classes. These lower-end eating places took the form of stands, lunchrooms, cafés, and cookshops and often represented ephemeral establishments that did not stay open for longer than a year or two. Menus specialized in "quick order" foods, such as sandwiches, that could be prepared quickly and cheaply. In many ways, these establishments had no nineteenth-century antecedents. They did not cater to an elite clientele, they did not bother with expensive décor or extensive menus, and they did not provide separate facilities for the accommodation of women.

The cultural diversity and novelty of these spaces prompted concern over their suitability and respectability. As more people depended on low-end eateries for their sustenance, cultural anxieties over their influence on public health and morality entered public discourse. For the poorest of southern society, the lack of sufficient nourishment threatened health and well-being, but as food practices evolved to fit the different pace of an urban environment, those who had plenty wondered if their overabundance and overindulgence might also lead to sickness of the body. Specifically, southerners adapting to new modes of consumption in city and town worried about indigestion caused by eating too quickly or consuming the wrong types of foods in public spaces. One Galveston, Texas, newspaper suggested that constantly eating out caused a myriad of contradictory digestive problems such as overeating, undereating, extravagance, frugality, indigestion, eating at odd hours, eating too quickly, eating too much meat, and unwise food choices.[26] National consumer markets offered solutions specifically designed for the working man forced to take lunch out. The Natural Food Company, for example, advertised shredded wheat as the solution to fast meals at the lunch counter.[27]

Such anxieties extended beyond the body, however, and permeated very basic concerns about the soul. Some southerners worried that eating places might serve as potential sites for activities considered immoral and that bodily pollution might result. This possibility was particularly disturbing in public locations where people consumed as if in their private homes. In fact, many early eating places advertised themselves as suitable replacements for home meals and, perhaps, sites that should uphold the same moral standards expected of the southern home. Still, public facilities were, in fact, public. Café proprietors would not, or could not, control activities within their establishments in the same way people might order their homes or in the way deemed appropriate by white urban authorities.

As public spaces, restaurants and cafés often served as scenes of crime and physical altercation. Authorities often arrested the Greek proprietors and employees for nonviolent offenses. In April 1909 Atlanta police arrested Jim Hanjaras, Jim Poulos, Tom Poulos, and Charlie Dordas for gambling in the basement of Hanjaras's eatery. All four either owned or worked at a café.[28] In February 1912 Atlanta police arrested Jim Favors and John Poulos for selling whiskey in contravention of local prohibition laws. Favors, the owner of a local restaurant, was convicted of running a "blind tiger," a term used to describe a lower-class establishment that sold illegal liquor.[29] In May 1914 Nick Caccans, Jim Poulos, George Poulos, and five others were arrested for gambling in the basement of Caccans's restaurant.[30] These arrests reveal more about the place of public eateries in the southern urban environment than they do about the alleged morality of any particular café owner or employee. As sites of legal consumption with a regular urban customer base, cafés and lunchrooms made excellent locations for offering extralegal goods and services as well.

City officials had good reason to fear disputes and criminal activities that occurred in public eating houses because such altercations often turned into violence in the city streets. In 1873 the small town of Decatur, Alabama, set the scene for a fatal confrontation between Samuel Weaver and a companion named Crenshaw. Crenshaw shot Weaver, presumably in self-defense, after Weaver pulled a knife on his opponent and ripped open his jaw in an effort to cut Crenshaw's throat. The deadly fight had started at the Bismarck Restaurant, where the two men were dining when an argument broke out. The scene spilled into the city streets and turned deadly. Although the fatal shot had not occurred at the Bismarck, public spaces with a diverse urban customer base and serving intoxicating beverages no doubt served as theaters in which violent fights often began.[31]

Physical altercation and robbery aside, urban authorities also worried that eating places might provide public space for less violent acts of supposed moral degradation, especially drinking. After Atlanta's city council ended the practice of serving meals in local saloons, restaurant proprietors began sending out for beer to serve to their patrons. Eating places often set up beside saloons and established a system whereby the restaurant keeper or patron might order drinks from the saloon to be delivered to the customer at the restaurant. Jim Brown, a Greek café owner in Atlanta, established a "push button" system with the saloon next door. When he wanted to order drinks for a patron, he simply pushed a button and placed the order. This system was similar to one used by every restaurant in the city until 1906, when the city council prohibited restaurants from serving alcohol. One way the city enforced this ordinance was to refuse business licenses to restaurants located too close to saloons.[32]

The struggle that southern cities undertook to reconcile eating and drinking in public places reveals the complicated merger of various value systems in a diverse urban environment. The governing, salaried classes worried that working-class whites, African Americans, and foreigners might use these spaces more as saloons than restaurants, thereby bypassing many of the regulations that specifically applied to saloons, such as the absence of women. If drinking was allowed, an assortment of patrons might linger in restaurants, becoming intoxicated and providing space for further public immorality and debauchery. City councils worried especially about eating places frequented by lower classes and African Americans.

The desire to separate eating and drinking by refusing to serve alcohol in restaurants had class and racial implications. In Atlanta, for example, the city council admitted that the regulation against drinking in restaurants specifically targeted those places that hosted African American customers. Despite this professed intention, the broadly applicable ordinance covered all public eating places. This more general application caused some white councilmen to initially oppose the law. One council member argued that men who did not frequent saloons nevertheless drank alcohol with their meals and joked that restaurant service "was the only way the prohibitionists could get a drink." The mayor opposed its wide applicability, stating that "there can be no harm in serving beer in such [eating] places as are in the center of the city [where the white restaurants were located]." Despite such protest, the council passed the law unanimously.[33]

Another solution for urban areas such as Atlanta was to do away with alcohol consumption entirely. One month after it took alcohol out of city restaurants, the Atlanta city council closed the city's saloons altogether and limited the purchase of alcohol in the city to a low-alcohol beverage called "near beer." The mayor recognized the incongruence of this action, commenting late in 1906, "The council recently refused to license certain restaurants because they were next door to saloons and then later closed up the very saloons which adjoined the objectionable restaurants."[34] For Atlanta, prohibition represented only the latest in a series of legislative attempts to govern the use and sale of inebriants in the city. The discourse and actions surrounding these events reveal white middle-class anxieties over the consumption of alcohol in public spaces, especially those designated for eating—and particularly by poor whites and African Americans.

Despite their best efforts, closing the saloons failed to solve the problem of drinking in public eating places and actually encouraged the emergence of cafés intended to circumvent the laws. Atlanta authorities continued to spend time and energy regulating the sale and consumption of alcohol in public spaces supposedly designated for eating. The city regulated the consumption of near beer with licensing provisions. The question of alcohol merged with concerns about other types of supposed immoral behavior in southern eating places. Atlanta went through various stages of prohibition and temperance in attempting to end crime and disorder in public spaces. In the absence of traditional saloons, many observers considered lower-class eating places to be fronts for the service of alcoholic beverages, illegal or otherwise.

The end of legalized alcohol in Atlanta did not mean the end to controversies over drinking and saloons. White middle-class authorities, who could no doubt afford to serve bootleg whiskey at home, believed alleged eating places that served alcohol attracted lower-class elements, which inherently led to trouble. In 1908, two years after Atlanta closed its saloons, local commentator J. Francis Keeley noted that he would rather see "a respectable saloon than a so-called café, selling 'near beer' and given to rowdyism."[35] After the city passed local prohibition laws, authorities continued to struggle with eating places and "near beer saloons" that continued to sell alcohol illegally or serve near beer to their customers in contravention of local licensing provisions.

Controversy stemmed from attempts to ban a substance that had a long connection with consumption and eating. In Montgomery, Alabama, the connection between eating and drinking alcohol was so common that proprietors assumed having a business license to serve meals also allowed them to serve alcoholic beverages. In 1875 Montgomery authorities convicted a local restaurateur named Nicrosi for selling alcoholic beverages without a license. Nicrosi apparently sold drinks to patrons eating on site and argued that his restaurant business license implied the ability to serve alcohol with meals. The Supreme Court of Alabama disagreed and affirmed Nicrosi's conviction, but this did not end the controversy.[36] In 1904 Montgomery's chief of police complained that a local ordinance allowing restaurants to conduct business on Sunday enabled the sale of alcohol despite laws against the practice. The connection between the sale of food and drink was so strong that the city's blue laws were threatened "where saloons are allowed to have restaurants attached and keep open all day Sunday to serve meals."[37] The struggles of urban areas such as Atlanta and Montgomery reveal the difficulties in regulating morality where a seemingly innocuous activity, such as eating, was involved.

Drinking in public spaces, illegal or otherwise, implicated other alleged moral infractions as well. Alcohol in public spaces often coincided with sexualized conduct between men and women, and again, restaurants and cafés served as sites for alleged transgressions. Unlike the higher-class restaurants and their "ladies cafés," lower-class eateries made little attempt to separate men and women. In fact, the ability to carouse with the opposite sex might have been an enticement. These spaces offered opportunities for men and women to meet, mingle, converse, and engage in sexualized activity that encompassed anything from drinking together to public displays of affection to actual intercourse. Atlanta police often raided cafés to halt sexual interactions considered to be improper. In May 1914 the College Inn served as the site for such a raid. Its proprietors faced charges related to illegal drinking and sexual mingling. The judge accused the café of circumventing local prohibition laws by purchasing near beer from local African American merchants who then delivered the drinks to the College Inn in violation of city ordinances. Worse still, men and women reportedly drank together at the College Inn, leading to a variety of different types of "disorderly conduct." Among other things, reports indicated that women sat in the laps of male companions and "embraced" them.[38] These eating establishments circumvented local law and cultural conventions that attempted to bound gendered conduct in the public sphere by separating men and women. Unlike the ladies' cafés of fine-dining restaurants, lower-class eateries failed to respect these principles in favor of more liberal interactions among men and women.

In addition to the relatively innocent intermingling of the genders in legitimate eating places, southern authorities worried that an eatery could serve as a front for a brothel. In 1903 black prostitutes arrested on vagrancy charges in Atlanta inevitably reported that they worked at "Old Lady Brown's Restaurant." Sarah Brown, a sixty-year-old African American woman, operated a café that authorities assumed was a front for prostitution. Police often visited her establishment for unspecified complaints of "disorder" and reportedly "drunken men [visited] at all hours of the day and night." Brown's café was located on Decatur Street, an area of Atlanta that was notorious for crime, drinking, prostitution, and other vices. She hired around forty women to work at her restaurant. In 1900 Brown had been brought up on charges for running a disorderly establishment, but the judge let her go with the promise that she would keep her customers in line. Despite this warning and the apparent illegal activities undertaken at Brown's café, there is no evidence that police shut her down. But city police did begin arresting any woman who reported working for Brown on "vagrancy" or prostitution charges.[39]

The fact that Mrs. Brown hired African American women as supposed waitresses illuminates another complicating factor with regard to public spaces designated for eating. For white southern authorities, the issue of race and the potential for race mixing in lower-class public eating establishments increased the potential threat associated with illegal drinking and illicit sexual interaction. Although southern eating places tended to implement some form of racial segregation even before formal Jim Crow laws took hold, interracial interactions nevertheless took place. Such interactions may have been exacerbated by the fact that café proprietors often came to the South unfamiliar with the region's racial mores. Albert P. Maurakis, the son of a Greek café operator, recalls his confusion over racial segregation when he moved from Pittsburgh to Danville, Virginia. He relied on family members with longer tenure in the South to elucidate the region's racialized eating rituals: "Uncle Steve explained the Southern Jim Crow practice of segregating the races in the use of all public facilities and that the 'colored' must enter back doors to eat in restaurant kitchens." The Maurakis family acquiesced to segregation culture. Although his uncle had no rear entrance, he served black customers through a small opening in the window. Maurakis's father opened the Central Café with an eight-foot partition to separate black and white dining areas and built separate entrances for each.[40]

Despite such concessions, evidence reveals that Greeks, perhaps because of their own experiences as the object of discrimination or their own darker pigmented skin, never entirely accepted southern racial mores as thoroughly as native-born southern whites. In Durham, North Carolina, the Lincoln Café, an African American eating place operated by Greek immigrants, reportedly received a threatening letter from the Ku Klux Klan alleging that white men and black women were meeting at the café and leaving together in automobiles. Specifically, the letter stated, "You are fraternizing with the Negroes and allowing a low element of whites to meet Nigger women in your place." In this letter, the Klan expresses their concerns that Greek immigrants were socializing with African Americans and that lower-class white men and black women were using the café as a meeting place for dates or sexual liaisons.[41]

These overt anxieties were complicated by less discernible issues. As an organization, the Klan in the 1920s was known for its nativist, as well as its racist, ideology. In this case, the apparent financial success of the immigrants may have provided fodder for the organization's xenophobic beliefs. Additionally, the name of the café represents an explicit reference to Abraham Lincoln and, by implication, to black emancipation. Collectively, the notion that immigrants and African Americans had the freedom to act independently in space open to the public may have exacerbated white anxieties that the Klan expressed through concerns about miscegenation and morality. The memories of Greek immigrant café owners also reveal a certain amount of ambivalence toward southern racial mores during the era of Jim Crow. In his memoir, Greek immigrant and South Carolina restaurateur John Katsos recalls an African American acquaintance asking him if he was Jewish. Katsos responded, "No. I thought you knew I was a Greek." The African American man answered that he was not aware of Katsos's ethnicity, "but I figured you ain't been no white man."[42] This story, assuming its authenticity, suggests that Greek immigrants may have treated African Americans subtly better or with more respect than native-born southern whites. If so, the important status of Greek immigrants within public food culture in the South might have served as a threat to the cultural system of racial segregation.

For southern white authorities, a potentially volatile situation ignited when illegal drinking and illicit sexual activity combined with race in the public sphere. City authorities across the South implemented programs in the early twentieth century to do away with so-called negro dives. A dive could take the legal form of a restaurant or saloon, but city authorities rarely made a distinction. Before Prohibition, the *Atlanta Constitution* explained that owners received a business license to operate a restaurant near a saloon. Throughout the day and night, black men and women hung out at the "restaurant" supposedly to eat but really to drink and mingle. The *Constitution* noted that this marked one way in which black women circumvented the city ordinance that prohibited women from patronizing saloons. In addition to drinking and sexualized activity, Atlanta authorities also complained about crime they associated with black restaurants.[43]

The question of black dives in early twentieth-century southern cities implicated many of the race, class, and gender issues that existed in the broader society. Southern white authorities took issue with several aspects of these inexpensive restaurants. First, although some black restaurants may have in fact been operated by whites, these establishments provided public space for poor African Americans to congregate without the oversight of a white employer or white authorities. Second, these public spaces implicated much broader concerns about social control in the urban environment. New people came into town on a regular basis who did not have any history in the area and about whom city authorities had no knowledge. Urban lifestyles differed from the daily and seasonal rhythms and traditions of agrarian routines. In particular, racialized rituals were less determined in young southern cities. For African Americans, negotiating the urban consumer landscape could bring escape from the normality of racial difference and prejudice. But such escape threatened white supremacy. White urban authorities strove to ensure that emerging consumer markets, which included cafés and restaurants, did not undermine racial difference in the city.

Other southern cities joined Atlanta's crusade against the supposedly demoralizing effect of black dives as well as the threat these establishments posed to white supremacy. In 1902 white Montgomery residents complained about "negro" dives operating just outside the city limits and violating Sunday liquor laws. These public spaces were variously described as saloons, stores, and "cookshops" (cafés operated by African American women). According to reports, these establishments, located in what the *Montgomery Advertiser* referred to as the "dive district," experienced good business on Sundays with patronage from black men and women and white men.[44] The presence of white men implicated another common trope reflecting the race-based anxieties of some white southerners: the fear of so-called race mixing. Miscegenation was no doubt at the heart of many food consumption issues with which urban authorities wrestled, from alcohol sales to female presence at cafés. In this case, Montgomery residents worried (as the Durham Ku Klux Klan would two decades later) that black eateries provided public space for lower-class white men and black women to mingle and date.

It was not just the presence of black women in public eating spaces that caused concern, or even the most concern, for southern white authorities. In the early twentieth century the presence of women of both races, even white women otherwise considered to be respectable, became an ordinary sight in common eateries that did not feature a separate ladies' café. This occurrence reflected the more public daily activities of southern women living in cities and towns. Women bore primary responsibility for their family's shopping, and stores were often located in downtown areas that may not be convenient to home. Also, professional men might take their wives out for a special treat. The *Atlanta Woman's Club Cook Book* advised that women who take primary responsibility for preparing the family's meals deserved a "half-holiday" on Thursday afternoons and a "dinner out."[45] Working-class women often could not return home in the short amount of time allocated for their lunch break. In the late 1930s Dorothy Dickins found that, although farm women and textile mill employees tended to eat lunch at home, female garment plant workers often purchased lunch in town because these factories were located farther away.[46] In addition to necessity, young women frequented public eating places for leisure and entertainment. When dating became a popular form of gendered interaction in the 1920s, women often visited soda fountains, cafés, or restaurants with their male companions.[47]

Even though they did not feature ladies' cafés, some lunchrooms attempted to provide a limited amount of protected space for female patronage. The Albert Restaurant in Birmingham offered to serve lunch to white women "at the tables." This condition implies that men had an option of eating elsewhere, perhaps at a counter or bar where they presumably would come into close contact with others as they ate. White women apparently had no such options, or perhaps Albert's simply meant to ensure them that they would have access to an eating place "safe" from close contact with unknown men dining beside them.[48] Such accommodations still would not have protected white women from contact with smoking, cursing, racial interactions, or similar activities common to ordinary lunchrooms.

The unease over accommodating white women as customers paled in comparison to the concerns prompted by white female servers. Despite their traditional role as purveyor of food at home, the notion of white women serving in public spaces was a foreign concept. In 1915 an unnamed northern restaurant chain brought its practice of hiring white waitresses to its location in Atlanta. The policy was considered to be so unusual that white Georgia natives initially refused to take the jobs, and the chain hired northern migrants to wait tables. Somewhat tongue-in-cheek, the *Atlanta Constitution* compared the practice to Sherman's march "shelling Dixie's hurtful menial traditions with a sweeping fire that is crumbling them as fast as they come under the range of the guns."[49] By the 1930s the use of white female servers proved to be more common but remained controversial because of the inherent sexuality that many southern men perceived. At the Peabody Hotel's grill room in Memphis, visiting North Carolina journalist Jonathan Daniels commented on the attractive face of his waitress. His companion, a Mississippi plantation owner, compared female food service to prostitution by noting that when poor white women were pushed off the farms, "the weakest and the dumbest go into the whore houses . . . but the pretty and smart ones get [waitressing] jobs like these."[50] The somewhat novel practice of white female food service in public places threatened some white southern sensibilities and revealed an anxiety connected with the greater white female presence in such spaces.

Formal Regulation of Public Eating Space

As the alcohol issue revealed, the anxieties and concerns of white authorities over the "appropriate" use of public space designated for consuming food generated a call for regulation at the state and local level. Prohibiting the consumption of alcohol represented only the first of the many ways in which southern white authorities regulated restaurants, cafés, and other public eating places over the course of the twentieth century. These regulations reflected many of the same issues that frustrated white urban authorities, especially the emerging presence of white women in public eating places. Because more white women frequented local eateries, separate spaces for men and women became impractical—even for establishments considered to be more respectable.

The increasing presence of women in restaurants encouraged politicians to call for protective legislation. In 1914 South Carolina governor Coleman L. Blease asked the state legislature to prohibit smoking in public eating places frequented by women. Such legislation would have been unnecessary in the nineteenth century when "ladies' cafés" kept women away from male influences considered to be inappropriate. Blease's concern involved secondhand smoke that might pollute the bodies of white women, who did not receive any particular protections in the common eatery. The governor based his appeal on vivid imagery, describing the bodily pollution inflicted on women exposed to smoking: "People in South Carolina (I will not say gentlemen, nor will I say true men) sit in our public dining rooms, restaurants and cafés and smoke cigars ... and whiff and puff and blow the smoke out through their nostrils, and this smoke is carried either by the natural breezes or the current of an electric fan into the eyes, mouths and nostrils of refined women." He requested that the South Carolina legislature prohibit smoking in public eating places patronized by women. This proposed law did not represent a general public health measure. Rather, it constituted legislation specifically designed to protect white women who participated in the leisure activity of eating out.[51]

Blease's speech reveals a southern culture transitioning from one that was based on private conduct, where behavior considered to be inappropriate could be regulated by family or community censure, to one that was much more public and therefore in need of official regulation. He longingly remembered "the time ... when, if a gentleman smoked a pipe ... while walking along the street by the side of a lady he was not regarded as well reared, and such a thing as smoking while riding in a buggy with a young lady would not have been tolerated." The opinions of family and community served as sufficient deterrents to prohibit actions that a cohesive class agreed were inappropriate—in this case, smoking in the presence of white women. However, Blease recognized that public censure could not regulate places of public accommodation. Specifically, Blease identified those from outside South Carolina "who have no respect for us or our ladies." Such individuals, according to the governor, "should be made to respect them," as should any residents "who are not decent enough to respect [South Carolina] women."[52] Here, Blease specifically referred to new populations of proprietors and customers who operated and patronized the new "quick order" cafés. The governor correctly understood that only legal requirements could force this motley urban assortment to respect the old cultural standards.

Although Blease decried the use of tobacco, smoking served as a metaphor for his greater anxieties over the racial purity of white women. The descriptive imagery the governor used to describe the alleged source of bodily pollution—the "whiff[ing] and puff[ing] and blow[ing]" of smoke out of the male body and into the various orifices of the female body—constitutes a thinly veiled sexual reference that is bolstered by his additional claim that women might be exposed to syphilis, among other diseases, through such contact.[53] Although Blease did not blame black men for smoke-filled southern cafés, other white southerners of the period openly theorized that African Americans carried and spread syphilis, and that black men did so by raping white women.[54] By referencing this common theme, Blease was not only relying on a well-defined southern trope to support his cause, he was connecting white cultural fears of bodily contamination and racial impurity to activities taking place in the relatively new consumer sphere of public eating places.

The anxieties reflected by Blease's speech inform legislative efforts across the South aimed at regulating public eating spaces, especially at the municipal level. City leaders implemented health codes that regulated sanitation, required inspections, constrained employee actions, and circumscribed patrons. Considering its early struggles over saloons and its aggressive policing of eating places, Atlanta's first health code emerged rather late. In 1924 the city council passed municipal ordinances that required restaurant inspections. Restaurants had to keep walls and floors clean and had to ensure access to a clean water supply. Bathrooms and sleeping quarters had to be located away from restaurant kitchens. Employees had to wear clean, washable clothing and could not work in restaurants if they had any communicable diseases.[55]

The most telling municipal ordinances related directly to race. In 1914, the same year that the South Carolina governor openly expressed his concerns over bodily pollution from tobacco smoke, the city of Birmingham added racial segregation ordinances to its restaurant health code. Birmingham's ordinance represented a relatively typical law for the period. The law prohibited proprietors from "conduct[ing] a restaurant or lunch counter at which white and colored persons are served in the same room." The Birmingham Board of Commissioners passed the law unanimously with very little explanation or public commentary.[56] The *Age-Herald* reported that Police Commissioner Judge A. O. Lane planned to introduce the ordinance to improve "the peace and happiness of the community"—even though cafés regularly sat each race on different sides of the dining room.[57] Because Birmingham included this racial segregation law as part of its health code and because de facto segregation was not sufficient, the Board of Commissioners seemed to be reflecting fears similar to those of Blease—in this case, that interracial eating might contribute to racial mixing and thereby implicate racial purity. In the second and third decades of the twentieth century, legislators in cities and small towns across the South reflected these same fears for the imagined threats over white women in public eating places by passing racial segregation laws.[58]

The result of such laws solidified a southern food culture that Atlanta had been attempting to achieve for years with its attacks on alcohol and black dives.[59] Although most segregation ordinances, like the Birmingham law, allowed for service to both races if each race had its own dining room, from a practical standpoint most café proprietors could not or did not invest in acceptable accommodations for nonwhites.[60] African Americans had to rely on service at black cafés—which were already under attack by many white southern authorities—or inferior take-out service, as Ollie's Barbecue implemented in Birmingham. Such treatment created an ethos in the South that identified whites as appropriate consumers of food and African Americans as secondary citizens in consumption culture. In eating places across the South, white supremacy prevailed, and over the next several decades, racial segregation laws united southern whites around a common ideology committed to the subjugation of black consumers.[61]

Southern Eating Space and Civil Rights

Starting on February 1, 1960, when four young men requested service at a lunch counter in Greensboro, North Carolina, the civil rights movement represented a direct challenge to the constructed image of African Americans as inferior within consumption spaces and to the culture of oppression that such representations sustained. Direct action campaigns of this type had actually taken place since World War II, when the Congress of Racial Equality (CORE) tried to end segregation in northern eating places.[62] But the Greensboro sit-ins represented the first attack on the racial-based laws that made segregation in southern eating places much more provocative. When white waitresses at the Greensboro Woolworth refused to serve the four African American students because of their race, the young people returned the next day and for many days thereafter. For weeks Greensboro became the site of civil rights protests at many downtown lunch counters and eating places. The demonstrations spread to student groups in other southern cities and resulted in the establishment of a new civil rights organization called the Student Nonviolent Coordinating Committee (SNCC), committed to, among other things, ending segregation in public eating places.[63]

The sit-in movement pressured southern lunch counters and restaurants to respect the rights of African American consumers and to provide African Americans with physical access to southern eating space. Yet the young activists who formed SNCC recognized that the contested space of eating places meant more than simply sitting down to a meal. As the white authorities in Atlanta, Birmingham, and other southern municipalities had recognized in the early twentieth century, access to consumption culture connected directly to other types of access in southern society. At the organizational meeting in Raleigh, North Carolina, SNCC advisor Ella Baker announced that lunch counter demonstrations were "bigger than a hamburger," aiming to end oppression and discrimination "not only at lunch counters, but in every aspect of life."[64] Certainly, since the end of World War II and the increase of American consumer culture in general, the ability to participate in conspicuous consumption became an important element of American democracy. Civil rights activists considered sit-ins and other forms of direct action protest toward discrimination in public eating places to be important elements for accessing these and other rights of citizenship.[65]

Because of the consolidation of white supremacy that had been encouraged and facilitated by decades of de jure racial segregation, many white southerners reacted critically, even violently, to the attempted desegregation of public eating places. Such spaces hosted literal conflict that differed only by degree from the contested nature of public eating space that had existed for most of the twentieth century. White supremacists continued to connect places where food was consumed to racial purity and to the decorum of the white southern home. In angry reaction to Senate committee hearings on the Civil Rights Act of 1964, Alabama constituent Lallage Longshore sent a vandalized picture of Martin Luther King Jr. to Senator Lister Hill. Over King's picture, Longshore wrote, "This is the Savage that Kennedy wants us to live with and take into our Homes."[66] The plain language of the civil rights act applied to places of public accommodation and did not make any demands on the private space of the home. Yet Longshore's statement reveals the connection that many white southerners continued to make between food consumption, racial purity, and—by implication—the home to which such matters ultimately alluded. Notions of food, sexuality, and the protection of white women, all of which implicated public and private spaces, continued to matter in southern politics and culture.

Despite strong southern opposition, President Lyndon B. Johnson signed the civil rights bill into law on July 2, 1964.[67] The final version of the act required that "all persons shall be entitled to the full and equal enjoyment of the goods, service, facilities, and privileges, advantages, and accommodations of any place of public accommodation ... without discrimination or segregation on the ground of race, color, religion, or national origin."[68] Among those establishments subject to the act were "any restaurant, cafeteria lunchroom, lunch counter, soda fountain, or other facility principally engaged in selling food for consumption on the premises."[69] In December 1964 the Supreme Court affirmed the act's constitutionality in a case brought by the owners of Ollie's Barbecue.[70] The law represented, for the first time since Reconstruction, federal recognition of the right of African Americans to fully participate in the South's consumer culture. Reverend Edward Gardner, vice president of the Alabama Christian Movement for Human Rights, recognized this when he said triumphantly, "There will be no more sit-ins, but from now on there will be walk-ins."[71]

Although, like the McClungs after the final court decision in their case, most white southern restaurant owners acquiesced to the law, the reaction of those who remained obstinate reveals the connection that white supremacists still made between segregation and the protection of white women.[72] Lester Maddox, owner of Atlanta's Pickrick Restaurant and the most notorious opponent of restaurant desegregation, feared the interaction of African American men and white women in his establishment. In 1962, in the midst of southern sit-in activism, Atlanta police arrested Tommy Lee Jordan, an African American employee at the Pickrick, after Jordan allegedly "tried to date" two white waitresses. Reportedly, Jordan had followed a Pickrick waitress into the ladies' room to ask her out. When she refused, he "had 'pulled on her coat' . . . when she brushed past him on her way out." Three weeks later, another waitress reported that Jordan had asked her to go to a nightclub with him. Atlanta police charged Jordan with disorderly conduct, disturbing the peace, and molestation. A year earlier, Maddox had accused Jordan of stealing a lady's purse, but he had not called the police at that time.[73] Maddox only contacted authorities when Jordan challenged Maddox's understanding of proper racial and gender conventions, even when no crime had occurred. In a politically motivated newspaper ad for his restaurant, Maddox directly connects the desegregation of eating places with the desegregation of southern bedrooms, writing, "I do hope you'll get your integration wishes—a stomach full of race mixing, and a lap full of little mulatto grandchildren."[74]

Interestingly, in December 1964, while the Supreme Court was considering their decision in *Katzenback v. McClung*, *The Citizen*, a national magazine published by the white supremacist Citizens' Councils of America, made no mention of the public accommodations section of the Civil Rights Act or of the Ollie's Barbecue case. Instead, the magazine devoted that month's edition to the imagined threats that white women faced in the event of so-called race mixing.[75] The common "black rapist" trope predominated. One editorial warned that "some drastic action is needed to protect whites from colored criminals—especially rapists" and continued by describing hundreds of alleged violent crimes committed by black men against white women. The list included the following examples: a "Negro gang" raped a white nurse in New Jersey; "a gang of about 10 Negro youths" raped white teenage girls in Memphis; "eight Negro youths . . . gang-raped" a white mother in Knoxville; "a Negro raped and murdered a young white housewife when she returned home from an early afternoon trip to the grocery store" in New Orleans; and in Mississippi "several white homemakers have been terrorized on their own premises by colored intruders evidently bent on rape." There is no indication that any of these alleged (and unsupported) atrocities occurred in public eating places or even occurred at all, but the timing makes the connection clear. While the eyes of the country focused on the Supreme Court as it decided the Ollie's Barbecue case, the Citizens' Councils of America focused on the so-called dangers of race mixing, and all supposed threats involved the well-being and racial purity of white women and, by extension, white families.[76]

Some white supremacists reacted to this culture of hyperbole with actions intended to protect white women. When Jimmy's Restaurant in Montgomery desegregated, the white owner reportedly fired the white waitresses and hired black men to wait tables because he did not think that it was proper for white women to serve black men.[77] In a more violent incident in Chattanooga, Tennessee, a white man shot and killed a black patron who allegedly "called a white waitress 'baby doll' . . . in a recently desegregated restaurant."[78] Like Lester Maddox's call for racial purity, these incidents demonstrate the white fear that interaction between blacks and whites in southern restaurants might lead to sexual relations between white women and black men. Because southern white supremacists could not comprehend that such interactions could be consensual, this ideology reinvigorated the notion of the black rapist.

In conclusion, history does not connect the periods between emancipation and racial segregation in southern eating places with a straight line. The 1910s seemed to have been a turning point of sorts when many southern cities implemented strict laws that regulated racial interactions in cafés and restaurants. Yet interracial mingling took place in public eating places before and after these laws took effect. The history of the development of public space, where eating represented the dominant activity, reveals a complicated history in which white southern authorities attempted to regulate the interactions of different races, classes, ethnicities, and genders. Notions of proper behavior according to class-based mores precipitated legislation that implicated deep-seated white anxieties over consumption, racial purity, and the protection of white women. This process found its most public incarnation during the civil rights movement of the early 1960s, in which civil rights activists attempted to establish equal access for African Americans to this public space. The Civil Rights Act of 1964 represented a significant victory for activists by requiring the desegregation of public eating space. This legislation allowed a more democratic consumption culture to prevail in common eateries.

NOTES

1. Transcript of September 1, 1964, McClung v. Katzenbach, 233 F. Supp. 815 (N.D. Ala.) (No. 64–448), 70–74, 80–81; "Barbecue and the Bar," *Newsweek*, September 28, 1964, 32; Ollie McClung Jr., interview by Joan Hoffman, November 5, 1975, tape and transcript LD81 B5381 A821 no. 2, Oral History Collection, Mervyn H. Sterne Library, University of Alabama at Birmingham, Birmingham, Alabama; General Code of Birmingham §369 (repealed July 23, 1963); Civil Rights Act of 1964, Pub. L. No. 88–352, July 2, 1964, §201; Katzenbach v. McClung, 379 U.S. 294 (1964). In addition to *McClung*, some of the many cases challenging the restaurants provision of the Civil Rights Act of 1964 include Willis v. Pickrick Restaurant, 231 F. Supp. 396 (1964); U.S. v. Johnson, 269 F. Supp. 706 (1967); Wright v. The Cork Club, 315 F. Supp 1143 (1970); and U.S. v. Boyd, 327 F. Supp. 998 (1970).

2. Grace Elizabeth Hale, *Making Whiteness: The Culture of Segregation in the South, 1890–1940* (New York: Vintage, 1999), 8–10. For earlier debates on racial segregation in the southern public sphere, see C. Vann Woodward, *The Strange Career of Jim Crow* (New York: Oxford University Press, 1955), and Joel Williamson, *The Crucible of Race: Black-White Relations since Emancipation* (New York: Oxford University Press, 1984), among others.

3. Elspeth Probyn, *Carnal Appetites: FoodSexIdentities* (New York: Routledge, 2000).

4. David Beriss and David Sutton, eds., *The Restaurants Book: Ethnographies of Where We Eat* (New York: Berg, 2007).

5. James Silk Buckingham, *Slave States of America* (London: Fisher, Son, & Co., 1842), 1:331–36.

6. Thomas Joseph Macon, *Life Gleanings* (Richmond: W. H. Adams, 1913), 25, accessed September 23, 2009, http://docsouth.unc.edu/fpn/macon/macon.html.

7. C. Vann Woodward and Mary Boykin Miller Chesnut, *Mary Chesnut's Civil War* (New Haven, Conn.: Yale University Press, 1981), 347.

8. "Thompson's Restaurant and Ladies' Dining Rooms," *Atlanta Constitution*, November 2, 1882; *Sholes' Atlanta Directory* (Atlanta: Sholes, 1880), 91. This and all subsequent references to the *Atlanta Constitution* were accessed at http://proquest.umi.com.libdata.lib.ua.edu.

9. "Pease and His Wife," *Atlanta Constitution*, December 9, 1868.

10. *Richmond Times Dispatch*, April 4, 1907, http://www.loc.gov/chroniclingamerica/lccn /sn85038615/1907–04–04/ed-1/seq-11.

11. See, e.g., the advertisement titled "The State House Saloon of Noonan & McGuire," *Atlanta Constitution*, August 28, 1868, describing "a free lunch . . . served every day."

12. "Alas and Alack Free Lunches Going," *Atlanta Constitution*, April 17, 1897; "Other 8—No Title," *Atlanta Constitution*, June 22, 1890; "Passing of the Pretzel," *Atlanta Constitution*, May 27, 1897; "Down with Free Lunch and Beer," *Atlanta Constitution*, June 12, 1897.

13. "Alas and Alack Free Lunches Going," *Atlanta Constitution*, April 17, 1897.

14. "Lunch Counters May Be Banished," *Atlanta Constitution*, June 8, 1897; "Foes to Free Lunch, These Saloon Men," *Atlanta Constitution*, June 9, 1897; "Council Names Free Lunch Bill of Fare," *Atlanta Constitution*, August 19, 1898; "Lunch Ordinance Is in Effect," *Atlanta Constitution*, August 21, 1898.

15. "Wail from Patrons of Free Lunch Counters," *Macon Telegraph*, June 27, 1901.

16. *Richmond Times Dispatch*, September 12, 1902, http://www.loc.gov/chroniclingamerica/lccn/sn85038614/1902–09–12/ed-1/seq-8; *Birmingham News*, April 15, 1902; *Richmond Times Dispatch*, July 14, 1907, http://www.loc.gov/chroniclingamerica/lccn/sn85038615/1907–07–14/ed-1/seq-11; *Birmingham News*, April 25, 1902; *Birmingham News*, April 15, 1902; *Richmond Times Dispatch*, July 14, 1907, http://www.loc.gov/chroniclingamerica/lccn/sn85038615/1907–07–14/ed-1/seq-11; *Louisville Courier*, Southern Prosperity Number, March 25, 1913, 7–8.

17. Switching from the American to the European plan was a national trend, as discussed in Richard Pillsbury's *From Boarding House to Bistro* (Boston: Unwin Hyman, 1990).

18. Charles C. Moskos, *Greek Americans: Struggle and Success* (New Brunswick, N.J.: Transaction, 2009), 25.

19. Henry Pratt Fairchild, *Greek Immigration to the United States* (New Haven, Conn.: Yale University Press, 1911), 258–59.

20. 1900 and 1910 United States Census, accessed through Ancestry.com.

21. Marios Christou Stephanides, *The History of the Greeks in Kentucky, 1900–1950*, vol. 1, The Early Pioneers of Louisville (Lewiston, N.Y.: Edwin Mellen, 2001), 30.

22. Oral History of Nicholas Christu by Sofia Petrou, February 3, 1977, 1–10, transcript and recording, Mervyn H. Sterne Library, University of Alabama at Birmingham (hereinafter referred to as "Christu interview").

23. Dino Thompson, *Greek Boy Growing Up Southern: A Myrtle Beach Memoir* (Myrtle Beach, S.C.: Snug Press, 1999), 1–2. Many other interviews and memoirs of southern Greeks describe moving around the country before settling down. See, e.g., from Oral Histories of Birmingham Greeks, Southern Foodways Alliance, University of Mississippi, Oxford, Mississippi, "Niki's Downtown," Oral History of George Sissa by Amy Evans, March 11, 2004, 4, http://www.southernfoodways.com/documentary/oh/greek/BG05_nikisdowntown.shtml, and "Zoe's," Oral History of Zoë Cassimus by Amy Evans, March 11, 2004, 2, http://www.southernfoodways.com/documentary/oh/greek/BG11_zoes.shtml.

24. Christu interview, 10.

25. Stephanides, *History of the Greeks in Kentucky*, 4–7.

26. "Some Mistakes of Restaurant Living," *Galveston Daily News*, March 17, 1915, http://newspaperarchive.com/. This is particularly ironic because in their original eighteenth-century French derivation, the primary purpose of a "restaurant" was to sustain customers

whose gastrointestinal tract could not handle the rigors of modern city life. The French term originally referred to a thick meat broth served to invalids whose weak constitutions could not handle heavier foods and only later came to apply to the public spaces where such fare could be consumed. Rebecca L. Spang, *The Invention of the Restaurant: Paris and Modern Gastronomic Culture* (Cambridge, Mass.: Harvard University Press, 2000), 1.

27. "Classified Ad 1—No Title," *Atlanta Constitution*, August 5, 1903.

28. "Negro Thief Escapes," *Atlanta Constitution*, April 6, 1909.

29. "Three Blind Tigers Get Limit of the Law," *Atlanta Constitution*, February 7, 1912.

30. "'Crap-Shooters' Pay Penalty of the Law in Recorder's Court," *Atlanta Constitution*, May 5, 1914.

31. "Alabama News," *Atlanta Constitution*, September 12, 1873.

32. "Can't Sell Beer in Restaurant: Recorder Broyles Hands Down an Interesting Opinion," *Atlanta Constitution*, April 17, 1906; "No More Liquor in Restaurants: City Council Has Adopted a New Rule for Future," *Atlanta Constitution*, September 27, 1906; "Many Matters Before Council. . . . License of Restaurants," *Atlanta Constitution*, May 21, 1907.

33. "No More Liquor in Restaurants: City Council Has Adopted a New Rule for Future," *Atlanta Constitution*, September 27, 1906; "Mayor Talks of Resolutions: All Restaurants Should Not Have Been Included, Says Woodward," *Atlanta Constitution*, September 28, 1906.

34. "Must Pay Debts Says the Mayor: Closing of Saloons Has Cut Down the Revenue," *Atlanta Constitution*, October 6, 1906.

35. J. Francis Keeley, "Keeley on the Correct Thing: General Comment on the Unique," *Atlanta Constitution*, May 24, 1908.

36. *Nicrosi v. The State*, 52 Ala. 336 (1875).

37. "Lays Blame on Council: Montgomery Chief Says He Needs More Laws," *Atlanta Constitution*, October 19, 1904.

38. "Orders College Inn Closed after Trial: Witnesses Declare Women Sat in Escorts' Laps, and That Couples Embraced," *Atlanta Constitution*, May 31, 1914.

39. "At the Police Matinee: Old Sarah Brown's Hashery," *Atlanta Constitution*, March 1, 1900; "All Worked for Old Woman: Nearly Every Female Negro Vagrant Arrested Said She Worked in 'Old Lady Brown's' Restaurant," *Atlanta Constitution*, September 3, 1903; Clifford M. Kuhn, Harlon E. Joye, and E. Bernard West, *Living Atlanta: An Oral History of the City, 1914–1948* (Athens: University of Georgia Press, 1990), 37; 1900 United States Census.

40. Albert P. Maurakis, *Never Saw Sunset* (Fredericksburg, Va.: Sheridan, 1998), 98, 131.

41. "Café Proprietors Receive Warning from Ku Klux," *Savannah Tribune*, February 5, 1921, http://infoweb.newsbank.com.libdata.lib.ua.edu/.

42. John Katsos, *The Life of John Katsos* (Greenville, S.C.: A Press, 1985), 127.

43. "Dives Are Run as Restaurants: Chief of Police Will Abolish Them," *Atlanta Constitution*, August 30, 1906,.

44. "Saloons on Red Bridge Road Violate the Sunday Law: Citizens Appeal to Courts for Relief," *Montgomery Advertiser*, March 17, 1902.

45. Home Economics Department, *Atlanta Woman's Club Cook Book* (Atlanta: Atlanta Woman's Club, 1921), 13.

46. Dorothy Dickins, *Some Contrasts in the Levels of Living of Women Engaged in Farm, Textile Mill, and Garment Plant Work* (State College: Mississippi Agricultural Experiment Station, 1941), 27.

47. For common attitudes toward dating among Alabama college coeds, see Lisa Lindquist Dorr, "Fifty Percent Moonshine and Fifty Percent Moonshine: Social Life and College Youth Culture in Alabama, 1913–1933," in *Manners and Southern History*, ed. Ted Ownby (Oxford: University Press of Mississippi, 2007), 45–75.

48. *Birmingham News*, April 26, 1902.

49. Britt Craig, "Shuffling Out 'Cakes' to Mr. Hungry Business Man Has Cotton Factory Beat Forty Ways, Says Mamie," *Atlanta Constitution*, January 10, 1915.

50. Jonathan Daniels, *A Southerner Discovers the South* (New York: Macmillan, 1938), 129.

51. Coleman L. Blease, "Message from the Governor," in *Journal of the House of Representatives of the General Assembly of the State of South Carolina Being the Regular Session, Beginning Tuesday, January 13, 1914* (Columbia, S.C.: Gonzales and Bryan, 1914), 37–38.

52. Ibid.

53. Ibid.; "Blease Shoots at Everything and Everybody: Annual Message of South Carolina Governor Loaded to Guards with Denunciation," *Atlanta Constitution*, January 14, 1914.

54. James Jones, *Bad Blood: The Tuskegee Syphilis Experiment* (New York: Free Press, 1993), 16–29; Lisa Lindquist Dorr, *White Women, Rape, and the Power of Race in Virginia, 1900–1960* (Chapel Hill: University of North Carolina Press, 2004), 98.

55. *The Charter and Ordinances of the City of Atlanta, Code of 1924* (Atlanta: Byrd, 1924), 673–78.

56. Ordinance No. 276-C, "An Ordinance to Prohibit the Condcuting [*sic*] of Resturants [*sic*] or Lunch Counters for White and Colored Persons in the Same Room," Regular Meeting of the Board of Commissioners of the City of Birmingham, SP-33, December 15, 1914, microfilm, Birmingham Archives, Birmingham Public Library, Birmingham, Alabama.

57. "To Stop Serving of Whites and Blacks in Same Restaurant: Judge Lane Will Introduce Ordinance Today Prohibiting Black and Tan Lunch Rooms," [Birmingham] *Age-Herald*, December 15, 1914.

58. Some racial segregation ordinances include *Code of the City of Montgomery, Alabama* (Charlottesville, Va.: Michie City Publications, 1952), §191:10:14; *Code of Ordinances City of Fairfield, Alabama* (Tallahassee, Fla.: Municipal Code Corporation, 1957), §14–29; *Code of the City of Eufaula, Alabama* (Eufaula: City Council, 1952), §346; *City Code of Gadsden, Alabama* (Charlottesville, Va.: Michie City Publications, 1946), §§12, 13; and *Code of the City of Bessemer, Alabama* (Charlottesville, Va.: Michie, 1944), §33ll.

59. This argument is consistent with C. Vann Woodward's notion that the implementation of de jure segregation contributed to a reinforced culture that advanced white supremacy in the South in *The Strange Career of Jim Crow*.

60. At a later date, the Birmingham city council amended its ordinance to require a seven-foot wall between the two dining rooms, and many other southern municipalities followed suit. Such specificity made it even more difficult to accommodate both races and less likely that proprietors would do so. Other cities, such as Atlanta, eliminated the two-dining-room option entirely by requiring a business license to serve either white or black customers.

61. This position is consistent with Grace Elizabeth Hale's understanding of segregation culture in *Making Whiteness*, in which the implementation of public images of blackness as servile was vital in reinforcing the supposed superiority of whiteness. Although Hale acknowledges that such representations were common nationally, they were most apparent in the South.

62. August Meier and Elliott M. Rudwick, CORE: *A Study in the Civil Rights Movement, 1942–1968* (New York: Oxford University Press, 1973).

63. Miles Wolff, *Lunch at the 5 & 10* (Chicago: Elephant Paperbacks, 1990), 8–13.

64. "Bigger than a Hamburger," *Southern Patriot* 18, no. 5 (May 1960): 4.

65. Lizabeth Cohen, *A Consumer's Republic: The Politics of Mass Consumption in Postwar America* (New York: Knopf, 2003), 190.

66. Lallage Longshore to Lister Hill, June 24, 1963, folder 121, box 495, Lister Hill Papers 1921–1968, W. S. Hoole Special Collections Library, University of Alabama, Tuscaloosa.

67. "Johnson Signs Civil Rights Bill, Allen Asks All to Obey Law Here," *Atlanta Constitution*, July 3, 1964.

68. Civil Rights Act of 1964, Pub. L. No. 88–352, July 2, 1964, §201(a).

69. Civil Rights Act of 1964, Pub. L. No. 88–352, July 2, 1964, §201(b)(2).

70. Katzenbach v. McClung, 379 U.S. 294 (1964).

71. Birmingham Police Department Inter-Office Communication, December 14, 1964, folder 987.1.14, Birmingham, Alabama, Law Department Civil Rights Files, Department of Archives and Manuscripts, Birmingham Public Library, Birmingham, Alabama.

72. "Mixing Incidents Are Few, Scattered," *Birmingham News*, July 4, 1964; "U.S. Responding Well to Rights Law, Says a Pleased President," *Atlanta Constitution*, July 4, 1964.

73. "2 Lester Maddox Waitresses Say Man Tried Dates," *Atlanta Daily World*, April 12, 1962.

74. Bruce Galphin, *The Riddle of Lester Maddox* (Atlanta: Camelot, 1968), 22.

75. Although several earlier editions of *The Citizen* attack the civil rights legislation pending in and later passed by Congress, the January 1965 edition interestingly makes no mention of *Katzenbach v. McClung*.

76. Editorial Opinion, "Who Needs Protection?" *The Citizen*, December 1964, 2, 23.

77. Virginia Foster Durr and Hollinger F. Barnard, *Outside the Magic Circle* (Tuscaloosa: University of Alabama Press, 1985), 276.

78. "Recently Desegregated—Negro Is Killed in Fight in Café," *Birmingham Post-Herald*, October 30, 1964.

PART 4
Material Cultures

DOES A CARROT GROWN TODAY taste the same as one grown a hundred years ago? Do the pots, pans, and cookbooks of our past represent the most or least used kitchen equipment? How do we "read" the food story if we have only have photographs and postcards? Can we approximate the sights and sounds and smells of the markets, kitchens, and tables? Can we account for their codification of southern cuisines? The articles in this section argue that all of these approaches are possible when using material cultures to study southern foodways.

A cast-iron pot from the 1890s; seven black-and-white photographs with unidentified subjects from the 1940s; and a collection of postcards depicting a vanished market of the 1820s: using these touchstones, Marcie Cohen Ferris, Psyche Williams-Forson, and Jessica B. Harris show us how to glean narratives from objects.

Their insights answer a persistent challenge. In "Recipes for Reading," a foundational 1989 piece published in the Modern Language Association's journal, Susan Leonardi recognized that literature often describes and prioritizes food. Yet she worried over how to discuss it without erasing ephemeral smells, tactile responses, and pleasures. Other authors, fearful that food studies could become too descriptive or too theoretically removed, have called for a correction. In 2008 Gerard Fitzgerald and Gabriella Patrick, writing in the *Journal of American History*, reminded scholars of the importance of the palate in history as well as in food studies. They cautioned that studies must not lose theoretical sophistication. At a time when food studies still struggles for a balance in its methods, Ferris, Williams-Forson, and Harris forge a middle ground in which the theoretical and the concrete are simultaneously present. From such a balance, productive intellectual questions emerge.[1]

In "The 'Stuff' of Southern Food: Food and Material Culture in the American South," Ferris challenges us to look at "what lies beneath" the food, arguing that while comestibles spoil, objects remain. Walking through her mother-in-law's Mississippi kitchen, Ferris notices that "a box of Texas grapefruit sits atop the beaten biscuit machine, alongside a large, worn wooden bowl." To contextualize the objects located by archaeologists, museum curators, photographers, visual artists, and musicians, Ferris turns to social historians, folklorists, media and cultural studies scholars, and African American theorists.

Psyche Williams-Forson is sympathetic to Ferris's efforts to "read" the material objects, but she interjects cautions. In "'Doing Our Part to Win the War': Using Historical Photography to Understand African American Performances with Southern Food," Williams-Forson presents a set of black-and-white photographs taken at a World War II training camp in Alabama. She proposes reading photographs against the background of the racial politics that contributed to their creation.

Her aim is to "use the visual record to consider the range of underlying interactions that exceed the descriptions we are often given about food preparation, presentation, and consumption." She urges all of us to seek the hidden transcripts in our sources. Can we read the silences? Does it matter if the silences are imposed by the white photographer, the army hierarchy, or the African American men who use such silences as protective cloaking to survive difficult situations? Williams-Forson answers with provisional affirmatives to all.

In "The Market Women of Louisiana: An Aural and Visual Archeology," Jessica B. Harris foregrounds a different issue of silence in the archives. She asks what we can know about the sounds, songs, and cadences of African American women in New Orleans's early nineteenth-century markets. And why, she asks, are those sounds important? By turning to postcards, scraps of song in literature, and folk lyrics, Harris reconstructs the world of the market women who worked the urban squares of New Orleans. Scholars outside of food studies actively debate the role of the aural in humanities research;[2] Harris applies such methods to the sounds and songs of southern food, making clear that not all ephemera have been lost through the years.

By exploring the tactile, the visual, and the aural—and by investigating carefully the silenced, erased, and forgotten—this section grounds our discussion of southern food methodology. Collectively, these essays remind us that, however theoretical our foodways discussions may be, food is a concrete object exchanged and consumed by physical bodies. To gain a full portrait of foodways import, we need to formulate questions that explore sensory responses to food, too.

NOTES

1. Susan Leonardi, "Recipes for Reading," PMLA 104, no. 3 (May 1989): 340–47. Gerard Fitzgerald and Gabriella Petrick, "In Good Taste: Rethinking American History with Our Palates," *Journal of American History* 95, no. 2 (September 2008): 392–404).

2. See, for instance, "Sound Clash: Listening to American Studies," ed. Kara Keeling and Josh Kun, special issue, *American Quarterly* 63, no. 3 (September 2011).

CHAPTER 12

The "Stuff" of Southern Food

Food and Material Culture in the American South

MARCIE COHEN FERRIS

If I could do it, I'd do no writing at all here. It would be photographs; the rest would be fragments of cloth, bits of cotton, lumps of earth, records of speech, pieces of wood and iron.

JAMES AGEE, *Let Us Now Praise Famous Men*, 1941

It is late December and bitterly cold on the farm where my husband grew up in Warren County, Mississippi. The sky is steely gray, and it feels like it may snow. Two horses graze in the field below the house. A screen door slams, and Bill calls to me, "Lunch is ready." I come downstairs, passing the old De Muth "Improved Dough and Beaten Biscuit Machine" that sits on the brick breezeway between the house and the garage. The porch swing stands idle in the cold weather. Cast-iron pots of different sizes are filled with parsley and chives, herbs that will last through the winter. A box of Texas grapefruit sits atop the beaten biscuit machine, alongside a large, worn wooden bowl that holds bright orange tangerines and clementines. I open the screen door to the kitchen, but then remember I wanted to photograph my mother-in-law's two freezers in the garage: one chest and one upright freezer. Inside the house, another chest freezer stands in the pantry, as well as the small freezers atop the two refrigerators in the kitchen. All are filled to capacity with frozen milk cartons of collard greens and yellow squash; plastic bags of butter beans, field peas, and okra; and casserole bowls labeled "CHICKEN TETRAZZINI" and "SWEET POTATOES." Bags of frozen quail and dove, venison sausage, and pork roasts are stacked next to tubs of crabmeat. A supply of ladyfingers—a light, sponge-cake biscuit—is kept for Shelby Ferris's famous chocolate icebox cake. These delicate cookies are hard to find in Vicksburg today, and when my mother-in-law sees them, she stocks up for the holidays. I check to be sure the freezers are closed tightly. A thawed freezer is a disaster on the farm, given the expense, labor, and time invested in their contents.

Inside the kitchen, Bill and his mother have already sat down at the table to eat. "Join us, Marcie," says Shelby. "Go get a plate." The meal of sautéed dove, butter beans, and rice was prepared by Liz Martin, who grew up in Warren County and has worked for more than thirty years as a cook and housekeeper for my mother-in-law. I spoon the dove onto my plate from a cast-iron frying pan, then I add a serving of butter beans and rice from the double boilers that keep these foods warm on two large ovens in the center of the kitchen. Shelby reminds me to get a piece of the Benton's bacon we sent her for Christmas. It's lying on a paper towel–covered plate on the electric food warmer that sits on the kitchen counter. Liz pulls a metal pan of hot biscuits from one of the ovens, and with a spatula she lifts them onto a plate and brings them to the table. "Take two, Marcie," Liz says.

A napkin ring with my name on it identifies my seat at the table. At the beginning of each holiday, Shelby places name stickers on napkin rings for visiting family members. The "regulars"—Bill and his sisters, their cousin Gene, and our niece Martha—can always find their napkin rings in the linen drawer. As an in-law, I note the fragility of the temporary labels and press mine tightly onto my napkin ring. Bill passes me the butter dish and a jar of Shelby's wild plum jelly. I squeeze a slice of lemon into my glass of iced tea, which Liz made earlier. She sweetens it with honey made from bees on the farm. Bill butters another biscuit and sighs with contentment. "There's some chess pie," says Shelby. "Would anybody like a little piece?"

I begin with this food memory from rural Mississippi because it is a story filled with familiar artifacts. (Note the screen doors, porch swings, frying pans, napkin rings, and butter knives.) These artifacts represent the material culture of food in a southern place where many of the objects have existed from the late nineteenth century to today. Inventor J. A. De Muth of St. Joseph, Missouri, proudly displayed his beaten biscuit machine in the agricultural exhibits at the World's Columbian Exposition in Chicago in 1893. The De Muth "kneader" and new food products such as Cracker Jack and Aunt Jemima's Pancake Mix were viewed by more than twenty-seven million visitors at the Columbian Exposition and nationally publicized by newspapers and magazines.[1] My husband's father, Bill Ferris, bought the antique De Muth beaten biscuit machine in Natchez for his wife Shelby soon after they married. A larger beaten biscuit machine with a marble top and cast-iron legs, "the one with a history," explains Shelby, came to her through her grandmother, Shelby Gibbs Flowers, and her mother, Hester Craig Flowers.

Liz Martin still uses the De Muth beaten biscuit machine three or four times a year, when she devotes most of a day to prepare a large tin of biscuits for the Ferris family. The De Muth, the lighter of the two machines, is more convenient for Liz to pick up and bring into the house. Before mechanization of the process, a simple dough of flour, lard, and milk was pounded with a mallet, as the dough was repeatedly folded and flattened.[2] This laborious process, replicated by the iron rollers of the kneader/beaten biscuit machine, creates a "short," flaky biscuit, perfect for serving with a salty bite of ham. But the presence of this patented device and the other objects in my Mississippi food memory—a wooden bowl, a cast-iron frying pan, casserole bowls, a dining table, iced tea glasses, food warmers, and napkin rings—reveals a more complicated story than a winter noontime meal or Liz Martin's biscuit recipe. The beaten biscuit machine's metal gears and rollers—which must be carefully cleaned after use—its handle that requires a skilled hand to turn it, the dough that needs a reliable oven, and the white family and guests who enjoy this special treat are part of a multilayered, evolving story of race, class, and gender in the American South.

What Is Southern?

In 2008 an unpublished essay by the late Edna Lewis, the African American doyenne of southern food, was discovered and published in *Gourmet* magazine. Titled "What Is Southern?," the essay is Lewis's poetic description of the foundational elements of southern food.[3] "How did southern food come into being?" she asks. "The early cooking of southern food was primarily done by blacks, men and women. It was then, and it still is now." If there is a "chestnut" of southern food, this is it. One could elaborate on agriculture, climate, geography, historical events, global economic forces, and the shifting of people from place to place to describe the history of southern food, but its roots lie in these twenty-one words.

Southern food and its regional artifacts—the material culture used in the production and consumption of food—are the cultural products of the interaction of white, black, and Native American people for more than four centuries. A walk through the period rooms of the Museum of Early Southern Decorative Arts in Winston-Salem, North Carolina, quickly reveals the historical artifacts of southern foodways.[4] There is a seventeenth-century court cupboard from southeastern Virginia passed down in the female line of a family because of its important domestic function as a place to store and display food-related ceramics, pewter, silver, and textiles.[5] Carved tea tables, dining tables, sideboards, chairs, pottery storage jars and jugs from the Carolinas, Moravian-style serving plates from Salem, Lowcountry sweetgrass baskets for winnowing rice, silver rice spoons for serving "Carolina Gold," imported china, and dishware are evidence of cultural systems of foodways production and consumption in the region.[6]

Sixteenth-century watercolors and engravings by John White and Theodor De Bry portray native people and their food artifacts on the Outer Banks of the Carolinas. Eighteenth- and nineteenth-century portraits of white plantation elite and paintings of their homes and estates feature food both at table and in the field to display wealth and status. Scenes of Civil War life described in diaries and illustrated in *Harper's Weekly* depict food shortages on the battlefield and in southern cities and villages. In the postbellum paintings of the South, and in the early twentieth-century work of Charleston Renaissance painters such as Alice Ravenel Huger Smith, food and its material culture capture the romantic South.

Photographic documentation of the material culture of southern food is equally rich, from Farm Security Administration (FSA) images in the 1930s to William Eggleston's color-saturated portraits of southern life. In his photograph of a dining table in a Mississippi Delta home, taken at the moment the meal was served, Eggleston captures the food and artifacts of a particular time—the white china plate of fried ham and green beans, a vase of white roses, yeast rolls served in a silver dish, a glass of iced tea, and vintage 1970s place mats.[7] William Christenberry's powerful photographs of Hale County, Alabama, a place to which he returns annually to document its changing material worlds, are filled with food imagery in faded painted advertisements, billboards, grocery stores, and café signs. Birney Imes's striking photographs of African American juke joints in the Mississippi Delta reveal a world energized by cold beer, catfish, dancing, and blues. Artists in the second half of the twentieth century, such as Walter Anderson (Mississippi Gulf Coast), Carroll Cloar (Arkansas Delta), William Dunlap (Central Mississippi/Virginia), and Glennray Tutor (Oxford, Mississippi), also have an eye for everyday food imagery, as seen in Tutor's photorealistic painting of jars of pickles.

Southern folk artists—also known as outsider, self-taught, or visionary artists—are careful observers of the daily worlds around them, and their approach to food is deeply shaped by their sense of place, family, and memory. Food becomes an iconic symbol in their work. Massive iron pots, cookstoves, frying pans, butter churns, and butchering tables are the subject of paintings by Clementine Hunter (Louisiana) and Minnie Smith Reinhardt (North Carolina), and of Emma Russell's quilt, *Memories of My Life on the Farm* (Mississippi).[8]

Drawing inspiration from Edna Lewis's evocation of the materiality of southern food, I explore the relationship between material culture and the study of southern foodways. To do so, a wide net must be cast because the three-dimensional "stuff" of southern foodways that we can touch—a cast-iron skillet, a canning jar, a jigger of bourbon, a deviled egg platter, a stoneware crock—is the tangible expression of these objects. These objects also exist in southern visual culture, consumer culture, history, memory, popular culture, and the southern literary tradition. The "stuff" of southern foodways, like food itself, is, as Richard Gray suggests, "the undertow of memory."[9] But can we "read" an iron pot, a rolling pin, or an apron—and why do these objects matter?

Richard Rabinowitz, curator of the slavery exhibition at the National Museum of African American History and Culture in Washington, D.C., describes the significance of an iron cooking pot for an enslaved family in the South. "You can imagine the rice pot sitting and cooking for most of the day," Mr. Rabinowitz said. "You have to try to evoke the quality of coming back and, even in the summertime, after a full day of work, it may be the last bits of twilight, and just having a chance to sit around that pot and to eat the food. Who's it been prepared by? What's said around that pot? You can really create a whole story around that."[10] Rabinowitz asks us to consider the people behind the object, as well as its relationship to sense of place, the phrase used by Eudora Welty to describe the "underlying bond that connects all the arts with place."[11]

Social History and Material Culture, Southern-Style

To decipher the coded language of material culture and southern food, we first turn to the definitions and methodologies developed by historians and folklorists in the newly emerging field of material culture during the turbulent social activism of the 1960s and 1970s. In his introduction to *New American History* (1990), Eric Foner reminds us that "in the course of the past twenty years, American history has been remade."[12] Social movements of the 1960s and 1970s spawned a generation of historians who rejected a vision of the past that celebrated the "Founding Fathers," ignoring ordinary Americans and their lives. With their new focus on the "everyday and everydayness," social historians embraced material culture as "the totality of artifacts in a culture, the vast universe of objects used by humankind to cope with the physical world, to facilitate social intercourse, to delight our fancy, and to create symbols of meaning."[13] Only by studying objects used in daily life can we reconstruct what social historians describe as the "whole landscape," or the total history of the past. "Material culture," writes anthropologist James Deetz, "is not culture, but its product."[14]

The study of material culture broadens our understanding of the past in many ways. Artifacts are often the only surviving evidence of the past; they provide a voice for marginalized people. In the context of southern food studies, these people were the enslaved cooks, house slaves, field hands, and white and black working poor whose lives were not presented in traditional written sources. As Ted Rosengarten explains, "One of the vexing problems about studying the southern plantation is that you come to know the masters better than you know the slaves."[15]

Objects reveal cultural perspectives from another time—the life experiences and *mentalité* of people whose lives are far different than our own.[16]

Folklorist and art historian Bernard Herman argues, "There are no innocent objects."[17] Every artifact has a history that lies beneath its surface. Those that survive in museums are more often the rare Chinese export porcelain platter than a common earthenware pot.[18]

Consider the broken or worn bits of objects found in the dooryards of late eighteenth- and early nineteenth-century kitchens and slave quarters in Charleston, South Carolina. Archaeologists uncovered fragments of sea grass baskets, decorative cowrie shells, beads, shards of English creamware, and African American colonoware bowls—pottery made by enslaved potters who melded African technology and European ceramic forms. This assemblage underscores the complex racial order in the urban South and the process of cultural retention and exchange that took place between enslaved people and slave owners. "The divided worlds of the house extended to the very cooking hearth where masters and mistresses often purchased separate provisions for their servants," states Herman, "and where the boundaries between those worlds were compromised every day in the very acts of cooking, tasting, and sampling."[19] Anthropologist Dell Upton argues that we must understand the complexities of the built environment—like the Charleston dooryard. Instead of viewing it as one uniform landscape, we must recognize that black and white Americans occupied distinct, separate landscapes that overlapped and intersected.[20] Within these historic landscapes lies the material culture of southern foodways.

Objects also allow scholars to reconsider past historical theories, such as the groundbreaking work in the Chesapeake region by social historians and archaeologists in the 1970s and 1980s.[21] Archaeological analysis of the common "Virginia House," a temporary structure set into the ground with wooden posts, and the contents of trash pits illustrated "the poverty of the country and want of necessaries here," as described in Virginia laws of 1647.[22] Until the collapse of the tobacco market after 1680, time, labor, and money went into tobacco crops, not housing or the dining table. The Chesapeake Bay country remained a "perpetual frontier" until a more stable, diversified agricultural economy was in place. The evidence of how and what people ate is an important material expression of this economic and cultural transformation.

Thomas Schlereth, one of the leading scholars to document material culture, published an important anthology on the field in 1982.[23] In *Material Culture Studies in America*, Schlereth noted that foodways was a topic largely ignored by material culturists. Folklorists and archaeologists were the leaders in the field of foodways, including scholars such as Jay Anderson, Charles Camp, James Deetz, Henry Glassie, and Don Yoder.[24] A visionary in the development of folklife studies, Yoder influenced a generation of scholars—including many who studied the South—to document food as another expression of American material life. Schlereth describes the era of material culture studies from 1965 to the 1980s as "the age of interpretation."[25] It was this period that most shaped the contemporary study of food and material culture in the American South.[26]

Southern Food History Comes of Age

Three landmark publications marked a turning point in the evolution of southern food history and material culture: Sam Bowers Hilliard's *Hog Meat and Hoecake: Food Supply in the Old South, 1840–1860* (1972), Joe Gray Taylor's *Eating, Drinking, and Visiting in the South: An Informal History* (1982), and John Egerton's *Southern Food: At Home, on the Road, in History* (1987). Hilliard states that the South has one of the strongest and most pervasive foodways traditions in the country, in large part due to the region's poverty, isolation, and historic small number of immigrants. He explores the foodways patterns of both black and white southerners and the ways in which these material worlds overlapped and separated. Black and white southerners ate similar foods, prepared in similar ways, using the same cast-iron pots and Dutch ovens, but the amount, variety, and quality of foodstuffs differed between the two groups. Robert St. George said of Hilliard, "He demonstrates that food—the only type of created artifact that men and women literally 'consume'—served at once to define the South as a cultural region and to demarcate recognized social boundaries."[27]

Any discussion of the material culture of southern foodways must consider the retention of African heritage, since food in the American South has been so strongly shaped by African Americans. In 1941 Melville Herskovits's groundbreaking study *Myth of the Negro Past* successfully demonstrated the existence of African retentions, what he called Africanisms, in African

American religion, magic, dance, black speech, and manners. He argued that little retention survived in material culture and suggested that this was the first area where slaves substituted New World forms for their African clothes, foodways, tools, and housing forms. In the 1960s and 1970s John Blassingame, Robert Farris Thompson, and John Vlach successfully demonstrated that African heritage survived in many forms of black material culture, sometimes in pristine African expressions, such as the banjo, and at other times in hybrid objects, such as baskets and pottery, that reflect the process of syncretism.[28]

Judith Carney, Eugene Genovese, Leland Ferguson, Jessica Harris, Karen Hess, Charles Joyner, Sidney Mintz, Philip Morgan, Frederick Opie, Dale Rosengarten, Psyche Williams-Forson, Peter Wood, Anne Yentsch, and other scholars broadened the scholarship of African heritage and its expression in African American material culture to include southern foodways.[29] Their work incorporated food in the cultural negotiation and exchange experienced by African American men and women—from slave ships to segregated trains of the Jim Crow South and the kitchens of 1950s white southerners. Jessica Harris states that while Africa was a distant memory to enslaved people in the South in the early nineteenth century, "Yet Africa remained. It remained in the shapes of the ceramic ware that was used on tables. It appeared in the foods that were on their plates."[30] Anne Yentsch explains, "Cultural identity does not require freedom to find expression."[31]

Rethinking the Boundaries and Landmarks of Southern Food

We return to Edna Lewis's question "What is Southern?" to explore the "stuff" of southern food. In the past, we would *first* define the borders of the South, then theorize about what makes the South distinctive, including its food and material culture.[32] The "old" map of the South traditionally referred to the eleven states of the former Confederacy, but today these rigid borders have changed. The South "is found wherever southern culture is found," existing "as a state of mind both within and beyond its geographical boundaries," including southern diasporic sites in Chicago, Cincinnati, Dallas, Detroit, Houston, Los Angeles, and New York City.[33] Fried catfish, greens, pork barbecue, and cast-iron skillets are an edible expression of southern identity in these cities and in many others outside the South that were terminus sites of the Great Migration.[34] Trucks from Georgia and the Carolinas appear on Atlantic Avenue in Brooklyn throughout the year, hauling southern produce and "seasoning meat" (smoked ham) to city residents who have roots in the South. In late December the trucks are filled with cabbage, collard greens, cornmeal, field peas, sweet potatoes, bags of peanuts and pecans, and jars of chowchow and honey, as well as the necessary seasonings and ham hock to prepare a proper southern New Year's Day feast.[35] Here we find material culture on wheels, a roving symbol of the power of taste, memory, and the African American heritage of southern foodways.

Beyond the question of what constitutes the South's borders, a new vision of southern studies challenges conventional tropes of southern identity, including what belongs in the canon of southern food and its bona fide artifacts.[36] The "new southern studies" considers landmarks of southern identity *other* than the Civil War and Reconstruction. These new landmarks include the civil rights movement and its material culture. Lunch counters in dime stores across the South where students protested segregation in the 1960s are now as important for southern food memory as an antebellum cast-iron pot. Kathleen Purvis, food editor for the *Charlotte Observer*, describes the simple white and gold Pyrex casserole dish on display in the Levine Museum of the New South. The bowl belonged to Maggie Ray, who led the biracial group of parents who developed the plan to integrate Charlotte's schools in the 1970s. Ray organized a yearlong series of supper meetings for the group. "Smart woman," wrote Purvis. "She not only got people to gather around a table, she also knew that it's hard to act hateful toward someone when you're eating their food."[37]

Rather than the old white and black South, the "new southern studies" recognizes the diverse cultures and ethnicities of the South, whose global influences shape the region. In this newly defined South the material culture of regional foodways includes Tampa's Columbia Restaurant (1905), with its classic Spanish-Cuban design; Atlanta's Buford Highway, a multiethnic commercial strip of vibrant food shops; and North Carolina's Latino tiendas and cafés. This rethinking of "what is Southern?" leads us to consider how southern food and its material culture relate to popular culture.

Mammy Goes to Hollywood

Generations of Americans, including native southerners, imagined the South as a made-for-Hollywood plantation setting of amiable white and black southerners enjoying traditional southern foods together: fried chicken, Virginia ham, crab, oysters, sweet potatoes, squash casserole, snap beans, Sally Lunn bread, hot biscuits, cornbread, sweet tea, and a tempting assortment of pies and cakes. This mythic world exists today in Turner Classic Movie (TCM) reruns of *Gone with the Wind* (1939), *Jezebel* (1938), and a 1935 series of Shirley Temple films set in the "Old South" that includes *The Littlest Rebel* and *The Little Colonel*.[38] In the height of the Depression, Hollywood producers David O. Selznick and William Wyler recognized the box office appeal of films that offered an escape to a southern "place out of time," filled with romance, feisty southern belles, handsome suitors, loyal servants, and evil carpetbaggers.[39] This celluloid mythic South locked images of southern hospitality—a material world of "groaning boards," gracious plantation picnics, and spoon-wielding black "mammies"—into the American mind.

Because the South and its history were so unfamiliar to the general public, executives at Metro-Goldwyn-Mayer Studio (MGM) worried that the plot of *Gone with the Wind* would confuse its audiences. A short trailer, *The Old South* (1940), directed by Fred Zinnemann, was produced to explain the rise of "King Cotton" and the South's devastation following the Civil War. Filled with images of a noble "Lost South," the trailer reinforced mythic images of southern material culture through lavish scenes of plantation dining, as described by the narrator: "There came to the South an era of wondrous beauty, of moonlight and magnolias and mint juleps—an era of chivalry and true hospitality, a gallantry of devil-may-care cavaliers and their lovely ladies fair."[40] Moviegoers loved a spectacle, and what scene better displayed the debauchery and wealth of elite white southerners than images of doting servants, grand candelabra, domed silver food warmers, fine china, and starched linens? These scenes also provided great drama for the money, since they were filmed in-house at MGM's back-lot studios.

Colonial Williamsburg's popular orientation film, *Williamsburg: The Story of a Patriot*, uses similar images of hospitality and fine living to depict the story of patriot-planters in the years leading up to the Revolution. Shot in 1956 by Academy Award–winning director George Seaton, the film is still shown at the museum today. In scenes filmed at Westover Plantation (1730) overlooking the James River, Virginia planters discuss their concerns about the British over glasses of Madeira and frosty mint juleps. Scenes set in Williamsburg's restored taverns display stoneware mugs, ceramic pipes, pewter bowls, glassware, and table linen, which are available for visitors to purchase in the museum's gift stores. In one scene fictional planter John Fry, played by Jack Lord of *Hawaii Five-O* fame, visits with his mother and his wife, as she unpacks a wooden barrel of goods recently arrived from Liverpool. The younger Mrs. Fry removes a set of English china and damask yardage from the barrel and excitedly shows the fine goods to her mother-in-law. Reinforcing the historic connection between gentility and consumption, the elder Mrs. Fry remarks, "English goods were ever the best."[41]

A Consumer World of "Plantation Flavor"

Motion pictures such as *The Story of a Patriot* were among the thousands of products available in the rapidly expanding consumer culture that shaped the American South in the first half of the twentieth century. Southern general stores, country stores, and, later, independent and chain grocery stores such as Piggly Wiggly offered a vast selection of newly branded food products to white and black consumers.[42] Grace Elizabeth Hale describes a "revolution in representation" that took place as national manufacturers used racial stereotypes and "racial nostalgia" that drew on the plantation myth to promote their products.[43]

In 1893 Nancy Green, a fifty-nine-year-old former slave working as a domestic worker in Chicago, was hired to promote Aunt Jemima pancake mix at the World's Columbian Exposition in Chicago.[44] Dressed in traditional "mammy" garb, Green stood in a giant flour barrel—twenty-four feet high and sixteen feet wide—where she greeted guests, sang songs, and told stories of the Old South. She reputedly served more than a million pancakes and took fifty thousand orders for the pancake mix. Noting the success of the Aunt Jemima trademark, other manufacturers followed suit as they realized the dollar value of advertisements that featured Rastus, the Cream of

Wheat chef, the Gold Dust Twins, the Luzianne Coffee Lady, Rinso's black housekeeper, and, in the 1940s, Uncle Ben's Rice.[45] "Spokeservants" such as these appeared on hundreds of domestic products, as well as on print advertisements and trade cards.[46] When this culturally coded material culture entered the homes of white southerners, the images of servile African Americans, the advertising copy and catchy jingles in black pidgin dialect reinforced ideas about black inferiority, especially for white children.[47] "Childhood was the crucial period when whites learned racial difference," says Hale. "The white home in the American South became a central site for the production and reproduction of racial identity."[48]

Black collectibles are the offspring of modern American advertising and mass marketing strategies developed at the turn of the twentieth century.[49] From the 1920s to the 1950s, American pottery companies such as McCoy, Red Wing, Shawnee, and Weller, as well as Japanese manufacturers, adopted "Mammy and her family" as they produced cookie jars, salt and pepper shakers, syrup pitchers, condiment sets, measuring cups, grocery reminder boards, linen dishtowels, and tablecloths. "Mammy" and her fictional partner "Uncle Mose" are never depicted at rest. Black figures raise eggs and candles aloft, release string through their mouths, store cookies in their skirts and straight pins in their stomachs. They were molded into human-shaped teapots, syrup pitchers, and dinner bells. Standing figurines held a broom, a spoon, a mixing bowl, or a platter. The inexpensive kitsch of their time, kitchen "collectibles," such as the "mammy" cookie jar, reinforced racial stereotypes in the South and throughout the nation. Through these domestic objects, white consumers, particularly women, reinforced a culture of segregation.[50] "Mammy" collectibles revived a never-never land of the "Old South" where middle-class, white housewives could momentarily ignore a changing American racial landscape.[51]

The civil rights movement of the 1960s and 1970s temporarily halted the production of "mammy" and other black stereotypical collectibles. In 1965 the NAACP called for an official boycott of Aunt Jemima, and Quaker Oats responded by removing her bandana and slimming her ample figure.[52] The Aunt Jemima stereotype was so familiar by this point that black Americans appropriated her as an insult in the urban street game of "Playing the Dozens" with the phrase, "Hey man, ain't ya' momma on the pancake box?"[53]

Many African Americans considered her a female version of Uncle Tom who sold both her soul and her secret pancake recipe to make money for the white man.[54]

At the center of racialized objects and southern foodways is the issue of power—the power of American manufacturers who sold domestic kitsch that reinforced racial stereotypes, and the power of white consumers who bought racist objects and displayed them in their kitchens. Black activists and collectors in the late twentieth century took back this power by using these objects in acts of protest, in art, and in their own collections as statements of resistance. Artist Betye Saar empowered "mammy" in her assemblage piece *The Liberation of Aunt Jemima* (1972), which incorporates black collectibles and advertising imagery. A smiling "mammy" figure in a red polka-dot kerchief stands inside a box, holding a broom in one hand and a rifle in the other. A bed of fluffy cotton lies beneath her feet. Positioned against a wall of "Aunt Jemima" faces, Saar's "mammy" is a "domestic soldier" who revolts against her enslavement and sexual oppression.[55]

Navigating the Segregated South: Food, Race, and Labor

Outside the home, the material culture of southern food and race symbolized the segregated South, and the physical evidence of that past remains today. Food-related guidebooks such as *The Negro Motorist Green Book* and Duncan Hines's *Adventures in Good Eating* provided restaurant recommendations for black and white travelers in the segregated South and throughout America. A former traveling salesman and native of Bowling Green, Kentucky, Hines published his guide from the 1930s to the 1950s. Drawing on his southern heritage for his culinary authority, Hines created a food empire based on his annual restaurant and lodging guides.[56] Being listed in the guide had serious financial benefits. When the High Hampton Inn in Cashiers, North Carolina, was left out of the guide in the 1950s, the hotel manager wrote Mr. Hines:

> Let me thank you for the recent publicity given High Hampton Inn and our oven broiled chicken in your recent column.... Another thing I wish to mention, and this has disturbed us considerably, is the report that High Hampton

Inn has been discontinued in your most recent issue of "Adventures in Good Eating." Have we sinned in some manner or was it just an oversight? We have always been proud of our listing among the good places to eat and regret very much that we have been dropped. Perhaps you can tell us the reason.[57]

Established in 1936 by Victor H. Green, *The Negro Motorist Green Book* provided an important service to African Americans who found Duncan Hines's segregated *Adventures in Good Eating* of no use to them in their travels.[58] For seventy-five cents, travelers could purchase this listing of businesses that served African Americans across the country, including restaurants, hotels, and taverns. Until the 1930s, lodging and concessions in Virginia's Shenandoah National Park were for "Whites Only." Pressure from Secretary of Interior Harold Ickes forced the National Park Service to develop facilities for African Americans, such as the Lewis Mountain Picnic Grounds for Negroes, which opened in 1939. Mr. Green wrote in the book's introduction, "The Jewish press has long published information about places that are restricted."[59] Green hoped a time would come when the guide would no longer be necessary. He ended the guide after the Civil Rights Act was passed in 1964.

Lewis Mountain Picnic Ground and other historically black sites such as Lincoln Beach in Louisiana, where African Americans were allowed to gather during the Jim Crow years, and Highland Beach in Maryland, the first African American–owned summer resort community, are iconic sites in the material record of southern foodways.[60] Picnic tables, benches, signage, postcards, and ephemera deserve a place of honor alongside other cultural symbols of this era such as the segregated lunch counter, bar stools, and pie rack at the Woolworth in Greensboro, North Carolina. The restricted bus station concession stand in Birmingham, Alabama, and the ubiquitous water fountains in southern courthouses and town squares were designated for use by the color of one's skin.[61] Natasha Trethewey, born in Gulfport, Mississippi, captures the poignancy of these remembered material worlds in her poem, "History Lesson":

> I am four in this photograph, standing
> on a wide strip of Mississippi Beach,
> my hands on the flowered hips

of a bright bikini....
I am alone except for my grandmother, other side
of the camera, telling me how to pose.
It is 1970, two years after they opened
the rest of this beach to us,

forty years since the photograph
where she stood on a narrow plot of sand
marked *colored*, smiling,

her hands on the flowered hips
of a cotton meal-sack dress.[62]

Documentarians included descriptions of southern food and its material culture in their work to illustrate the South's incessant struggles with race. From John Dollard's *Caste and Class in a Southern Town* (1937), a sociological study of race in Indianola, Mississippi, to Anne Moody's *Coming of Age in Mississippi* (1968), the classic memoir of a young black woman's movement from oppression to activism, food and its material culture offer compelling ways to chronicle the South.[63] Moody wrote,

One Saturday the white lady let Mama bring us to her house. We sat on the back porch until the white family finished eating. Then Mama brought us in the house and sat us at the table and we finished up the food. It was the first time I had seen the inside of a white family's kitchen. That kitchen was pretty, all white and shiny. Mama had cooked that food we were eating, too. "If Mama only had a kitchen like this of her own," I thought, "she would cook better food for us, too."[64]

The material culture of food is also emblematic of labor and reform movements in the early twentieth century New South. Lewis Hine documented child labor in his photography of textile mills in the Carolinas, as well as in the oyster and shrimp canneries of the Gulf Coast, where children stood on boxes to reach the work. After the early twentieth-century switch from waterpower to electricity, and the subsequent "speedup" of mechanized looms, textile mill workers could no longer go home for a midday meal and rest breaks. "Sometimes you'd start up several looms, then you'd eat a little," mill worker Lloyd Davidson recalled. "After you'd started two or three, then you'd eat a little more. You couldn't take any time to amount to anything for eating. You just had to work your eating in with your work."[65] "Dope carts" were a fixture of southern mill life.[66] These rolling food carts carried pimiento cheese sandwiches, cold drinks, candy bars, packages of Nabs, and BC "Headache" Powder and provided sustenance for workers, whose schedules and bodies were controlled by mill management and their visiting "efficiency experts."

In the mountain South, Progressive Era northern-trained teachers described ill-provisioned kitchens in their settlement schools and complained bitterly about the cornbread. Convincing local women to switch to "light" bread and beaten biscuits was next to impossible when cornbread required so little to prepare—just an iron skillet, a bowl, a spoon, and a source of heat.[67] In the tobacco-growing Carolina Piedmont, female home demonstration agents showed rural girls how to use pressure cookers and canning machines to prepare and sell their homegrown tomatoes.[68]

Throughout the South, the unrelenting poverty of the Depression was captured in the FSA photographs of housewives and mothers "making do" in spare kitchens, and images of the lean meals eaten by laborers and families in the 1930s. Works Progress Administration (WPA) state guides and *America Eats*—both projects of the Federal Writers' Project in the 1930s and 1940s—included descriptions of southern food and its artifacts and architecture by writers and folklorists such as Zora Neale Hurston and Stetson Kennedy.[69]

WPA interviewers collected more than two thousand narratives of slavery from older, largely rural, black southerners in the 1930s. A significant number of the interviews included descriptions of slave rations and the material culture of food in the slave quarters, in the fields, and in the "Big House." WPA interviewer Grace McCune recorded the following story from Benny Dilliard of Athens, Georgia, using the interviewing style of the late 1930s to recreate the black vernacular:

> De fireplaces was a heap bigger dan dey has now. . . . 'Taters and cornpone was roasted in de ashes and most of de other victuals was biled [boiled] in de big old pots what swung on cranes over de coals. Dey had long-handled fryin' pans and heavy iron skillets wid big, thick, tight-fittin' lids, and ovens of all sizes to bake in. . . . De wooden bowls what slave chillun et out of was made out of sweetgum trees. Us et wid mussel shells 'stid of spoons . . ."[70]

Discussing the merits and challenges of using former slave narratives as archival sources, historian C. Vann Woodward argued that some interviewees' nostalgia for plantation slavery was shaped by their difficult experiences in the Great Depression. Many of the former slaves were hungry and suffering during the interviews conducted in the 1930s. Woodward noted the words of a former enslaved man from North Carolina: "It's all hard, slavery and freedom, both bad when you can't eat."[71]

Southern Food as Signifier in Contemporary Culture

In the 1960s and 1970s food and its material culture symbolized the South in many popular southern-themed television programs such as *The Andy Griffith Show*, *The Beverly Hillbillies*, *Green Acres*, *Petticoat Junction*, and *The Waltons*, and musical variety shows such as *Hee Haw* and the *Grand Ole Opry*. This tradition continues today in "reality" television programs set in the South, where meal-time scenes with duck-call carvers, alligator wrestlers, catfish "noodlers," and working-class white families, like that of Alana "Honey Boo Boo" Thompson, signify the bizarre South. In practically any contemporary film set in the South—*Norma Rae*, *Steel Magnolias*, *The Big Easy*, *The Color Purple*, *Fried Green Tomatoes*, *Driving Miss Daisy*, *Mississippi Masala*, *O Brother, Where Art Thou?*, *Cold Mountain*, *Junebug*, *Beasts of the Southern Wild*—scenes of food and iconic culinary artifacts help audiences examine the South portrayed on screen.[72] Joe York's documentary films on southern food and its material culture are available through the Southern Foodways Alliance.[73] Filmmakers Les Blank, William Ferris, and Stan Woodward (*It's Grits*) also explore the material worlds of southern food in their work, much of which can be found on Folkstreams.[74]

Many celebrity chefs on television's Food Network are southerners whose programs feature regional food and a southern "patois," such as Cat Cora (Mississippi), Paula Deen and her sons Bobby and Jamie Deen (Georgia), Tyler Florence (South Carolina), Emeril Lagasse (a native of Massachusetts, but a devotee of Creole cuisine), and Patrick and Gina Neely (Tennessee). The sets for these programs are filled with the imagined material culture of southern food, from cast-iron skillets to family silver to suburban kitchens with granite countertops. Viewers read these "made-for-TV" worlds as authentically southern, or at least "southern-style." Similarly, *Southern*

Living magazine has played a tremendous role in the popularization of what a southern home and, most importantly, a southern kitchen should look like.[75] In John Shelton and Dale Volberg Reed's *1001 Things Everyone Should Know about the South*, Nicholas Lemann observed "for affluent southern whites today, 'the southern way of life' no longer means 'white supremacy' but includes a list of material essentials such as the 'totally planned community' around a golf course, cheese grits and honey-baked ham at the pre-game brunch," and "a five-year subscription to *Southern Living*."[76]

Southern music provides a rich cache of regional food and its material culture.[77] In toe-tapping fiddle tunes, sexually explicit blues lyrics, hip-hop poetry, biscuit-filled country music, barbecue-basted beach music, and southern-themed musical scores for films and television, food denotes regional identity. James Whitcomb Riley's "Shortnin' Bread" (1900) was a musical expression of the plantation myth and a nostalgic southern world of "mammies," kitchens, and skillets.[78] The Andrews Sisters recorded a popular version of "Shortnin' Bread" in 1938. Bob Wills and His Texas Playboys recorded an ode to the mythic Lost South in their 1942 version of "That's What I Like about the South," which includes "fryin' eggs and boiling hammy" and "basements full of berry jams."[79] Bobbie Gentry's "Ode to Billie Joe" (1968) is a ballad of the white working-class South. Over dinner, a cotton-farming family talks about the recent suicide of a young boy, Billie Joe McAllister, in the Mississippi Delta.

> And Papa said to Mama as he passed around the black-eyed peas,
> "Well, Billie Joe never had a lick of sense, pass the biscuits, please.
> . . .
> I'll have another piece of apple pie, you know it don't seem right,
> I saw him at the sawmill yesterday on Choctaw Ridge,
> and now you tell me Billie Joe's jumped off the Tallahatchie Bridge."[80]

The narrative unfolds in verses marked by food and place names in Mississippi, such as Carroll County, Choctaw Ridge, the Tallahatchie Bridge, and Tupelo.

JJ Grey & MOFRO, a contemporary southern rock band from Florida, recorded "Ho Cake" (2007), an ode to southern soul food.

My Granny makes the best cracklin' ho cake.
It taste so good I can't wait to dip my plate.
She's cookin' ham hocks in some white-acre peas.
She's cookin' turnip greens and macaroni and cheese.

Get on out my way, I got to ease up to that pot.
I like my cornbread while it's still piping hot.
I love this food, Lord. I can't get enough.
Stick ya hands near my plate, you'll draw back a nub.[81]

The Material Worlds of Southern Food and Southern Fiction

Writers of southern fiction would be hard pressed to tell a story without food and its material worlds. In Eudora Welty's *Delta Wedding* (1946), set in Mississippi in the 1920s, two cakes become characters in the story: a white coconut cake prepared from the recipe of a long-dead ancestor, Great Aunt Mashula, and a spicy, dark "patticake" made by Partheny, an African American cook, who adds voodoo to the mix—"a little white dove blood in it, dove heart, blood of a snake—things."[82] There are caramel cakes and a fantastical wedding cake shipped from Memphis, too. With this "extensive vocabulary of cakes," states Ann Romines, Welty used domestic ritual to describe the intricate relationships of the white and black women of Shellmound Plantation.[83] Southern writers Harper Lee, Ernest Gaines, Minrose Gwin, Randall Kenan, Lee Smith, and Elizabeth Spencer, to name but a few, turn to the South's domestic worlds to speak of much more than recipes and housekeeping. Descriptions of the rituals of mealtime, hot ovens, rolling pins, mortar and pestles, cake pans, and nutmeg graters reveal the daily dance of white and black families, related by blood, by place, and by the legacy of racism.

In Ralph Ellison's *Invisible Man* (1953), the nostalgic, powerful pull of food draws the black protagonist back south in his memory. As the southern-born narrator searches for meaning, he is stopped in his tracks when he encounters a vendor in Harlem selling baked yams from a street cart.

I stopped as though struck by a shot, deeply inhaling, remembering, my mind surging back, back. At home we'd bake them in the hot coals of the fireplace, had carried them cold to school for lunch; munched them secretly, squeezing the sweet pulp from the soft peel as we hid from the teacher behind the largest book, the *World's Geography*. Yes, and we'd love them candied, or baked in a cobbler, deep-fat fried in a pocket of dough, or roasted with pork and glazed with the well-browned fat; had chewed them raw—yams and years ago. More yams than years ago, though the time seemed endlessly expanded stretched thin as the spiraling smoke beyond all recall. I moved again. "Get yo' hot, baked Car'lina yam," he called.[84]

The South's rigid codes of race and class come to life in Harper Lee's Pulitzer Prize–winning novel of the segregated South, *To Kill a Mockingbird* (1960). Set in fictional Maycomb, Alabama, in the 1930s, the effects of post–Civil War poverty and the Depression were visible in the material worlds Lee created, including the southern table. This New South is a world of want but also an evolving consumer culture that Lee illustrates through commercial products such as Coca-Cola, tins of sardines, and Tootsie Rolls. In a pivotal scene, Scout Finch learns an important lesson about respect and manners from the family's African American housekeeper, Calpurnia. The simple artifacts of a southern meal—a syrup pitcher, the dining table, a glass of milk, a tablecloth—are at the center of the drama. Scout and her brother Jem realize their schoolmate Walter Cunningham has no lunch and invite him home for noontime dinner. Walter represents white, working-class poverty. His bare feet, watery, red-rimmed eyes, and colorless face are clear signs of hookworms—"he looked as if he had been raised on fish food." After the meal is put on the table, Walter timidly asks for some molasses. Calpurnia brings a syrup pitcher on a small silver platter to the table.

> Walter poured syrup on his vegetables and meat with a generous hand. He would probably have poured it into his milk glass had I not asked what the sam hill he was doing. . . .
> Atticus shook his head at me. . . . "But he's gone and drowned his dinner in syrup," I protested. "He's poured it all over—"
> It was then that Calpurnia requested my presence in the kitchen. . . . "There's some folks who don't eat like us," she whispered fiercely, "but you ain't called on to contradict 'em at the table when they don't. That boy's yo' comp'ny and if he wants to eat up the table cloth you let him, you hear?"[85]

Larry Brown creates a different material setting in his fiction, centered on the "rough South" of working-class whites in a Mississippi that is changing from the civil rights movement to the economic downturn of the contemporary South. His work is filled with food, but not the "meat and three" square meals of Welty and Lee's fiction. Brown's characters exist in a world of beat-up trucks, a six-pack of beer, and heat lamp–warmed fried chicken or pork ribs from a "Quick Mart." When a proper sit-down meal is served, usually a mother, a girlfriend, or an ex-wife has prepared it. Brown's novel, *Father and Son* (1996), opens as Glen Davis has been released from prison and goes home to visit his estranged father. Brown sets the scene of a decaying South through objects that speak of its agrarian past, food, memory, and loss.

> Glen opened the back door of the car and brought out the rest of the beer. He walked across the yard and set it on the porch at his father's feet. Virgil watched him for a few moments and then reached down slowly and got one. There was an opener hanging from a nail driven into a post. He opened the can, his big hands flexing, and white foam spewed out. He waited for it to stop, holding the opener out for somebody to take. Glen took it, opened two more beers, handed one to Puppy, and stood in the yard drinking silently, looking around. In the garden out by the coupe, turnips the size of softballs rested their purple heads against the dry ground. Rotted bean stakes still leaned against a rusted piece of barbed wire, sheathed in dead vines. Dried catfish heads littered the dirt.... He was thinking of the days he had worked in this garden with his mother, of wandering its rows of tomatoes with a jar in his hand for the worms that crawled over the young green globes . . . his mother cooking in the kitchen and their cousins and uncles drinking beer with his father at the table. Old voices and old times gone by and the memories of them like faded photos on a screen.
>
> He looked up at his daddy. "You still look like an old drunk to me," he said.[86]

Our literary journey through the material worlds of food and southern culture closes with the postapocalyptic, southern gothic vision of Pulitzer Prize–winning author Cormac McCarthy, who grew up in east Tennessee. McCarthy's father was an attorney for the Tennessee Valley Authority (TVA), the New South institution founded by President Franklin Roosevelt in the

1930s to bring conservation, electricity, and jobs to a recovering yet modern-izing South. In *The Road* (2006), McCarthy follows the futuristic journey of a father and son as they make their way "south" after a global catastrophe has destroyed most life on earth—like the devastated post-Depression South that McCarthy's father rebuilt at the TVA and the twenty-first century's post-Katrina Gulf Coast. They are alone—not unlike Larry Brown's characters of Glen and his father, who also lost their mother and wife—and must fend for themselves in a southern world with no domestic comforts. McCarthy creates an even bleaker, rougher South than Brown's, but both writers tie the region to its past through a material description of the remnants of a "world that once was."

As father and son search for food and warmth, they come upon a "once grand house . . . tall and stately with white Doric columns across the front," only to find unspeakable horrors inside—again, an allusion to the historic South where gracious facades covered the nightmare of slavery. They escape and eventually find an underground bunker of food and supplies where they can rest. The boy finally sleeps, and then he wakes to the smell of his father cooking breakfast.

> "What is that?" he said.
> "Coffee. Ham. Biscuits."
> "Wow," the boy said. . . .
> He set out a bowl of biscuits covered with a hand towel and a plate of butter and a can of condensed milk. Salt and pepper. He looked at the boy. The boy looked drugged. He brought the frying pan from the stove and forked a piece of browned ham onto the boy's plate and scooped scrambled eggs from the other pan and ladled out spoonfuls of baked beans and poured coffee into their cups. The boy looked up at him.
> "Go ahead," he said. "Dont let it get cold."
> "What do I eat first?"
> "Whatever you like."
> "Is this coffee?"
> "Yes. Here. You put the butter on your biscuits. Like this." . . .
> "Do you think we should thank the people?"
> "The people?"
> "The people who gave us all this."

"Well. Yes, I guess we could do that."

"Will you do it?"

"Why don't you?"

"I don't know how."

"Yes you do. You know how to say thank you."

. . . The man was about to speak when he said: "Dear people, thank you for all this food and stuff. We know that you saved it for yourself and if you were here we wouldnt eat it no matter how hungry we were and we're sorry that you didnt get to eat it and we hope that you're safe in heaven with God."

He looked up. "Is that okay?" he said.

"Yes. I think that's okay."[87]

What Lies Beneath

McCarthy returns us to where we began, a southern memory of cast-iron frying pans, of serving food to family, of hot biscuits slathered with butter, and good manners. His work and that of other writers, scholars, artists, and filmmakers help us understand the complex history that *lies beneath* food and its material culture in the American South. Southern letters, diaries, journals, and ephemera are filled with descriptions and images of food and its material culture, from the early South through the civil rights movement.[88] Expressive language describing the hominy and pottery cooking vessels of Algonquian Indians on North Carolina's Outer Banks, described by Thomas Harriot in 1590, speaks of cultural exchange, colonization, and, ultimately, exploitation and disease. The influence of European culture and increasing immigration to the South, including a significant Jewish population, frames an 1833 letter from Judah P. Benjamin to a colleague in New York. Benjamin, the Jewish secretary of state and secretary of war for the Confederacy, included directions for preparing proper "Creole coffee" in a "biggin," an enamelware extraction pot like those used in France to make drip coffee.[89]

Plantation codes of race and the inner workings of slavery are the subtext of letters from visiting teachers and nannies who describe meals and food preparation. Ruth Hastings wrote from a Society Hill, South Carolina, plantation to her mother in New Hampshire: "The negroes are making sausages out in the smokehouse, chopping the meat. They killed 15 or 20 hogs before now, and now 20 more. They eat the brains and I don't know all that don't seem fit to eat, too, and they chop out the whole backbone and eat it fresh instead of salting it as we do. I have been out to see them cut up the meat."[90]

In the New South, the enduring hold of the Lost South and the resistance to post-Reconstruction change is palpable in a 1921 menu from a reunion dinner in New Orleans honoring Confederate veterans. The evening began with a bugle call and processional march, followed by elaborate "rations" of "Vicksburg Roast Turkey and Lookout Mountain Oyster Dressing."[91]

A series of photographs from the 1940s documents the entrenched disparity of South Carolina's segregated schools. Lunchrooms in the white schools are notable for the floral tieback curtains at the windows, freshly painted walls, flowers on the tables, fruit, and individual bottles of milk for each student. Few of these amenities exist in the "colored" lunchroom, where children sit on simple benches at crowded, rough-hewn tables.[92] In 1964 Mississippi newspapers reported daily accounts of civil rights activists' attempts to desegregate "whites only" cafés and restaurants, including the Pinehurst-Travel Inn strategically located across the street from the police station in Laurel, Mississippi. "The arrests came as Governor Paul B. Johnson declared in Jackson that the U.S. Supreme Court gave a 'green light to anarchy' by upholding the public accommodations section of the 1964 Civil Rights Law."[93]

Material worlds of southern food are as meaningful today as they were in the historic moments described above. "The South is continually coming into being," writes Edward Ayers, "continually being remade, continually struggling with its pasts." Ayers warns us not to "exoticize" the South by attempting to freeze it in a mythic past that seems more authentic—a Cracker Barrel world of past "treasures" nailed into place.[94] There is no more authentic time in the American South than the present. The "stuff" of southern food—its cast-iron skillets, celery holders, Dutch ovens, iced tea pitchers, beaten biscuit machines, pottery bowls, canning jars, stoneware crocks, choppers, sugar molds, oyster culling hammers, bread bowls, backyard sheds for peanut boils and fish fries—all bear meaning.[95]

In their film *Beasts of the Southern Wild* (2012) filmmaker Benh Zeitlin and writer Lucy Alibar introduce us to a doomsday world set in "the Bathtub," the flooded worlds of southeast Louisiana where rising sea waters and climate change have retaken watery lands, unsuccessfully controlled—and ultimately harmed—by human interaction.[96] The central figures, a father, Wink (Dwight Henry), and his six-year-old daughter, Hushpuppy (Quvenzhané Wallis), move through the apocalyptic landscape in which they live, attempting to care for one another, notably by feeding each other from the lush bayous that surround them. Like the father in Cormac McCarthy's story, Wink knows he must teach his child how to survive once he is gone, and learning to feed oneself is at the heart of these lessons. Lucy Alibar, a native of rural Florida who wrote the original play that became *Beasts*, fills scenes with foods and material objects that suggest the region's natural abundance and hospitality as well as its brutality and racial violence—not unlike the Cajun worlds of Ernest Gaines's Louisiana childhood. Food shared together—teeming tables of crab and crawfish, raw chickens pulled from hurricane-indestructible plastic coolers and cooked roughly on a grate over an open fire, plates of spicy fried fish—and food eaten alone (Hushpuppy dispassionately prepares a meal of dog food in one scene) reveal an age-old South of love and survival despite inconsolable loss and change.

Together these works speak of an evolutionary South, a place continually pulled back by the past and at the same time wrenched forward into a changing present. Material culture surrounds us in the South speaking of food's power. It's time we listened.

NOTES

I am indebted to my friends and colleagues Elizabeth Engelhardt, Ted Ownby, and John T. Edge for their groundbreaking work in the field of southern food studies, expressed in their vision for this anthology. Many thanks to Lori Rider and Sara Camp Arnold for their editorial guidance on this essay.

1. Andrew F. Smith, *Eating History: Thirty Turning Points in the Making of American Cuisine* (New York: Columbia University Press, 2009), 100–101; M. M. Manring, *Slave in a Box: The Strange Career of Aunt Jemima* (Charlottesville: University of Virginia Press, 1998), 75.

2. John Egerton, *Southern Food: At Home, on the Road, in History* (New York: Knopf, 1987), 218.

3. Edna Lewis, "What Is Southern?" *Gourmet* (January 2008): 24–30. This essay draws heavily from Lewis's earlier book, *The Taste of Country Cooking* (New York: Knopf, 1983). This cookbook/memoir explores the evocative foodways of Lewis's childhood in Freetown,

Virginia, named for free blacks who purchased land in the area and began to farm after emancipation. *The Taste of Country Cooking* is an iconic text in the canon of southern culinary history. Lewis's editor at Knopf, Judith Jones, worked with many great food writers, including Julia Child.

4. See work of culinary historian Nancy Carter Crump for a detailed analysis of the material culture of southern foodways in the early South, including fireplace equipment, cookware, dinnerware, furniture, recipes, and descriptions of meals from period diaries, letters, and travel accounts. Nancy Carter Crump, "Foodways of the Albemarle Region: Indulgent Nature Makes Up for Every Want," *Journal of Early Southern Decorative Arts* 19, no. 1 (May 1993): 1–36; Nancy Carter Crump, *Hearthside Cooking: Early American Southern Cuisine* (Chapel Hill: University of North Carolina Press, 2008).

5. Gary J. Albert, *Southern Perspective: A Sampling from the Museum of Early Southern Decorative Arts* (Winston-Salem, N.C.: Museum of Early Southern Decorative Arts, 2005), 10–11.

6. "The Museum of Early Southern Decorative Arts," special issue, *The Magazine Antiques*, January 2007.

7. William Eggleston, *Sumner, Mississippi*, dye transfer print, ca. 1972, printed 1986 (Museum of Modern Art, New York), in Elizabeth Sussman and Thomas Weski, *William Eggleston Democratic Camera: Photographs and Video, 1961–2008* (New Haven, Conn.: Yale University Press, 2008), 59.

8. Patti Carr Black, *Art in Mississippi, 1720–1980* (Jackson: Mississippi Historical Society, 1998), 214; Emma Russell, *Memories of My Life on the Farm*, cotton appliqué on cotton, 1979, collection of Roland L. Freeman, Washington, D.C.

9. Richard Gray, "Recorded and Unrecorded Histories: Recent Southern Writing and Social Change," in *The Southern State of Mind*, ed. Jan Nordby Gretlund (Columbia: University of South Carolina Press, 1999), 75.

10. Kate Taylor, "The Thorny Path to a National Black Museum," *New York Times*, January 23, 2011, 23.

11. Eudora Welty, "Place in Fiction," *The Eye of the Story: Selected Essays and Reviews* (New York: Vintage International, 1990), 119.

12. Eric Foner, "Introduction," *New American History* (Philadelphia: Temple University Press, 1997), ix.

13. Henri Lefebvre, "The Everyday and Everydayness," trans. Christine Levich, *Yale French Studies* 73 (1987): 7–11; Thomas J. Schlereth, "Material Culture Studies in America, 1876–1976," in *Material Culture Studies in America*, ed. Thomas J. Schlereth (Nashville: American Association for State and Local History, 1982), 2. This definition of material culture came from anthropologist Melville Herskovits.

14. James Deetz, *In Small Things Forgotten: The Archeology of Early American Life* (New York: Anchor Books, 1977), 24.

15. Theodore Rosengarten, *Tombee: Portrait of a Cotton Planter with the Journal of Thomas B. Chaplin (1822–1890)* (New York: McGraw-Hill, 1987), 9.

16. The new social history of the 1970s and 1980s, influenced by the French Annales School of historians, focused their analyses of the concept of *mentalité*—the thought processes, values, and beliefs shared by members of a social or cultural community—to understand human actions and historical experience.

17. Bernard L. Herman, "Ideologies of the Ordinary and the Urban Domestic Landscape," in *Shaping the Body Politic: Art and Political Formation in the Early Nation, ed.* Maurie McInnis and Louis P. Nelson (Charlottesville: University of Virginia Press, 2011).

18. See the 2009 Prop Master exhibit at the Gibbes Museum of Art in Charleston, South Carolina, curated by artists Susan Harbage Page and Juan Logan, who radically reinterpret the role of the museum as a "prop master" and the museum's collections as "props" chosen to represent another time. In the exhibit, Page and Logan juxtapose museum objects from the Gibbes collection with works of their own creation. Paintings and furniture associated with the white elite of Charleston's plantocracy are joined by other "props," such as tied fabric bundles, suggesting the simple belongings of enslaved people whose presence speaks of the invisible labor behind the wealth of the planter society. http://www.southernspaces.org/2009/prop-master-charlestons-gibbes-museum-art.

19. Bernard L. Herman, *Town House: Architecture and Material Life in the Early American City, 1780–1830* (Chapel Hill: University of North Carolina Press, 2005), 152–54.

20. Dell Upton, "White and Black Landscapes in Eighteenth-Century Virginia," *Material Life in America, 1600–1860*, ed. Robert Blair St. George (Boston: Northeastern University Press, 1988), 357–69.

21. Thad W. Tate and David L. Ammerman, eds., "Preface," *The Chesapeake in the Seventeenth Century: Essays on Anglo-American Society* (Norton, 1979), viii. This scholarship identified the impermanent, fragile character of early seventeenth-century Chesapeake society, the strong cultural imprint of the British Isles, and the eighteenth-century transformations that led to a plantation economy based on enslaved labor; James Deetz, *Flowerdew Hundred: The Archaeology of a Virginia Plantation, 1619–1864* (Charlottesville: University of Virginia Press, 1995).

22. Cary Carson, Norman F. Barka, William M. Kelso, Gary Wheeler Stone, and Dell Upton, "Impermanent Architecture in the Southern American Colonies," in St. George, *Material Life in America,* 135.

23. Schlereth, *Material Culture Studies in America.*

24. Ibid., 71. James Deetz and Henry Glassie were two of the first material culturists to address foodways in their groundbreaking studies on the historical archaeology of early American life and the patterns of regional culture in material folklife. James Deetz, *In Small Things Forgotten: The Archaeology of Early America* (New York: Anchor Books, 1977); Henry Glassie, *Patterns in the Material Folklife of the Eastern United States* (Philadelphia: University of Pennsylvania Press, 1968).

25. A sampling of folklorists who have studied southern folk culture, including its foodways: Barbara Allen, Jay Anderson, Roger Abrahams, John Burrison, Charles Camp, William

Ferris, Henry Glassie, Bernard Herman, Glenn Hinson, Charles Joyner, Lynwood Montell, Dan and Beverly Patterson, Judy Peiser, Kathy Roberts, Robert Farris Thompson, Maude Wahlman, John Vlach, and Terry Zug.

26. Schlereth, *Material Culture Studies in America* 32–40. The "age of interpretation" in material culture studies was, again, informed by the new social history of the 1970s and 1980s that was influenced by the French Annales School and British labor historians, structuralists such as Claude Lévi-Strauss, folklife programs and the concern for regional culture (as seen in the founding of the University of Mississippi's Center for the Study of Southern Culture [1977] and the Southern Foodways Alliance [1999]), the history of technology, the study of consumption, and academic/museum partnerships with museums such as Plimoth Planta-tion, Old Sturbridge Village, and St. Mary's City. Institutions created in this phase such as the American Association of Museums, the American Association for State and Local History, the National Endowments for the Arts and the Humanities, and the American Folklife Center also affected growing scholarship in material culture studies and social history.

27. Robert Blair St. George, Introduction to essay by Sam Hilliard, "Hog Meat and Corn-pone: Foodways in the Antebellum South," in St. George, *Material Life in America*, 311.

28. John W. Blassingame, *The Slave Community: Plantation Life in the Antebellum South* (New York: Oxford University Press, 1972); Robert Farris Thompson, "African Influence on the Art of the United States," in *Black Studies in the University*, ed. Armstead L. Robinson, Craig Foster, and Donald H. Ogilvie (New Haven, Conn.: Yale University Press, 1969), 122–70; John Vlach, *Afro-American Tradition in the Decorative Arts* (Athens: University of Georgia Press, 1978); John Vlach, *By the Work of Their Hands: Studies in African American Folklife* (Charlottesville: University Press of Virginia, 1991); John Vlach, *Back of the Big House: The Architecture of Plantation Slavery* (Chapel Hill: University of North Carolina Press, 1993). In syncretism, similar patterns in two different cultures are combined to produce a new hybrid object. This process helped maintain cultural identity while making sense of a new culture.

29. Judith A. Carney, *Black Rice: The African Origins of Rice Cultivation in the Americas* (Cambridge, Mass.: Harvard University Press, 2001); Eugene D. Genovese, *Roll, Jordan, Roll: The World the Slaves Made* (New York: Vintage Books, 1972); Leland Ferguson, *Archaeology and Early African America, 1650–1800* (Washington, D.C.: Smithsonian Institution Press, 1992); Jessica B. Harris, *High on the Hog: A Culinary Journey* (New York: Bloomsbury, 2011); Karen Hess, *The Carolina Rice Kitchen: The African Connection* (Columbia: University of South Carolina Press, 1992); Charles Joyner, *Down by the Riverside: A South Carolina Slave Community* (Urbana: University of Illinois Press, 1984, 2009); Sidney W. Mintz and Richard Price, *The Birth of African-American Culture: An Anthropological Perspective* (New York: Beacon, 1972, 1992); Sidney W. Mintz, *Tasting Food, Tasting Freedom: Excursions into Eating, Culture, and the Past* (Boston: Beacon, 1996); Philip D. Morgan, *Slave Counterpoint: Black Cul-ture in the Eighteenth-Century Chesapeake and Lowcountry* (Chapel Hill: University of North Carolina Press, 1998); Frederick Douglass Opie, *Hog and Hominy: Soul Food from Africa to America* (New York: Columbia University Press, 2009); Dale Rosengarten, Ted Rosengarten,

and Enid Schildkrout, *Grass Roots: African Origins of an American Art* (New York: Museum for African Art, 2008); Psyche Williams-Forson, *Building Houses out of Chicken Legs: Black Women, Food, and Power* (Chapel Hill: University of North Carolina Press, 2006); Peter H. Wood, *Black Majority: Negroes in Colonial South Carolina from 1670 through the Stono Rebellion* (New York: Norton, 1974); Anne Yentsch, *A Chesapeake Family and Their Slaves: A Study in Historical Archaeology* (New York: Cambridge University Press, 1994); Anne Yentsch, "Excavating the South's African American Food History," in *African American Foodways: Explorations of History & Culture*, ed. Anne Bower (Urbana: University of Illinois, 2007), 59–98. Jessica Harris has published extensively on the food of African Americans, its connections with global cuisines, and the food of Africa and its American diaspora.

30. Harris, *High on the Hog*, 107.

31. Yentsch, *A Chesapeake Family and Their Slaves*, 166.

32. C. Vann Woodward (*The Burden of Southern History* [New York: Vintage, 1960]) and W. J. Cash (*The Mind of the South* [New York: Vintage, 1941]) argued that the South was made distinctive by its history. In *Shared Traditions: Southern History and Folk Culture* (Urbana: University of Illinois Press, 1999), historian-folklorist Charles Joyner argues that it is both history and folk culture that have produced the South's distinctive identity. The dynamic product of this interaction is southern folk culture, which is most strongly expressed in the region's music, folk art, foodways, language, and architecture.

33. Charles Reagan Wilson and William Ferris, "Introduction," *Encyclopedia of Southern Culture* (Chapel Hill: University of North Carolina Press, 1982), xv.

34. Isabel Wilkerson, *The Warmth of Other Suns: The Epic Story of America's Great Migration* (New York: Random House, 2010), 531. Wilkerson documents the lives of three individuals among the six million people who left the South for northern and western cities from the 1910s to the 1970s, seeking opportunity and an escape from segregation and the deeply imbedded racial codes of the region. The Great Migration brought southern culture—its language, literature, music, and food—to the rest of the nation. Wilkerson states, "The Migration changed American culture as we know it."

35. Kim Severson, "Brooklyn's Flavor Route to the South," *New York Times*, December 30, 2009.

36. "The New Southern Studies: What's So New about It?" Center for the Study of Southern Culture, University of Mississippi, http://www.olemiss.edu/depts/south/NewSST.html (no longer available), accessed August 10, 2008; Ted Ownby, "Director's Column," *The Southern Register*, Center for the Study of Southern Culture (Summer 2008): 2–3.

37. Kathleen Purvis, "A Decent Meeting Calls for Eating," *Charlotte Observer*, January 26, 2005.

38. See the documentary *Moving Midway* (2008) by film critic Godfrey Cheshire for a discussion of the plantation myth in popular culture and American film, beginning with Thomas Dixon and D. W. Griffith's controversial *Birth of a Nation* (1915), which portrays Reconstruction as a violent period of racial chaos, which ends with the restoration of white rule.

Godfrey Cheshire returned from New York City to his childhood home of Raleigh, North Carolina, where his cousin Charlie Silver decided to relocate the family ancestral home, Midway Plantation, to escape urban sprawl on Highway 64. During this unfolding story, Cheshire is introduced to NYU history professor Robert Hinton, whose grandfather was born a slave at Midway Plantation. Together, Cheshire and Hinton discover more than one hundred African American cousins in the process of moving Midway Plantation. For further discussion of the plantation myth in popular culture, see Thomas Cripps, *Slow Fade to Black: The Negro in American Film, 1900–1942* (New York: Oxford University Press, 1977); Catherine Clinton, *Tara Revisited: Women, War, and the Plantation Legend* (New York: Abbeville, 1995); Tara McPherson, *Reconstructing Dixie: Race, Gender, and Nostalgia in the Imagined South* (Durham, N.C.: Duke University Press, 2003); and Karen L. Cox, *Dreaming of Dixie: How the South Was Created in American Popular Culture* (Chapel Hill: University of North Carolina Press, 2011).

39. Edward D. C. Campbell Jr., "Plantation Film," *Encyclopedia of Southern Culture*, ed. Charles Wilson Reagan and William R. Ferris (Chapel Hill: University of North Carolina Press, 1989), 922–24; see Clinton, *Tara Revisited*, 21, 205. For more information on the Jewish immigrant generation who romanticized the plantation South in ragtime of the 1920s and films of the 1930s and 1940s, see Stephen Whitfield, "Is It True What They Sing about Dixie?" *Southern Cultures* (Summer 2002): 8–37.

40. *The Old South*, Fred Zinnemann, film, MGM Studios, 1940.

41. *Williamsburg: The Story of a Patriot*, George Seaton, dir., Emmet Lavery, writer, starring Jack Lord. Colonial Williamsburg Foundation, Paramount Pictures, 1957.

42. Grace Elizabeth Hale, *Making Whiteness: The Culture of Segregation in the South, 1890–1940* (New York: Pantheon, 1998), 169; see also Lisa C. Tolbert, "The Aristocracy of the Market Basket: Self-Service Food Shopping in the New South," *Food Chains: From Farmyard to Shopping Cart*, ed. Warren Belasco and Roger Horowitz (Philadelphia: University of Pennsylvania Press, 2009), 179–195, for a discussion of Clarence Saunders, who founded the Piggly Wiggly franchise, one of the first self-service grocery stores in the nation, in 1916. Tolbert examines the changing social geography of food shopping in the evolving commercial landscape of the New South.

43. Hale, *Making Whiteness*, 137.

44. Ibid., 150–52; Manring, *Slave in a Box*, 75.

45. Hale, *Making Whiteness*, 160–64; Manring, *Slave in a Box*, 91, 112, 115, 116, 140. Kentucky-born James Webb Young developed the Aunt Jemima campaign at J. Walter Thompson, the advertising firm hired by Quaker Oats. His Aunt Jemima ads of the 1920s featured N. C. Wyeth's romanticized illustrations of a mythic plantation South. Young believed the images of elite white southerners would appeal to middle-class, white female consumers, who increasingly labored in their own households without the help of black domestic workers. Company executives at Quaker Oats hoped housewives would imagine themselves as the mistresses of their own households and Aunt Jemima their loyal servant—as Manring suggests, their "slave in a box." For further discussion on the "mammy" stereotype and its evolution from

the plantation South to the contemporary South, see Eugene D. Genovese, *Roll, Jordan, Roll: The World the Slaves Made* (New York: Vintage, 1972), 353–65; Deborah Gray White, *Ar'n't I a Woman: Female Slaves in the Plantation South* (New York: Norton, 1985), 189; Micki McElya, *Clinging to Mammy: The Faithful Slave in Twentieth-Century America* (Cambridge, Mass.: Harvard University Press, 2007); Rebecca Sharpless, *Cooking in Other Women's Kitchens: Domestic Workers in the South, 1865–1960* (Chapel Hill: University of North Carolina Press, 2010); Doris Witt, *Black Hunger: Food and the Politics of U.S. Identity* (New York: Oxford University Press, 1999).

46. Hale, *Making Whiteness*, 164.

47. Manring, *Slave in a Box*, 60, 72. The most recognizable, longest-lived "mammy" stereotype is the Aunt Jemima trademark, registered by Chris Rutt and Charles Underwood in 1890, soon after their purchase of a bankrupt flour mill in St. Joseph, Missouri. Aunt Jemima began her life as a white male minstrel player in blackface dressed as an enslaved woman, singing Billy Kersand's hit tune of 1875, "Old Aunt Jemima." After seeing this 1880s minstrel number, Rutt believed a southern, black "mammy" could best sell his new pancake mix, and not just as a face on a package but as advertising's first living trademark.

48. Ibid., 94–96.

49. See Patricia A. Turner, *Ceramic Uncles and Celluloid Mammies: Black Images and Their Influence on Culture* (Charlottesville: University of Virginia Press, 2002).

50. Hale, *Making Whiteness*, 164–65.

51. Ibid., 101.

52. Manring, *Slave in a Box*, 165.

53. Ibid., 160.

54. Ibid., 160–61.

55. Renee Montagne, "Life Is a Collage for Artist Betye Saar," National Public Radio, December 28, 2006. The appropriation of racially stereotyped commercial objects by black activists and artists culminated in the 1982 exhibit "Ethnic Notions: Black Images in the White Mind" at the Berkeley Art Center in Berkeley, California, and the release of Marlon Riggs's Emmy-winning documentary film *Ethnic Notions* (1987).

56. Egerton, *Southern Food*, 41. See Louis Hatchett, *Duncan Hines: The Man Behind the Cake Mix* (Macon, Ga.: Mercer University Press, 2001); Damon Talbott, "Duncan Hines' Consumption Community and the Geography of American Gastronomy, 1936–1956," 2008, http://digitalcommons.unl.edu/cgi/viewcontent.cgi?article=1031&context=historyrawleyconference.

57. F. J. Schermerhorn letter to Duncan Hines, July 16, 1956, Cashiers, N.C., collection of High Hampton Inn.

58. Cotton Seiler, *Republic of Drivers: A Cultural History of Automobility in America* (Chicago: University of Chicago Press, 2008), 115–16.

59. Celia Magee, "The Open Road Wasn't Quite Open to All," *New York Times*, August 22, 2010.

60. See artist Juan Logan's work, which examines how race and power have shaped, and

continue to shape, the physical, cultural, and political landscapes of America. Leisure Space, a 2009–10 exhibit at the Harvey B. Gantt Center for African-American Arts and Culture in Charlotte, North Carolina, featured Juan Logan's paintings of America's many historically black segregated beaches, such as Chicken Bone Beach (Atlantic City, New Jersey), Inkwell Beach (Martha's Vineyard, Massachusetts), Lincoln Beach (New Orleans, Louisiana), and Chowan Beach (North Carolina). http://www.ganttcenter.org/web/page.asp?urh=Exhibitions Viewer&id=2.

61. In Greensboro, North Carolina, the original lunch counter, bar stools, and pie rack are centerpieces in the city's new International Civil Rights Center and Museum, located in the Woolworth where the sit-in took place on February 1, 1960. The lunch counter and stools have never been moved from their location. http://www.sitinmovement.org/home.asp.

62. Natasha Tretheway, "History Lesson," *Domestic Work* (St. Paul, Minn.: Graywolf, 2000), 45.

63. John Dollard, *Caste and Class in a Southern Town* (New Haven, Conn.: Yale University Press, 1937); Anne Moody, *Coming of Age in Mississippi* (New York: Dell, 1968).

64. Moody, *Coming of Age*, 34.

65. Jacquelyn Dowd Hall, James Leloudis, Robert Korstad, Mary Murphy, Lu Ann Jones, and Christopher B. Daly, *Like a Family: The Making of a Southern Cotton Mill World* (Chapel Hill: University of North Carolina Press, 1987), 209; Betty and Lloyd Davidson, interview by Allen Tullos, Burlington, N.C., February 2 and 15, 1979; see also Emily Wallace, "Pimento Cheese in the North Carolina Piedmont: From Home to Work and Back Again," *Gravy* 39 (Winter 2011): 13–16.

66. Hall et al., *Like a Family*, 209. "Dope" was a nickname for Coca-Cola.

67. Elizabeth S. D. Engelhardt, "Beating the Biscuits in Appalachia: Race, Class, and Gender Politics of Women Baking Bread," in *Cooking Lessons: The Politics of Gender and Food*, ed. Sherrie Inness (Lanham, Md.: Rowman & Littlefield, 2001), 160.

68. Elizabeth Engelhardt, "Canning Tomatoes, Growing 'Better and More Perfect Women': The Girls' Tomato Club Movement," *Southern Cultures* (Winter 2009): 78–92; see also Engelhardt, *A Mess of Greens: Southern Gender and Southern Food* (Athens: University of Georgia Press, 2011).

69. See Pat Willard, *America Eats: On the Road with the* wpa (New York: Bloomsbury, 2008).

70. Herbert C. Covey and Dwight Eisnach, *What the Slaves Ate: Recollections of African American Foods and Foodways from the Slave Narratives* (Santa Barbara, Calif.: Greenwood, 2009), 57.

71. C. Vann Woodward, review of *The American Slave: A Composite Autobiography* by George P. Rawick, in *American Historical Review* 79, no. 2 (April 1974): 474–75.

72. For more on food in American film, see Anne L. Bower, "Watching Food: The Production of Food, Film, and Values," in *Reel Food: Essays on Food and Film*, ed. Anne L. Bower

(New York: Routledge, 2004), 1–13; Steve Zimmerman, "Food in Films: A Star Is Born," *Gastronomica* (Spring 2009): 25–34.

73. http://www.southernfoodways.com/documentary/film/index.html; http://www.folkstreams.net.

74. Blank and Ferris both recorded scenes of eating, food preparation, family, and festival in their films on music and other folklore topics as a record of everyday life and community. Stan Woodward has a large body of foodways films documenting southern regional dishes, such as burgoo, Brunswick stew, barbecue, "Carolina Hash," grits, and rockfish muddle.

75. John Shelton Reed, "Southern Living," *Encyclopedia of Southern Culture* (Chapel Hill: University of North Carolina Press, 1989), 973–74. The Progressive Era roots of the magazine are reflected in its publisher, Southern Progress Corporation of Birmingham, Alabama. Founded in 1886 in North Carolina, Southern Progress's first publication was *The Progressive Farmer*, whose mission was to improve farming methods and education for white working-class farmers and their families. In 1985 Southern Progress was purchased by Time Warner for $480 million.

76. John Shelton Reed and Dale Volberg Reed, *1001 Things Everyone Should Know About the South* (New York: Doubleday, 1996), 294.

77. See Roy Blount, "You Can't Eat 'Em Blues: Cooking Up a Food Song Movie," *Cornbread Nation* (Chapel Hill: University of North Carolina Press, 2002), 106–9; Amy Evans, "Blues in the Kitchen," *Delta Magazine* (July–August 2005): 64–65.

78. "Shortnin' Bread," attributed to Reese Dupree in an unpublished version from 1925. See James J. Fuld, *The Book of World-Famous Music: Classical, Popular, and Folk* (Mineola, NY: Dover, 2000), 497–98. Shortnin' bread is a variation of cornbread, fried in a cast-iron skillet.

79. Andy Razaf, "That's What I Like about the South," Southern Music Publishing Co., 1944, popularized by Phil Harris. See Nat Shapiro and Bruce Pollock, eds., *Popular Music, 1920–1979: A Revised Cumulation* (Detroit, MI: Gale, 1985), 1804.

80. Bobbie Gentry, "Ode to Billie Joe," 1967. This single sold three million copies after its release in August 1967. Bobbie Gentry was nominated for three Grammy Awards in 1968 and was also named the Academy of Country Music's Best New Female Vocalist.

81. JJ Grey and MOFRO, "Ho Cake," *Blackwater* (Alligator, 2007).

82. Ann Romines, "Reading the Cakes: *Delta Wedding* and Texts of Southern Women's Culture," *Mississippi Quarterly* 50 (Fall 1977): 608–11; Eudora Welty, *Delta Wedding* (New York: Harcourt, 1946), 172.

83. "Ann Romines on Eudora Welty's Cake," GW *English News*, Department of English, George Washington University, April 9, 2007, http://gwenglish.blogspot.com/2007/04/ann-romines-on-eudora-weltys-cakes.html; Ann Romines, *The Home Plot: Women, Writing, and Domestic Ritual* (Amherst: University of Massachusetts Press, 1992), 8.

84. Ralph Ellison, *Invisible Man* (New York: Random House, 1947), 262–63.

85. Harper Lee, *To Kill a Mockingbird* (New York: Warner, 1960), 23–24.

86. Larry Brown, *Father and Son* (New York: Holt, 1996), 24.

87. Cormac McCarthy, *The Road* (New York: Vintage, 2006), 144–46.

88. Culinary historian Nancy Carter Crump has examined foodways manuscripts, including many descriptions of food-related material culture, in the University of North Carolina's Southern Historical Collection. These examples are largely of the white southern elite from the colonial South to the end of the nineteenth century. See Nancy Carter Crump, *Hearthside Cooking: Early American Southern Cuisine* (Chapel Hill: University of North Carolina, 2008).

89. Judah P. Benjamin, letter to Dr. Barton, New Orleans, April 28, 1833. Historic New Orleans Collection, New Orleans, Louisiana.

90. Ruth Hastings to Mary Anne Hastings, November 29, 1859. Ruth Newcomb Hastings Papers, William L. Clements Library, University of Michigan. In an essay on the material culture of antebellum southern travel, Eric Plaag examines the "collective memory" of northerners, such as Ruth Hastings, whose food writing in letters and diaries he describes as "ephemeral souvenirs." See Eric W. Plaag, "There Is an Abundance of Those Which Are Genuine": Northern Travelers and Souvenirs of the Antebellum South," in *Dixie Emporium: Tourism, Foodways, and Consumer Culture in the American South*, ed. Anthony J. Stanonis (Athens: University of Georgia Press, 2008), 27.

91. Association of the Army of Tennessee. Louisiana Division. 44th Annual Reunion, Hotel DeSoto, April 6, 1921. New Orleans, La. TX 739.A7 Historic New Orleans Collection, New Orleans, Louisiana.

92. Rich Hill Colored School, Lancaster, South Carolina, 1946, 12363.14; Blacksburg Grammar Lunchroom, Blacksburg, South Carolina, 3/13/1946, 12363.7. South Caroliniana Collection, University of South Carolina, Columbia.

93. "Four Negroes and Two White Civil Rights Workers," December 16, 1946, UPI, Jackson, Mississippi. Joan Harris Trumpauer Civil Rights Scrapbooks III, folder 1 of 2, z 22 74.000s, 1961–1964.

94. Edward L. Ayers, "What We Talk about When We Talk about the South," in *All Over the Map: Rethinking American Regions*, ed. Edward L. Ayers, Patricia Nelson Limerick, Stephen Nissenbaum, and Peter S. Onuf (Baltimore: Johns Hopkins University Press, 1995), 82, 65, 69.

95. This list of southern food "things" was the result of a query sent to colleagues in southern food studies. Many thanks to Sheri Castle, North Carolina (glass canning jar); Nathalie Dupree, South Carolina (beaten biscuit machine, celery holder, sugar molds); John T. Edge, Mississippi (McCarty's pottery highball glasses); Jessica Harris, New York/New Orleans (paternal grandmother's cast-iron skillet and Dutch oven, maternal grandmother's iced tea pitcher; "they were lovingly given to my mother as a legacy from two women who had little else to give"); Bernie Herman, North Carolina/Eastern Shore of Virginia (oyster culling hammer); April McGreger, North Carolina/Mississippi ("Daddy's shed . . . where everything magical and mysterious happened: peanut boils, fish frys, venison, quail, and fish cleaning, and beer drinking"); Kathleen Purvis, North Carolina (parent's bread bowl); Fred Sauceman, Tennessee (stoneware crock and two-bladed chopper for making sauerkraut). Tom Hanchett

of the Levine Museum of the New South added a 78 RPM recording of Robert Johnson's blues ode to tamales, "They're Red Hot" (1937). My southern food "thing" is a wooden rolling pin for making noodle dough, brought by my grandmother Luba Tooter Cohen to Blytheville, Arkansas, from Russia via New York in 1912.

96. Benh Zeitlin and Lucy Alibar, *Beasts of the Southern Wild*, Fox Searchlight Pictures, 2012. The film was nominated for four Academy Awards in 2013.

CHAPTER 13

The Dance of Culinary Patriotism

Material Culture and the Performance
of Race with Southern Food

PSYCHE WILLIAMS-FORSON

It's not that photographs are not good. They're too good....
They contain everything. We have worked out techniques for digesting
verbal data, but what can we do with photographs?
JOHN COLLIER, *Visual Anthropology* (1986)

World War II powerfully influenced American farming and food production. Shortly after the war began, food rationing became mandatory. Ration books were the order of the day. Continuing the World War I theme of
"Food will win the war," farmers and factories increased production to grow
"army and navy men [of] rugged health and courage." As medical doctor
Thomas Parren made clear, "every drop of milk, every egg, every legume, every pound of meat and of fish [that could be produced] for Anglo-American
nutrition, plus substantial quantities of animal and vegetable fats, fish liver
oils, and certain vitamins [were needed]."[1] Farms and production facilities
across the country helped satisfy this need.[2]

World War II catalyzed a multifaceted food distribution system, defined
by specific methods of preparation, precise measurements, and large quantities, all designed to produce wholesome and nutritious meals for soldiers.
Patricia Prell writes,

Service men stationed in America were issued the maximum possible fresh
meat, fruit and vegetables. Overseas units still depended largely on canned
food, dehydrated fruits and powdered eggs. Both at home and overseas, the
military attempted not only to feed the troops, but also to feed them well. Food
was generally worse closer to the front lines, though extraordinary efforts were

made to get holiday food to combat areas on Thanksgiving and Christmas Day.[3]

In the South, and specifically at Craig Field Southeastern Air Training Center in Selma, Alabama, the "manifesto of security" included a "food for defense" nutrition program. According to menus from that era, soldiers ate an array of seasonal foods including, but not limited to, strawberries, eggs, bacon, potatoes, cabbage, tomatoes, lettuce, pickles, and peas. They were also fed the hallmark of southern cuisine: fried chicken.

Craig Field obtained its chickens from farms that held contracts with the Food for Defense program, a division of the Farm Security Administration. John Collier, a staff photographer for the FSA/OWI (Office of War Information), traveled south to document the work being done on these poultry farms. He traced the process from production to a fried chicken dinner cooked for the white cadets at Craig Field.[4]

The archive contains a series of photographs by Collier that tell an interesting story of gender, race, food, and power during World War II. This essay considers how material culture artifacts such as photographs can be used to understand the tensions, power dynamics, and overall complexities of food and eating in the wartime South.

Doing Food Analysis with Material Culture

In her essay "Dances with Things: Material Culture and the Performance of Race," Robin Bernstein calls for an examination of "things" as scripters of action. She explains, "the term *script* denotes not a rigid dictation of performed action but, rather, a necessary openness to resistance, interpretation, and improvisation" [emphasis in original]. Bernstein suggests "that agency, intention, and racial subjectivation co-emerge through everyday physical encounters in the physical world."[5] In short, people perform evocative dances with things. In the case of the Craig Field photographs, such dances reflect how racial practices were constructed and enacted.

Scholars of material culture distinguish between "objects" and "things." Objects enable people to transmit and communicate meaning. People use objects "to establish and negotiate identities; establish or challenge one's place in society; signify one's social affinities, perceived social status, or oc-cupation; facilitate one's relationship with other individuals or groups; and facilitate changes of self-identity or reconcile a current self-identity."[6] While objects in general are useful for what they reveal, scholars of thing theory from Martin Heidegger to Bill Brown intimate that objects are simply "mat-ter that one looks through or beyond to understand something human," while things "script actions."[7] The difference between the two is considered "situational and subjective" by Bernstein.

Both objects and things are performative. They do something. They invite humans to move, and they shape human behaviors.[8] A thing like a photo-graph is scripted, and it scripts behavior. Photographs enable us to make in-ferences about the past. Bernstein argues, "By reading things' scripts within historically located traditions of performance, we can make well-supported claims about normative aggregate behavior."[9] For material culturalists, reading the photograph as a thing enables us to delve into the performative scripts captured by the camera. We ask a series of questions to interpret behaviors exhibited in the photographs. Using objects in the photos, such as clothing, cooking, and eating implements, we can better understand the complex dance in which the actors engaged. We can also grasp the role that food played in that process.

Scripting Behavior

Things script behaviors through both determined and implied (or prompted) actions. An example of the latter appears in the food photographs that John Collier took at Craig Field Air Force Base in Selma, Alabama, in 1941. Collier was recruited by Roy Emerson Stryker, head of the documen-tary photography operation of the FSA/OWI, and instructed to spotlight different kinds of American life.[10] Unlike better-known Depression-era pho-tographers, such as Dorothea Lange, Marion Post Wolcott, Jack Delano, and Gordon Parks, Collier was not hired to report on the plight of the farmer in rural America. By the time he arrived at the agency, the assignments were more random. Collier documented a wide range of subjects, including coal miners in Pittsburgh. In a 1965 interview, Collier explained:

[The government] had information specialists of every region in the United States who were feeding into the newspapers, into magazines, into government reports the reality of what was going on. I wouldn't call them propagandists, I think they were more fairly considered historians of what was happening. They were the eyes and ears that fed material into the [photo] files and it was very clear what our role was, because whenever we'd get back from any interesting field trip we'd all be shipped across the street to the Department of Agriculture. And we would be pumped dry by specialists who couldn't care less about our photographs. They were interested in our eyewitness experiences.... And they were interested in conversations, they were interested in our impressions as observers, so we operated as a corps of intelligence for desk-rooted specialists across the street. And they'd always milk us whenever we got back from the field.[11]

With war imminent, and the attack on Pearl Harbor on the horizon, the federal government worked to bolster patriotism by documenting war preparations at home. Collier recalled, "Food for victory was the greatest goal of the Department of Agriculture, and shortly ... we were officially made a member of the Office of War Information.... I found myself photographing 'Food for Victory' projects in the South, in terms of food for army camps, increased farming activity, of supervised credit farmers, and FSA rehabilitation projects."[12]

Collier, the youngest son of a social activist who later served as the commissioner of Indian affairs, was socially conscious and interested in photographing marginalized people. Early in his life, he had struggled with hearing loss and learning disabilities. Those struggles helped shape his inclusive worldview. After the war, Collier would go on to be a pioneer in the field of visual anthropology, publishing the influential volume *Visual Anthropology: Photography as Research Method* in 1967.[13] Collier made important contributions to the documentation of black life. He captured on film a Food for Defense dinner that took place in the summer of 1941. Several of the photographs from this series command attention.[14]

Collier was encouraged to organize the photographs as he saw fit, so the narrative does not precisely follow the order in which he shot the events.[15]

In the photographic composite we learn about the farms where some of the chickens, also called "fryers for flyers," were raised. We also learn how they were killed, dressed, weighed, iced, crated, and transported to the air base. Following the sequential numbering of the images on the Library of Congress's American Memory website, the narrative follows the purchasing and handling processes of the fowl, as well as the daily life of some white cadets and officers stationed at Craig Field. Collier provided pictures of cadet living quarters and their work and leisure routines. He captured their habits of preparing for Sunday dinner. Statements relayed in captions tout the "real home-cooked chicken" and "there's hardly room for cake after dinner." The cadets were evidently "well satisfied" after their "hearty meal."

In the photographs, we see instructors charting their afternoon flights. We see cadets boarding their planes, following their afternoon dinner. Those not performing drills practice archery, read, or otherwise relax. In almost all of the captions, Collier, or whoever processed the images, emphasized the satiation of the white military men. They were "smiling and chuckling over their hearty meal of fried chicken supplied by FSA clients through the 'Food for Defense'" program (figs. 17 and 18).[16]

Scattered throughout this ensemble of images are pictures of the African American men who managed domestic life on the base. Clad in aprons instead of uniforms, their faces show focus and concentration (fig. 19). We first encounter African American soldiers as they load platters of fried chicken to serve the cadets. Later images reveal that they also unloaded boxes of frozen chicken, thawed the meat, and prepped it for frying. They set the tables and cleared the dishes after the meal. In sum, as one caption explains, these men worked "all morning preparing a feast . . . for the Craig Field training center for flying cadets."[17] The pictures suggest that African American cooks also washed dishes and stored and discarded remainders (fig. 20). In the name of *their* country, these African American men worked from morning until afternoon catering to their white counterparts who flew planes in the name of *their* country.

It would be easy to celebrate the patriotism and work of the white cadets as they prepared to fight. But this overlooks the invisible labor of those who "worked all morning" to help make the job of the cadets possible. Like women, who provided essential household labor, the role of black men—

FIGURE 17. Cadet E. A. Peresich Jr. takes his third helping of fried chicken. Craig Field, Southeastern Air Training Center, Selma, Alabama. Library of Congress, Prints & Photographs Division, FSA/OWI Collection, [LC-USF34-080306-D].

FIGURE 18. Chicken raised by FSA (Farm Security Administration) borrowers is good right down to the bone. Craig Field, Southeastern Air Training Center, Selma, Alabama. Library of Congress, Prints & Photographs Division, FSA/OWI Collection, [LC-USF34-080491-E].

FIGURE 19. Craig Field cooks loading up platters of crisp fried chickens, supplied through the FSA (Farm Security Administration) "Food for Defense" program. Craig Field, Southeastern Air Training Center, Selma, Alabama. Library of Congress, Prints & Photographs Division, FSA/OWI Collection, [LC-USF34-080304-E].

FIGURE 20. Nothing left but the bones of these chickens raised by FSA (Farm Security Administration) borrowers. Craig Field, Southeastern Air Training Center, Alabama. Library of Congress, Prints & Photographs Division, FSA/OWI Collection, [LC-USF34-080488-E].

supporting the troops through culinary patriotism—cannot be overstated. A material culture approach compels us to evaluate the photographs as historical evidence of the contributions of African Americans to the World War II homefront effort. It focuses our attention on the historical and social memory preserved in these images.

The remainder of this essay examines the photographs in more detail, considering the range of interactions and complex dances people do with things and revealing the power dynamics that inform food preparation, presentation, and consumption.[18]

Mapping Black Masculinities on the Kitchen Landscape

Images from World War II portrayed young, white, male muscled bodies as the ideal American body politic prepared for war. They also communicated ideas about America's national identity. To maintain their physique and their strength, white men needed hearty meals. In contrast, images of black men propagated and promoted by government institutions and popular culture suggested they were a social problem. African American males were accused of being diseased, dirty, lazy, infantile, and illiterate, and thus unfit to wear American military uniforms or serve in combat. Black men were aware of these negative stereotypes and understood the connections between combat duty, service work, and masculinity. Bill Stevens of the 25th Infantry Regiment of the all-black 93rd Division recalled:

> Black troops were just naturally suspected of cowardice, stealing, rape, the whole racial-stereotype lie. White commanders had no respect for black soldiers. . . . The general opinion of white officers was that black units made excellent labor battalions. . . . Blacks were not going to be given a chance to prove themselves in combat in the Pacific. . . . From where I sat they weren't going to get a chance even if it caused the death of every cracker in the Pacific to keep it that way. The glory boys had to be white![19]

Placing black troops in domestic positions, where they donned aprons and washed other men's clothes, reinforced beliefs that African American men were servile, cowardly, and lacking in manhood. These gender-transgressive performances were heavily scripted by Jim Crow policies that relegated African Americans to the lowest rungs of civilian and military society. Many white men also donned aprons and served as mess hall cooks. But the implications for African American men were very different, precisely because of the racial politics. Photographs of African American men, working in aprons alongside white men in uniform, highlighted the dichotomies and power configurations.

Historically, when masculinity and virility are attached to food, it is through the symbolism of meat that has been hunted, killed, butchered, and eaten — preferably rare. Chicken does not fall comfortably within this rubric. There is very little hunting or aggression involved in catching, plucking, and cutting a chicken. The sliminess of chicken in its raw state also makes it difficult to handle. Chicken is also considered a lighter option than red meat. At the same time, chickens generally have meaty breasts, thighs, and legs, which can make for a substantial meal.[20]

In the absence of red meat during wartime rationing, chicken became a viable alternative. Cooking wholesome meals to "win the war" at home was the work of women and wives. In the segregated army, however, cooking was also the duty of many African American men. Amy Bentley asserts,

> During World War II, black men in the military were assigned to kitchen duty (and other noncombatant positions) in grossly disproportionate numbers, and they deeply resented being put in this decidedly subordinate and traditionally female position. The behind-the-lines, female-identified job of food preparation, could never compare with the masculine-identified soldiering on the battlefront. That one's race, a characteristic having nothing to do with the ability to be a good soldier, determined who performed which duty made the job of army cook all the more insulting.[21]

Regardless of their occupations prior to entering the military, African Americans were unable to escape the institutionalized racism created by Jim Crow policies. Blacks in the armed forces were, for the most part, considered unfit and incompetent for combat and were denied opportunities to take up arms like their white counterparts. Only a few were promoted, and then they were placed in charge of all-black units, which were usually poorly trained. When placed under the command of white officers, African Americans often fared worse.

Military leaders often treated black soldiers with disrespect, expecting the men to fail. Clubs for officers were segregated, as were most barracks and mess halls. Most African Americans in the army were relegated to the roles of stevedoring, digging ditches, hauling lumber, burying bodies, cleaning latrines, doing laundry, and cooking. They accepted these roles because they believed that, if they performed these duties with dignity and skill, they would prove themselves worthy of contributing more. For many, the military offered possibilities for travel and other kinds of personal advancement. Others resisted consignment to such positions while "whitey [went] off to class at technical school and [the] blacks [went] nowhere but to mess cooking duty, laundry, and bilge cleaning!"[22]

By examining the images against this backdrop, we can ask how African American men in service positions distinguished their masculinized bodies from the feminine-identified act of cooking. More interesting to consider is the question of how African American men recast and rescripted the kitchen landscape and debunked racist and sexist stereotypes. Using the scripts of masculinity available to them at that time, one can argue that they performed the work with the same precision, skill, and accuracy as if they were training for combat. More than simply drawing on the available scripts, they expanded the possibilities as they performed the kitchen work they were assigned.[23]

Foods are embedded in the social processes captured on film at Craig Field in 1941. To map black masculinities on the kitchen landscape, we must be attentive to the ways in which race and gender tensions, food perceptions, and people intertwine. Fried chicken, especially in a southern context, is a totemic food (fig. 21). During enslavement, black women often cooked the chicken on many plantations. They lined the "southern groaning boards" with heaping platters of fried chicken. They were continuously praised for the taste of the poultry they cooked, but they seldom received credit for the effort involved in preparation.[24] Captions from the photographs at Craig Field minimize the domestic labor of the servicemen. One caption reads: "[The chickens] is [sic] so well raised, they fry themselves—when one's cooked—they're all cooked" (fig. 22).[25]

Chicken raises complex issues. Many whites in the 1940s bought into the stereotypes that all black people not only loved chicken but could cook it well. Under a minimally publicized decree, "Negro Mess Attendant" training

FIGURE 21. A hot tray of crisp chicken. Craig Field, Southeastern Air Training Center, Alabama. Library of Congress, Prints & Photographs Division, FSA/OWI Collection, [LC-USF34-080339-D].

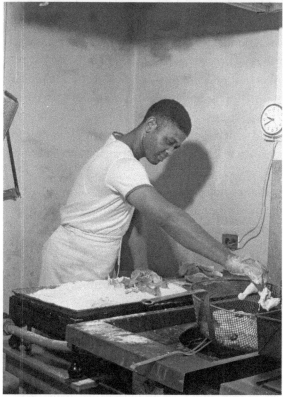

FIGURE 22. Craig Field cook says, "They is so well raised, they fry themselves—when one's cooked—they're all cooked." Craig Field, Southeastern Air Training Center, Selma, Alabama. Library of Congress, Prints & Photographs Division, FSA/OWI Collection, [LC-USF34-080311-D].

began in 1932 at Norfolk, Virginia's naval operating base. Lloyd Prewitt, who heard that the navy was "signing up 'colored' men to be mess attendants," was among the first to arrive for the new training program. In an interview with Daniel Miller for *Messmen Chronicles*, Prewitt recalled: "There were twenty men in our class from six southern states. We were the first group of blacks to go into the navy since 1919. They recruited only us Southerners because they believed we would be more accepting of the servant role they had in mind for us than would blacks from the North. We were all farm boys or unemployed and just glad to get off the street—to have food and a place to sleep." Miller goes on to point out that some whites believed the South was a "reservoir" filled with well-trained "house Negroes."[26]

Some whites wanted and needed to think of servile blacks as normal. But they also needed to be able to distinguish black frying and eating from white claims that fried chicken was one of the hallmarks of southern cuisine. Cooking and preparing foods does not necessarily grant one ownership. And when access is allowed or given, it is not always equitable. In times of war, for example, food is rationed and guarded. Segregation mandated separate dining facilities, which were not necessarily equal. African American servicemen had to break culinary and social boundaries to share in the consumption of the food, especially in the presence of whites. Cultural demarcations became necessary to symbolically separate the South between white and black.

Food and domestic rituals separated the cook from the consumer. African Americans were compelled to remember their "natural" place as servants and not as "social equals." These temporal and spatial prescriptions fostered feelings of inferiority among black men and feelings of superiority among white men. These feelings would also be the catalyst for black men's recasting what was considered black women's work in terms that were suitably masculine. Considering the dinner at Craig Field in this context, the "hearty chicken meal" is part of a social institution, shaped by racial and gendered complexities. Social segregation, therefore, is represented in the relationships of the period as well as the food.[27] And fried chicken becomes a contested social marker of "Old South" mores.

Southern fried chicken, in this context, is an object that "hails." Robin Bernstein explains:

Scriptive things leap out within a field, address an individual, and demand to be reckoned with. . . . Things *hail*. And they do so persistently, constantly, when we are alone and in groups, when we think about them and when we do not . . . when we individually or collectively accept the invitation to dance, refuse it, accept but improvise new steps, or renegotiate, deconstruct, or explode roles of leader and follower. A hail demands a bodily response.[28]

The dance here was between African Americans and southern fried chicken. In the process they reclaimed their subjecthood through gesture, posture, and verbal retort. And they rejected the dominant script, which suggested they were less important to the war effort than white soldiers.

Service, not Servitude: Opposition in the Kitchen

In 1935's *Mules and Men*, Zora Neale Hurston wrote:

The Negro, in spite of his open faced laughter, his seeming acquiescence, is particularly evasive. You see we are a polite people and we do not say to our questioner, "Get out of here!" We smile and tell him or her something that satisfies the white person because, knowing so little about us, he doesn't know what he is missing. The Indian resists curiosity by a stony silence. The Negro offers a feather bed resistance, that is, we let the probe enter, but it never comes out. It gets smothered under a lot of laughter and pleasantries.[29]

Throughout African American history, men and women have used nonviolent opposition to confront obstacles to their advancement. From household workers in Atlanta, Georgia, to the Pullman Porters who rejected the condescending name "George," blacks have engaged in acts of resistance. How can we rethink black masculine work in the kitchens of Craig Field in the 1940s to encompass such actions?[30]

In countless cases, African American men and women have employed oppositional food practices. From early entrepreneurs who engaged in forestalling and huckstering to domestic workers who crushed glass, burned food, or refused to cook, daily acts have countered racism and sexism. Acts of resistance in the military are a bit harder to understand, because behavior was controlled and direct insubordination usually met with swift repercussions—from court-martial to execution. But stories exist of uncooked food, broken dishes, and direct defiance. Chester Wright told Daniel Miller about a "head boy" named Matt Alfonso "Scarface" Davis:

> [There was a wide, concrete space . . . where the midshipmen held their meal-time formations and where we messmen] marched in and marched out to form up platoons after we finished serving. . . . One of the two white chief commissary stewards . . . came out and told [Scarface Davis] that the officer of the day had ordered us not to march out the front door. . . . They were having a big football game. He didn't want the guests . . . to see us. . . . Instead, we were to march out the back door.
>
> Scarface Davis said, "They ain't *been* marchin' out the back door, and as long as I'm the head boy . . . they're not *going* to march out the back door!" . . .
>
> We went right in front like we usually did. We lined up, counted off, pivoted, swung around, and marked time.
>
> You know, Negroes are dramatic. We didn't march with the little *ba bum, ba bump* that the midshipmen had. On "forward march" those dudes were beating those kettledrums like wild men: BOOM, BUBBA BOOM, BUBBA BOOM, BOOM, BOOM! Everybody stopped and started looking down there at us.[31]

The soldiers here engaged in a specific kind of resistance. The loud, differently cadenced drumming is part of the "hidden transcript" described by Robin D. G. Kelley in "We Are Not What We Seem." Kelley writes that some forms of resistance are composed of a "'hidden transcript,' a dissident political undercurrent running through daily conversation, folklore, jokes, and songs. It may include theft, foot-dragging, destruction of property, or, more rarely, open attacks on individuals, institutions, or symbols of domination."[32]

We do not have records of the conversations that took place among the African American men at Craig Field as they worked. They may have talked about what they were going to eat and with whom. They may have recalled and shared conversations they were not supposed to hear. That was the case for many domestic employees, considered present but invisible by their employers. They may have been "talking back" or using other kinds of objectionable language. As Hurston observed, people in service positions sometimes cursed about their situations while smiling in the face of their oppressor.[33] No direct evidence shows how assertive these men were

FIGURE 23. Craig Field cooks setting out plates for chicken dinner. Craig Field, Southeastern Air Training Center, Selma, Alabama. Library of Congress, Prints & Photographs Division, FSA/OWI Collection, [LC-USF34-080348-E].

or whether they overtly questioned authority. The photographs suggest the tensions of the Craig Field kitchen landscape.

The gaze of the men in the photographs compels our attention. In each photograph, at least one black man looks directly into the camera. What are we to make of this gaze? It is direct and, in some cases, defiant (fig. 23). We also glimpse segregated military culture. The kitchen space is divided unequally. We do not know if there were any white kitchen workers, because Collier does not include them in the frame. What is apparent, however, is the dichotomy that Collier suggests by framing a photograph of a soldier facing the cooks around the kitchen station. Here the photographer played a role in grafting the oppositional stance (fig. 24).

Looking only at one or two of the images, it might be hard to discern the racial inequality of the kitchen landscape. In many of the photos, the emphasis is on the chicken frying. The photographs used here, however, focus primarily on the men who performed the labor. They point to disparities in status.

Collier established an oppositional stance by photographing the men

FIGURE 24. Untitled. Craig Field, Southeastern Air Training Center, Selma, Alabama. Library of Congress, Prints & Photographs Division, FSA/OWI Collection, [LC-USF34-080355-D].

from the side or behind, as when the two black men are seen sitting on the trash cans. Though they sit on the garbage cans, wearing the aprons assigned to them by the military, their posture does not suggest that they see themselves as anything other than comfortable in their own subjecthood (fig. 25). They are not slouching or leaning, looking idle, looking downcast. Rather, they appear to be men who are physically, psychologically, and emotionally tired. Mistrustful of the photographer's gaze, they are engaged in conversations that sustain and reify their sense of self.

Reading "Between the Lines"

In a 1965 interview, John Collier explained what makes this photographic collection historically valuable, calling it "photographing between the lines." Collier argued that most of the FSA photographers were artists first. Their

FIGURE 25. Untitled. Craig Field, Southeastern Air Training Center, Selma, Alabama. Library of Congress, Prints & Photographs Division, FSA/OWI Collection, [LC-USF34-080346-E].

goal was to capture the subjective while appearing to present the objective point of view. He said,

> You find a voluminous amount of material, maybe up to 90% of the file that was all photographed between the lines. They had nothing whatsoever to do with the stated policy of the FSA Division of Information.... All the photographers spent some of their time, some photographers spent all their time ... photographing culturally between the lines.... And the richness of the file is the fact that it is very non-objective ... [but] you have two levels of important data, in the file. Something's on the firing line right in the middle of a dust storm and the Okie camps, or you find highly non-objective records of what was going on in America at that time, usually faced in the other direction from the government project.

Collier's point is well taken. By including photographs of the African American cooks, he highlighted how African Americans in the military, serving as supply men, waited for their chance to fight and to be treated as first-class citizens. By drawing our attention to these few men at Craig Field, Collier redefined and rescripted black masculinities. He read between the lines to tell the untold stories. He encouraged the viewer to embrace the many possible ways that black masculinity can be defined.

Perhaps African American men were not the primary subjects of his Craig Field assignment. Given that the captions emphasize the Food for Defense program and the various farms from which the poultry came, Collier probably planned to focus on poultry production and the readiness of the cadets. The photographer could have secured this information without including the African American soldier-cooks. Collier's social conscience, combined with his artist's eye, provides the viewer with a rare glimpse of the experiences of some African American military men. Collier made this point in the same 1965 interview:

> [FSA photographers] had faith in the visual record that this nonverbal evidence might do something where nothing else would. Therefore, they were social and did a social welfare job, and all the ones that I knew, any of them, whether it be Delano or Lee or Post, they all had this thought in the background, that every photograph they made had some essential and secret purpose and would do something for somebody someday.... And I would say that this was the real core of the spirit of the Farm Security Administration. That they believed that their photographs were effectual and purposeful. This is different from saying, were they interested in culture? They were interested in communication, and they felt that what was going on should be communicated.

Through his lens, gender, race, region, food, and power in American society during World War II unfold, and we get a better understanding of the tensions that existed during that time. Collier said, "That much data on one thing is bound to have power, is bound to tell you things about culture you can't get in any other way."[34]

Many might read these images as depictions of black menial labor. But we can "read around in them" to hear a different narrator. The subtextual story that Collier captures illustrates the ways cooks prepared the meal. Hearing a different voice, we understand that a complex social interaction—a dance— took place and was embodied by the fried chicken. The fried chicken symbolizes different things to everyone involved in this story. For the cadets it is a hearty meal. For the photographer it is an opportunity to document diverse Americans working together to "fight the enemy." For the cooks it is work, which alleviates hunger, and definitely represents discrimination.

Collier's employment of the oppositional gaze challenges us to look directly at the cooks. Through these photographs, Collier helps us recast this kitchen space in a way that does not feminize these black men but invests in their definitions of masculinity in ways that defy the standard script.

NOTES

Many thanks to Jessica Walker, Fabio Parasecoli, and Francis Robb for commenting on various parts of this essay, and to the staff in the Reference Section of the Prints and Photographs Division at the Library of Congress, in particular Jeff Bridgers, and to Amy Purcell, Associate Curator, Special Collections, Ekstrom Library, University of Louisville, for archival assistance.

1. Thomas Parren, "The Job Ahead," *Survey Graphic* 30, no. 7 (July 1941). Food for Defense Poster, 1941. Farm Security Administration—Office of War Information Photograph Collection from the Library of Congress, accessed August 25, 2002, http://lcweb2.loc.gov/cgi-bin /query/D?fsaall:6:./temp/~ammem_AXKZ:: [USF345– 007702-ZA-A].

2. Turkeys and chickens were the only foods not rationed during World War II. Because the Eastern Shore of Maryland and Virginia (Delmarva area) dominated the commercial broiler industry at this time, the federal government, through the War Food Administration, placed a "freeze" on the chicken supply from other vendors. The government had sole access to the chickens from this area. With the close of the war, the government abruptly cancelled their contracts for chickens. Coupled with a greater demand for beef in the postwar era, this move severely affected the economic status of the region. See John Steele Gordon, "The Chicken Story: The History of the U.S. Poultry Industry," *American Heritage* 47, no. 5 (September 1996): 52–64; Gordon Sawyer, *The Agribusiness Poultry Industry: A History of Its Development* (New York: Exposition, 1971).

3. Patricia Prell, "Every Chow Line Leads to Natick: All Military Menus Are Tested and Approved at Natick," November-December 1998 issue of *The Warrior*, accessed January 2009, http://www.seabeecook.com/cookery/recipes/Natick.htm.

4. Photos taken by FSA photographer Jack Delano affirm that there were some African American FSA farmers. Of those he photographed in Woodville, Georgia (Greene County), none were shown actually preparing their goods for sale. Most of these photographs show the farmers waiting for a FSA meeting to begin. It is doubtful, given Jim Crow policies in the South, that these farms were used to supply the army air force base. Delano, "At a Meeting of Negro FSA Borrowers," [LC-USF34–044163-D to LC-USF34–044200-D].

5. Robin Bernstein, "Dances with Things: Material Culture and the Performance of Race," *Social Text 101* 27, no. 4 (Winter 2009): 67–94.

6. Jeff Miller and Jonathan Deutsch, "Using Material Objects in Food Studies Research," in *Food Studies: An Introduction to Research Methods* (London: Berg, 2010), 182.

7. Bernstein, "Dances with Things," 69; see also Martin Heidegger, "The Thing," in *Poetry, Language, Thought,* trans. Albert Hofstadter (New York: Harper & Row, 1971), 174–82; Bill Brown, "Thing Theory," *Critical Inquiry* 28 (Autumn 2001): 1–22.

8. Bernstein, "Dances with Things," 70.

9. Ibid., 79.

10. The Farm Security Administration photographs are part of the best-known but highly underutilized collections. Its images depict the living and social conditions of Americans in suburban, urban, and rural areas during the Depression and World War II. Initiated in 1935 as the documentary arm of the Resettlement Administration under Rexford Tugwell, the goal was to document loans to farmers provided by the RA/USDA. Tugwell appointed Roy Stryker to direct the project, which he did until 1943. The entire collection at the Library of Congress includes more than a hundred thousand images from the RA/FSA/OWI (Office of War Information). Photographers such as Dorothea Lange, Walker Evans, Marion Post Wolcott, and Gordon Parks were major contributors. The photographer of the images under study here, John Collier Jr., played a significant role, too. Quite a bit has been written on the photographs. The pictures often referred to are those of white individuals and communities. For one of the best overviews of the collection as it pertains to African American people, see Nicholas Natonson, *The Black Image in the New Deal: The Politics of FSA Photography* (Knoxville: University of Tennessee Press, 1992).

11. Richard Doud, "John Collier interview," January 18, 1965, Archives of American Art, Smithsonian Institution, accessed June 8, 2005, http://artarchives.si.edu/oralhist/collie65.htm.

12. Oral history interview with John Collier, January 18, 1965, Archives of American Art, Smithsonian Institution, 9.

13. John Collier Jr. obituary, *New York Times*, March 5, 1992, accessed February 22, 2013, http://www.nytimes.com/1992/03/05/arts/john-collier-jr-78-a-teacher-writer-and -photographer.html.

14. Collier downplays his reputation, compared to Jack Delano, Dorothea Lange, and other better-known FSA photographers. Collier, however, focused a high percentage of his photographs on black life. See Natonson, *Black Image in the New Deal,* 72–74.

15. In his interview, Collier says that he took the suggestion made by cataloguer Paul Vanderbilt to put his photographs together to form a complete experience. In Library of Congress parlance this is called a lot, which is an organized set of photographs designed to convey a message as conceived by the photographer. Neither the caption sheet nor the microfilm for this lot could be located at the Library of Congress.

16. According to Collier we cannot trust the captions that accompany the images. Once the file was reorganized, captions were added, and it was categorized by like subject matter. Oral history interview with John Collier, 11.

17. This is the caption for several of the images in this series.

18. The notion that objects have a cultural biography relates to the history of its ownership and how it passes from hand to hand. This approach asks about the status of an object as it moves from place to place and person to person. Examining these sociological contexts enables a better reading of how people relate to objects and how those objects carry various meanings. See Arjun Appadurai, ed., *The Social Life of Things: Commodities in Cultural Perspective* (Cambridge: Cambridge University Press, 1988), 4–5; Igor Kopytoff, "The Cultural Biography of Things," in Appadurai, *Social Life of Things*, 64–91. Barbara Carson also provides a perspective on this method in her article "Interpreting History through Objects," *Journal of Museum Education* 10, no. 3 (1985): 129–33.

19. Quoted in Mary P. Motley, ed., *The Invisible Soldier: The Experience of the Black Soldier, World War II* (Detroit: Wayne State University Press, 1987), 77.

20. Given this latter point, one would be hard pressed not to see connections between the "bird" or the "chick" and the female body. From the standpoint of gender-typing food, chicken is considered feminine. On this point, see Psyche Williams-Forson, *Building Houses Out of Chicken Legs: Black Women, Food, and Power* (Chapel Hill: University of North Carolina Press, 2006), especially chapter 2, and Jane Dixon, *The Changing Chicken: Chooks, Cooks, and Culinary Culture* (Sydney: University of New South Wales Press, 2009).

21. Amy Bentley, *Eating for Victory: Food Rationing and the Politics of Domesticity* (Urbana: University of Illinois Press, 1988), 80. Richard Allen Burns recalls the reservations he had when he joined the U.S. Marine Corps and learned that he had been assigned the "rather effeminate job" of field cook. Like Burns in 1969, some white men were assigned to the mess hall in the 1940s at Craig Field. Some of these men can be seen in Collier's photographs. See Richard Allen Burns, "Foodways in the Military," *Digest: An Interdisciplinary Study of Food and Foodways* 18 (1998): 21–26; Collier, "Private Sykes, Assistant Mess Sergeant" [LC-USF34-080310-D]; and also Jonathan Deutsch, "'Please Pass the Chicken Tits': Rethinking Men and Cooking at an Urban Firehouse," *Food and Foodways* 13, nos. 1–2 (2005): 91–114.

22. Emmitt Tidd quoted in Gerald Astor, *The Right to Fight: A History of African Americans in the Military* (Cambridge, Mass.: Da Capo, 2001). Several books use oral histories to detail the experiences of African Americans in the military. Among them are Motley, *Invisible Soldier*; Bernard Nalty, *Strength for the Fight: A History of Black Americans in the Military* (New York: Free Press, 1989). Though several others include minor comments related to mess halls and food handling, only one seemed to fully detail the life of the "invisible soldier" from this standpoint: Richard Miller, *The Messman Chronicles: African American in the U.S. Navy, 1932–1943* (Annapolis, Md.: Naval Institute Press, 2004).

23. While many African American men were assigned the job of cook or mess attendant, they possessed other knowledge as well. Many knew how to fire guns prior to their arrival in the military. Others received training while in the military, though it may have been less than equal to that of white soldiers.

24. The image of the heavy-set, bandanna-wearing black woman with a spatula or some other cooking implement dominated southern literature and advertisements (see Williams-

Forson, *Building Houses Out of Chicken Legs*, chapter 3). Classics such as Harriet Beecher Stowe's *Uncle Tom's Cabin* and Margaret Mitchell's *Gone with the Wind* feature black women as this kind of illustrative cook. On this point and more about African Americans and chicken, *Building Houses out of Chicken Legs* and John T. Edge, *Fried Chicken: An American Story* (New York: Putnam, 2004) for other perspectives.

25. Collier, Craig Field Cook. [LC-USF34-080311-D].

26. Miller, *Messman Chronicles* 10–23.

27. Titus, "'Groaning Tables and Spit in the Kettles': Food and Race in the Nineteenth-Century South." *Southern Quarterly* 20, no. 2–3 (1992): 13–21. Excellent examples of how food is a marker of social segregation include the incidents at the Woolworth lunch counter in Greensboro, North Carolina. See William Yeingst and Lonnie Bunch, "Curating the Recent Past: The Woolworth Lunch Counter, Greensboro, North Carolina," in *Exhibiting Dilemmas: Issues of Representation at the Smithsonian*, ed. Amy Henderson and Adrienne Kaeppler (Washington, D.C.: Smithsonian Institution Press, 1997), 143–56.

28. Bernstein, "Dances with Things," 73.

29. Zora Neale Hurston, *Mules and Men* (New York: J. B. Lippincott, 1935).

30. Because little, if any, material exists on the men who cooked at the army air force base during the era of Jim Crow, I draw examples from other regiments of the military where such actions and their actors have been documented.

31. Miller, *Messmen Chronicles*, 71.

32. Robin D. G. Kelley, "'We Are Not What We Seem': Rethinking Black Working-Class Opposition in the Jim Crow South," *Journal of American History* 80, no. 1 (June 1993): 75–112.

33. Chris Rock makes a similar point about old black men and the ways in which they play the Janus-faced role of servant-resistor: "There's nothing more racist than an old black man. You know why? 'Cause an old black man went through some real racism. He didn't go through that I-can't-get-a-cab shit. He was the cab.... You know what's wild about the old black men? An old black man, he ain't gonna let you fuck up his money. Whenever an old black man sees an old white man ... the old black man always kisses the old white man's ass. 'How you doing, sir? Pleased to meet you. Whatever I can get you, you let me know.' As soon as the white man get out of sight, he's like: 'Cracker-ass cracker!' ... The white man come back. 'Howdy, sir?'" http://www.script-o-rama.com/movie_scripts/c/chris-rock-bigger-and-blacker-script.html (January 2009). *Bigger and Blacker*, HBO Studios, 1999.

34. Doud, Collier interview.

CHAPTER 14

"I'm Talkin' 'Bout the Food I Sells"

African American Street Vendors and the Sound of Food from Noise to Nostalgia

JESSICA B. HARRIS

Food easily appeals to four of the five senses: the feel of the soft fuzz of a ripe peach, the juicy taste of a sun-heated tomato, the sight of a dew-drenched bush laden with blueberries, or the pungent aroma of a fiery habanero. Sound, though, is usually left out of the culinary equation. The sizzle of a steak on the grill or the tinkling sound of Moroccan mint tea poured from on high or the clink of glasses in a toast may well be evocative. But the best "text" waiting to be discovered comes from the generations of vendors, both enslaved and free, who hawked their wares in the country's urban areas and rural byways for more than three centuries.

A woman strolls across the stage at the beginning of act 3 of George Gershwin's folk opera *Porgy and Bess*.

> Oh dey's so fresh an' fine
> An dey's just off the vine
> Strawberry, strawberry, strawberry.[1]

The composer uses the woman's plangent call to signal daybreak over Catfish Row. As the community emerges to face the day, the cry of the honey man and the crab seller follow that of the strawberry seller.

Street vendors such as those evoked by Gershwin and his librettist, DuBose Heyward, were longtime fixtures on the streets and in the street markets of the United States. The vendors each used a specific cry to extol their wares. They were so much a part of the South's character that travelers wrote home about them and magazine illustrators profiled them.

In South Carolina, the street cries of Charleston were typical of major cities across the globe in the seventeenth, eighteenth, and nineteenth centuries. Old etchings show various Parisian street vendors, including the hot chocolate seller, the chestnut vendor, and the notions peddler. In the late seventeenth century, Marcellus Laroon the Elder etched the street criers of London. The cries of Dublin streets are remembered in the folk song "Molly Malone," who sold "cockles and mussels alive, alive-o." The vendors of London were immortalized more recently in the Broadway musical *Oliver!* with the song "Who Will Buy?"

Charleston's street cries were different. They offered a New World twist on an Old World theme. In most of the urban areas of the American South, well into the nineteenth century, the majority of the street vendors were of African descent. Whether freedmen, newly emancipated, or enslaved, they brought a verve, a verbal dexterity, and an ingenuity to marketing their wares that was all their own (fig. 26).

Market women in Africa have wielded both economic and political power for centuries. In the upheaval of the transatlantic slave trade, they brought their marketing traditions to the Western Hemisphere and transformed its vending habits. West Africa had traditional markets that were fixed and well organized. Itinerant vendors existed, but the majority of women vendors worked in well-established markets, divided according to the wares they sold and stratified by the status of the vendors. More prosperous vendors sold wholesale to smaller retailers, who transported the wares to outlying regions and often sold door to door. Different sections of the large markets offered different items, ranging from metal goods to fabric, from calabashes to portable grills. The markets also had dedicated sections for food, and some markets dealt with food exclusively. They, too, had their hierarchy of stall holders, itinerant vendors, and occasional or illegal vendors. These were places for commerce and also for news-gathering, gossip, and assembly.[2]

These types of markets also existed in the New World context. They could be found in major urban areas throughout the United States. Africans and their descendants played the same roles they had on the African continent. In the New World, though, the Africans who marketed their wares did so as street vendors. Early on in the New World, "higglers," or "hucksters," as itinerant vendors are called in the English-speaking Caribbean, appeared in the markets.

16801—Shrimp Vender

FIGURE 26. Antique postcard of a male shrimp vendor, from the author's personal collection.

In the first quarter of the eighteenth century, Barbados planters were inundated with enslaved street vendors. Huckstering was so endemic that it was made punishable by law. So many engaged in the practice that several types of hucksters could be determined, according to Hilary McDonald Beckles in *Natural Rebels: A Social History of Enslaved Black Women*. Beckles identifies men and women who sold goods for their masters or mistresses and who were required to wear a metal collar with the name of their master engraved on it. She also identifies freedmen who sold on their own account. They sold many things, including household services, from sweeping chimneys to day labor. Mainly, they sold food.

Slave vending came to be associated with pilfering and theft. This entrepreneurship was challenged by white businessmen. In response, street vending was confined in the Slave Code of 1688 and outlawed in 1708. Eventually, planters had to acknowledge the necessity of slave commerce and accept slave vending as legal.[3]

In what were then the northern colonies, the same street-vending economy prevailed. Early in the colonial period, women of African descent cornered the market on homemade goods. A black woman selling sweetmeats or savories on the street was as common a sight in New York or Philadelphia or Charleston as in Barbados. Free, they worked for themselves; enslaved, they worked for their mistresses and were occasionally allowed to keep a small portion of their earnings.

Blacks, both free and enslaved, dominated street vending until a new wave of European immigrants made inroads in the mid-nineteenth century. African American street vendors in the North and South gave the streets of fledgling cities an African inflection. Vendors hawked their wares with loud cries designed to lure customers. Musicologist Thomas Brothers has defined African cultural legacies, present on plantations, to include "dancing, gestures, verbal sparring, storytelling, linguistic patterns, architecture, textile designs, outdoor decoration (bottle trees, raked-dirt yards), crop cultivation, and diet."[4]

Speaking well is still important on the African continent. A recent guidebook to Senegal explains: "Discussion is a way of being.... When it comes to bargaining, negotiating, or arguing, discussion becomes 'tchatche.' The Senegalese are known throughout West Africa as first-class speakers."[5] The African tradition of verbal sparring can be heard in the street cries of competing vendors who worked to lure clientele in colonial, federal, and antebellum America. African American vendors approached their task with a cacophonous zeal and were often argumentative and rude. In Charleston, where the custom of wearing badges parallels that of the metal collars in Barbados, slave vendors were particularly insubordinate.

On March 26, 1823, a letter to the editors of Charleston's *Post and Courier* signed by "A Warning Voice" noted: "The legalized audacity of the negros [*sic*] who hawk their wares, &c. about our streets, should no longer be permitted.... The public cries should be regulated. The negro [*sic*] should be taught to announce what he has to sell and to suppress his wit. A decency and humility of conduct should pervade all ranks of our colored population."[6]

Similar charges were leveled at African American street vendors in New

York and other cities along the Eastern Seaboard. In New York, "Human-itas," a pseudonymous social commentator, complained of the same nui-sance created by noisy street vendors, or hucksters. In 1820 he grumbled that the oyster stands and numerous tables of foods that lined the streets made easy passage all but impossible. In certain areas of the city, cries such as "He-e-e-e-e-ere's your fine Rocka-a-way clams" and seasonal additions such as the autumnal "H-au-ut corn," "H-a-u-r-t Ca-irrne" [hot corn] were common.[7]

The street cries of African American vendors emerged as an identify-ing aspect of the urban culture. American pamphlets, which followed the European model of works such as the *Street Cries of London*, documented the vendor calls. *Cries of New York*, published in 1809, was one of the first such works. The cries of the street vendors, initially considered bothersome noise, became aural symbols of various cities. Leon Frémaux, an engineer and former Confederate officer, was one of the first artists to capture the im-ages of the peddlers in New Orleans. Frémaux's *New Orleans Characters*, a collection of drawings, first appeared in 1876. His captions reflect the biases of his time; his drawings, however, reveal just how lively the street vendors were.

Lafcadio Hearn, patron saint of all things New Orleans, carried on Frémaux's tradition. Hearn worked for the *Daily City Item*. During his two-year tenure with the paper, he produced multiple woodcuts and articles that celebrated street vendors: the tignoned vegetable seller with her basket over her arm or balanced precariously on her head; the knife grinder, bell in hand, bent under his wheel. Hearn advanced Frémaux's description. In a July 21, 1881, article in the *Item*, "Voices of Dawn," he showcased the aural component that vendors added to street life.

> With the first glow of sunlight the street resounds with their cries; and, really, the famous "Book of London Cries" contains nothing more curious than some of these vocal advertisements—these musical announcements sung by Ital-ians, negroes, Frenchmen, and Spaniards. The vendor of fowls pokes in his head at every open window with cries of "Chick- en, Madamma, Chick-en!" and the seller of "Lem-Ons—fine Lem-Ons!" follows in his footsteps. The peddlers of "Ap-Pulls!" of "Straw-BARE-eries!" and "Clack-Brees!"—all own sonorous voices.[8]

Hearn went on to detail the cries and accents of the various sellers, from the fresh fig vendor to the person selling "ochre-A"—which he jokingly suggested sounded as though the peddler was selling grade-A paint supplies. Frémaux and Hearn, while admiring the innovation and the ingenuity of the salesmanship, both seemed to be looking at the vendors as "other." Frémaux saw them as characters from a past era, while Hearn found them objects of curiosity who contributed to the uniqueness of his favored city.

With the turn of the twentieth century, the African American street vendors became folkloric fixtures in several southern cities. Charleston became known for its vendors. Their calls and demeanor were the subjects of thorough documentation. In 1910 Harriette Kershaw Leiding published *Street Cries of an Old Southern City*, which added musical transcriptions for the cries as well as notes on the vendors and their demeanor. She spoke both admiringly and condescendingly:

> "Ole Joe Cole, good old soul," who does a thriving business in lower King Street under the quaint sign of "Joe Cole & Wife" is the bright, particular, tho fast-waning star of our galaxy of street artists. He sets the fashion, so to speak, in "hucksterdom." Joe has many imitators, but no equals, for he looks like an Indian Chief, walks with a limp that would "do a general proud," and uses his walking stick like a baton, while bellowing like the "Bull of Bashan." It's a Never to be forgotten occasion when Joe lustily yells:

> Old Joe Cole—Good old Soul
> Porgy in the Summer-time
> An e Whiting in the Spring
> 8 upon a string.
> Don't be late, I'm watin [sic] at de gate
> Don't be mad—Heres [sic] your shad
> Old Joe Cole—Good Ole Soul."[9]

Joe was joined in the streets of Charleston by vegetable vendors, according to Leiding, "wonderful wide-chested big-hipped specimens of womanhood that balance a fifty pound basket of vegetables on their heads and ever and anon cry their goods" (fig. 27).[10]

In 1925 R. Emmett wrote of New Orleans in *Mellows: A Chronicle of Unknown Singers*: "Among the many quaint old customs which still prevail,

FIGURE 27. A female
vendor. From the author's
personal collection.

there, perhaps the most characteristic is the going about of Negro street
vendors with their plaintive melodious cries by which they announce their
wares." Lyle Saxon, Robert Tallant, and Edward Dreyer documented New
Orleans of the 1930s for the Works Progress Administration. They devoted
an entire chapter of their work *Gumbo Ya-Ya* to a history of the city's street
cries, including those of coffee vendors, a waffle man, a lemonade seller, and
peddlers of *calas* (deep-fried rice cakes).[11]

The cries were not limited to the South. Street vendors found voice in the
African American urban enclaves of the North in the early to mid-twentieth
century. In New York's Harlem, street vendors sold cooked foods such as
baked sweet potatoes and boiled pigs' feet. They also peddled fresh fruits
and vegetables. Harlem was a mecca not only for migrants from the South
but also for immigrants from the Caribbean. The street cries were multi-
lingual:

Yo tengo guineas
Yo tengo cocoas
Yo tengo piñas tambien[12]

Well into the twentieth century, cries continued in cities south and north. Rhythm and blues singer Sam Cooke gave some of his first public performances while crying wares on a watermelon vendor's truck in Chicago.[13]

Now, in the early years of the twenty-first century, itinerant street vendors and their cries have all but disappeared. The excitement generated by an ice cream truck's distinctive sounds is one of the last vestiges of door-to-door food vending. Street vendors of old are remembered fondly, and the few remaining street vendors are living artifacts of times past. In present-day New Orleans, an African American vendor plies his trade under the sobriquet of Mr. Okra. He drives his truck, decorated like a Haitian tap tap, through the city's neighborhoods, crying out, "I got ya okra! I got you pineapples! I got ya sweet corn!" through a loudspeaker. Mr. Okra is a throwback to the time when the freshest fruit, vegetables, and fish came with a rhythm and a rhyme and a cry that said "I'm Talkin' About the Food I Sell!"

NOTES

1. George Gershwin and DuBose Heyward, *Porgy and Bess*, Houston Grand Opera, RCA Houston Grand Opera Company RCD3-2109, 1977, 33 ⅓ rpm.

2. Thierry Paulais and Laurence Wilhelm, *Marchés d'Afrique* (Paris; Karthala, 2000); Jessica Harris, *High on the Hog: A Culinary Journey from Africa to America* (New York: Bloomsbury, 2010), 86–91.

3. Hilary McDonald Beckles, *Natural Rebels: A Social History of Enslaved Black Women in Barbados* (New Brunswick, N.J.: Rutgers University Press, 1989), 72–75.

4. Thomas Brothers, *Louis Armstrong's New Orleans* (New York: Norton, 2006), 138.

5. "La palabre est un art de vivre.... La palabre devient '*tchatche*' lorsqu'il est question de marchander, de négocier, ou de s'embrouiler. Les Sénégalais sont connus partout dans l'ouest de l'Afrique pour être des embrouilleurs de première." Dominique Auzias, Jean Paul Labourdette et al., *Sénégal 2011–2012* (Paris: Petit Futé, 2010), 73.

6. Harlen Greene, Harry S. Hutchins Jr., and Brian E. Hutchins, *Slave Badges and the Slave Hire System in Charleston, South Carolina, 1783–1865* (Jefferson, N.C.: McFarland, 2004), 43.

7. Shane White, "Black Life in Freedom: Creating a Popular Culture," in *Slavery in New York*, ed. Ira Berlin and Leslie M. Harris (New York: New Press, 2005), 157–58.

8. Lafcadio Hearn, "Voices of Dawn," *Daily City Item*, July 21, 1881.

9. Harriette Kershaw Leiding, *Street Cries of an Old Southern City*, 2nd ed. (Charleston, S.C.: Dagett, 1927), 3.

10. Ibid., 9.

11. Lyle Saxon, Robert Tallant, and Edward Dreyer, *Gumbo Ya-Ya: A Collection of Louisiana Folk Tales* (New York: Bonanza, 1945).

12. Harris, *High on the Hog*, 179.

13. Mavis Staples, interview, CBS Sunday Morning, May 8, 2011.

PART 5

On Authenticity

THE FINAL PIECES in this collection, Andrew Warnes's "Edgeland *Terroir*: Authenticity and Invention in New Southern Foodways Strategy" and the conclusion by Ted Ownby, take a close and critical look at the southern food studies enterprise. Both explore the role of theory and metacriticism in the methodologies of food studies.

Warnes finds much to celebrate and much to approach with caution. He points out a collective temptation to see functioning communities, to romanticize easy cross-racial, cross-gender, cross-class affiliations, and to overstate the connections fostered by the study and consumption of food. Warnes criticizes the increasingly common misreadings of American studies scholar Benedict Anderson's idea of imagined communities.[1]

It is a familiar criticism to food studies scholars. Warren Belasco's careful exploration of how identical data can fuel predictions of both Malthusian food shortage and golden-breadbasket food excess complements Warnes's interrogation of popular foodways narratives.[2] Just as we hope to inspire future colleagues by this anthology, we hope Warnes's challenge inspires constructive debate about our collective project.

In kindred spirit, Ted Ownby offers a dispassionate concluding analysis of the current foodways field. He sidesteps prevailing assumptions about the South, labeling them "too simple, static, or misleading," preferring, instead, to think about how these essays raise a number of issues including ethnicity, leveraging the knowledge that, like language, food offers Americans an accepted forum to think about ethnicity while also raising questions about creativity. Ownby argues individually, as these pieces argue collectively, that scholars working in the field of food studies no longer need to justify their work but can, instead, focus their energies and intellects on elaborating the various yields of interdisciplinary approaches to studying food and cultural life.

NOTES

1. Benedict Anderson, *Imagined Communities: Reflections on the Origin and Spread of Nationalism* (New York: Verso, 1983, 2006).

2. Warren Belasco, *Meals to Come: History of the Future of Food* (Berkeley: University of California Press, 2006).

CHAPTER 15

Edgeland *Terroir*

Authenticity and Invention in New Southern Foodways Strategy

ANDREW WARNES

Precious soil, I say to myself, by what singular custom of laws is that thou wast made to constitute the riches of the freeholder? What should we American farmers be without the distinct possession of the soil? It feeds, it clothes us, from it we draw even a great exuberancy, our best meat, our richest drink, the very honey of our bees comes from this privileged spot.

J. HECTOR ST. JOHN DE CRÈVECOEUR, *Letters of an American Farmer* (1784)

Trains afford us the best views of allotments, a secret landscape.... Allotments signal that you are now passing through the edgelands as emphatically as a sewage works or a power station. They thrive on the fringes, the in-between spaces; on land left over (or left behind) by the tides of building and industrial development, in pockets behind houses or factories, and in ribbons along the trackbeds of railways.... Seen from the train, they seem to hark back towards feudal, swineherd England, subsistence strips for the poor outside the pasture land and deer parks. They are gardens that make no secret of their physics and chemistry, blowsily revealing an infrastructure of water butts and pipework, all the ad hoc plastic groundsheets and carpet offcuts. They flaunt their functionality; the domestic garden with its hands dirty, busy and raddled with agriculture's businesslike clutter. They don't fit in. Minutes after leaving a central station, and the privatised shiny surfaces of the city, and there they lie, a cobbling together, like a refugee camp for those fleeing consumerism.

PAUL FARLEY and MICHAEL SYMMONS ROBERTS, *Edgelands: Journeys into England's True Wilderness* (2011)

In the pages that follow I would like to reflect a little on my monograph *Savage Barbecue: Race, Culture, and the Invention of America's First Food* (2008). I would like to do this in order to offer some ideas about an area to which, I believe, the emerging discipline of southern food studies would do well to give deep thought over the coming years. Focusing on what I now recognize to be a source of scholarly confusion reflected in *Savage Barbecue*, the following observations in particular concern the relationship between this emerging discipline and the neighboring fields of southern studies and postnationalist American studies.

The area of confusion that I have in mind lies in the vague hinterland between two keywords—buzzwords, even—now familiar to us all. These buzzwords, *authenticity* and *invention*, really do crop up everywhere nowadays. Although its modern usage is sometimes traced to advertising, *authenticity* today just as often appears on commodities themselves, on the skin of the thing itself asserting the integrity of spice rubs and sauces, sunglasses and skateboards, record companies and sporting merchandise galore.[1] And *invention*, if a little less ubiquitous, still gets plenty of airtime in commodity capitalism, and appeals most especially to the authors and editors working in the diverse and multifaceted world of history publishing; *The Invention of America's First Food*, indeed. And yet, although already the subject of some academic debate, the sheer ubiquity of these buzzwords suggests that their relationship to each other requires still more attention. Quite how they reflect on each other remains, for many of us, unclear.

If true generally, moreover, this need grows all the more urgent when critical attention turns to the American South. On southern grounds, after all, ideas of authenticity and invention at once acquire added urgency and develop new character. In no other American region does quite so much kitsch or knowingly ersatz culture flourish in such close proximity with so many traditions that present themselves as time honored and anything but invented. But the blossoming, on the same southern grounds, of all manner of appeals to the "real" America and all manner of flagrantly invented Americana tends, I think, to place a particularly strong temptation before so-called southernists. The habit, widespread among English speakers, of treating *authenticity* and *invention* as mutually exclusive and almost as opposites of each other tends, I think, to encourage us to deal with the bewildering variety of southern culture by placing some of it into one and some into the other camp. Southernists, of course, are far from alone in this. For many different reasons, however, the opposition between *authenticity* and *invention* cuts especially deeply into their discourse, sometimes drawing up battle lines before discussions can be had, and often urging individuals to pick sides. And many of these individuals, it has to be said, oblige. Some embrace this opposition, identify themselves accordingly, and develop an archival or otherwise historical mode of scholarship that aims to legitimize an order they suppose to be "immemorial and 'natural.'"[2] Faced with their resonant statements, on the other hand, other southernists grow iconoclastic. They deploy a smart and withering critique against the nostalgic yearning to which many of their fellow southerners succumb. They debunk like there's no tomorrow. And finally they grow so withering about *authenticity*, so altogether skeptical about it, as to suggest that everything is invented—as though the Delta blues, for example, were no more "real" than Dollywood.

I am suggesting, then, that academic conferences about southern culture aren't always quite as cordial as the annual symposia that the Southern Foodways Alliance has been holding at the University of Mississippi since 1998. But I am also suggesting that, elsewhere in academia, some would attribute the cordiality of these symposia to the fact that its participants belong to the first of the two groups that I just mentioned. They would not necessarily see the Southern Foodways Alliance as what it is: an academic organization, founded by John Egerton, among others, dedicated to the study as well as the affirmation of "the diverse food cultures of the changing American South."[3] They might instead suspect, in this formulation, that affirmation outweighed scrutiny—that the SFA's symposia are instead gatherings of the likeminded, invested in a dubious idea of cultural authenticity, at which panelists might wax nostalgic about the grits of their youth, might sentimentalize preindustrial life, but without ever really settling into anything like critique.[4] My own experience of the SFA's symposium strongly belies this impression and confirmed that debate at the SFA is nothing like as introspective or unthinkingly affirmative as this caricature might suggest. Nonetheless, in future strategy the SFA would do well to reflect on this caricature, expose the misapprehensions that produce it, and more generally reflect on the state of southern cultural studies.

The critique of authenticity is now gathering speed in southernist discourse. Tara McPherson's *Reconstructing Dixie: Race, Gender, and Nostalgia in the Imagined South* (2003) and Scott Romine's *The Real South: Southern Narrative in the Age of Reproduction* (2008) are just two important studies determined to insist, as McPherson puts it, that there "is no pure South—

indeed, there never was—so specific understandings of how the South is represented, commodified, and packaged become key."[5] The influence of this academic approach, moreover, is now apparent in more popular books. Elijah Wald's *Escaping the Delta* (2004) and Greg Milner's *Perfecting Sound Forever* (2009) voyage into the manufacturing of southern blues authenticity in particular, in the process debunking what Romine calls "the premise that some deep but ultimately legible or recoverable code underwrites the South, lending it coherence and providing it with territorial integrity."[6] In the light of this powerful critique, the fact that southern food studies all but inaugurated itself in the desire to "recover" the "deep" and "ultimately legible ... code" of southern cooking now seems open to question. Much of John Egerton's foundational *Southern Food* (1987), not to mention his later calls for an SFA that could "preserve and enhance the great food heritage of the South," would seem to require critique.[7]

> What remains of the South that now seems worth saving and preserving? What is left that is authentic and valuable and representative of the best that Southerners could do? It is a short list: some of the literature and music and the arts, the oral tradition, the speech patterns, some of the traits of character and personality—and some of the food. There probably is very little that anyone can do to assure that these dwindling treasures will keep their vitality and usefulness. As long as people value them, they will last. How many is enough, and what constitutes value? No one can say. You can only do your part and hope for the best.[8]

Nostalgic, full of Jeffersonian touches and moments of confided intimacy, *Southern Food*'s language can make the need to engage with McPherson and Romine appear obvious. But it can also explain the desire to ignore them. That is to say, given its origins and ongoing investment in what Egerton called "an old Southern skill" that "deserves to last as long as the corn grows tall," it would hardly be surprising if the members of the SFA started to present a more or less allergic response to the kind of argument Romine offers in *The Real South*.[9] Nor, given the aforementioned pleasures of the SFA's annual symposium, is it hard to think of Romine and McPherson as spoilsports: the kind of bookish killjoys who, far from enjoying the party, stand in the kitchen critiquing it. Turning a blind eye to *The Real South* and other critiques of authenticity must certainly seem a tempting option to any southern scholar who has been building an archive in a vernacular tradition and who wants to continue doing so.

My purpose in this essay is twofold. First and foremost, I encourage the students of southern food to continue to fight against this understandable temptation, to uphold the SFA's traditions of open intellectual inquiry, and to respond further to the southernist critique of authenticity. But I am also seeking to contribute to that response. I am urging students of southern food to continue engaging with the southernist critique of authenticity, in other words, for reasons that go beyond mere matters of intellectual propriety. Engagement of this kind, I believe, will in fact enable SFA practitioners to reflect on their theory as well as their practice. It will allow them to articulate still more clearly the distance that stands between their work and the essentializing impulses lying latent in so many other responses to the southern past.

If we were to compare *The Real South* and the SFA only on the basis of their headline messages, we would quickly find ourselves in the realm of intellectual confrontation. Jon Smith's funny comment, on the back of Romine's book, that *The Real South* could cure those who "have read far too much *Southern Living*" and who feel "pleased that in today's high-tech, fast-paced world . . . the South still offers manners, memory, 'foodways,' family, a sense of place, and a sense of community" clearly throws the gauntlet down at an SFA he assumes to be committed to retrograde notions of cultural purity. Yet such sound bites simplify—and hide as much as they inform. Just as the SFA's values statement actually affirms that "we value funk," so the Louisiana State University Press's promotion of *The Real South* doesn't dwell on those moments where Romine adopts a slightly confessional tone (of a kind also to be found in McPherson's *Reconstructing Dixie*) and admits to his own occasional proclivity to succumb to southern yearning.[10] Neither Jon Smith's winning sneer on the back of *The Real South* nor the summary provided on its inside sleeve prepares us for the delicious prospect of Romine suggesting that "the discursive and tacitly ironized play of authenticity" might in fact constitute "a soft stop between the excesses of atavistic essentialism and banal pluralism."[11] Romine's willingness to entertain these promising possibilities reveals that *The Real South*, like *Recon-*

structing Dixie, doesn't simply deride or mock fantasies of authenticity. It doesn't seek to "cure" students of their love of southern food. Nor does it oblige them, effectively or otherwise, to abandon their pursuit of grassroots foodways—of "real" gumbo, hard-to-find boudin, barbecue trails, and the like—as signs of their naive or antediluvian investment in ideas of cultural purity. Far from it: *The Real South* instead, I believe, implores the students of such things to reflect—to relate their ethnographic enterprise to the critique of authenticity, and to think about which of its findings hit home and which fall short. And it is through such self-examination, I believe, that SFA practitioners can develop a fuller sense of why these vernacular foodways, from barbecue to boudin, matter so much to them, and appear to them in need of protection against outside forces. When SFA practitioners light out for these down-home foods, what is at stake? What histories do they oppose, and what traditions do they bear? What do they find precious in these imperiled foodways, and what are they protecting them from? How, in other words, might SFA practitioners articulate the ethical and intellectual imperatives of their community activities against the gathering academic critique of authenticity?

The Reinvention of Invention

Invention, on the other hand, now seems no less ubiquitous. Today, indeed, it appears so often on the covers of new books that you could be forgiven for thinking it referred to an academic discipline in its own right. However, delving into some of these books would quickly apprise you of your mistake. Little links Donna Landry's *The Invention of the Countryside* (2001) with Shlomo Sand's *The Invention of the Jewish People* (2009), after all; and still less connects Rebecca L. Spang's *The Invention of the Restaurant* (2000) with Sarah McNamer's *Affective Meditation and the Invention of Medieval Compassion* (2010). The differences not just in period and subject matter but also in the methodologies that these books employ as a matter of fact make it hard to say exactly why all of them should echo each other in their titles. No doubt, like all the riffs on Cornel West's *Race Matters* (1993) that now litter our world, the ubiquity of *invention* today has quite a lot to do with something like the academic equivalent of brand recognition. But it also owes much to the versatility that the term has acquired over the last twenty or so years. The term can certainly seem stunningly open today. It appears to spotlight more or less any spontaneous cultural phenomena occurring in more or less any context.

This openness, in turn, reveals the invention—or perhaps it would be better to say reinvention—of *invention* itself. That is to say, to a large extent we can trace the present ubiquity of the term to Eric Hobsbawm and Terence Ranger's seminal work *The Invention of Tradition* (1983). Soon after its publication, this seminal essay collection began to amass the huge number of citations that it commands today. Quickly, however, when we trace *invention*'s odyssey through these subsequent scholarly citations, two important transformations become apparent. One of the earliest significant responses to Hobsbawm and Ranger's book, Werner Sollors's edited collection *The Invention of Ethnicity* (1989), demonstrates that scholars quickly abbreviated the original concept of the *invented tradition* in order to talk of mere invention in the manner customary today. And second, while this condensing of *invented tradition* into *invention* has evidently brought several advantages for writers and publishers alike, helping their titles become less wordy, it by no means contradicts, but very much complements, the concurrent intellectual desire to ditch the political overtones that the term carries in Hobsbawm and Ranger's original collection.

Looked at one way, the transformation of *invented tradition* into *invention* resembles that of *binary opposition* into *binary*: an obvious distillation that, convenient and sensible, helps fluency along without loss of nuance or meaning. Only the fussiest of copyeditors, in this view, could object to the change, and any attempt to restore *invention* to *invented tradition* would smack of academic pedantry. Against this familiar objection, however, I would insist that it is only right for us, as academics, to take forensic care over our language. Words are our tools of trade, and we cannot afford to be indifferent to the fact that, unlike *binary* and *opposition*, *invention* and *tradition* are not even remotely synonymous. On the contrary: Because *invention* and *tradition* are, if anything, opposites of each other, the preservation of the former and the disappearance of the latter has left us with a keyword—*invention*—that can, and usually does, mean something very different indeed from the original phrase that it continues to echo.

To repeat, the sheer scale of the move to *invention* likely owes much to the exigencies of book publishing. But it is rooted in a clear and tangible intellectual impulse not just to adopt Hobsbawm and Ranger's keyword but to open it out and allow it to refer no longer to the artificial manufacture of authentic tradition but to more or less any spontaneous cultural phenomenon occurring in more or less any context. As such, although it involves a lexical distillation so subtle as to grow invisible, the shift away from *invented tradition* in effect "reinvents" *invention*. Easily overlooked, the effects of this terminological movement become apparent if we set Hobsbawm's original introduction alongside a statement of intent that Spang delivers about halfway through her magisterial *The Invention of the Restaurant*. Here is Hobsbawm:

> "Invented tradition" is taken to mean a set of practices, normally governed by overtly or tacitly accepted rules and of a ritual or symbolic nature, which seek to inculcate certain values and norms of behaviour by repetition, which automatically implies continuity with the past. In fact, where possible, they normally attempt to establish continuity with a suitable historical past.... Inventing traditions, it is assumed here, is essentially a process of formalization and ritualization, characterized by reference to the past, if only by imposing repetition. The actual process of creating such ritual and symbolic complexes has not been adequately studied by historians. Much of it is still rather obscure. It is presumably most clearly exemplified where a "tradition" is deliberately invented and constructed by a single initiator.[12]

And here is Spang:

> From the guidebook writers of 1800 to an American journalist covering the Revolution's bicentennial, from the French aesthete brothers Jules and Edmond Goncourt to the British Marxist Eric Hobsbawm, rumor and received wisdom have inextricably linked the origin of restaurants to the political, economic and cultural upheavals of 1789.
>
> In the highly charged political aftermath of early nineteenth-century France, as well, observers from across the ideological spectrum invoked the Revolution's aftermath in order to account for the proliferation of restaurants. Restaurants featured in the analyses of counter-revolutionaries and radicals alike: the aristocratic Madame de Genlis ... saw the spread of restaurants and

the development of gastronomic literature as further signs of revolutionary barbarism; the writer Louis Sébastien Mercier, whose republican fervor only cooled with his imprisonment under the police-state of the Terror, denounced restaurants for breaking up the family meals (real and imagined) that had characterized the Revolution's great fraternal moments. . . .

What all these writers somehow managed to overlook . . . is, of course, that restaurants had actually first appeared in the 1760s. Invented by the inexhaustible entrepreneur Mathurin Roze de Chantoiseau . . . , the restaurant did not require the Revolution to make it a fixture in Paris life.[13]

Encapsulated in these citations, I would suggest, is the unremarked but radical shift of meaning that has tended to accompany our move toward *invention*. *Invented traditions* are defined and understood in unmistakably political terms in Hobsbawm's introduction. Here the "invention of tradition" is presented to the reader as a planned and purposeful act, and involves the imposition of a manufactured truth over a prior way of life that Hobsbawm goes on to associate with "custom."[14] Hobsbawm approaches that new tradition, indeed, as if it were the second script being written on a palimpsestic surface, an obliterating message that overwrites original code. Any committed cultural history, for him, must accordingly attempt to expose, if possible, the imposing second script and to recover, if possible, the original code that it has rendered all but illegible. On these quite specific terms, then, *the invention of tradition* is carried out, if not by governments necessarily, then certainly by institutions or individuals that possess social authority of some kind. An almost idealistic commitment not just to justice and equality but also to the possibility of some kind of authentic tradition as such seems a prerequisite of Hobsbawm's approach. In his introduction and elsewhere, Hobsbawm and his contributors grant to vernacular or folk traditions something like authenticity; they indict invented traditions for producing something like propaganda, and as a result they present readers, time after time, with what cannot be mistaken for anything but a form of moral struggle.

In *The Invention of the Restaurant*, by way of contrast, Spang in a single phrase acknowledges Hobsbawm's influence and distances herself from it. Her use of "Marxist" here has that American smell of suspicion about it, allowing her to move back into an intellectual context that releases *invention* from any attendant associations with an awkward, essentialized truth. Put another way, while many academics nowadays cannot employ such terms without reaching for the scare quotes, Spang here avoids the problem by dislodging *invention* from political analysis and treating it as a spontaneous and ungovernable phenomenon. The subsequent transformation is all but total. *Invented traditions*, for Hobsbawm, are the handiworks of authority and can be thought of, among other things, as a kind of attack on the diverse indigenous cultures and customs of the general population. But *invention*, for Spang, if anything lies in the hand of those diverse cultures themselves and certainly refers to them far more than it does to any kind of political command. Even revolutionary politicians, Spang is suggesting, were powerless to control a process of cultural invention very like that which Hobsbawm once attributed to authority itself.

This journey, this compacting of the *invention of tradition* into *invention*, offers an object lesson in how scholarship since about 1990 has tended to adopt a radical or leftist vocabulary but used it for cultural rather than political purposes. Like those who talk of reification but do not cite Georg Lukács, scholars today who talk in general terms about *invention* can look as though they are wanting to associate themselves with the radical without wishing to commit themselves to any full-blown leftist politics. But the real drawback of this rhetorical ploy is that the hard political edge it seeks to appropriate is blunted by its concurrent drive toward lexical efficiency. The concentration on *invention* comes at the price of a largely secret disinvestment in *tradition*. Its popularization is also a disarming, a dilution, which leaves the concept powerless to carry out its original work of spotlighting and exposing forms of cultural appropriation.

Ideas of authenticity, like truth and purity, are always at risk of implementing a simplification or distortion of culture. But we can only use a word like *distortion* if we remain committed to the category of truth itself. Many modern habits of academic argument, and not just the frequent recourse to scare quotes, tend to shun or repudiate ideas of truth or purity, but do so in a manner that suggests a continuing belief in justice—and, therefore, in truth. Nowhere is this contradictory, if understandable, habit of argument more prominent than in discussions of the American South. McPherson and Romine, among others, allow us to see that ideas of *authenticity* are particularly awkward in southern culture, and not least because such notions of cultural essence always remain liable to fall under the shadow of race.[15] And yet, as their works continue to pursue ultimate notions of truth and justice, it becomes apparent that both are treating this historic entanglement of racial and cultural authenticity as a problem that can only be solved through the complete abolition of authenticity as a category or value. But both can seem to assume more than demonstrate this need for outright abolition, and perhaps we can still ask the question: Must our rejection of racial purity necessitate a rejection of *purity* altogether? If so, how are we to handle the fact that purity continues to exist as a meaningful scientific category, not to mention its continuing widespread use in everyday speech? Language commits us to thought. We "use semantics to create a reality to go beyond semantics, and semantics to create powers that go beyond semantic powers."[16] Academia should do far more than attempt to decontaminate everyday speech.

In the second chapter of *Savage Barbecue*, I offer an analysis of the barbecue that the London journalist Edward Ward described as happening in his home city as early as 1707. I observe:

> Something about the feast at the New Dock clearly caught Ward's fancy. Something about its savagery, something about its ability to offer outlet to the masculine desires that the civilizing process had started to drive from London life, apparently captivated Ward, drawing him to visit further examples of this scene that happenstance had put before him on the road to Horn Fair. From the transition between *A frolick to Horn-fair* (1700) and *The Barbacue Feast* (1707), then, we can deduce that Ward learned to refer to this "Savage Piece of Cookery" as *barbacue* only some years after his alleged Caribbean sojourn. But we can also start to see that Ward, throughout *The Barbacue Feast*, is trying to cover up this inconvenient fact. Here, then, is a maneuver akin to the way in which *Jamaica Viewed* withholds italics from this word, presenting it as a commonplace and silencing any etymological speculation. A similar emptying out occurs: *The Barbacue Feast* bears witness to another commodity that we are asked to accept as American, but which seems strangely bare of any evidence to confirm this authentic status. Now the Americanness of barbecue

transpires ... out of the sheer necessity to believe in the existence of savagery and its foods. The word and the idea that it conveys can once more "behave ... as though we knew it already." No provenance needs to be given, no attribution offered, to support this impulse to know that savagery resides and is perfected in the world abroad.

Not least because it is the first work to name and report a barbecue as we know and eat it today, *The Barbacue Feast* is thus of major importance to this book, of major importance to the invention of this more or less "American" food.[17]

Hearing writers talk about past mistakes is often quite a bore and can be almost as bad as hearing them complain about being misunderstood. Perhaps the context of this essay, however, might permit me to name some of the regrets I have about *Savage Barbecue*. At least for present purposes, there are two. I do wish I had found a way to avoid mere *invention* and weave the full phrase *invented tradition* into my subtitle. Connectedly, however, I now realize that by situating the work even more squarely in Hobsbawm's tradition of socialist thought, I could have done more to trumpet the particular invention of tradition that my research uncovered. Before *Savage Barbecue*, nobody had ever dwelt for too long on the minor writings, or hackwork, of Ned Ward. Even a bare acknowledgement of the existence of his *Barbacue Feast* seemed fairly absent from the bibliographies I consulted. Yet the research I completed for the work made it apparent that Ward's pamphlet was in fact of seminal importance to the development of barbecue in the English-speaking world and that its importance, specifically, lay in the form of his invention of a tradition. The disingenuous transformations that occur over the course of Ward's career certainly require us to turn to the categories of true and false. If not a liar, Ward was on free and easy terms with facts. The rhetorical flourish by which, describing the outdoor feasts held in London's purlieus, he decided to call one a *barbecue* was the act of one of semantic liberty. Naming the *invention of tradition* in full in *Savage Barbecue*'s title would thus have enabled me to underline my thesis that *barbecue* was a manufactured, artificial tradition, to be contrasted, at least in terms of its ultimate origins, from other culinary genealogies. But such a contention, too, would have betrayed my continuing investment in authenticity—and it is to this contentious notion, the subject of so much recent critique, that I must now turn.

Edgeland *Terroir*

More than thirty years have now passed since, in Michel de Certeau's *The Practice of Everyday Life* (1980), Luce Giard paid tribute to domestic French cooking and the "innumerable anonymous women" who practice it every day.[18] In France, in the years since the publication of those words, a lot of concrete has been poured. Innumerable delicatessens and boulangeries have closed, and McDonald's and Carrefours have opened. As a result of these changes, *The Practice of Everyday Life*'s affirmation of the tactile aptitude, "multiple memory," and "creative ingenuity of cleverness" of unknown and unpaid French cooks can start to look a little anachronistic.[19] But in the South in particular, so many years after the bulldozer revolution, Giard's affirmation of the "tang of the soil," or *terroir*, can seem irrelevant, the stuff of a foreign nostalgia.

> Stated differences are often attributed to a *regional cultural history* with obscure particularities, when it is really a question of material necessities established little by little through tradition, a way of adapting to local agricultural production: when one harvest this fruit or that vegetable is in abundance, one must learn to prepare and preserve it. Thus, as of the second half of the eighteenth century, junior high school menus presented a rather clear regional aspect: cabbage and sauerkraut in Alsace, white beans and chestnuts in Auch. Similarly, if Alsatian cuisine made a specialty for itself out of sauerkraut and of recourse to turnips, it is because great quantities of those vegetables were available that were adapted to the region's soils and climate, and thus ways had been found to preserve them through curing and fermentation. . . .
>
> In the past, foreign travelers admired the subtleties of southern China, whose cuisine is based on poorly refined rice, peppers, green vegetables, soy, and fish; but the elements in this composition were imposed by the situation: these products were at once the least costly and the most nutritious in the area. Often, a dish's flavor stems from the unique nature of a local product: prepared with Californian apples, *tarte Tatin* loses the delicate balance of acidity (due to *pommes de reinettes*) and caramelized sugar that give it its charm, and Mexican *pollo negro* is unfeasible without (unsweetened) cocoa powders.[20]

Reading Giard in twenty-first-century Mississippi or Georgia could feel like taking a "voyage" into anything but the "ordinary."[21] And I would imagine that, if read from a southern perspective, the *terroir* she emphasizes here could seem a little like fresh bread or fast trains: a good idea that, for one reason or another, hasn't transplanted too well onto American soil.[22] That soil, indeed, can prove hard to find amid the strip malls and parking lots of the still newer South of 2011. Proportionately fewer people here, in the absence of a Common Agricultural Policy or EU subsidies, actually know farming life, or have firsthand knowledge of the kinds of unexpected agricultural highs and lows that help animate Giard's remarks.

And yet, before concluding that southern soil is today too hard to find for us to speak of its "tang," we ought to remember that Giard, too, is approaching *terroir* as a culinary culture under threat. We ought to remember that she is not writing in the France of Brillat Savarin, not even in the France of Elizabeth David, but in Paris during the years of Pompidou's aggressive modernization schemes and amid the rise of the suburbs whose apparent lack of authenticity earned them the mocking soubriquet *faubourgs*. Even in France in the 1970s, in other words, soil felt pretty hard to find, and plenty of concrete was already being poured.

> In the end, every regional cuisine loses its internal coherence, this money-saving spirit whose inventive ingenuity and rigor make up all its strength; in their place remains only an insignificant succession of "typical dishes" whose origin and function are longer understood.... In our cities, a thousand hired cooks fabricate simplified exotic dishes that are adapted to our prior habits and to the laws of the market. Thus, we happily eat shreds of local cultures that are disintegrating, or a material token of a past or future voyage; thus, the West is biting with gusto into the pale copies of these subtle and tender marvels established throughout the slow movement of centuries by generations of anonymous artists.[23]

A continuing investment in the possibility of an integrated cultural tradition becomes apparent in these remarks. For Giard, something very like an atmosphere of authenticity surrounds particular foods, and nowhere does it grow more tangible than in the grim instant when responsibility for their preparation passes from domestic space into the hands of "hired cooks." Nostalgia of a recognizable kind at this moment threatens to undo the commentary. *Terroir*, as Giard treats it, can start to look like a classic instance of what Zygmunt Bauman, in his 1995 work *Life in Fragments*, calls a "*modern* 'problem of identity,'" a pure and traditional myth of selfhood that Giard cannot quite protect against the benighted and destabilizing forces of modernity.[24] And yet the innovative culinary resourcefulness of the "innumerable anonymous women" that Giard celebrates elsewhere in her essay always stands as a very interesting counterweight to this "modern" and nostalgic understanding of *terroir*. For Giard these anonymous women, far from subscribing to any static understanding of "modern" identity, practice an open and ever innovative form of cultural work that would, if anything, evoke the "postmodern 'problem of identity'" that *Life in Fragments* sets in opposition to it. Giard's exhortation of everyday cooking—the tributes she pays to its endless new beginnings and to the incessant and happy destruction of the private masterpieces it produces—certainly seem in keeping not with any modern predicament but with the need to avoid fixation, to remain mobile and "keep our options open," by which Bauman suggests we negotiate postmodern experience.[25]

In the work of these unknown women, Giard finds hope. These Frenchwomen, like anyone who cooks every day, daily arrive at adaptations and reach creative solutions very like those that, in her view, shaped the human tradition of *terroir* in the first place. In the account of *terroir* that Giard delivers, the essence of the dish incarnates no ideal—it is not forged in purity—but lies instead in the record of adaptation and inspired compromise that we can recover from its composition. The resourceful activity of these women places them, and could place us all, into a long line of brilliant but anonymous cooks. *Terroir*, then, is authentic. But it offers no dream of purity. No unattainable ideal lies within it. And, as much as modernity threatens it, great ancestors do not inevitably dwarf its modern legacies. Like southern pit barbecue, it achieves this authenticity because of reinvention: because of the heritage of process and technique we can recover from it. Not least because the "moral significance" of material work lies "in the simple fact that such things lie outside the self," it is real—in every sense of the word but the academic.[26] That authenticity, moreover, grows in the hands. To the extent that it emanates from the land, it emanates from the transformation of the land that those hands have been able to achieve. Consequently, and because it arises from knowable and repeatable human activity, *terroir* incarnates a form of cultural authenticity over which we maintain control. Interventions can hold in check its disappearance from ordinary life, enabling us to transform it into new forms.

Here are the intellectual grounds for the protection of particular foods that, thanks to EU law as well as an extension of the traditional system of *appellation d'origine contrôlée*, now prevails throughout France. Brie, champagne, Roquefort, *tarte Tatin*: these foods are now deemed authentic, and the subsequent protection that they receive helps small producers to thrive. In each case, however, their authenticity refers not to any lost purity but to the moments of brilliant historical invention that have produced the existing and recoverable composition accessible to us today. It is a matter of ingredient and technique more than myth.

We live in an age of fast and frightening change. A defining feature of our period is that our capitalist system is at once growing stronger and weaker, extending into new areas of life and widening inequality even as its inflationary and monopolizing tendencies leave it prone to perpetual crisis. Many academics now offer brilliant Marxist or leftist critiques of this situation, but the radical tenor and the sheer difficulty of our terminology can sometimes prevent us from connecting with a public who might nevertheless agree that governments should help small businesses get a fighting chance against the multinationals. At the same time, those multinationals are growing ever more adept at hiding their power from consumers, and they often do this by harnessing invented traditions that echo some of the SFA's rhetoric about family businesses and foodways.[27]

Under these circumstances, in 2011, the objectives of John Egerton's original foodways writings now look, if anything, even more powerful. But they also require constant reexamination. In particular, I believe that students of southern food ought to continue asking themselves to what extent Egerton's investment in the pastoral and the southern farm helps or hinders the SFA's ongoing efforts to protect southern cooking in its fullest sense. It cannot be doubted that the SFA already offers a rare example of humanities academia, which so often talks the talk, engaging in meaningful community activity; or that it has already made a significant contribution in ensuring that, as Tara McPherson points out, "touring the South reminds us that the much bemoaned homogenization of American culture is not total."[28] But today, when global corporations present an agrarian face to the world, harnessing the language of family and farm, the southern soil that has always been contentious is also becoming increasingly elusive. At the same time, Giard's very human analysis of *terroir* might help students to consider how southerners have put that soil to use, made it productive, and developed authentic foodways as a result of their use of it. And these circumstances, if placed together, could suggest a need to think in more formal ways about the different kinds of southern soil that lie beyond the plantation and the pastoral farm. What of the briar patch, the working garden, the southern equivalents to those places that Farley and Symmons call "the fringes, the in-between spaces," the "land left over (or left behind)" in English life? Here, could we find another *terroir*—a *terroir* of the edgelands, authentic and organic, where the hands of southerners continue to connect them to a difficult, yet unavoidably collective, working past?

NOTES

1. Scott Romine, *The Real South: Southern Narrative in the Age of Reproduction* (Baton Rouge: Louisiana State University Press, 2008), 4.

2. Michel de Certeau, *The Practice of Everyday Life*, trans. Steven Rendall (Berkeley: University of California Press, 1988), 26.

3. The mission statement of the Southern Foodways Association is available at http://southernfoodways.org/about/mission.html, accessed March 9, 2012.

4. Jennifer Jensen Wallach, "The Marketing of Southern Identity," *Reviews in America History* 38, no. 2 (June 2010): 295–300. Wallach, for example, acknowledges the "wildly successful" events of the SFA but suggests that "the relationship between foodways and identity construction requires much more scrutiny through a scholarly gaze" ("The Marketing of Southern Identity," 298). Other powerful scholars attempt to exile the SFA from the world of bona fide scholarship in much more candid terms.

5. Tara McPherson, *Reconstructing Dixie: Race, Gender, and Nostalgia in the Imagined South* (Durham, N.C.: Duke University Press, 2003), 18. Press reports and previous conference papers suggest that Jon Smith's *Alabama and the Future of American Culture Studies*, forthcoming with the University of Georgia Press, will interestingly inhabit and extend this body of critique.

6. Romine, *Real South*, 103; passages of this kind appear in Elijah Wald, *Escaping the Delta: Robert Johnson and the Invention of the Blues* (New York: Amistad, 2004), 250–64; and Greg Milner, *Perfecting Sound Forever: The Story of Recorded Music* (London: Granta, 2009), 80–108.

7. John Egerton, "Founder's Letter," June 16, 1999, http://www.southernfoodways.com/about/history.html, accessed February 22, 2011.

8. John Egerton, *Southern Food: At Home, on the Road, in History* (New York: Knopf, 1987), 46.

9. Ibid., 345.

10. On the inner sleeve of *The Real South* we read: "Where earlier critics have tended to *assume* a real or authentic South, Romine questions such assumptions and whether the 'authentic South' ever truly existed." Broadly speaking, in this article, I am suggesting that the southernist critique of authenticity long predates even McPherson's *Reconstructing Dixie* (2003), and that the distinction of Romine's work in fact lies in the empathy he brings to his examination of the impulses and anxieties that produce these "assumptions."

11. Romine, *Real South*, 235.

12. Rebecca L. Spang, "Introduction: Inventing Traditions," in *The Invention of the Restaurant: Paris and Modern Gastronomic Culture* (Cambridge, Mass.: Harvard University Press, 2000), 1–4.

13. Spang, *Invention of the Restaurant*, 91–92.

14. Spang, "Introduction," 6.

15. McPherson, *Reconstructing Dixie*, 30.

16. John R. Searle, *Making the Social World: The Structure of Human Civilization* (Oxford: Oxford University Press, 2010), 14.

17. Andrew Warnes, *Savage Barbecue: Race, Culture, and the Invention of America's First Food* (Athens: The University of Georgia Press, 2008), 69–70.

18. Michel Certeau, *The Practice of Everyday Life*, vol. 2: *Living and Cooking* (Minneapolis: University of Minnesota Press, 1998), 155.

19. Ibid., 2:157.

20. Ibid., 2:177–78.

21. Ibid., 2:xxxix.

22. Ibid., 2:178.

23. Ibid.

24. Zygmunt Bauman, *Life in Fragments: Essays in Postmodern Morality* (Oxford: Blackwell, 1995), 94.

25. Certeau, *Practice of Everyday Life*, 2:158.

26. Matthew Crawford, *The Case for Working with Your Hands: Or Why Office Work Is Bad for Us and Fixing Things Feels Good* (London: Penguin, 2011), 16. As Crawford suggests, Richard Sennett offers some important observations about the radical value of manual work. Both Crawford and Sennett, however, seem to conceive of craftwork in mechanical terms, and often assume that it results in permanent and less disposable items. It would be interesting to see them engage a bit more deeply with the cyclical, messy business of domestic cooking.

27. The website of Jack Daniels, for example, goes to extraordinary lengths to present users with the image of a small and family-run southern company; see http://www.jackdaniels.com/JackDaniel/FamilyTree.aspx.

28. McPherson, *Reconstructing Dixie*, 254.

CHAPTER 16

Conclusion

Go Forth with Method

TED OWNBY

I write to offer a few reflections on these essays, not as a scholar with training or teaching experience in foodways, but as a southern historian who has been observing the rise of southern foodways as a field. Some years ago, when the Southern Foodways Alliance began offering programming that challenged the boundaries between academics and others, I was excited by the possibilities of scholars, journalists, food professionals, and everyone else sharing discussions of food and the questions food can raise. I still find that exciting, and the good news is there are far more foodways scholars now, far more classes and academic programs connecting food and culture, and a wider range of good scholarship. Suspicions from some scholars that food study is somehow not serious are not a thing of the past, but it seems likely that this book will be one of the last collections of academic essays in which any scholars feel the need to explain or defend their choice of foodways as a topic. Above all, I hope this volume is one of many steps in making clear the potential of interdisciplinary approaches in studying food and cultural life.

As a historian interested in academic movements, I can suggest a few reasons for the increased scholarly engagement with food and its context. First, food is obviously important, and anyone should be able to see that; one might more usefully offer a list of why so many historians and other scholars have traditionally ignored the subject. Second, the growing and passionate interest among many people, especially younger people, in food choices as a vital part of their own politics has encouraged new and better scholarly questions about food and markets, food and labor, justice and access to food, and food and health. Third, scholarship in gender studies has encouraged excellent scholarship on people who cook, raising questions about both family members and household workers who prepare food, and also challenging some people's conceptions of women as cooks and men as chefs. Fourth, scholarly efforts to see beyond national borders have encouraged the study of both products and laborers that make broad connections. Food scholars brought us big books about sugar and salt and fish and rice— all topics that have to take a global perspective to adequately address their subjects.

Turning to this volume, one simple conclusion is that the essays emphasize complexity, multiplicity, and change. Any quick assumptions that southern food starts with corn and pork, or food with British and African roots, or food from the gardens of our grandparents, quickly fall apart as too simple, static, or misleading. The fact that this book focuses not on food but on food*ways* signals that the essays concern the range of social issues we can study through food, and those issues, like food itself, change and vary. While the scholars assembled here are interested in complexity, they show little interest in the nostalgia that characterizes, whether subtly or directly, a good deal of writing about food.

If there is no food or food experience that typifies southern foodways— not dinner on the grounds or community barbecue, no biscuits or gumbo that only the elders can make—then scholars do not need to spend energy revering or rejecting particular foods and what they represent. If there is no clearly central experience or starting place, scholars do not have to decenter or hurry to the margins looking for new topics. Instead, scholars can get on with the project of asking a wide range of questions about a wide range of topics related to food and culture.

As I read the essays, one recurring and intellectually exciting theme is the profound difference between studying foodways and ethnicity and studying foodways and race. Studying foodways and ethnicity is open-ended, with strong potential for multiple experiences, many of them positive. Ethnic studies scholars have long had a great interest in food choices as ways to study cultural continuity, change, assimilation, and creativity. Along with language, food is one of the most immediate ways that many Americans think about ethnicity. And America's extraordinary spread of ethnic cuisines, promising variety, change, and maybe surprise, is one of the constitutive features of its food scene—perhaps rivaled only by the popularity of chain restaurants that promise continuity and predictability. Studying ethnicity often means analyzing ongoing processes of influence and image, and it consistently involves redefinition, both within a group and in relations among groups.

On the other hand, when scholars discuss foodways scholarship and its relation to race—generally conceived as a construction that tries to divide complex social groups into permanent dichotomies, with privileges for one group and disrespect and discrimination for the other—they are discussing power and limitations, injustice, dependent labor, and insult. People claiming the privileges of whiteness have not wanted redefinition, variety, change, and surprise; they want clear categories with clear privileges, and they want those categories and privileges to seem inherited and beyond questioning.

Many scholars would agree with at least three ideas about the relationship between southern ethnicity and the concept of race. First, in contrast to many parts of the United States, the American South has neither a myth nor historical ideal of the region as a land of welcome and opportunity for all people. No Emma Lazarus poem speaks of people arriving in the South "yearning to breathe free," in substantial part because many of the people who lived in the South's ports of entry came to Charleston and New Orleans as slaves. Second, at numerous points in southern history, some people wanted to reduce most human categories to two, to call those categories white and black, and to claim clear benefits for the former. People claiming those benefits have shown intense interest in race as a construction that serves a range of purposes that elevate some at the expense of others. Third, despite the first two points, there is always more variety and complexity than there might seem, and there are recurring questions about how people outside a white-black dichotomy operate inside, outside, and on the edges of a world some people have tried to define as white and black.

Several scholars in this volume write with a mission to overturn the idea of the South as a place with a biracial society with biracial foodways. Rayna Green's essay argues that Native American foods and food techniques have been a vital element in southern life, long after many people noticed that fact or identified certain foods as having Native American backgrounds.

And Thomas Hanchett's article displays at least two crucial concepts of ethnic foodways in the modern South. There are many opportunities for variety outside a simple white-and-black paradigm, and new combinations of people (immigrants cooking the food in restaurants owned by other immigrants) and new ethnic identifications both offer great novelty. Both discuss ways that ethnic diversity complicates and challenges any effort to categorize people as belonging to one of only two groups.

This book is full of discussions of ethnic cuisines that developed outside the boundaries of the American South, in Africa, Greece, Sicily, and elsewhere. Often the cooks themselves choose or make note of ethnic diversity. Perhaps as much as anything, the two articles on cookbooks by Rebecca Sharpless and Rien Fertel show how a global South has long lived in kitchens, and in our understandings of inherited recipes and recipes that are Mexican, Italian, Middle Eastern, northern European, English and Welsh, Chinese, Spanish, French, and German.

If studying ethnicity and foodways first brings up the concept of variety (and, in the South, uses that concept to challenge notions of race), it also raises issues of creativity. Thinking about ethnicity is one of the oldest ways scholars of the South discussed specific West African cultural continuities and how they changed in America, as enslaved people raised, cooked, and consumed rice, for example, and okra. Scholars appreciate the creativity of people who find ways to keep food practices alive in new and sometimes stealthy ways. Other forms of creativity, some of it available only at the margins, abound. Jessica B. Harris details the ways Africans and African Americans have combined the selling of food items with verbal skills that retain broad patterns but always change to fit new circumstances. Harris shows that street vendors exemplified a broad pan-African tradition, working with and for people who loved their food and often their salesmanship but also with people who feared the freedom their sales represented. By depicting efforts by Greek restaurateurs to live outside the rigid categories of the Jim Crow system, Angela Cooley's paper discusses another form of creativity on the margins.

Justin Nystrom's paper on the muffuletta examines another aspect of creativity—the definition of certain foods and practices as ethnic cuisine. In the muffuletta, Nystrom shows some Italians in New Orleans finding a niche, building on preexisting knowledge, creating something more or less new. And then that more-or-less new dish became part of the definition of food in New Orleans—sometimes considered something that generations of folks might have been making and eating back in the old country. Creativity can come in identifying a wide range of food practices and ingredients as ethnic cuisine—taking food from an extraordinary diversity of places and calling a few dishes and ingredients the keys to Middle Eastern or Mexican or Chinese or Italian food. Often the experience of immigrants in the midst of nonimmigrants helps establish something as identifiably ethnic food. Certainly people did not eat in the South just as they had eaten somewhere else, but they could continue to contribute a few key ingredients or techniques or emphases, and those keys, identified both by the immigrants and by others, became the way to mark ethnic food.

In general, thinking about the multiethnic nature of southern foodways can be an exciting and even uplifting way to mark the creative meeting of tradition and new circumstances. If multiplicity and creativity characterize a great deal of the discussions of ethnicity and foodways, the concept of race places limits on people's behavior and on their claims of division and duality and essential and permanent difference. While "ethnic cuisine" is a useful if complicated concept, no one seems to write or speak of "racial cuisines," and for good reason.

The essays in this volume that discuss race analyze efforts to limit multiplicity, creativity, and possibility. Psyche Williams-Forson shows how the U.S. military during World War II tried, without complete success, to keep African American men in servile positions preparing chicken. The street vendors Jessica Harris describes faced repeated efforts to criminalize parts of their work. In Angela Jill Cooley's essay, the emerging institution of the restaurant, like other relatively new institutions, became a place where segregationist leaders wanted to enforce segregation. One of the wild cards is that the Greek restaurateurs who came to the United States faced pressure to claim the identities and privileges of white people by enforcing Jim Crow rules. Later, those restaurants were battlegrounds for civil rights era discussions of racial privilege.

In each of those cases, the concept of race was a force for division. Race trumped class, at least for a while on some topics, and duality won out over multiplicity, for a time. The Greek restaurant owners Cooley analyzes did not get to choose. In Rien Fertel's paper on the *Picayune Creole Cook Book*, the concept of race intruded into the extraordinary complexity people find in the various definitions of the term "Creole." On the other hand, the hopefulness of Thomas Hanchett's paper emerges from his argument that a multiethnic cuisine in Charlotte could develop only after the biracial traditions of the city were overcome.

The essays in this volume address issues of foodways and labor, but most do so in ways that diverge from many older approaches. For years corn and hogs were central figures to southern historians who were debating the degree to which southern farming people were self-sufficient and analyzing the meanings different southerners saw in that concept. Many southerners have claimed independence from the control of other people, or the goal of gaining freedom from dependence, as central to their understanding of themselves and perhaps southern or American history. Whether discussed as the yeoman ideal, or republican principles, or the promised land ideal, or even an image of the South as a mythic garden, the close connection between the products of farm life and freedom from control has been important as some combination of political language, ideal for the future, or nostalgia about an imagined past.

The essays in this volume address foodways and labor from a range of perspectives, none of which start with questions about independence emerging from the products of farm life. Wiley Prewitt's essay on hunting probably comes closest, but instead of contrasting an old day when people hunted game for home use to a new day when few hunt and even fewer eat game, his essay stresses that hunting has changed in essential ways—what is hunted, how, and why—with major changes in southern agricultural practices. David Shields's article on oil begins with Thomas Jefferson and like-minded elites wanting to develop cooking oils in part to secure their independence from distant exporters. The intriguing twist is that while olive oil efforts had little success, it was benne oil that succeeded, in large part because of the West African background to its production and consumption. In her essay, Marcie Cohen Ferris includes the assertion by Edna Lewis that "the early cooking of southern food was primarily done by blacks, men and women. It was then, and it still is now." Ferris's essay almost immediately expands beyond that point by showing the multiple forms of work that make up southern cooking. And the essays by Rien Fertel and Rebecca Sharpless complicate the issue of cooking by detailing how white women and men collected recipes, many of which came from the work done by African Americans.

In much of southern history, the coming of the machine and perhaps the corporation means the end of something important—the end of skilled labor, maybe independence, maybe even work itself. The essays by Carolyn de la Peña and Katie Rawson complicate those possibilities. De la Peña explores the possibility that southerners may have been especially drawn to machine-made doughnuts because they could see the whole process. The doughnuts did not emerge in packages from mysterious corporate structures. In the same way, Rawson's paper argues that one of the reasons so many southerners identify with Waffle House is that cooking is visible to the patrons, who are close in many ways to the cooks.

A final point comes from the perspective of a southern studies scholar. Although all of these essays are about topics in the South, few are centrally concerned with issues of southern identity. Numerous scholars have noticed that we may have moved into an age of studying people in the American South without always seeking southern identity. In part, we want to study everyone's identities, all of them, and not just the ways some people, most often those with a conservative political perspective, have claimed southern identity for themselves. In part, we want to study all of life, without always asking for the "southern" parts, however defined. And in large part, scholars want to study things without a center—without dichotomies of race and class, continuity and change, burden or innocence, essential South or diminished South, having the intellectual potential to hold the range of their questions. Few, if any, are searching for a central theme in southern food history.

In her article on the cookbook in Waco, Rebecca Sharpless describes the inclusion of food named for Robert E. Lee and Stonewall Jackson, as well as a cake recipe from Mrs. Robert E. Lee, and also some dishes the cookbook organizers referred to as "southern," but she situates those points in a thorough discussion of a much wider range of identities. Saying certain foods were "southern," in her essay, did not seem particularly important to the people making the claim. Marcie Cohen Ferris's paper makes a similar point, that there is simply too much diversity of experience to allow us to identify anything comfortably as southern food.

Beth Latshaw notes that identifying with southern food does not necessarily correlate with eating foods associated with the South. She argues that African Americans eat more foods associated with the South than anyone else, but she points out that those eating habits do not necessarily lead to celebrations of southern identity. In fact, she writes, food choices may have more to do with "the presence of unknown factors" than self-conscious regional identification. Andrew Warnes suggests that food scholars should continue to move away from old definitions of southern foodways as rooted in farming communities and virtues some people associate with pastoral life, both to escape outdated and troubling notions of authenticity and to take a fuller view of the South, past and present.

Most of the authors in this book, I suspect, would accept Warnes's suggestion to study foodways without having a fixed point for judging authenticity. The scholars have moved away from notions that some key elements defined the South at one time and their job is to describe which of those elements, positive or negative or both, live on. That kind of end-of-the-South thinking has declined along with the search for southern identity. One feature that unifies most, and perhaps all, of the articles is the lack of nostalgia—or in many cases, even affection—for the food itself. In truth, it is hard to tell whether most of these scholars enjoy eating southern food and even harder to see if that question matters. But they clearly think it worthy of study. What emerges is a decentered southern foodways scholarship asking numerous questions, with numerous starting and ending points. Reading such a collection of essays may not encourage food metaphors—it's not a feast, not a gumbo, certainly not a home-cooked meal—but I think it's healthy.

Contributors

Angela Jill Cooley was a postdoctoral fellow at the Center for the Study of Southern Culture at the University of Mississippi from 2011 to 2013, where she collaborated with the Southern Foodways Alliance to develop curriculum that explores connections among southern foodways, history, and culture. Her current book manuscript examines changes to food culture in the twentieth-century South.

Carolyn de la Peña is professor of American studies and interim vice-provost for undergraduate education at the University of California at Davis. She is the author of two books: *Empty Pleasures: The Story of Artificial Sweeteners from Saccharin to Splenda* and *The Body Electric: How Strange Machines Built the Modern American.*

John T. Edge is the director of the Southern Foodways Alliance. He holds an MA in southern studies from the University of Mississippi and an MFA in nonfiction from Goucher College. He is the editor of the Foodways volume of *The New Encyclopedia of Southern Culture* and the series editor of *Cornbread Nation.*

Elizabeth Engelhardt is a professor of American studies and women's and gender studies at the University of Texas–Austin. She received her PhD in women's studies from Emory University. She is the author, most recently, of *A Mess of Greens: Southern Gender and Southern Food.*

Marcie Cohen Ferris is an associate professor in the Department of American Studies at the University of North Carolina at Chapel Hill, where she directs the southern studies concentration. She is the author of *Matzoh Ball Gumbo: Culinary Tales of the Jewish South.* Her forthcoming book, *The Edible South: Food and History in an American Region,* examines the expressive power of food in narrative and material culture from the plantation South to the struggles of the civil rights movement.

Rien T. Fertel graduated from Tulane University's History Department with a PhD in the spring of 2013. He writes for several magazines on the subjects of food, culture, and travel, and he collects oral histories for the Southern Foodways Alliance and Foodways Texas.

Rayna Green, a reformed academic specializing in both American Indian cultural history and food, has been a program director and curator at the National Museum of American History, Smithsonian Institution since 1984. Her most recent exhibition there is "FOOD: Transforming the American Table, 1950–2000" (2012).

Tom Hanchett earned a history PhD at the University of North Carolina at Chapel Hill and joined the Levine Museum of the New South in Charlotte as staff historian in 1999. He is the author of *Sorting Out the New South City: Race, Class, and Urban Development in Charlotte, 1875–1975.*

Jessica B. Harris is the author of eleven books on the foodways of the African diaspora, most recently *High on the Hog: A Culinary Journey from Africa to America.* She is a professor of English at Queens College of the City University of New York.

Beth A. Latshaw is an assistant professor of sociology at Appalachian State University in Boone, North Carolina, where she teaches courses on gender, families, and relationships. Her work on foodways in the American South was made possible through funding from the Center for the Study of the American South at UNC-Chapel Hill, where she completed her PhD in sociology.

Justin A. Nystrom is an assistant professor of history at Loyola University New Orleans, where he also directs the Center for the Study of New Orleans and the Documentary and Oral History Studio. He is the author of *New Orleans after the Civil War: Race, Politics, and a New Birth of Freedom.*

Ted Ownby is a professor of history and southern studies at the University of Mississippi, where he is also the director of the Center for the Study of Southern Culture. He received his PhD in history from Johns Hopkins University. He is the author of *American Dreams in Mississippi: Consumers, Poverty, and Culture, 1830–1998.*

Wiley C. Prewitt Jr. earned an MA in history at the University of Mississippi. He cooks his kills outside Oxford, Mississippi.

Katie Rawson recently completed her PhD at the Institute of Liberal Arts at Emory University, where she was managing editor of the online journal *Southern Spaces.*

Rebecca Sharpless, a professor of history at Texas Christian University, focuses her work on women in Texas and the American South. She is the author of *Cooking in Other Women's Kitchens: Domestic Workers in the South, 1865–1960* and *Fertile Ground, Narrow Choices: Women on Texas Cotton Farms, 1900–1940*, and she has edited or coedited numerous other scholarly volumes.

David S. Shields is McClintock Professor of Southern Letters at the University of South Carolina and chair of the Carolina Gold Rice Foundation. His book-length history of southern cookery and the place of Lowcountry cuisine is slated for publication in 2014.

Andrew Warnes is the author of *Savage Barbecue: Race, Culture, and the Invention of America's First Food*. He is a reader in American studies at the University of Leeds in the United Kingdom.

Psyche Williams-Forson is associate professor of American studies at the University of Maryland College Park. She specializes in African American studies and women's and gender studies. She is the author of *Building Houses Out of Chicken Legs: Black Women, Food, and Power* and the coeditor of *Taking Food Public: Redefining Foodways in a Changing World*.

Index